ALTERNATIVE DISPUTE RESOLUTION

By

Stephen J. Ware
Professor of Law
Samford University
Cumberland School of Law

HORNBOOK SERIES®

WEST
GROUP

ST. PAUL, MINN., 2001

West Group has created this publication to provide you with accurate and authoritative information concerning the subject matter covered. However, this publication was not necessarily prepared by persons licensed to practice law in a particular jurisdiction. West Group is not engaged in rendering legal or other professional advice, and this publication is not a substitute for the advice of an attorney. If you require legal or other expert advice, you should seek the services of a competent attorney or other professional.

Hornbook Series, *WESTLAW*, and the West Group symbol
are registered trademarks used herein under license.

 TEXT IS PRINTED ON 10% POST CONSUMER RECYCLED PAPER

For Catherine K. and R. Timmis Ware

*

Preface

The term "Alternative Dispute Resolution" is still fairly new. Prior to the 1970's, lawyers did not talk about "ADR". They did, however, practice ADR. They negotiated settlement agreements and they represented clients in arbitration. Such activities have long been performed by lawyers. Only recently, though, has ADR emerged as a distinct field of study in law school. This book is an outgrowth of that emergence.

This book surveys ADR. It is written with one overriding goal, to serve as a clear and reliable statement of the law and concepts central to ADR.

The literature on ADR is large and growing. Not only does the ADR literature represent a wide variety of views, it represents a wide variety of approaches. Much of what is written on ADR consists of prescriptive guidance for practitioners, containing suggestions on "how to be a better mediator", for example. Other ADR writings are descriptive or empirical, in the manner of social science. Finally, some ADR writings are theoretical, even philosophical, and occasionally theological.

In the midst of all this rich diversity, law can get lost. Law does not get lost in this book, however. This is a law book, written by a lawyer, for lawyers and law students.

There is a body of legal doctrine—from statutes, judicial decisions, and other sources—focused on ADR. This doctrine is prominent throughout this book, even in the sections addressing the practice of ADR, because the practice of ADR is pervasively influenced by the law of ADR. This book is written with the conviction that the law of ADR is every bit as important and challenging as the law of other fields. In short, the time has come for ADR to have its own Hornbook.

The list of people who contributed to this book is long. Thanks to Tom Berg, Mike Floyd, Henry Strickland, Bob Goodwin, Chris Drahozal, Rick Bales, Susan Nielsen, Nicole Scozzi, Thomas Gould, William Meador, Tyler Vail, Ekta Patrawala, Todd Burkett, Kimberlee Wisniewski, Susan Isbister, Marty Plummer, Monica Warmbrod Sargent, Craig Stephens, and Tammy McClendon Stokes. This book was written with the support of research grants by Samford University's Cumberland School of Law.

As I expect that there will be future editions of this book, I welcome comments on this first edition and suggestions for the future.

STEPHEN J. WARE

*

Acknowledgments

The following authors and publishers gave permission to reprint excerpts from copyright material.

Ian R. Macneil, Richard E. Speidel & Thomas J. Stipanowich, Federal Arbitration Law § 32.7.1. (1994). Reprinted by permission. Copyright © 1994 by Aspen Law and Business.

Reprinted by permission of the publisher from Game Theory and the Law by Douglas G. Baird, Robert H. Gertner, and Randall C. Picker, Cambridge, Mass.: Harvard University Press, Copyright © 1994 by the President and Fellows of Harvard College.

Guidelines for Christian Conciliation ¶ 21 (Revision 4.1 2000). Reprinted by permission. Copyright © 2000 by The Institute for Christian Conciliation™, a division of Peacemaker® Ministries.

Restatement (Second) of Contracts §§ 90 & 211 cmt.b (1981). Copyright © 1981 by The American Law Institute. Reprinted with permission.

Reprinted from Legal Negotiation: Theory and Applications, Donald G. Gifford 94 (1989) with permission of the West Group.

Jay E. Grenig, West's Legal Forms: Alternative Dispute Resolution § 2.42 (1998). Reprinted by permission. Copyright © 1998 by West Group.

8 Charles A. Wright et al., Federal Practice and Procedure § 2035 (2d ed.1994). Reprinted by permission. Copyright © 1994 by West Group.

Nancy H. Rogers & Craig A. McEwen, Mediation Law, Policy, & Practice § 2:02 (2d ed.1994). Reprinted by permission. Copyright © 1994 by West Group.

American Bar Association, Model Rules of Professional Conduct, Rule 4.1, Rule 1.7, Rule 1.7, comment 5, Rule 1.7., comment 12, and Rule 2.2 (1999). Reprinted by permission of the American Bar Association. Copyright © 1999 American Bar Association. All rights reserved. Copies of ABA Model Rules of Professional Conduct are available from Member Services, American Bar Association, 750 North Lake Shore Drive, Chicago, IL, 60611-4497, (312)988-5522.

John S. Murray, Alan Scott Rau & Edward F. Sherman, Processes of Dispute Resolution: The Role of Lawyers (2d ed.1996). Reprinted by permission. Copyright © 1996 by West Group, Foundation Press.

Leonard L. Riskin, Mediation and Lawyers, originally published in 43 Ohio St. L.J. 29, 45 (1982). Copyright © 1982 by Leonard L. Riskin and the Ohio State Law Journal.

*

WESTLAW® Overview

Alternative Dispute Resolution offers a detailed and comprehensive treatment of basic rules, principles and issues relating to alternative dispute resolution. To supplement the information contained in this book, you can access Westlaw, a computer-assisted legal research service of West Group. Westlaw contains a broad array of legal resources, including case law, statutes, expert commentary, current developments and various other types of information.

Learning how to use these materials effectively will enhance your legal research abilities. To help you coordinate the information in the book with your Westlaw research, this volume contains an appendix listing Westlaw databases, search techniques and sample problems.

THE PUBLISHER

*

Summary of Contents

*

Table of Contents

CHAPTER 3. NEGOTIATION

A. NEGOTIATION CONTEXTS

   **APPENDIX.   RESEARCHING ALTERNATIVE DISPUTE
                 RESOLUTION ON WESTLAW**

ALTERNATIVE DISPUTE RESOLUTION

*

Chapter 1

INTRODUCTION

Table of Sections

1

Research References:

Key Number System: Arbitration ☞ 1 et seq. (to(33)); Exchanges ☞ 11(11) (160k11(11); Insurance ☞ 3265–3332 (217XXVII(B)7); Labor Relations ☞ 411–500 (232AVIII); Partnership ☞ 82 (289k82)

Am Jur 2d, Actions § 138; Administrative Law §§ 395–403; Alternative Dispute Resolution §§ 1 et seq.; Appellate Review §§ 213–215; Contractors' Bonds § 239; Corporations §§ 1118, 2778; Declaratory Judgments § 157; Federal Courts §§ 2486–2488; Insurance §§ 1688–1699; Job Discrimination §§ 2317, 2318, 2648, 2654, 3015, 3045, 3072; Labor and Labor Relations §§ 162–231, 461–480, 519–565, 845–891, 3352–3510; Partnership §§ 529–541; Private Franchise Contracts §§ 389–391, 806–820

Corpus Juris Secundum, Arbitration §§ 1 et seq.; Contracts § 242; Exchanges §§ 19–43; Insurance §§ 1355–1384, 1638–1641, 1691–1695; Joint Ventures § 44; Labor Relations §§ 402–500; Mandamus § 118; Partnership §§ 92, 163, 343; Workmens' Compensation §§ 929, 930, 1136, 1137, 1230, 1238, 1247, 1264

ALR Index: Alternative Dispute Resolution; Arbitration and Award

ALR Digest: Arbitration §§ 1 et seq.; Appeal and Error §§ 721–725

Am Jur Legal Forms 2d, Arbitration and Award §§ 1 et seq.; Contracts §§ 68:199, 68:200; Labor and Labor Relations §§ 159:1347–159:1372; Physicians and Surgeons §§ 202:74, 202:75; Real Estate Sales §§ 219:841–219:844; Uniform Commercial Code §§ 253:1088–253:1112

Am Jur Pleading and Practice (Rev), Alternative Dispute Resolution §§ 1 et seq.; Arbitration and Award §§ 1 et seq.

61 Am Jur Trials 357, Trials over Arbitration Clauses in Securities Broker Contracts; 57 Am Jur Trials 555, Mediation as a Trial Alternative: Effective Use of the ADR Rules; 52 Am Jur Trials 209, Alternative Dispute Resolution: Construction Industry

31 POF3d 495, Invalidity of Foreign Arbitration Agreement or Arbitral Award; 27 POF3d 103, Establishing Statutory Grounds To Vacate an Arbitration Award In Nonjudicial Arbitration

4 POF2d 709, Bias of Arbitrator

§ 1.1 Overview

This book surveys Alternative Dispute Resolution ("ADR"). Accordingly, this introductory chapter begins by defining *dispute*,[1] then discusses what constitutes *resolution* of a dispute.[2] With the concept of *dispute resolution* thus introduced, the remainder of this chapter focuses on *processes* of dispute resolution. It notes that litigation is a process of dispute resolution and defines ADR as encompassing all legally-permitted processes of dispute resolution other than litigation.[3] It then introduces the major ADR processes (arbitration, negotiation, mediation and other processes in aid of negotiation), and suggests that arbitration is fundamentally different from all other ADR processes.[4] Much of this discussion addresses whether particular processes can produce legally-binding results and what is required for them to do so. This chapter concludes by introducing some broader perspectives on ADR.[5]

§ 1.1

1. See § 1.2.
2. See § 1.3.
3. See § 1.5.
4. See §§ 1.6 & 1.7.
5. See § 1.8.

§ 1.2   Disputes

A dispute involves at least two parties, the *disputants*. The disputants can be individuals, corporations, governments, or other entities. A dispute does not occur until one party (the *claimant*) makes a *claim* against another (the *respondent*). A claim is more than the communication of dissatisfaction. A claim asserts that the respondent has a duty to do something about the source of the claimant's dissatisfaction.

Consider, for example, an individual consumer who recently bought a shirt at a local store and seeks to return it in exchange for credit toward future purchases at that store. The consumer's request for credit might or might not constitute a claim, depending on how the consumer acts. Is the consumer asserting that the store has a duty to grant credit? Or is the consumer asking the store to do that which, the consumer concedes, the store is not obligated to do? The former is a claim, while the latter is not.

Not all claims produce disputes. Suppose the consumer asserts that the store has a duty to grant credit and the store in fact grants credit to the consumer. No dispute arises because the consumer's claim is satisfied. But if the consumer insists upon a cash refund and the store refuses, offering "store credit only", then a dispute has arisen. The respondent's rejection of a claim creates a dispute.[6]

Some disputes involve only a single claimant and a single respondent, while other disputes involve multiple claimants, multiple respondents or both. Often, respondents assert claims of their own so that some or all disputants are both claimants and respondents with respect to the same dispute.[7]

§ 1.3   Resolution of Disputes

Once a dispute arises, then what happens? The respondent's preferred answer will typically be "nothing". Disputing consumes the time, and perhaps other resources, of the respondent and rarely produces any benefits for the respondent. So unless the claimant initiates activity regarding a dispute, no such activity is likely to occur. And in many disputes, perhaps most disputes, nothing does occur. The claimant simply moves on with life. Once the claim is rejected by the respondent, the claimant drops the matter. The claimant concludes, after much deliberation or none at all, that disputing is more trouble than it is worth.[8]

§ 1.2

6. For similar definitions of *claim* and *dispute*, *see, e.g.*, Richard E. Miller & Austin Sarat, Grievances, Claims, and Disputes: Assessing the Adversary Culture, 15 Law & Soc'y Rev. 525, 526–27 (1980–81).

7. One might characterize each rejected claim as a separate dispute, but if two or more claims arise from the same transaction or occurrence they can be characterized as part of the same dispute.

§ 1.3

8. This may be a tragedy. It may be that the claimant is suffering horribly and that the respondent has a clear duty—legal and/or moral—to do something that will end the claimant's suffering.

Sometimes claimants do initiate activity regarding a dispute. The sorts of activity they initiate are varied. Some claimants violently attack respondents. Some claimants stop inviting respondents to social events. Some claimants hire lawyers to sue respondents. Similarly varied are the sorts of activities engaged in by respondents. The possible means of disputing are limited only by disputants' imaginations. So disputing takes many forms.

A dispute can last as long as the disputants last. If the disputants die, their successors, heirs or assigns can replace them as disputants.[9] So what causes a dispute to end? There are only two possibilities. Either the respondent satisfies the claim or the claimant gives up, *i.e.*, takes no further action regarding the dispute.

Ending a dispute might be synonymous with *resolving* it. But other definitions of dispute *resolution* entail more than merely ending the dispute. *Resolving* a dispute might be defined as ending the dispute:

—in such a way that the claimant is satisfied with the result,

—in such a way that all parties are satisfied with the result,

—with a just result,

—through a fair process, or

—some combination of the foregoing.[10]

Achieving any of these goals may be difficult. Even merely ending a dispute may be difficult. For example, a claimant who loses a courtroom trial and unsuccessfully appeals to higher courts may not give up. Even though the court system rules that the respondent has not breached any duty to the claimant, the claimant may continue to assert the contrary and may continue to engage in disputing activity, such as violently attacking the respondent.

§ 1.4   Processes of Dispute Resolution

As discussed in the previous section,[11] there are a variety of views about what constitutes *resolution* of a dispute. It follows from this that there are a variety of views about what constitutes a *process* of dispute resolution. If, for example, you believe that merely ending a dispute constitutes resolving it, then you must recognize violence as a process of dispute resolution. After all, violence can end a dispute by killing the claimant(s). In contrast, if you believe that dispute resolution requires not just ending a dispute, but ending it in such a way that the claimant is satisfied with the result, then you will not see the violent death of the claimant(s) as a process of dispute resolution.

---

9. This might describe the feuding between the Hatfields and McCoys or the Arabs and Israelis.

10. This list does not exhaust the possible definitions of dispute resolution.

§ 1.4

11. See § 1.3.

Because there are a variety of views about what constitutes a process of dispute resolution, it is not possible to make a list of such processes that will satisfy everyone. A typical list of dispute-resolution processes might include some or all of the following:

—adjudication,

—arbitration,

—conciliation

—early neutral evaluation,

—litigation,

—mediation,

—"med-arb",

—mini-trial,

—negotiation,

—non-binding arbitration,

—private judging,

—settlement conference, and

—summary jury trial.

Some of these processes overlap with others. Indeed, some are examples of others. To provide a structure for understanding various processes, the following sections of this chapter provide definitions and categories for the major processes of dispute resolution.

§ 1.5   Definitions of Litigation and ADR

(a) ADR as Alternatives to Litigation

Lawyers call the process by which courts decide cases *litigation*. Litigation can be defined to include all *adjudication*[12] in a government forum, whether that forum be a court or some other government body, such as an administrative agency. Litigation is a process of dispute resolution.

ADR can be defined as encompassing all legally-permitted processes of dispute resolution other than litigation.[13] While this definition (or

---

§ 1.5

12. Adjudication is the process by which somebody (the adjudicator) decides the result of a dispute. Rather than the disputing parties agreeing on the result of the dispute, as in negotiation, adjudication is the adjudicator telling the parties the result. *See, e.g.,* John S. Murray, Alan Scott Rau & Edward F. Sherman, Processes of Dispute Resolution: The Role of Lawyers 16 (2d ed.1996)(" 'Adjudication' refers to the process by which final, authoritative decisions are rendered by a neutral third party who enters the controversy without previous

knowledge of the dispute."); Lon Fuller, The Forms and Limits of Adjudication, 92 Harv.L.Rev. 353, 364 (1978)("the distinguishing characteristic of adjudication lies in the fact that it confers on the [disputing] party a peculiar form of participation in decision, that of presenting proofs and reasoned arguments for a decision in his favor.")

13. Limiting ADR to "legally-permissible" alternatives to litigation generally excludes violence, for example, from the realm of ADR.

something like it) is widely-used, ADR proponents may object to it on the ground that it privileges litigation by giving the impression that litigation is the normal or standard process of dispute resolution, while alternative processes are aberrant or deviant. That impression is false. Litigation is a relatively rarely used process of dispute resolution. Alternative processes, especially negotiation, are used far more frequently. Even disputes involving lawyers are resolved by negotiation far more often than by litigation.[14]

So ADR is not defined as everything-but-litigation because litigation is the norm. Litigation is not the norm. ADR is defined as everything-but-litigation because litigation is, as a matter of law, the default process of dispute resolution.

(b) Litigation as the Default Process

Litigation produces legally-binding results, *i.e.*, results enforced by government. Litigation produces judgments by courts and these judgments are enforced, ultimately, by sheriffs and marshals with guns and badges.[15] Parties who fail to comply with a court's judgment may find themselves imprisoned or find their property forcibly taken from them.

Not only does litigation produce legally-binding results, but its results are binding even on parties who never contracted to have their disputes resolved in litigation. This distinguishes litigation from ADR. ADR processes can produce legally-binding results, too.[16] But the results of an ADR process bind only those parties who have *contracted* to be bound by the results produced by that process.[17] To put it another way, litigation is the default process of dispute resolution. Parties can contract into alternative processes of dispute resolution, but if they do not do so then each party retains the right to have the dispute resolved in litigation.

§ 1.6   Introductions to Major ADR Processes

(a) Negotiation

To negotiate is to "communicate or confer with another to arrive at the settlement of some matter."[18] So defined, negotiation is pervasive. Nearly everyone negotiates the resolution of disputes. Lawyers do so especially frequently. Negotiation is the most frequently used process of dispute resolution and is the foundation for other important processes, including mediation.

(b) Mediation and Other Processes in Aid of Negotiation

Mediation is facilitated negotiation. A mediator is someone who

---

14. See § 3.5, n.18.

15. Jack H. Friedanthal, Mary Kay Kane & Arthur R. Miller, Civil Procedure ch.15 (3d ed.1999).

16. See § 1.7(a).

17. Id.

§ 1.6

18. Webster's Third New International Dictionary 1514 (Merriam–Webster 1971). Negotiation is the subject of Chapter 3.

helps the negotiators negotiate.[19] While negotiation involves only the parties and their agents, such as their lawyers, mediation adds the mediator, who is not an agent of either party. The mediator is a neutral.

While mediation is the most important process in aid of negotiation, there are other such processes. They include: early neutral evaluation, the mini-trial, non-binding arbitration, and the summary jury trial. What all these processes (including mediation) have in common is that they do not by themselves resolve disputes. Rather, they help the parties negotiate a resolution to the dispute. Accordingly, they are called "processes in aid of negotiation".

Many of these processes are encouraged, and sometimes even required, by courts and other government agencies. As a result, these processes become intertwined with litigation.

(c) Arbitration

Like *litigation*,[20] arbitration is a form of binding adjudication. *Adjudication* is a process by which somebody (the adjudicator) decides the result of a dispute.[21] Rather than the disputing parties agreeing on the result of the dispute, as in negotiation, adjudication is the adjudicator telling the parties the result. Judges and jurors are the adjudicators in litigation, which is adjudication in a court or other government forum. Arbitration is adjudication in a private, *i.e.*, non-government, forum.[22]

§ 1.7   The Basic Division Within ADR: Arbitration vs. Everything Else

Arbitration is profoundly different from all other forms of ADR. All other forms of ADR, while they differ from each other in some respects, are fundamentally similar. The basic division within ADR is between arbitration and everything else. This division relates to the manner in which particular processes produce legally-binding results.

(a) All ADR Processes Can Produce Binding Results

While all ADR processes can produce legally-binding results, they all require a contract to do so. Each ADR process binds only those parties who have contracted to be bound by the results produced by that process.

(1) Negotiation

Negotiation is sometimes said to be a non-binding process. But negotiation can lead to legally-binding results. Negotiation often produces an agreement between the disputants. That agreement is often legally-enforceable.[23] Settlement agreements are binding. Like court

---

19. See § 4.2. Mediation is discussed in §§ 4.1—4.30.

20. See § 1.5.

21. See § 1.5, n.12.

22. Arbitration is discussed in §§ 2.1—2.53.

§ 1.7

23. See § 3.39.

judgments, settlement agreements are enforced, ultimately, by sheriffs and marshals with guns and badges. By contrast, negotiation that does not produce a settlement agreement produces no legally-binding result. In short, a contract is required to make negotiation binding.

(2) Mediation and Other Processes in Aid of Negotiation

Binding results can be produced by mediation (and other processes in aid of negotiation) in the same manner that binding results can be produced by negotiation, by forming a settlement agreement. Also like negotiation, a process in aid of negotiation that does not produce a settlement agreement produces no legally-binding result. Mediation and other processes in aid of negotiation require a contract to be binding.

(3) Arbitration

Arbitration is a legally-binding process. Once an arbitrator renders a decision, that decision can be enforced in court.[24] The arbitrator's decision is enforced in the same manner as court judgments produced by litigation.

Disputes do not go to arbitration unless and until the parties have contracted to comply with the arbitrator's decision.[25] In other words, a contract is required for arbitration to occur at all and, therefore, for arbitration to be binding. Arbitration binds only those who contracted for it.

(b) Arbitration is the Only ADR Process that Can Produce Binding Results Without a Post–Dispute Contract

The previous paragraphs explained that all ADR processes are capable of producing legally-binding results.[26] In contrast to the results of litigation, however, the results of an ADR process bind only those parties who have contracted to be bound by that process.[27] In a significant respect then, all ADR is closely connected to the use of contracts. There is an important distinction among ADR processes, however, regarding the *time* at which the relevant contract is formed.

In all ADR processes other than arbitration, parties do not contract for a binding result until *after* the dispute has arisen. In contrast, parties can (and often do) form *pre-dispute* arbitration agreements. These are contracts containing a clause providing that, if a dispute arises, the parties will submit that dispute to arbitration and comply with the arbitrator's decision.[28] By the time a dispute arises, arbitration has replaced litigation as the default process of dispute resolution.[29] Disput-

---

24. See § 2.40.

25. See § 2.3(a).

26. See § 1.7(a).

27. See id.

28. These arbitration clauses typically are written broadly to cover any dispute the parties' transaction might produce, but also can be written more narrowly to cover just some potential disputes. See §§ 2.29—2.31. Arbitration clauses appear in a wide variety of contracts including those relating to employment, credit, goods, services and real estate.

29. See § 1.5(b)(discussing litigation as the default process of dispute resolution).

ing parties who have previously agreed to arbitrate can contract into some other process of dispute resolution, but if they do not do so then each party has the right to have the dispute resolved in arbitration.

From the post-dispute perspective then, arbitration resembles litigation more than it resembles any other ADR process. From the post-dispute perspective, either arbitration or litigation is the default process, the one process capable of producing a legally-binding resolution without further agreement between the parties. All other ADR processes (negotiation and processes in aid of it) are incapable of achieving this status, *i.e.*, of being the post-dispute default process. It cannot be said of negotiation, or a process in aid of negotiation, that it is capable of producing a legally-binding resolution without further agreement between the parties. That is because a stubborn party can easily prevent any of these processes from reaching a resolution by simply refusing all proposed settlements. Negotiation and processes in aid of it are powerless against a party who just refuses to settle.

Consider a respondent who has breached a duty to the claimant. The respondent might be a thug who has brutally beaten the claimant or a merchant who has not paid its debt for goods received from the claimant. Either way, the respondent may prefer that the claimant remain unsatisfied. The respondent may recognize that it has breached a duty to the claimant and may want to avoid liability for that breach. In short, the respondent may want to avoid justice.

Negotiation and processes in aid of it are powerless against such a respondent. They pose no threat to the respondent. In contrast, litigation and arbitration threaten the respondent with the prospect of being imprisoned or having its property forcibly taken.[30] Litigation and, from the post-dispute perspective, arbitration impose results on the respondent. Negotiation and processes in aid of it produce only those results agreeable to respondent. Negotiation and processes in aid of it are just talk. Litigation and arbitration are physical force.

(c) Arbitration or Litigation Casts the Shadow in Which Negotiation and Processes in Aid of it Occur

The previous section explained that, from the post-dispute perspective, either litigation or arbitration can be the default process, the one process capable of producing a legally-binding result without further agreement between the parties.[31] All other ADR processes (negotiation and processes in aid of it) are incapable of becoming the default process.[32] However, negotiation and processes in aid of it are often heavily influenced by the default process. The following paragraphs, which explain that influence, are phrased in terms of negotiation, but their reasoning also applies to processes in aid of negotiation, such as mediation.

30. See §§ 1.5(b) & 1.7(a)(3).   **32.** See id.
31. See § 1.7(b).

Most dispute negotiation occurs without the involvement of lawyers. Usually, the disputants—such as family members or co-workers—negotiate on their own. Lawyers are likely to be involved in only the negotiation of a narrow class of disputes: those in litigation or arbitration, and those that are likely to go to litigation or arbitration if negotiation fails to reach a settlement. Negotiation of these disputes can be called *settlement negotiation*. Because of its importance to lawyers, settlement negotiation is emphasized in this book.

Settlement negotiation is negotiation about the sale of a claim by Claimant to Respondent. Claims, though, differ from other saleable assets in the legal consequences of not agreeing on price. If a car, for example, is not sold because the negotiators do not agree on price, the potential buyer will keep its money and the potential seller will keep its car. Nobody will force a sale. In contrast, if a claim is not sold because the negotiators do not agree on a price, the claimant can force a sale through litigation or arbitration, whichever is the default process.[33] The court's or arbitrator's decision will transfer (or "sell") the claim from Claimant to Respondent and will set the price Respondent must pay. This impending "forced sale" looms over settlement negotiation. Settlement negotiation is conducted "in the shadow of the law" because the negotiators' expectations about the results of litigation or arbitration, *i.e.*, the forced sale, shape the negotiators' attitudes toward various settlement terms.[34] Negotiators' expectations about the price of a forced sale, if it comes to that, influence the price at which they will agree to settle. The "price" of a claim, whether agreed to in settlement or imposed by litigation or arbitration, is not necessarily an amount of money. The price includes whatever the claimant receives in exchange for the claim.

(d) Implications for Categorizing and Comparing Processes

This section's discussion thus far[35] suggests a two-step analysis of processes for resolving a dispute that has already arisen. The first step is to determine whether litigation or arbitration is the default process. Litigation is the default process unless the parties have formed an enforceable arbitration agreement covering the dispute in question.[36] Once the default process has been identified, each party can try to predict the likely results of the default process.[37] Doing so informs that party's decisions regarding negotiation and processes in aid of negotiation.

This analysis suggests that arbitration and litigation are substitutes for each other. It also suggests that negotiation and processes in aid of it are (1) substitutes for each other,[38] and (2) not substitutes for arbitration

---

33. See §§ 1.5(b)(discussing litigation as the default process) & 1.7(b)(discussing arbitration replacing litigation as the default process).

34. See § 3.11.

35. See §§ 1.7(a)-(c).

36. See §§ 1.5(b) & 1.7(b).

37. See § 3.5.

38. See § 4.30(b). See also Nancy H. Rogers & Craig A. McEwen, Mediation Law, Policy, & Practice § 2:02 at 12 (2d ed.1994).

or litigation. Arbitration and litigation fall into the category of default processes, processes that cast "the shadow of the law".[39] Negotiation and processes in aid of it, such as mediation, fall into the category of non-default processes, processes that occur in the shadow cast by litigation or arbitration.[40]

It is, therefore, useful to compare arbitration and litigation to each other as if they were competing products on a store's shelf. It is similarly useful to compare negotiation and mediation to each other,[41] or to compare mediation with some other process in aid of negotiation.

Far trickier is to try to compare a default process with a non-default process. Those who compare mediation to arbitration, for example, must be especially careful. Such comparisons often go awry due to a failure to appreciate the basic difference between a process that casts the shadow of the law and a process that occurs in that shadow.

§ 1.8   Broader Perspectives on ADR

(a) ADR Diversity

As this introductory chapter has shown, ADR encompasses a variety of quite different processes. It is, therefore, difficult to generalize about ADR. One too often hears statements beginning with phrases like "One of ADR's strengths is * * *", or "One of ADR's weaknesses is * * *". Such statements usually over-generalize because there are few traits common to all ADR processes. The only thing all ADR processes have in common is that they are not litigation.[42] To completely oppose ADR, therefore, one would have to believe that litigation is the one right way to resolve every dispute. Similarly, it is rare to find people whose support for ADR is so all-encompassing that they believe litigation is never the best way to resolve any dispute.

Many ADR proponents are enthusiastic about some, but not all ADR processes. Other ADR proponents are enthusiastic about ADR only as long as it is voluntarily chosen by the parties. These opponents of mandatory ADR, however, have a variety of views about what is mandatory and what is voluntary.[43] Other ADR proponents are enthusiastic about the "multi-door courthouse" where individual disputes would be matched with appropriate processes so the "forum fits the fuss."[44] In sum, there is a great diversity of views among ADR proponents.

39. See § 1.7(c).

40. Id.

41. See § 4.24.

§ 1.8

42. See § 1.5.

43. Compare, e.g., Stephen J. Ware, Employment Arbitration and Voluntary Consent, 25 Hofstra L.Rev. 83 (1996), with commentators cited therein at nn. 102–04.

44. See, e.g., Frank E.A. Sander & Stephen B. Goldberg, Fitting the Forum to the Fuss: A User–Friendly Guide to Selecting an ADR Procedure, 10 Neg.J. 49 (1994). The idea of a multi-door courthouse is generally traced to Frank Sander, who originally referred to it as a Dispute Resolution Center. See Frank E.A. Sander, Varieties of Dispute Processing, 70 F.R.D. 111 (1976) (envisioning Dispute Resolution Center, with several specialized departments, in which a screening clerk would direct a grievant to the appropriate process).

(b) Cool and Warm Themes; The Cost and Quality of Dispute Resolution

The previous paragraphs emphasize the diversity of ADR and the diversity of views among ADR proponents.[45] One can, however, see themes in the ADR movement. One way to categorize these themes is as "cool" and "warm".[46] The "cool" theme of the ADR movement focuses on the *cost* of dispute-resolution. "Cool" proponents of ADR emphasize that litigation is a costly process of dispute resolution. Time and money typically can be saved by using a different process. In contrast, the "warm" theme of the ADR movement focuses on the *quality* of dispute resolution. Quality can be measured in many ways. Some see quality in a resolution to the dispute which is "responsive * * * to the underlying needs and interests of the parties."[47] Others see quality in a process that replaces "adversary conflict" with "reconciliation" and "mutual understanding."[48] When quality is defined along these lines, warm-theme proponents of ADR see little quality in litigation.

There may be a tradeoff between the cost of dispute resolution and the quality of dispute resolution. Higher quality processes of dispute resolution may tend to cost more than lower quality processes, just as higher quality cars tend to cost more than lower quality cars. Not all proponents of ADR will concede this point. Some cool-theme ADR proponents argue that their preferred processes reduce costs without sacrificing any quality. Some warm-theme ADR proponents argue that their preferred processes increase quality without adding cost. Some ADR proponents even argue that their preferred processes both lower costs and raise quality. Regardless of how persuasive one finds these arguments, it is useful to compare dispute-resolution processes in terms of their cost and quality.

(c) Lawyers and ADR

While everyone can compare dispute-resolution processes in terms of their cost and quality in general,[49] the lawyer representing a client in a particular dispute must take a more narrow perspective. The lawyer must seek to advance the client's interests so, from this perspective, the quality of a process is measured by how well the client is likely to fare in

Along these lines, some ADR proponents say the "ADR" they favor stands for *appropriate* dispute resolution, rather than *alternative* dispute resolution. *See, e.g.,* Leonard L. Riskin & James E. Westbrook, Dispute Resolution and Lawyers 51 (2d ed.1997). This usage emphasizes the ability to "choose or design the most appropriate methods to resolve a dispute." Id. While nobody says he or she opposes "appropriate" dispute resolution, there is disagreement over who gets to decide which process is most appropriate for which dispute. This book is written with the conviction that the parties to each dispute should be free to decide for themselves which process is most appropriate. The contrary view is perhaps most famously expressed in Owen Fiss, Against Settlement, 93 Yale L.J. 1073 (1984).

45. See § 1.8(a).

46. See Murray, Rau & Sherman, supra note 12, at 45–46.

47. Id.

48. Id.

49. See § 1.8(b).

that process.[50] Will my client receive a higher award of money damages from a jury than an arbitrator? Will mediation rebuild a relationship important to my client? Will negotiating a settlement cost my client less than going to trial? These are the sorts of questions lawyers must ask and answer. The answers will change from client to client and dispute to dispute. Often the answers will be difficult judgment-calls about which reasonable people (including reasonable lawyers) can disagree. But a lawyer who fails even to ask these questions, because of an assumption that litigation is the only option, has committed malpractice.

To reiterate, two perspectives must be distinguished. One is the perspective of the person considering various processes of dispute resolution based on their costs and quality, generally. The other is the perspective of the lawyer considering various processes based on their suitability in advancing the interests of a particular client with a particular dispute. The lawyer may, as a person, believe that a particular process of dispute resolution is generally very costly and low in quality. But that lawyer may have a professional obligation to use that process if doing so appears to be in the client's interests.

Finally, we can ask about the lawyer's own interests. Various processes of dispute resolution affect lawyers—individual lawyers and lawyers as a whole—in different ways. Lawyers have an interest, in every sense of that word "interest", in the extent to which various processes of dispute resolution are used. Do the interests of lawyers, in this regard, diverge from the interests of society as a whole?[51]

50. See, e.g., James E. Westbrook, The Problems with Process Bias, 1989 J.Disp.Resol. 309, 313, 316.

51. See, e.g., Murray, Rau & Sherman, supra note 12, at 49.

Chapter 2

ARBITRATION AND SIMILAR PROCESSES

Table of Sections

A. OVERVIEW

B. SOURCES OF CONTEMPORARY AMERICAN ARBITRATION LAW

C. FAA PREEMPTION OF STATE LAW

1. THE FAA's EVOLUTION FROM PROCEDURAL TO SUBSTANTIVE LAW

2. PREEMPTION OF STATE LAW IMPEDING CONTRACT ENFORCEMENT

Research References:

Key Number System: Arbitration ☞ 1 et seq. (to(33)); Exchanges ☞ 11(11) (160k11(11); Insurance ☞ 3265–3332 (217XXVII(B)7); Labor Relations ☞ 411–500 (232AVIII); Partnership ☞ 82 (217k82)

Am Jur 2d, Actions § 138; Administrative Law §§ 395–403; Admiralty §§ 15–17; Alternative Dispute Resolution §§ 1 et seq.; Appellate Review §§ 213–215; Automobile Insurance §§ 604–611; Contractors' Bonds § 239; Corporations §§ 1118, 2778; Declaratory Judgments § 157; Federal Courts §§ 2486–2488; Insurance §§ 1688–1699; International Law §§ 124, 139, 157; Job Discrimination §§ 2317, 2318, 2648, 2654, 3015, 3045, 3072; Labor and Labor Relations §§ 162–231, 461–480, 519–565, 845–891, 3352–3510; Partnership §§ 529–541; Patents §§ 1156–1160; Pollution Control §§ 1306–1320, 1756–1779; Private Franchise Contracts §§ 389–391, 806–820; Wrongful Discharge § 203

Corpus Juris Secundum, Arbitration §§ 1 et seq.; Attorney and Client § 204; Contracts § 242; Exchanges §§ 19–43; Insurance §§ 1355–1384, 1638–1641, 1691–1695; International Law § 61; Joint Ventures § 44; Labor Relations §§ 402–500; Mandamus § 118; Partnership §§ 92, 163, 343; Workmens' Compensation §§ 929, 930, 1136, 1137, 1230, 1238, 1247, 1264

ALR Index: Alternative Dispute Resolution; Arbitration and Award

ALR Digest: Arbitration §§ 1 et seq.; Insurance § 619; Attorneys § 52

Am Jur Legal Forms 2d, Arbitration and Award §§ 1 et seq.; Building Contracts §§ 47:154–47:162; Community Property § 61:215; Contracts §§ 68:199, 68:200; International Business Transactions §§ 150B:59, 150B:60; Labor and Labor Relations §§ 159:1347–159:1372; Physicians and Surgeons §§ 202:74, 202:75; Real Estate Sales §§ 219:841–219:844; Uniform Commercial Code §§ 253:1088–253:1112

Am Jur Pleading and Practice (Rev), Alternative Dispute Resolution §§ 1–4; Arbitration and Award §§ 1 et seq.; Automobile Insurance §§ 147–195; Building and Construction Contracts §§ 12–15; Insurance §§ 751–777; Labor and Labor Relations, Forms 81, 87, 102, 113

61 Am Jur Trials 357, Trials over Arbitration Clauses in Securities Broker Contracts; 57 Am Jur Trials 255, Alternative Dispute Resolution: Employment Law; 56 Am Jur Trials 529, Strategies for Effective Management of Crossborder Recognition and Enforcement of American Money Judgments; 52 Am Jur Trials 209, Alternative Dispute Resolution: Construction Industry; 46 Am Jur Trials 231, Alternative Dispute Resolution for Banks and Other Financial Institutions; 44 Am Jur Trials 507, Alternative Dispute Resolution: Commercial Arbitration; 27 Am Jur Trials 621, Resolving Real Estate Disputes Through Arbitration; 11 Am Jur Trials 327, Arbitration of a Labor Dispute–Management Representation

31 POF3d 495, Invalidity of Foreign Arbitration Agreement or Arbitral Award; 27 POF3d 103, Establishing Statutory Grounds To Vacate an Arbitration Award In Nonjudicial Arbitration; 9 POF3d 687, Invalidity of Judgment of Court of Foreign Country

4 POF2d 709, Bias of Arbitrator

A. OVERVIEW

Table of Sections

§ 2.1 Arbitration Defined

Arbitration is private adjudication.[1] *Adjudication* is a process by which somebody (the adjudicator) decides the result of a dispute.[2] Rather than the disputing parties agreeing on the result of the dispute, as in *negotiation*[3] or *mediation*,[4] adjudication is the adjudicator telling the parties the result. Judges and jurors are the adjudicators in *litigation*, which is adjudication in a government forum, typically a court. Arbitration is adjudication in a private, *i.e.*, non-government, forum.

In addition to being "private" in the sense of non-governmental, arbitration is also usually "private" in the sense of secret or confidential. But it does not have to be. Arbitration could occur on a busy city sidewalk in full view of the public. It would still be *private* adjudication. In short, the essence of arbitration is that it is a private-sector alternative to government courts. It is to the court system what private schools are to public schools, or what private housing is to government housing projects.

§ 2.2 Contractual Arbitration and Non–Contractual Arbitration; Constitutional Right to Jury Trial

There are two types of arbitration, contractual and non-contractual.[5] The duty to arbitrate a dispute can be created by contract or by other law. If the duty to arbitrate is created by contract, then enforcing that duty is unlikely to violate the constitutional right to a jury trial. Courts typically hold that, by forming a contract to arbitrate, a party waives its right to a trial by jury.[6] In contrast, the parties to non-contractual

---

§ 2.1

1. See, e.g., Ian R. Macneil, Richard E. Speidel & Thomas J. Stipanowich, Federal Arbitration Law § 2.6.1, at 2:37 n.1 (1994); John S. Murray, Alan Scott Rau & Edward F. Sherman, Processes of Dispute Resolution: The Role of Lawyers 500–22 (2d ed.1996).

2. See § 1.5(a), n.12.

3. See Chapter 3.

4. See Chapter 4.

§ 2.2

5. See § 2.55(a).

6. See, e.g., Dillard v. Merrill Lynch, Pierce, Fenner & Smith, Inc., 961 F.2d 1148, 1155 n. 12 (5th Cir.1992); In re Ball, 236 A.D.2d 158, 665 N.Y.S.2d 444, 447 (N.Y.App.Div.1997); Mugnano–Bornstein v. Crowell, 42 Mass.App.Ct. 347, 677 N.E.2d 242 (Mass.App.Ct.1997); Long v. DeGeer, 753 P.2d 1327, 1329 (Okla.1987); Madden v. Kaiser Foundation Hospitals, 17 Cal.3d 699,

131 Cal.Rptr. 882, 891, 552 P.2d 1178 (1976). But cf. Moore v. Fragatos, 116 Mich. App. 179, 321 N.W.2d 781, 785 (Mich.Ct. App.1982)(no waiver of jury trial right); Jean Sternlight, Rethinking the Constitutionality of the Supreme Court's Preference for Binding Arbitration, 72 Tul.L.Rev. 1, 47–48 (1997)("Courts' willingness and even eagerness to conclude that parties have, by accepting binding arbitration, waived their constitutional rights cannot be reconciled with the protective attitude usually displayed by courts toward the waiver of constitutional rights.")

The Seventh Amendment, preserving the right to jury trial, is one of the few provisions of the Bill of Rights that constrains only federal, not state, government. See Curtis v. Loether, 415 U.S. 189, 192 n. 6, 94 S.Ct. 1005, 39 L.Ed.2d 260 (1974). The Seventh Amendment applies in federal, not state, court. While many state constitutions contain a provision that similarly protects the right to trial by jury, see Martin H.

arbitration have rarely waived the right to a jury trial. Therefore, non-contractual arbitration generally must be non-binding to avoid violating this right.[7]

Non-contractual, yet binding, arbitration is discussed at the end of this chapter, under the heading "Processes Similar to Arbitration."[8] Otherwise, the term "arbitration" is used throughout this chapter to mean "contractual arbitration."

Non-binding arbitration has less in common with arbitration than it does with mediation and other processes in aid of negotiation. Accordingly, non-binding arbitration is discussed, not in this chapter, but in Chapter 4.[9]

§ 2.3 Arbitration Law Summarized

(a) Post–Dispute and Pre–Dispute Agreements to Arbitrate

A dispute goes to arbitration only when the parties have contracted to send it there.[10] Sometimes parties with an existing dispute contract to send that dispute to arbitration. Such *post-dispute* arbitration agreements (or "submission agreements") are relatively rare and non-controversial.[11] More common, and more controversial, are *pre-dispute* arbitration agreements. These are contracts containing a clause providing that, if a dispute arises, the parties will resolve that dispute in arbitration, rather than litigation. These arbitration clauses typically are written broadly to cover any dispute the parties' transaction might produce, but also can be written more narrowly to cover just some potential disputes.[12] Arbitration clauses appear in a wide variety of contracts including those relating to employment, credit, goods, services and real estate.

(b) Enforcement of Arbitration Agreements

In the case of most contracts containing arbitration clauses, like most contracts generally, the parties never have any dispute. If the parties do have a dispute, however, the arbitration clause likely will be enforceable, so that a party who would rather litigate than arbitrate will

Redish, Legislative Response to Medical Malpractice Insurance Crisis: Constitutional Implications, 55 Tex.L.Rev. 759, 797 (1977), the Federal Arbitration Act prevails in a conflict between it and a state constitutional provision. See U.S. Const. art. VI, § 2 (the Supremacy Clause). Thus, an arbitration agreement's effectiveness as a waiver of the right to jury trial is determined solely by federal, rather than state, law.

7. See § 2.55.

8. See id.

9. See § 4.32.

§ 2.3

10. See, e.g., First Options of Chicago, Inc. v. Kaplan, 514 U.S. 938, 943, 115 S.Ct. 1920, 131 L.Ed.2d 985 (1995)("arbitration is simply a matter of contract between the parties"); United Steelworkers v. Warrior & Gulf Nav. Co., 363 U.S. 574, 582, 80 S.Ct. 1347, 4 L.Ed.2d 1409 (1960)("arbitration is a matter of contract and a party cannot be required to submit to arbitration any dispute which he has not agreed so to submit.")

11. Post-dispute arbitration agreements resemble settlement agreements, which are discussed in Chapter 3. By agreeing to arbitrate a particular dispute that has already arisen, the plaintiff agrees to give up her claim against the defendant in exchange, not for something specified, but for whatever the arbitrator decides to award her.

12. See §§ 2.29—2.31 & 2.53(c)(3).

have to perform its agreement to arbitrate. If, for example, Seller sues Buyer despite an arbitration agreement between them, Buyer can get a court to stay or dismiss Seller's lawsuit.[13] The court enforces Seller's agreement to arbitrate by relegating Seller's claim to arbitration; Seller's only forum to pursue its claim is arbitration.[14] Another possibility is that Seller asserts a claim against Buyer in arbitration but Buyer simply refuses to participate in arbitration. Seller can get a court order compelling Buyer to participate.[15] In this manner, the court enforces Buyer's agreement to arbitrate.

(c) The Arbitration Process

Not only does the parties' contract determine *whether* a dispute goes to arbitration, the contract also determines *what occurs* during arbitration.[16] Arbitration, like any *adjudication*,[17] involves the presentation of evidence and argument to the adjudicator. The presentation of evidence and argument in *litigation* is governed by rules of procedure and evidence enacted by government. In contrast, the rules of procedure and evidence in arbitration are, with few exceptions, whatever the contract says they are. Arbitration agreements commonly provide for less discovery and motion practice than is typical of litigation and commonly provide for fewer rules of evidence than are typical of litigation. But the parties are free to draft their agreement almost any way they like. Arbitration privatizes procedural law by allowing parties to create their own customized rules of procedure and evidence. In short, arbitration is a creature of contract.

(d) Enforcement of Arbitrator's Decision or "Award"

Once an arbitrator renders a decision, that decision can be enforced in court. Judicial enforcement may not be needed because the party losing at arbitration often voluntarily complies with the arbitrator's decision. Nevertheless, the winning party can get a court order *confirming* the arbitration award; confirmation converts the award into a judgment of the court.[18] A confirmed arbitration award in favor of the plaintiff (or "claimant") is enforced in the same manner as other court judgments, through judgment liens, execution, garnishment, etc. Arbitration awards also are enforced through the preclusion of subsequent court actions. An arbitration award in favor of the defendant (or "respondent") precludes the plaintiff from litigating the claim that was already resolved in arbitration.[19]

---

13. See § 2.4(b).

14. With respect to this dispute, arbitration has replaced litigation as the default process of dispute resolution. Disputing parties who have previously agreed to arbitrate can contract into some other process of dispute resolution, but if they do not do so then each party has the right to have the dispute resolved in arbitration. See § 1.7(b).

15. See § 2.4(b).

16. See §§ 2.35—2.39.

17. See § 1.5(a), n.12.

18. See § 2.40.

19. See § 2.41.

Judicial enforcement of arbitrators' decisions is simply an example of courts enforcing contracts. The parties agreed to comply with the arbitrator's decision and if a party refuses to do so then that party is in breach of contract. To put it another way, the arbitrator's decision is, with few exceptions,[20] final and binding.

B. SOURCES OF CONTEMPORARY AMERICAN ARBITRATION LAW

Table of Sections

§ 2.4   Federal Law

The Federal Arbitration Act ("FAA")[21] is by far the most important source of arbitration law. There are other sources of federal arbitration law but they govern only specific types of arbitration, such as labor arbitration[22] and international arbitration.[23] State arbitration law is much less important than the FAA because the FAA has a broad reach and preempts state law that conflicts with it.[24]

(a) Pro–Contract

The FAA, enacted in 1925, is resolutely pro-contract. FAA § 2 says that arbitration agreements "shall be valid, irrevocable, and enforceable, save upon such grounds as exist at law or in equity for the revocation of any contract."[25] This language reflects an intent to place arbitration agreements "upon the same footing as other contracts" and to reverse judicial hostility to the enforcement of arbitration agreements.[26] The FAA's enactment was "motivated, first and foremost, by a congressional desire to enforce agreements into which parties had entered."[27]

---

20.   See §§ 2.43—2.46.

§ 2.4

21.   9 U.S.C. §§ 1–16, 201–08, 301–07 (1994).

22.   See § 2.53.

23.   See § 2.48.

24.   See §§ 2.6—2.18.

25.   The full text of § 2 is as follows:

A written provision in any maritime transaction or a contract evidencing a transaction involving commerce to settle by arbitration a controversy thereafter arising out of such contract or transaction, or the refusal to perform the whole or any part thereof, or an agreement in writing to submit to arbitration an existing controversy arising out of such a contract, transaction, or refusal, shall be valid, irrevocable, and enforceable, save upon such grounds as exist at law or in equity for the revocation of any contract.

9 U.S.C. § 2 (1994).

26.   H.R.Rep.No. 68–96, at 2 (1924).

27.   Volt Info. Sciences, Inc. v. Board of Trustees, 489 U.S. 468, 109 S.Ct. 1248, 103 L.Ed.2d 488 (1989); Dean Witter Reynolds v. Byrd, 470 U.S. 213, 220, 105 S.Ct. 1238, 84 L.Ed.2d 158 (1985).

(b) Court Orders to Arbitrate; Specific Performance of Arbitration Agreements

The FAA requires courts to use an especially powerful remedy in enforcing arbitration agreements. While money damages are the ordinary remedy for breach of contract,[28] specific performance is the FAA's remedy for breach of an arbitration agreement. An example will illuminate the point.

Suppose that Seller sues Buyer despite an arbitration agreement between them. If Seller's suit occurred prior to the enactment of the FAA,[29] the court would allow Seller's litigation to proceed.[30] The court would deny Buyer's motion to stay or dismiss Seller's case. The only remedy available to Buyer for Seller's breach of the arbitration agreement would be money damages. But how would the amount of those damages be calculated? To put the non-breaching party in the position it would have been in had the contract had been performed,[31] the court would have to predict the results of both arbitration and litigation, then award as damages the difference (in terms of value to the non-breaching party) between the two. The speculativeness of such an approach is daunting. And courts did not use such an approach. A court might award nominal damages of one dollar or so,[32] but Buyer would receive no meaningful remedy for Seller's breach. In short, Seller could breach its arbitration agreement without legal consequence.

Alternatively, suppose that Seller asserted a claim against Buyer in arbitration but Buyer simply refused to participate in arbitration. Prior to the FAA, Seller could not get a court order compelling Buyer to participate in arbitration.[33] If Seller wanted to pursue its claim against Buyer, Seller would have to do so in litigation. There would be no meaningful remedy for Buyer's breach of the arbitration agreement. Buyer could breach its arbitration agreement with impunity.

The FAA changes the result in both of the Seller/Buyer scenarios. Under the FAA, the remedy for breach of an arbitration agreement is specific performance, *i.e.*, an order to arbitrate.

---

28. See John D. Calamari & Joseph M. Perillo, Contracts § 14.1 (4th ed.1998)

29. Suits brought in the courts of two states, New York and New Jersey, are exceptions to this generalization. These two states enacted statutes providing specific enforcement for arbitration agreements a few years before the FAA's 1925 enactment. See Ian R. Macneil, American Arbitration Law: Reformation, Nationalization, Internationalization 34–47 (1992).

30. See Macneil, Speidel & Stipanowich, supra note 1, § 4.3.2.2 (explaining that in the period 1800–1920, agreements to arbitrate future disputes were not enforced with remedy of specific performance); Wesley A. Sturges, Commercial Arbitration and Awards § 87 (1930).

31. This is the way to calculate the "expectation damages" normally awarded for breach of contract. See Restatement (Second) of Contracts §§ 344 & 347 (1981).

32. See Munson v. Straits of Dover S. S. Co., 102 F. 926 (2d Cir.1900) (holding that plaintiff, who sought damages in the form of lawyer's fees and costs incurred in defending a lawsuit for breach of agreement to arbitrate, was entitled to nominal damages only.)

33. Two states, New York and New Jersey, enacted statutes providing specific enforcement for arbitration agreements a few years before the FAA's 1925 enactment. See Macneil, supra note 29.

Consider, first, Seller's suit against Buyer. A plaintiff who sues, despite an arbitration agreement with the defendant, is in breach of that agreement. By staying the lawsuit, a court effectively orders the plaintiff to perform the agreement to arbitrate. This stay follows from FAA § 3, which says:

> If any suit or proceeding be brought in any of the courts of the United States upon any issue referable to arbitration under an agreement in writing for such arbitration, the court in which such suit is pending, upon being satisfied that the issue involved in such suit or proceeding is referable to arbitration under such an agreement, shall on application of one of the parties stay the trial of the action until such arbitration has been had in accordance with the terms of the agreement, providing the applicant for the stay is not in default in proceeding with such arbitration.[34]

Now consider the second scenario, Buyer's refusal to arbitrate Seller's claim against it. A defendant who refuses to participate in arbitration will be ordered by a court to do so. This order follows from FAA § 4, which says, in part:

> A party aggrieved by the alleged failure, neglect, or refusal of another to arbitrate under a written agreement for arbitration may petition any United States district court * * * for an order directing that such arbitration proceed in the manner provided for in such agreement * * * . The court shall hear the parties, and upon being satisfied that the making of the agreement for arbitration or the failure to comply therewith is not in issue, the court shall make an order directing the parties to proceed to arbitration in accordance with the terms of the agreement * * * .[35]

To summarize, FAA §§ 3 and 4 require courts to enforce arbitration agreements with orders of specific performance. Rather than ordering the payment of money, courts order parties in breach of arbitration agreements to perform their agreements, *i.e.*, to arbitrate. Failure to obey such an order is contempt of court,[36] punishable by financial sanctions or even imprisonment.

(c) Broad Applicability

The FAA applies to a written[37] arbitration agreement "in any maritime transaction or a contract evidencing a transaction involving commerce."[38] FAA § 1 defines "commerce" to mean interstate or international commerce.[39] The Supreme Court interprets this language broad-

---

34. 9 U.S.C. § 3 (1994).

35. 9 U.S.C. § 4 (1994).

36. See Wal–Mart Stores, Inc. v. PT Multipolar Corp., 202 F.3d 280, 1999 WL 1079625, *2 (9th Cir.1999).

37. An oral arbitration agreement may be unenforceable. The FAA requires courts to enforce only "written" arbitration agreements, as do most state arbitration stat-

utes. See Unif. Arbitration Act § 2, 7 U.L.A. 1, 109 (1997). This statute of frauds can be satisfied by conduct manifesting an intent to submit disputes to arbitration.

38. 9 U.S.C. § 2 (1994).

39. "Commerce" is defined as:

commerce among the several States or with foreign nations, or in any Territory of the United States or in the District of

ly to reach all transactions affecting interstate or international commerce.[40] So interpreted, FAA § 1's definition of commerce is extremely broad, bringing the vast majority of arbitration agreements within the coverage of the FAA.[41]

There is, however, an exception to the FAA's extremely broad reach. FAA § 1 says "nothing herein contained shall apply to contracts of employment of seamen, railroad employees, or any other class of workers engaged in foreign or interstate commerce."[42] Arbitration agreements falling within this "employment exclusion" are not governed by the FAA.[43] On the other hand, collective bargaining arbitration agreements falling within this exclusion are made enforceable by another federal statute, the Labor Management Relations Act ("LMRA").[44] The important area of labor arbitration is governed primarily by the LMRA, rather than the FAA.

§ 2.5   State Law

(a) Arbitration Law

Prior to the 1925 enactment of the FAA, only two states required courts to enforce pre-dispute arbitration agreements with the remedy of specific performance, *i.e.*, orders to arbitrate.[45] The 1925 law in all other states provided no meaningful remedy against a party in breach of its promise to arbitrate. Since 1925, nearly every state has changed its law to require courts to order performance of arbitration agreements. Now, only Alabama, and, perhaps, Mississippi and West Virginia still refuse such enforcement of pre-dispute arbitration agreements.[46]

Many states have adopted the Uniform Arbitration Act ("UAA").[47] The UAA is similar to the FAA. There are few, if any, inconsistencies

---

Columbia, or between any such Territory and another, or between any such Territory and any State or foreign nation, or between the District of Columbia and any State or Territory or foreign nation, but nothing herein contained shall apply to contracts of employment of seamen, railroad employees, or any other class of workers engaged in foreign or interstate commerce.

9 U.S.C. § 1 (1994).

40. Allied–Bruce Terminix Co. Inc., v. Dobson, 513 U.S. 265, 115 S.Ct. 834, 130 L.Ed.2d 753 (1995).

41. For rare exceptions, see Sisters of the Visitation v. Cochran Plastering Co., 2000 WL 681066 (Ala.2000); City of Cut Bank v. Tom Patrick Construction, Inc., 290 Mont. 470, 963 P.2d 1283 (Mont.1998).

42. 9 U.S.C. § 1 (1994).

43. Most employment arbitration agreements do not fall within this exclusion. In other words, most employment arbitration

agreements are governed by the FAA. See § 2.51.

44. See § 2.53.

§ 2.5

45. Macneil, supra note 29.

46. Macneil, supra note 29, at 57; Henry C. Strickland et al., Modern Arbitration for Alabama: A Concept Whose Time Has Come, 25 Cumb.L.Rev. 59, 60 n.4 (1994)(listing statutes). See also Ala. Code § 8–1–41(3) (1975)("The following obligations cannot be specifically enforced: * * * An agreement to submit a controversy to arbitration"); Miss. Code Ann. § 11–15–1 (1972)(enforcing only post-dispute arbitration agreements); IP Timberlands Oper. Co., v. Denmiss Corp., 726 So.2d 96, 104 (Miss.1998)("this Court will respect the right of an individual or an entity to agree in advance of a dispute to arbitration").

47. The UAA, drafted by the National Conference of Commissioners on Uniform

between the two statutes. But the UAA is longer than the FAA, covering some topics not addressed by the FAA.[48] Originally drafted in 1955, the UAA was recently revised for the first time.[49]

This book discusses state arbitration law only where that law differs from federal law. Where state and federal arbitration law are the same, nothing turns on the question of which applies.

(b) Non–Arbitration Law

Neither the FAA, nor the UAA, nor any other arbitration statute, is a complete statement of all the law governing arbitration.[50] These statutes presuppose, and often incorporate, existing law in areas such as contract, property, agency and tort.[51] In other words, lots of non-arbitration law applies to arbitration. Most of this non-arbitration law is state common law. Especially important to arbitration is the common law of contracts. Much of arbitration law is merely an application of general contract law to a particular sort of contract, the arbitration agreement.[52]

C. FAA PREEMPTION OF STATE LAW

Table of Sections

1. THE FAA's EVOLUTION FROM PROCEDURAL TO SUBSTANTIVE LAW

2. PREEMPTION OF STATE LAW IMPEDING CONTRACT ENFORCEMENT

State Laws, has been enacted in 34 states, plus the District of Columbia. See Unif. Arbitration Act, 7 U.L.A. 281–83 (1997); See also 7 U.L.A. 1 (1997)(table of jurisdictions adopting the act).

48. Macneil, Speidel & Stipanowich, supra note 1, § 5.4.2.

49. For the latest draft, see <www.law.upenn.edu/bll/ulc/ulc.htm#uaa>.

50. Macneil, Speidel & Stipanowich, supra note 1, § 10.6.2.1.

51. Id.

52. See §§ 2.19—2.46. For that reason, much of the language of this chapter and even some of its organization is borrowed from contract law.

1. THE FAA'S EVOLUTION FROM PROCEDURAL TO SUBSTANTIVE LAW

Table of Sections

§ 2.6 The Original FAA as Procedural Law

The relationship between federal and state law is one of the most important and complex topics in arbitration law. The starting point is the Supremacy Clause of the United States Constitution, which says that federal law is supreme over state law.[53] In a conflict between federal and state law, the federal law governs. Consider, for example, a case in which Defendant is liable to Plaintiff under state tort and contract law. If Defendant can show that enforcement of that state law would conflict with a federal statute, the Employee Retirement Income Security Act ("ERISA"), then Defendant wins the case.[54] What would have been the result under state law is reversed by federal law. What has just been said about the preemptive effect of ERISA can also be said about all federal *substantive* law. Federal substantive law preempts state law, and this is true whether the case is heard in federal or state court. In contrast, federal *procedural* law does not preempt state law. For instance, the Federal Rules of Civil Procedure do not preempt inconsistent state law because the Federal Rules of Civil Procedure only apply in federal court and the "inconsistent" state law, the state rules of civil procedure, only apply in state court. There is no conflict because each governs in its own forum.

The same was true of federal and state arbitration law prior to the FAA's 1925 enactment. Federal arbitration law governed only in federal court and state arbitration law governed only in state court.[55] The FAA

---

§ 2.6

53. U.S. Const. art. VI, cl. 2.

54. See, e.g., Pilot Life Insurance Co. v. Dedeaux, 481 U.S. 41, 50, 107 S.Ct. 1549, 95 L.Ed.2d 39 (1987).

55. Macneil, supra note 29, at 21–24; Macneil, Speidel & Stipanowich, supra note 1, § 10.1.

was apparently enacted with this understanding. Those who enacted the FAA apparently thought they were enacting a *procedural* law governing only in federal courts,[56] unlike *substantive* federal law which governs in both federal and state courts.

The original understanding of the FAA as governing only in federal court prevailed in the case law for many decades after 1925.[57] But the Supreme Court gradually changed the FAA from procedural law (governing only in federal courts) to substantive law (governing in both federal and state courts). This change is discussed in the following section.

§ 2.7 *Erie* and its Consequences for the FAA

The FAA's evolution into substantive law was a result of non-arbitration decisions by the Supreme Court, including *Erie Railroad Co. v. Tompkins*.[58] *Erie* was a 1938 landmark decision dealing with how federal courts decide claims for recovery based on state-created law. (Federal courts often have jurisdiction over such state claims because federal courts have jurisdiction over "diversity cases," *i.e.*, cases in which the parties are citizens of different states, even if these cases involve no federal claims.[59]) *Erie* held that in such cases federal courts must apply state law, rather than create their own federal law.[60] *Erie* declared that there is "no federal general common law."[61] One rationale for *Erie* is that the result of a case should be the same regardless of whether the plaintiff brings the case in state or federal court. Any other rule would encourage forum-shopping by plaintiffs. So *Erie* requires federal courts to apply the same law that state courts apply.[62]

This requirement, however, applies only to *substantive* law. While *Erie* requires federal courts to apply the state law that creates a claim,

---

56. Macneil, supra note 29, chs. 7–12, especially 97–98 (citing the House Judiciary Committee Report, H.R.Rep.No. 68–96 (1924), 110–11 (citing J.H. Cohen's brief to the Senate–House subcommittee, Bills to Make Valid and Enforceable Written Provisions or Agreements for Arbitration of Disputes Arising out of Contracts, Maritime Transactions, or Commerce Among the States or Territories or with Foreign Nations: Joint Hearings on S. 1005 and H.R. 646 Before the Subcommittee of the Committees on the Judiciary, 68th Cong., 1st Sess. (1924))); Macneil, Speidel & Stipanowich, supra note 1, § 10.2; Southland Corp. v. Keating, 465 U.S. 1, 104 S.Ct. 852, 79 L.Ed.2d 1 (1984) (O'Connor, J., dissenting); Allied–Bruce Terminix Co. Inc., v. Dobson, 513 U.S. 265, 115 S.Ct. 834, 130 L.Ed.2d 753 (1995)(Thomas, J., dissenting). For a contrary (and much-criticized) view of the FAA's legislative history, see Southland Corp. v. Keating, 465 U.S. 1, 104 S.Ct. 852, 79 L.Ed.2d 1 (1984).

57. Macneil, supra note 29, chs. 7–12.

§ 2.7

58. 304 U.S. 64, 58 S.Ct. 817, 82 L.Ed. 1188 (1938).

59. 28 U.S.C. § 1332(a) (1994). Federal courts also have jurisdiction over state claims when those claims are pendent to federal claims. 28 U.S.C. § 1367(a) (1994). The *Erie* analysis in the text, phrased in terms of diversity jurisdiction, also applies to pendent jurisdiction. See, e.g., Mangold v. California Public Util.Comm'n, 67 F.3d 1470, 1478 (9th Cir.1995) ("The Erie principles apply equally in the context of pendent jurisdiction."); Maternally Yours v. Your Maternity Shop, 234 F.2d 538, n. 1 (2d Cir.1956)("the Erie doctrine applies, whatever the ground for federal jurisdiction, to any issue or claim which has its source in state law.")

60. The *Erie* Court stated that:

Except in matters governed by the Federal Constitution or by Acts of Congress, the law to be applied in any case is the law of the State. * * * There is no federal general common law. Congress has no power to declare substantive rules of common law applicable in a State * * *. And no clause in the Constitution purports to confer such a power upon the federal courts.

304 U.S. at 78.

61. Id.

62. Id.

Erie permits federal courts to use federal procedures for resolving that claim. *Erie* permits federal rules of procedure that differ from state rules of procedure. Thus *Erie* requires a line between "substance" and "procedure." The Supreme Court provided such a line in the 1945 case of *Guaranty Trust Co. v. York*,[63] which put on the substantive side any law that was "outcome determinative."[64] The Supreme Court then used that line in *Bernhardt v. Polygraphic Co. of America*,[65] to conclude that arbitration is substantive for *Erie* purposes.[66] Thus *Erie, Guaranty Trust* and *Bernhardt* moved the FAA from the procedural side of the law, where it was originally understood to be, to the substantive side.

Once arbitration was understood as substantive, a troubling issue arose about the FAA's constitutionality. *Erie* held that it was unconstitutional for federal courts to make substantive common law governing in federal courts' diversity cases but not in state court. Is it similarly unconstitutional for Congress to make substantive statutory law governing in federal courts' diversity cases but not in state court?[67] If so, then the FAA, as originally understood, was rendered unconstitutional by *Erie, Guaranty Trust* and *Bernhardt*.

After *Bernhardt* held that the FAA was substantive, the Supreme Court had three choices. First, it could hold that the FAA, although constitutional when enacted, had been rendered unconstitutional by *Erie, Guaranty Trust* and *Bernhardt*. Second it could hold that the FAA governed only in federal courts and there only in non-diversity cases.[68] (This would have interpreted the FAA more narrowly than the original understanding of applying in all federal cases.) Third, it could hold that the FAA governed in both federal and state courts. (This would have interpreted the FAA more broadly than the original understanding of applying only in federal cases.)

---

63. 326 U.S. 99, 65 S.Ct. 1464, 89 L.Ed. 2079 (1945).

64. Guaranty Trust, 326 U.S. at 109. The "outcome determinative" test classifies virtually all law as "substantive" and has not been followed strictly by the Supreme Court. See, e.g., Hanna v. Plumer, 380 U.S. 460, 468, 85 S.Ct. 1136, 14 L.Ed.2d 8 (1965) ("in this sense every procedural variation is 'outcome-determinative.' ").

65. 350 U.S. 198, 76 S.Ct. 273, 100 L.Ed. 199 (1956).

66. Id. at 203 ("If the federal court allows arbitration where the state court would disallow it, the outcome of litigation might depend on the courthouse where the suit is brought. * * * The nature of the tribunal where suits are tried is an important part of the parcel of rights behind a cause of action.").

67. At least one thoughtful scholar suggests that it is. See Linda R. Hirshman, The Second Arbitration Trilogy: The Federalization of Arbitration Law, 71 Va.L.Rev. 1305,

1316 (1985)(*Erie* implied that Congress lacked the constitutional power to enact rules of decision for state-created rights in diversity cases).

68. This was the suggestion of Justice Frankfurter's concurring opinion in *Bernhardt*:

> it would raise a serious question of constitutional law whether Congress could subject to arbitration litigation in the federal courts which is there solely because it is 'between Citizens of different States', U.S.Const. Art. III, § 2, in disregard of the law of the State in which a federal court is sitting. Since [the FAA] does not obviously apply to diversity cases, in the light of its terms and the relevant interpretive materials, avoidance of the constitutional question is for me sufficiently compelling to lead to a construction of the [FAA] as not applicable to diversity cases.

350 U.S. 198, 208, 76 S.Ct. 273, 100 L.Ed. 199 (Frankfurter, J., dissenting).

The Supreme Court committed itself to the third choice in the 1967 case of *Prima Paint Corp. v. Flood & Conklin Mfg. Co.*[69] The *Prima Paint* Court applied the FAA to a diversity case. By doing so, the Court implicitly ruled out the first and second choices above. *Prima Paint* "did not quite say that the FAA governs in state court, but its reasoning left little room for any other result."[70] It took another seventeen years, however, before the Court finally applied the FAA to a state court case, *Southland Corp. v. Keating*.[71] The 1984 *Southland* case, discussed in a later section,[72] began the era of FAA preemption of state law.[73]

Unfortunately, *Southland* did not acknowledge the original understanding of the FAA as procedural law governing only in federal court.[74] Chief Justice Burger's opinion for the majority in *Southland* asserted that the FAA had, from its enactment, been substantive law applicable in state, as well as federal, court.[75] Justice Stevens' concurring opinion, by contrast, more aptly conceded that "the legislative history of the Federal Arbitration Act demonstrates that the 1925 Congress that enacted the statute viewed the statute as essentially procedural in nature."[76] Nevertheless, Justice Stevens concluded "that the intervening developments in the law compel the conclusion that the Court has reached."[77] Those intervening developments are *Erie, Guaranty Trust, Bernhardt*, and *Prima Paint*.

The *Southland* majority's failure to concede that the FAA had evolved from procedural law (governing only in federal courts) to substantive law (governing in both federal and state courts) has led to complications in arbitration law. These complications relate to whether *all* of the FAA applies in state court, or just *some* of it.[78]

---

69.   388 U.S. 395, 404–05, 87 S.Ct. 1801, 18 L.Ed.2d 1270 (1967). This case is discussed in § 2.19.

70.   Macneil, Speidel & Stipanowich, supra note 1, § 10.4.2.

The Prima Paint Court said:

It is true that the Arbitration Act was passed 13 years before this Court's decision in Erie R. Co. v. Tompkins, supra, brought to an end the regime of Swift v. Tyson, 41 U.S. 1, 16 Pet. 1, 10 L.Ed. 865 (1842), and that at the time of enactment Congress had reason to believe that it still had power to create federal rules to govern questions of 'general law' arising in simple diversity cases—at least, absent any state statute to the contrary. If Congress relied at all on this 'oft-challenged' power, see Erie R. Co., 304 U.S., at 69, it was only supplementary to the admiralty and commerce powers, which formed the principal bases of the legislation.

388 U.S. at 415 n.13.

71.   465 U.S. 1, 11, 104 S.Ct. 852, 79 L.Ed.2d 1 (1984).

72.   See § 2.12.

73.   That preemption is discussed in §§ 2.9—2.14.

74.   Macneil, Speidel & Stipanowich, supra note 1, § 10.5.3.

75.   465 U.S. 1, 15, 104 S.Ct. 852, 79 L.Ed.2d 1 (1984)("we cannot believe Congress intended to limit the Arbitration Act to disputes subject only to federal court jurisdiction.")

76.   465 U.S. 1, 17, 104 S.Ct. 852, 79 L.Ed.2d 1 (Stevens, J., concurring).

77.   Id.

78.   The cases discussed throughout §§ 2.9—2.14 clearly hold that FAA § 2 applies in state court. Whether FAA §§ 3 and 4 apply in state court is discussed in § 2.11.

§ 2.8   The FAA Creates No Federal Jurisdiction

While the FAA has evolved from procedural to substantive law,[79] it is unusual federal substantive law in that it creates no federal jurisdiction.[80] Ordinarily, a party asserting its federal rights is entitled to have a federal court hear its claims. But that is not true of parties asserting their FAA rights. These parties are relegated to state court unless they can point to some other source of federal jurisdiction.[81]

2.   PREEMPTION OF STATE LAW IMPEDING CONTRACT ENFORCEMENT

Table of Sections

§ 2.9   Generally

The FAA is resolutely pro-contract. FAA § 2 says that arbitration agreements "shall be valid, irrevocable, and enforceable, save upon such grounds as exist at law or in equity for the revocation of any contract."[82] This language reflects an intent to place arbitration agreements "upon the same footing as other contracts" and to reverse judicial hostility to arbitration agreements.[83] The FAA's enactment was "motivated, first and foremost, by a congressional desire to enforce agreements into which parties had entered."[84] Accordingly, the Supreme Court has repeatedly

---

§ 2.8

79. See § 2.7.

80. Southland, 465 U.S. 1, 16 n. 9, 104 S.Ct. 852, 79 L.Ed.2d 1 (1984).

While the Federal Arbitration Act creates federal substantive law requiring the parties to honor arbitration agreements, it does not create any independent federal-question jurisdiction under 28 U.S.C. § 1331 (1976) or otherwise. This seems implicit in the provisions in § 3 for a stay by a "court in which such suit is pending" and in § 4 that enforcement may be ordered by "any United States district court which, save for such agreement, would have jurisdiction under Title 28, in a civil action or in admiralty of the sub-

ject matter of a suit arising out of the controversy between the parties." Ibid. Id. (citations omitted). In contrast, the international sections of the FAA, 9 U.S.C. §§ 201–208 and 301–307, do create federal jurisdiction.

81. See Macneil, Speidel & Stipanowich, supra note 1, § 9.2.1.

§ 2.9

82. 9 U.S.C. § 2 (1994).

83. H.R.Rep. No. 68–96, at 2 (1924).

84. Volt Info. Sciences, Inc. v. Board of Trustees, 489 U.S. 468, 109 S.Ct. 1248, 103 L.Ed.2d 488 (1989); Dean Witter Reynolds v. Byrd, 470 U.S. 213, 220, 105 S.Ct. 1238, 84 L.Ed.2d 158 (1985).

emphasized that it seeks "to ensure the enforceability, according to their terms, of private agreements to arbitrate."[85]

The resolutely pro-contract stance of the FAA frequently conflicts with state law. In the event of such a conflict, the state law is unenforceable because it is preempted by the FAA.[86]

The following sections discuss the most important area of FAA preemption, the enforceability of executory arbitration agreements.[87] Other issues relating to FAA preemption of state law are discussed throughout this chapter as they arise amidst various topics.

§ 2.10 State Law Prohibiting Courts From Enforcing Arbitration Agreements

The clearest case for FAA preemption is state law making arbitration agreements unenforceable. For example, Alabama courts have declared that pre-dispute arbitration agreements are "void."[88] The Supreme Court held in *Allied-Bruce Terminix Cos. v. Dobson*,[89] that the FAA preempts this Alabama law.

§ 2.11 State Law Prohibiting Courts From Enforcing Arbitration Agreements With the Remedy of Specific Performance

Alabama has a statute prohibiting courts from enforcing arbitration agreements with the remedy of specific performance, *i.e.*, orders to arbitrate.[90] The Supreme Court held in *Allied-Bruce Terminix Cos. v. Dobson*,[91] that the FAA preempts this Alabama statute. Justice Thomas's dissent in *Allied-Bruce* pointed out that this Alabama statute does not, by its terms, make arbitration agreements unenforceable but merely limits the remedies courts can use in enforcing arbitration agreements.[92]

---

85. Mastrobuono v. Shearson Lehman Hutton, Inc., 514 U.S. 52, 57, 115 S.Ct. 1212, 131 L.Ed.2d 76 (1995)(quoting Volt Info. Sciences, Inc. v. Board of Trustees, 489 U.S. 468, 476, 109 S.Ct. 1248, 103 L.Ed.2d 488 (1989)); see also Dean Witter Reynolds, Inc. v. Byrd, 470 U.S. 213, 221, 105 S.Ct. 1238, 84 L.Ed.2d 158 (1985) ("the preeminent concern of Congress in passing the [FAA] was to enforce private agreements into which parties had entered, and that concern requires that we rigorously enforce agreements to arbitrate.").

86. U.S. Const. art. VI, cl. 2 (the Supremacy Clause).

87. See §§ 2.10—2.14.

§ 2.10

88. See, e.g., Wells v. Mobile County Bd. of Realtors, 387 So.2d 140, 144 (Ala.1980).

89. 513 U.S. 265, 281, 115 S.Ct. 834, 130 L.Ed.2d 753 (1995).

§ 2.11

90. Ala.Code § 8–1–41(3)(1975)("The following obligations cannot be specifically enforced: * * * An agreement to submit a controversy to arbitration").

91. 513 U.S. 265, 281, 115 S.Ct. 834, 130 L.Ed.2d 753 (1995).

92. See 513 U.S. at 293 (Thomas, J. dissenting)("A contract surely can be 'valid, irrevocable, and enforceable' even though it can be enforced only through actions for damages."); id. at 294 ("the [Alabama] statute does not itself make executory arbitration agreements invalid, revocable, or unenforceable").

For example, the Alabama statute permits courts to award money damages for breach of an arbitration agreement. Therefore, Justice Thomas concluded, the Alabama statute does not conflict with the FAA's requirement that arbitration agreements be "valid, irrevocable and enforceable."[93]

On behalf of the *Allied-Bruce* majority, one can note that the ineffectiveness of money damages as a remedy for breach of arbitration agreements is the very problem the FAA was enacted to solve.[94] Central to the FAA is its requirement that courts enforce arbitration agreements with the remedy of specific performance. Accordingly, the FAA directly conflicts with, and therefore preempts, a state law precluding specific performance as a remedy for breach of an arbitration agreement.

Here, however, the text of the FAA stands out. The portions of the FAA requiring courts to enforce arbitration agreements with the remedy of specific performance are FAA §§ 3 and 4.[95] The text of these provisions indicates that they apply only in federal, not state, court. FAA § 3 covers "any suit or proceeding * * * brought in any of the courts of the United States."[96] FAA § 4 is even clearer, applying to "any United States district court."[97] These provisions reflect the original understanding of the FAA as procedural law governing only in federal, not state, court.[98]

The Supreme Court gradually changed the FAA from procedural law (governing only in federal courts) to substantive law (governing in both federal and state courts).[99] This evolution culminated in 1984 when the Supreme Court applied the FAA to a state court case, *Southland Corp. v. Keating*.[100] While the FAA's evolution into substantive law is defensible as a response to the Supreme Court's landmark constitutional decision, *Erie Railroad Co. v. Tompkins*,[101] that evolution conflicts with the plain language of FAA §§ 3 and 4. Probably for this reason, the Supreme Court has muddled around the question of whether FAA §§ 3 and 4 apply in state court.

In 1983, the year preceding *Southland*, the Court said that "state courts, as much as federal courts, are obliged to grant stays of litigation under § 3 of the Act."[102] But *Southland* backtracked: "we do not hold that §§ 3 and 4 of the Arbitration Act apply to proceedings in state courts."[103] And in 1989, the Supreme Court stated: "we have never held that §§ 3 and 4, which by their terms appear to apply only to proceed-

---

93. 9 U.S.C. § 2 (1994).

94. See § 2.4(b).

95. See id.

96. 9 U.S.C. § 3 (1994).

97. 9 U.S.C. § 4 (1994).

98. See § 2.6.

99. See §§ 2.6—2.8.

100. 465 U.S. 1, 11, 104 S.Ct. 852, 79 L.Ed.2d 1 (1984).

101. 304 U.S. 64, 58 S.Ct. 817, 82 L.Ed. 1188 (1938). That defense is outlined in § 2.7.

102. Moses H. Cone Memorial Hospital v. Mercury Construction Corp., 460 U.S. 1, 26 n. 34, 103 S.Ct. 927, 74 L.Ed.2d 765 (1983).

103. See Southland, 465 U.S. 1, 16 n. 10, 104 S.Ct. 852, 79 L.Ed.2d 1 (1984).

ings in federal court, are nonetheless applicable in state court."[104] The 1995 *Allied-Bruce* case did not discuss whether FAA §§ 3 and 4 apply in state court. Notice, however, that the effect of *Southland* and *Allied-Bruce* is to require state courts to enforce arbitration agreements with the remedy of specific performance, *i.e.*, orders to arbitrate. In effect, *Southland* and *Allied-Bruce* have made the substance of FAA §§ 3 and 4 applicable in state court even while maintaining that it is still an open question whether those provisions technically apply in state court.[105]

§ 2.12 State Law Making Arbitration Agreements Unenforceable With Respect to Certain Claims

The FAA preempts state law making arbitration agreements unenforceable with respect to certain claims. An example of such a law appeared in *Southland Corp. v. Keating*,[106] which involved an arbitration clause in a franchise agreement for a 7–11 Store. Franchisees sued Southland alleging a variety of claims including torts, breach of contract, and breach of the disclosure requirements of a California statute, the California Franchise Investment Law ("CFIL").[107] The trial court granted Southland's motion to compel arbitration of all claims except those based on the CFIL.[108] The trial court ruled that the dispute should be split, with one claim litigated and other claims arbitrated.[109] The Supreme Court of California agreed, enforcing the arbitration agreement with respect to all claims except for one.[110] In other words, it held that the franchisees' tort and contract claims were *arbitrable* but their CFIL claims were not.[111]

The rationale for treating CFIL claims differently from tort or contract claims is the language of the CFIL, which says that "any stipulation purporting to waive compliance with any provision of this law is void."[112] The California Supreme Court interpreted this language to

104. Volt Information Sciences, Inc. v. Board of Trustees of the Leland Stanford Junior University, 489 U.S. 468, 477 n. 6, 109 S.Ct. 1248, 103 L.Ed.2d 488 (1989).

105. See Southland, 465 U.S. at 24 (O'Connor, J., dissenting)("the Court reads [FAA] § 2 to require state courts to enforce § 2 rights using procedures that mimic those specified for federal courts by FAA §§ 3 and 4."); Macneil, Speidel & Stipanowich, supra note 1, § 10.8.2.4 ("although the Court holds that FAA §§ 3 and 4 do not govern state courts, it is equally clear that FAA § 2, which does govern them, carries with it duties indistinguishable from those imposed on federal courts by FAA §§ 3 and 4.")

§ 2.12

106. 465 U.S. 1, 104 S.Ct. 852, 79 L.Ed.2d 1 (1984).

107. See Cal.Corp.Code Ann. §§ 31000 et seq. (West 1977).

108. 465 U.S. at 4.

109. This raises questions about whether one action should be stayed while the other proceeds and about possible conflicting rulings in the two actions. See Dean Witter Reynolds Inc. v. Byrd, 470 U.S. 213, 105 S.Ct. 1238, 84 L.Ed.2d 158 (1985).

110. 465 U.S. at 5.

111. This is an issue of statutory arbitrability, not contractual arbitrability. While state inarbitrability law is preempted by the FAA, federal inarbitrability law is not. See § 2.27(a). Contractual arbitrability is discussed in §§ 2.29—2.31.

112. Cal.Corp.Code § 31512 (West 1977).

void an agreement to arbitrate CFIL claims.[113] Whether the California court was correct in treating an arbitration clause as a waiver of statutory compliance is an interesting question.[114] But the United States Supreme Court did not address it in *Southland*. The United States Supreme Court deferred to the California Supreme Court as the highest interpreter of California statutes. The United States Supreme Court considered only whether the California statute, as interpreted by California's highest court, was preempted by federal law.

The United States Supreme Court concluded in *Southland* that the California statute, as interpreted by California's highest court, was preempted by the FAA. FAA § 2 says that arbitration agreements "shall be valid, irrevocable, and enforceable, save upon such grounds as exist at law or in equity for the revocation of any contract."[115] The Supreme Court in *Southland* explained that the CFIL conflicts with, and is therefore preempted by, FAA § 2.

> We agree, of course, that a party may assert general contract defenses such as fraud to avoid enforcement of an arbitration agreement. We conclude, however, that the defense to arbitration found in the California Franchise Investment Law is not a ground that exists at law or in equity "for the revocation of any contract" but merely a ground that exists for the revocation of arbitration provisions in contracts subject to the California Franchise Investment Law.[116]

Justice Stevens' dissent in *Southland* argued that "a state policy of providing special protection for franchisees * * * can be recognized without impairing the basic purposes of the federal statute."[117] But the majority strongly rebutted Stevens' analysis.

> If we accepted this analysis, states could wholly eviscerate Congressional intent to place arbitration agreements "upon the same footing as other contracts," simply by passing statutes such as the Franchise Investment Law. We have rejected this analysis because it is in conflict with the Arbitration Act and would permit states to override the declared policy requiring enforcement of arbitration agreements.[118]

This reasoning is solid.[119] Courts may decline to enforce arbitration agreements only on "such grounds as exist at law or in equity for the revocation of any contract."[120] In other words, the FAA requires parties

---

113. 465 U.S. at 10.

114. Compare § 2.45(a)(courts confirm and enforce arbitration awards that do not apply the law), with Shearson/American Express, Inc. v. McMahon, 482 U.S. 220, 229, 107 S.Ct. 2332, 96 L.Ed.2d 185 (1987)("[b]y agreeing to arbitrate a statutory claim, a party does not forgo the substantive rights afforded by the statute.")

115. 9 U.S.C. § 2 (1994).

116. Southland, 465 U.S. at 16.

117. Southland, 465 U.S. at 21 (Stevens, J., dissenting).

118. Southland, 465 U.S. at 16 (quoting H.R.Rep. No. 68–96, supra note 83).

119. It is solid once one accepts the (controversial) evolution of the FAA into substantive law applicable in both state and federal courts. See §§ 2.6—2.8.

120. 9 U.S.C. § 2 (1994).

who attack an arbitration agreement to find their weapons in contract law, not in some other body of law.

Many states have law analogous to the California law held preempted in *Southland*. That is, many states' laws prohibit enforcement of pre-dispute arbitration agreements with respect to certain categories of claims, such as personal injury claims or medical malpractice claims.[121] These laws are preempted by the FAA because they create a ground for denying enforcement to arbitration agreements that is not a ground "for the revocation of any contract."[122]

§ 2.13 State Law Making Arbitration Agreements in Certain Types of Transactions Unenforceable

The law of many states makes unenforceable arbitration agreements in certain types of transactions. For instance, many states' laws prohibit enforcement of arbitration clauses in consumer contracts, adhesion contracts, insurance contracts, or employment contracts.[123] These laws (with the possible exceptions of those relating to insurance[124] and employment[125]) are preempted by the FAA because they create a ground for

121. See, e.g., Ala.Code § 6–5–485 (1993)(medical malpractice); Ark.Code Ann. § 16–108–201 (Michie Supp.1995)(personal injury); Ga.Code Ann. § 9–9–2(c)(Supp.1996)(personal injury); Iowa Code Ann. § 679A.1 (West 1987)(personal injury); Kan.Stat.Ann. § 5–401(c) (Supp.1995)(personal injury); La.Rev.Stat. Ann. § 9:4232 (West 1991) (medical malpractice); Mont.Code Ann. § 27–5–114 (1995)(personal injury); Neb.Rev.Stat. § 25–2602 (1995)(workers' compensation); S.C.Code Ann. § 15–48–10 (Law.Co-op. Supp.1995) (medical malpractice); Tex.Civ. Prac. & Rem.Code Ann. § 171.001 (West Supp.1997) (personal injury).

122. 9 U.S.C. § 2 (1994). In addition to Southland, see also Perry v. Thomas, 482 U.S. 483, 490–91, 107 S.Ct. 2520, 96 L.Ed.2d 426 (1987) (FAA preempts state law denying enforcement of agreements to arbitrate California Labor Code claims); Macneil, Speidel & Stipanowich, supra note 1, § 16.6.1 ("[S]tate public policy defense law is the clearest possible example of state arbitration law, which is superseded by the FAA."). Macneil, Speidel & Stipanowich, use the term "public policy defense" to refer to the argument that claims arising under a particular body of law are inarbitrable. The defense to enforcement of the arbitration agreement is that it would violate public policy to send those claims to arbitration without the parties' post-dispute consent.

§ 2.13

123. See, e.g., Ark.Code Ann. § 16–108–201 (Michie Supp.1995) (insurance contracts); Ga.Code Ann. § 9–9–2(c) (Supp. 1996) (insurance contracts, consumer contracts); Iowa Code Ann. § 679A.1 (West 1987) (adhesion contracts, employment contracts); Kan.Stat.Ann. § 5–401(c) (Supp. 1995) (insurance contracts); Baxter v. John Weitzel, Inc., 19 Kan.App.2d 467, 871 P.2d 855 (Kan.Ct.App.1994) (employment contracts); Ky.Rev.Stat.Ann. § 336.700 (Michie 1995) (employment contracts); id. § 417.050 (Michie Supp.1996) (insurance contracts); Mo.Ann.Stat. §§ 435.350, 435.460 (West 1992) (adhesion contracts, insurance contracts); Mont.Code Ann. § 27–5–114 (1995) (insurance contracts, property contracts); N.Y.Gen.Bus.Law § 399–c (McKinney 1996)(consumer contracts); Ohio Rev.Code Ann. § 2711.01 (Anderson 1992) (rental contracts); id. § 2711.23 (medical contracts); Okla.Stat.Ann.tit. 15, § 802 (West 1992) (insurance contracts except those between insurance companies); R.I.Gen.Laws § 10–3–2 (Supp.1995) (employment contracts, insurance contracts); S.C.Code Ann. § 15–48–10 (Law.Co-op.Supp.1995) (employment contracts); S.D.Codified Laws Ann. § 21–25A–3 (Michie 1987) (insurance contracts); Vt.Stat.Ann.tit. 12, §§ 5652, 5653 (Supp.1995) (insurance contracts).

124. See § 2.18.

125. See § 2.51.

denying enforcement to certain arbitration agreements that is not a ground "for the revocation of any contract."[126]

§ 2.14   State Law Raising the Standard of Assent for Contract Formation

Formation of a contract requires a manifestation of assent by each party.[127] Assent is typically manifested by signing a document or saying certain words, but can be accomplished in other ways as well. Mutual manifestation of assent is required to form an arbitration agreement, just as it is required to form any contract.[128]

Contract law has long grappled with assent issues in the context of form contracts presented take-it-or-leave-it to consumers. For example, a comment to the Restatement (Second) of Contracts says that:

> A party who makes regular use of a standardized form of agreement does not ordinarily expect his customers to understand or even to read the standard terms * * * . Customers do not in fact ordinarily understand or even read the standard terms. They trust to the good faith of the party using the form and to the tacit representation that like terms are being accepted regularly by others similarly situated. But they understand that they are assenting to the terms not read or not understood, subject to such limitations as the law may impose.[129]

One such limitation holds that the consumer does not assent to a form contract term if the "other party has reason to believe that the [consumer] would not have accepted the agreement if he had known that the agreement contained the particular term."[130] This doctrine protects consumers from a form contract term which is "bizarre or oppressive," "eviscerates the non-standard terms explicitly agreed to," or "eliminates the dominant purpose of the transaction."[131]

States may apply to arbitration agreements this sort of contract law regarding assent without risking FAA preemption. Because this sort of law applies to all contracts, states may apply it to arbitration agreements while remaining faithful to the FAA's goal of placing arbitration agreements "upon the same footing as other contracts."[132] Indeed, states would be unfaithful to this goal if they applied a lower standard of assent to arbitration agreements than to other contracts. Conversely, states may not apply a higher standard of assent to arbitration agreements than to other contracts.

For example, the FAA preempts the following Montana statute: "Notice that a contract is subject to arbitration * * * shall be typed in

---

126. 9 U.S.C. § 2 (1994).

§ 2.14

127. See generally E. Allan Farnsworth, Contracts ch.3 (3d ed.1999).

128. See § 2.22.

129. Restatement (Second) of Contracts § 211 cmt. b (1981).

130. Id. § 211 cmt. f.

131. Id.

132. See § 2.9.

underlined capital letters on the first page of the contract; and unless such notice is displayed thereon, the contract may not be subject to arbitration."[133] *Doctor's Associates, Inc. v. Casarotto,*[134] involved a franchise agreement that did not comply with this statute because the arbitration clause was on page nine and in ordinary type.[135] The Supreme Court held that the Montana statute is preempted by the FAA because the Montana statute "conditions the enforceability of arbitration agreements on compliance with a special notice requirement not applicable to contracts generally."[136] The FAA "precludes States from singling out arbitration provisions for suspect status, requiring instead that such provisions be placed 'upon the same footing as other contracts.'"[137] Other state laws preempted on the reasoning of *Casarotto* are numerous.[138]

3. CHOICE–OF–LAW CLAUSES

Table of Sections

§ 2.15 Introduction

Because of the United States Constitution's Supremacy Clause, when there is a conflict between federal and state law, the federal law prevails. In this regard, federal arbitration law is no different from any

---

133. Mont.Code Ann. § 27–5–114(4)(1995). This language was deleted from the statute in 1997.

134. Doctor's Assocs., Inc. v. Casarotto, 517 U.S. 681, 116 S.Ct. 1652, 134 L.Ed.2d 902 (1996).

135. Id. at 684–85.

136. Id. at 687.

137. Id.

138. With the possible exceptions of state statutes relating to insurance, see § 2.18, and employment, see § 2.51, other statutes preempted on the reasoning of *Casarotto* include: Cal.Bus. & Prof.Code § 7191 (Deering Supp.1996) (arbitration clauses in certain residential contracts shall contain prescribed notice in at least ten-point roman boldface type or if in red print in at least eight-point boldface type); Colo. Rev.Stat.Ann. § 13–64–403 (West Supp. 1996) (arbitration clauses in agreements for medical services shall contain prescribed notice in at least ten-point boldface type); Ga.Code Ann. § 9–9–2(c)(8) and (9) (Supp. 1999) (arbitration clause must be initialed);

N.Y.Pub. Health Law § 4406–a(2), (3) (McKinney Supp.1996) (arbitration provisions of health maintenance organization contracts must be "in at least twelve point boldface type immediately above spaces for the signature"); R.I.Gen.Laws § 10–3–2 (Supp.1995) (arbitration clauses in insurance contracts must be "immediately before the testimonium clause or the signature of the parties"); S.C.Code Ann. § 15–48–10 (Law.Co-op.Supp.1995) (arbitration clause must be underlined and capitalized, or rubber-stamped prominently, and on first page); S.D.Codified Laws Ann. § 21–25B–3 (Michie 1987) (arbitration clauses relating to medical services must be in twelve-point boldface type immediately above the space for signature); Tenn.Code Ann. § 29–5–302 (Supp.1996) (arbitration clause in certain contracts must be signed or initialed by the parties); Tex.Civ.Prac. & Rem.Code Ann. § 171.001 (West Supp.1997) (arbitration clauses in certain contracts must be signed by parties and their attorneys); Vt.Stat. Ann.tit. 12, § 5652 (Supp.1995) (arbitration clause must be signed by parties and displayed prominently).

other federal law.[139] The FAA preempts many state laws.[140]

What makes FAA preemption of state law unusual, however, is that the parties to an arbitration agreement can contract out of it. Parties can form an enforceable arbitration agreement providing that any dispute they have will be governed by state arbitration law, instead of by the FAA. The parties' power to do this is found in the Supreme Court's opinion in *Volt Information Sciences, Inc. v. Board of Trustees of the Leland Stanford Junior University*.[141]

§ 2.16　The *Volt* Case

Volt involved an arbitration clause in a construction contract. The California trial court stayed arbitration pending resolution of related litigation.[142] A California statute permits such a stay.[143] The FAA probably does not permit such a stay.[144] The California Court of Appeal held that California arbitration law, rather than the FAA, applied because the construction contract included a choice-of-law clause which stated that the contract would be "governed by the law of the place where the project is located."[145] The project at issue was located in California.[146] The California Court of Appeal stated that the parties "have agreed, as we interpret their choice of law provision, that the laws of California, of which [the stay provision] is certainly a part, are to govern their contract."[147] The California Court of Appeal held "that enforcement of the arbitration agreement in accordance with the chosen California rules of procedure does not create a conflict with the [FAA], since the purpose of the [FAA] was to ensure that private agreements to arbitrate are enforceable contracts."[148] The United States Supreme Court agreed and affirmed.[149]

While there was a dissent in *Volt*, the Supreme Court was unanimous in ruling that parties can make an enforceable agreement that California arbitration law, rather than the FAA, governs. The majority in *Volt* affirmed the holding that the parties in *Volt* had made such an agreement. While the dissent did not agree that these particular parties had made such an agreement, the dissent agreed that parties "are free if they wish to write an agreement to arbitrate outside the coverage of the FAA. Such an agreement would permit a state rule, otherwise preempted

§ 2.15

139. See §§ 2.6—2.8.

140. See §§ 2.9—2.14.

141. 489 U.S. 468, 109 S.Ct. 1248, 103 L.Ed.2d 488 (1989).

§ 2.16

142. Board of Trustees of the Leland Stanford Junior Univ. v. Volt Info. Sciences., Inc., 240 Cal.Rptr. 558, 559 (Ct.App. 1987), aff'd, 489 U.S. 468, 109 S.Ct. 1248, 103 L.Ed.2d 488 (1989).

143. Cal.Civ.Proc.Code § 1281.2(c)(4). This provision is quoted in § 2.33, n.362.

144. See § 2.33.

145. Volt, 240 Cal.Rptr. at 559.

146. Id.

147. Id.

148. Id.

149. Volt Info. Sciences, Inc., v. Board of Trustees of the Leland Stanford Junior Univ., 489 U.S. 468, 479, 109 S.Ct. 1248, 103 L.Ed.2d 488 (1989).

by the FAA, to govern their arbitration."[150] The Court was unanimous in ruling that parties may contract out of FAA preemption.

The majority and dissent differed on a narrower issue. The majority in *Volt* did not review, but accepted as a matter of state law, the California Court of Appeal's interpretation of the choice-of-law clause "to mean that the parties had incorporated the California rules of arbitration into their arbitration agreement."[151] In contrast, the Supreme Court's dissent stated "I can accept neither the state court's unusual interpretation of the parties' contract, nor this Court's unwillingness to review it."[152]

The dissent correctly pointed out that "the normal purpose of such choice-of-law clauses is to determine that the law of one State rather than that of another State will be applicable; they simply do not speak to any interaction between state and federal law."[153] The choice-of-law clause in *Volt* is best interpreted as the parties' choice of California law over other state law, rather than California law over federal law. The California Court of Appeal mis-interpreted the contract.

The most challenging question for the Supreme Court in *Volt* was whether to correct the California court's mis-interpretation of the contract. Ordinarily, the Supreme Court reviews *de novo* state court rulings on federal law but defers to state courts on matters of state law.[154] Contract interpretation is usually a matter of state law. But certain contracts, arbitration agreements, are also the subject of federal law, the FAA. The FAA presupposes, and often incorporates, state contract law.[155] In effect, state contract law becomes federal law when the contract in question is an arbitration agreement.

Suppose, for example, that Alabama courts interpreted every arbitration agreement before them as choosing to be governed by Alabama arbitration law, rather than the FAA. Alabama law holds that pre-dispute arbitration agreements are void.[156] So if Alabama courts interpreted all arbitration agreements before them as choosing to be governed by Alabama law, then the FAA's primary command—that arbitration agreements be enforced—would not apply in Alabama courts. By ruling on contract interpretation, ordinarily a matter of state law, Alabama courts would effectively nullify a federal statute. Surely, the Supreme Court would review contract interpretation by Alabama courts in this example even though it refused to review contract interpretation by the California court in *Volt*.[157]

150. Id. at 485 (Brennan, J., dissenting).

151. Id. at 474.

152. Id. at 481 (Brennan, J., dissenting).

153. Id. at 488 (Brennan, J., dissenting)(citing authority).

154. Erwin Chemerinsky, Federal Jurisdiction § 10.1 (3d ed.1999)("The Court may decide only questions of federal law. The Court has no authority to decide matters of state law in reviewing the decisions of state courts.")

155. See § 2.5(b).

156. See § 2.10.

157. Cf. § 2.25(b)(discussing Supreme Court decisions constraining state courts' discretion regarding what is usually a state-law issue, unconscionability).

There is an important distinction between the Alabama example and *Volt*. Alabama arbitration law is diametrically opposed to the FAA, while California arbitration law is fairly similar to the FAA. California arbitration law is generally supportive of arbitration and enforcement of arbitration agreements.[158] *Volt* expressly noted that California arbitration law is "manifestly designed to encourage resort to the arbitral process."[159] *Volt* can be read as deferring to state court contract misinterpretations when those mis-interpretations result in the application of pro-arbitration state law, but not when they result in the application of anti-arbitration state law.[160]

§ 2.17   The *Mastrobuono* Case

Since *Volt*, the Supreme Court has addressed only once the question whether parties had contracted out of FAA preemption. *Mastrobuono v. Shearson Lehman Hutton, Inc.*,[161] involved a contract between investors and their securities broker. The contract contained both an arbitration clause and a New York choice-of-law clause.[162] New York law, at the time of the case, prohibited arbitrators from awarding punitive damages.[163] When the arbitrator awarded punitive damages to the investor, the broker (citing *Volt*) asked the court to vacate that portion of the arbitrator's award on the ground that New York law governed.[164] The Supreme Court rejected the broker's argument and confirmed the award of punitive damages.[165]

Unlike *Volt*, which began in state court, the *Mastrobuono* case went to federal court. So in *Mastrobuono* the Supreme Court could interpret the contract as it wished, without considering whether to defer (as it did in *Volt*) to a state court's interpretation of the contract.[166] The *Mastrobuono* Court rightly interpreted the contract as not requiring application of New York's law prohibiting arbitrators from awarding punitive damages. The Court's reasoning, however, is murky.

158. Cal.Civ.Proc.Code §§ 1281—1281.9 (West 1982).

159. Volt, 489 U.S. at 476.

160. With less justification, *Volt* can be read as enforcing agreements contracting out of the FAA into pro-arbitration state law, but not anti-arbitration state law. See Macneil, Speidel & Stipanowich, supra note 1, § 10.9.2.2 (discussing cases). *Volt*'s emphasis on party autonomy counsels against this reading, *i.e.*, supports an inference that courts must enforce even agreements contracting out of the FAA into anti-arbitration state law. Consider, however, the unlikelihood of parties actually doing this. Why, for example, would parties put an arbitration clause in their contract and agree to be governed by Alabama arbitration law? By agreeing to be governed by Alabama arbitration law, the parties would have effectively nullified the arbitration clause. If courts are to interpret all clauses of a contract as consistent with each other, see Restatement (Second) of Contracts § 202(5)(1981), then they must not interpret contracts with arbitration clauses as choosing to be governed by Alabama arbitration law.

§ 2.17

161. 514 U.S. 52, 115 S.Ct. 1212, 131 L.Ed.2d 76 (1995).

162. Id. at 52.

163. Id. at 55.

164. Mastrobuono, 514 U.S. at 54–55.

165. Id. at 64.

166. Whether to do so defer is the issue that split the majority and dissent in *Volt*. See § 2.16.

The Court began by suggesting that the choice-of-law clause was simply a choice of New York law over the law of other states, rather than a choice to avoid FAA preemption of New York law. The Court did this by pointing out that the broker interpreted the contract's choice of "the laws of the State of New York" to "include[] the caveat, 'detached from otherwise-applicable federal law.' "[167] The Court could have simply interpreted the contract not to include this caveat. This interpretation would have been consistent with the ordinary understanding of such choice-of-law clauses as choices among states, not choices between state and federal.[168] And this interpretation would have led easily to the conclusion the Court reached, that the parties did not contract out of FAA preemption, so the arbitrator could award punitive damages.

Instead of stopping with the point that the choice-of-law clause did not address the relationship between state and federal law, the Court spoke further on its interpretation of the contract.[169] In other words, the Court did not rely squarely on its interpretation of the choice-of-law clause but also relied on other grounds.[170] By adding these other grounds, the Court left unclear when choice-of-law clauses will be held to contract out of FAA preemption of state law.

4. INSURANCE ARBITRATION

Table of Sections

§ 2.18 McCarran–Ferguson and the FAA

FAA preemption of state law has an added complication in the insurance context because of the McCarran–Ferguson Act,[171] which states:

(a) State regulation

167. Mastrobuono, 514 U.S. at 55.

168. Volt, 489 U.S. at 488 (Brennan, J., dissenting)(citing authority).

169. The Court pointed out that the contract's arbitration clause authorized arbitration in accordance with the rules of the National Association of Securities Dealers and a manual provided to NASD arbitrators contained this provision: "The issue of punitive damages may arise with great frequency in arbitrations. Parties to arbitration are informed that arbitrators can consider punitive damages as a remedy." Mastrobuono, 514 U.S. at 61 (quoting Mastrobuono v. Shearson Lehman Hutton, Inc., 20 F.3d 713, 717 (7th Cir.1994)). Thus the Court found that the arbitration clause "contradicts * * * the conclusion

that the parties agreed to foreclose claims for punitive damages." Mastrobuono, 514 U.S. at 61. The Court then went on to cite two further reasons for interpreting the contract to permit arbitrators to award punitive damages: (1) "the federal policy favoring arbitration," which means that "ambiguities as to the scope of the arbitration clause itself are resolved in favor of arbitration", id. at 62, and (2) "the common-law rule of contract interpretation that a court should construe ambiguous language against the interest of the party that drafted it." Id. at 62–63.

170. Id.

§ 2.18

171. 15 U.S.C. §§ 1011–1015 (1994).

The business of insurance, and every person engaged therein, shall be subject to the laws of the several States which relate to the regulation or taxation of such business.

(b) Federal regulation

No Act of Congress shall be construed to invalidate, impair, or supersede any law enacted by any State for the purposes of regulating the business of insurance, * * * unless such Act specifically relates to the business of insurance. * * * [172]

Some state laws that would otherwise be preempted by federal law are protected from that preemption by McCarran–Ferguson. For example, McCarran–Ferguson precludes application of the FAA to certain insurance cases, leaving those cases to state arbitration law. The challenge then, is to identify which state laws are protected from FAA preemption by McCarran–Ferguson.

The Supreme Court says that, to be protected from preemption by McCarran–Ferguson, a state "law must not just have an impact on the insurance industry, but be specifically directed toward that industry."[173] For this reason, McCarran–Ferguson does not protect from FAA preemption state laws regulating arbitration generally, even when those laws are applied to insurance arbitration.[174] In contrast, McCarran–Ferguson protects from FAA preemption a Kansas statute providing that arbitration clauses in insurance policies are unenforceable, while arbitration clauses in other contracts are enforceable.[175] McCarran–Ferguson also protects from FAA preemption certain state law regarding insurance company liquidations and receiverships.[176]

---

172. 15 U.S.C. § 1012(a),(b) (1994).

173. Pilot Life Insurance Co. v. Dedeaux, 481 U.S. 41, 50, 107 S.Ct. 1549, 95 L.Ed.2d 39 (1987).

174. See Miller v. National Fidel. Life Ins. Co., 588 F.2d 185, 187 (5th Cir. 1979)(where state insurance code contains no provisions relating to arbitration, applying the FAA to an insurance arbitration clause does not—to use McCarran–Ferguson's language—"invalidate, impair, or supersede any state law regulating the business of insurance."); Hart v. Orion Ins. Co., 453 F.2d 1358, 1360 (10th Cir.1971); Hamilton Life Ins. Co. v. Republic Nat'l Life Ins. Co., 408 F.2d 606, 611 (2d Cir. 1969)("arbitration statutes * * * are not statutes regulating the business of insurance, but statutes regulating the method of handling contract disputes generally."); Ainsworth v. Allstate Ins. Co., 634 F.Supp. 52 (W.D.Mo.1985).

175. Mutual Reinsurance Bureau v. Great Plains Mutual Insurance Company, Inc., 969 F.2d 931 (10th Cir.1992), cert. denied, 506 U.S. 1001, 113 S.Ct. 604, 121 L.Ed.2d 540 (1992). See also Friday v. Trinity Universal of Kansas, 262 Kan. 347, 939 P.2d 869 (Kan.1997). But see Little v. Allstate Ins. Co., 167 Vt. 171, 705 A.2d 538 (Vt.1997).

176. See Corcoran v. Universal Reinsurance Corp., 713 F.Supp. 77 (S.D.N.Y.1989); Ideal Mut. Ins. Co. v. Phoenix Greek Gen'l Ins. Co., 1987 WL 28636 (S.D.N.Y.1987); Washburn v. Corcoran, 643 F.Supp. 554 (S.D.N.Y.1986).

D. FORMATION OF ENFORCEABLE ARBITRATION AGREEMENTS

Table of Sections

1. SEPARABILITY

The FAA is not a complete statement of all the law governing arbitration.[177] The FAA presupposes, and often incorporates, state law in areas such as contract, property, agency and tort. In other words, lots of general state law applies to arbitration. The area of general state law with the most frequent application to arbitration is contract law. This chapter surveys the law regarding formation of enforceable contracts as that law applies to arbitration agreements.[178] Before doing so, however, it discusses a special twist of contract law that arises only when the contract has an arbitration clause. That twist is the separability doctrine.

1. SEPARABILITY

Table of Sections

---

177. See § 2.5(b).   **178.** See §§ 2.22—2.26.

§ 2.19   The *Prima Paint* Case

The separability doctrine can be understood by starting with the Supreme Court case adopting it, *Prima Paint Corp. v. Flood & Conklin Manufacturing Co.*[179] F & C sold to Prima Paint a list of F & C's customers and promised not to sell paint to these customers for six years.[180] F & C also promised to act as a consultant to Prima Paint during these six years.[181] This consulting agreement included an arbitration clause.[182] Prima Paint did not make payments provided for in the consulting agreement.[183] Prima Paint contended that F & C had fraudulently represented that it was solvent and able to perform its contract, but, in fact, was insolvent and intended to file for bankruptcy shortly after executing its consulting agreement with Prima Paint.[184]

F & C served upon Prima Paint a "notice of intention to arbitrate."[185] Prima Paint then sued in federal[186] court seeking rescission of the consulting agreement (due to the alleged misrepresentation) and an order enjoining F & C from proceeding with arbitration.[187] F & C cross-moved to stay the suit pending arbitration.[188] The trial court granted F & C's motion, staying Prima Paint's suit pending arbitration.[189] The Supreme Court affirmed.

Although the Court ruled against Prima Paint, the Court did not reject Prima Paint's argument that F & C fraudulently induced Prima Paint to sign the consulting agreement. The Court did not address this argument. In fact, the Court held that no court should address this argument. This argument should be addressed by the arbitrator.

The Court said that its result is compelled by FAA § 4 which provides that if

> [a] party [claims to be] aggrieved by the alleged failure * * * of another to arbitrate * * * [t]he court shall hear the parties, and upon being satisfied that the making of the agreement for arbitration or the failure to comply therewith is not in issue, the court shall make an order directing the parties to proceed to arbitration * * * . If the making of the arbitration agreement or the failure, neglect, or refusal to perform the same be in issue, the court shall proceed summarily to the trial thereof.[190]

§ 2.19

179. 388 U.S. 395, 87 S.Ct. 1801, 18 L.Ed.2d 1270 (1967).

180. Id. at 397.

181. Id.

182. Id. at 398.

183. Id.

184. Id.

185. Id.

186. The federal court had diversity jurisdiction. See § 2.7. The Prima Paint case is important to the FAA's evolution from procedural law governing only in federal courts to substantive law governing in both federal and state courts. See id.

187. 388 U.S. at 398–99.

188. Id. at 399.

189. Id.

190. 9 U.S.C. § 4 (1994).

This provision says that the court shall not order the parties to arbitration if "the making of the arbitration agreement" is in issue.[191] If the making of the arbitration agreement is in issue then the court proceeds to trial on that issue. If the trial determines that an arbitration agreement was made then the court orders the parties to arbitration. Conversely, if the trial determines that an arbitration agreement was not made then the court does not order the parties to arbitration. In short, FAA § 4 rests on the basic premise that the parties should be ordered to arbitration if, but only if, they have contracted to be there.

The Supreme Court held in *Prima Paint* that there would be no trial on the question of whether an arbitration agreement was made.[192] Prima Paint was not entitled to such a trial because its allegations of fraudulent inducement did not put in issue the question of whether an "arbitration agreement" was made. That is because the term "arbitration agreement", as used in FAA § 4, refers specifically to the arbitration clause itself, not more broadly to the consulting contract of which the arbitration clause was a part.[193] If Prima Paint had argued that there was fraud "directed to the arbitration clause itself",[194] then the making of the arbitration agreement would have been at issue and Prima Paint would have been entitled to a trial on that issue.[195] But FAA § 4, the Supreme Court held, "does not permit the court to consider arguments of fraud in the inducement of the contract generally."[196]

This holding is known as the separability doctrine because it treats the arbitration clause as if it is a separate contract from the contract containing the arbitration clause, *i.e.*, the "container contract."[197] The *Prima Paint* Court held that:

> arbitration clauses as a matter of federal law are "separable" from the contracts in which they are embedded, and that where no claim is made that fraud was directed to the arbitration clause itself, a broad arbitration clause will be held to encompass arbitration of the claim that the contract itself was induced by fraud.[198]

In other words, the separability doctrine is a legal fiction that, in addition to the container contract, the parties also formed a second contract consisting of just the arbitration clause. This fictional second contract requires arbitration of disputes over whether the container contract was induced by fraud. Courts applying the separability doctrine enforce the fictional second contract when they send to arbitration disputes over whether the container contract was induced by fraud.

191. Id.

192. Prima Paint, 388 U.S. at 404.

193. See § 2.19.

194. 388 U.S. at 402.

195. See, e.g., Moseley v. Electronic & Missile Facilities, Inc., 374 U.S. 167, 83 S.Ct. 1815, 10 L.Ed.2d 818 (1963)(cited in Prima Paint); Engalla v. Permanente Medical Group, Inc., 15 Cal.4th 951, 64 Cal. Rptr.2d 843, 938 P.2d 903 (Cal.1997).

196. Prima Paint, 388 U.S. at 404.

197. Id. at 402.

198. Id.

§ 2.20   Assessing *Prima Paint* and Separability

FAA § 4's phrases, "arbitration agreement" and "agreement for arbitration", are ambiguous. They could refer specifically to the arbitration clause or they could refer more broadly to the contract containing the clause, the "container contract". The *Prima Paint* Court correctly interpreted these statutory phrases to refer specifically to the arbitration clause and not more broadly to the container contract. If these statutory phrases referred to the container contract, then every breach of the container contract would constitute a "failure to comply" with the "agreement for arbitration." In other words, nearly every breach of contract claim, *e.g.*, "buyer did not pay" or "seller breached a warranty", would require a court's trial on whether that breach occurred. Thus, no breach-of-contract case would ever be ordered to arbitration over a party's objection until a court had determined that the breach did not occur.[199]

So the *Prima Paint* Court correctly read § 4's use of the terms "agreement for arbitration" and "arbitration agreement" to refer specifically to the arbitration clause and not more broadly to the container contract. This reading, however, does not compel the Court's conclusion that courts should hear only claims "that fraud was directed to the arbitration clause itself" and not claims that the container contract as a whole was induced by fraud.[200] The Court could have held that the making of an arbitration clause is in issue whenever the making of the container contract is in issue.[201] Consider, though, the consequences of this "anti-separability" approach.

In the absence of the separability doctrine, if Prima Paint alleges fraudulent inducement of the consulting agreement then a court would "proceed summarily to a trial thereof."[202] A court would decide whether F & C made a fraudulent misrepresentation. If the answer is no, then the court would refer to arbitration F & C's claim for payment. But Prima Paint's defense to payment *is* misrepresentation, so the court would have already decided the issue being sent to arbitration.

In the absence of the separability doctrine, courts deciding whether to send disputes to arbitration often would, as in this example, become entangled with the merits of the dispute. If the court sent a dispute to arbitration after effectively ruling on the merits, the arbitrator would have two choices. The arbitrator could reconsider the merits *de novo*,

---

§ 2.20

199. Macneil, Speidel & Stipanowich, overstate it slightly when they say: "The arbitration clause would be nullified in every case, and the FAA would have been a nullity." Macneil, Speidel & Stipanowich, supra note 1, § 15.2 n.13. The arbitration clause would "only" be a nullity in cases in which one party alleges breach of the con-

tract. The vast majority of arbitration cases include such an allegation.

200. 388 U.S. at 402.

201. Macneil, Speidel & Stipanowich, supra note 1, § 15.2 n.13.

202. 9 U.S.C. § 4 (1994).

which would require the parties to adjudicate the merits twice and create the possibility of inconsistent results. Or the arbitrator could rubber-stamp the court's view of the merits, which would make the arbitration agreement effectively unenforceable because the parties would get a court's, rather than an arbitrator's, decision on the merits. So there is an important practical rationale for the separability doctrine.[203]

§ 2.21   Applications of Separability

The Supreme Court case adopting the separability doctrine, *Prima Paint Corp. v. Flood & Conklin Manufacturing Co.*,[204] was decided in 1967. Despite this long-standing ruling from the highest court in the land, many courts do not apply the separability doctrine. There are "a wide range of cases where *Prima Paint* issues were in fact present, but where the courts have refused to apply them or simply ignored their presence."[205] This could be because many courts do not understand the separability doctrine, do not like the separability doctrine, or some combination of the two reasons. Presumably, as more and more lawyers gain familiarity with arbitration law and argue the separability doctrine, more and more courts will fall in line behind the Supreme Court. But these cases will confront many unresolved issues about the scope of the separability doctrine.

Prima Paint was a misrepresentation case and misrepresentation is a common allegation in arbitration cases. The separability doctrine, however, has been applied beyond misrepresentation to other contract defenses, including duress.[206] Suppose Prima Paint had alleged that its president signed the consulting agreement with F & C because there was a gun to his head. Would the Supreme Court have required Prima Paint to arbitrate the question of duress on the ground that the duress allegations were not "directed to the arbitration clause itself" but to the container contract as a whole?[207] That reasoning follows from the Court's opinion in *Prima Paint* unless there is some reason to distinguish between misrepresentation and duress.

What was just said about duress can also be said of several other contract law defenses to enforcement, including undue influence or overreaching, mistake, impracticability, frustration of purpose, illegality and the statute of frauds. The reasoning of *Prima Paint* seems to apply to them in the same manner that it applies to misrepresentation.[208]

---

203. For a critique of the separability doctrine, see Stephen J. Ware, Employment Arbitration and Voluntary Consent, 25 Hofstra L.Rev. 83, 128–38 (1996).

§ 2.21

204. 388 U.S. 395, 87 S.Ct. 1801, 18 L.Ed.2d 1270 (1967).

205. Macneil, Speidel & Stipanowich, supra note 1, § 15.3.2.

206. See Merrill Lynch, Pierce, Fenner & Smith, Inc. v. Haydu, 637 F.2d 391 (5th Cir.1981)(duress and undue influence).

207. Prima Paint, 388 U.S. at 402.

208. Macneil, Speidel & Stipanowich, supra note 1, § 15.3.2 (citing cases applying separability doctrine in instances other than fraudulent misrepresentation).

A distinction has been drawn, however, between legal doctrines relating to the enforceability of contracts and legal doctrines relating to whether a contract is formed. Parties alleging misrepresentation, duress and the other doctrines listed above do not dispute that a contract was formed. Rather, these parties argue that the contract is voidable at the option of the party or parties aggrieved by misrepresentation, duress, or the like. In contrast, other cases involve parties who dispute whether a contract was formed. These parties may argue, for example, that they never manifested assent to a contract. Such an argument is made, for instance, by a party who asserts that its alleged signature on a document is actually a forgery.

Suppose Prima Paint had alleged that its president never signed (or otherwise manifested assent to) the consulting agreement with F & C; the alleged signature was a forgery. Would the Supreme Court have required Prima Paint to arbitrate the question of assent on the ground that the forgery allegations are not "directed to the arbitration clause itself" but to the container contract as a whole?[209] That reasoning follows from the Court's opinion in *Prima Paint* unless there is some reason to distinguish between voidable-contract arguments, like misrepresentation, and no-contract arguments, like forgery.

Some courts have made this distinction, applying *Prima Paint* to voidable-contract arguments but not to no-contract arguments.[210] These courts would hold a trial on allegations of forgery or other questions relating to assent and then send the merits of the case to arbitration only if the trial determines that the parties did manifest assent to the container contract.

2. FORMATION

Table of Sections

Leaving aside the separability doctrine,[211] the general state law of contract formation applies to arbitration agreements. The general requirements to form a contract are: (1) mutual manifestations of assent, (2) consideration, and (3) terms that are sufficiently definite or certain.[212] These contract-formation requirements apply to arbitration agreements.

209. Prima Paint, 388 U.S. at 402.

210. Jolley v. Welch, 904 F.2d 988 (5th Cir.1990); Three Valleys Mun. Water Dist. v. E.F. Hutton & Co., 925 F.2d 1136, 1140–41 (9th Cir.1991); Rainbow Investments, Inc. v. Super 8 Motels, Inc., 973 F.Supp. 1387, 1390–91 (M.D.Ala.1997); Allstar Homes, Inc. v. Waters, 711 So.2d 924, 927 (Ala.1997). These cases are criticized, as inconsistent with *Prima Paint*, by Macneil, Speidel & Stipanowich, supra note 1, § 15.3.3.

211. See §§ 2.19—2.21.

212. Farnsworth, supra note 127, ch.2–3.

§ 2.22 Mutual Manifestations of Assent

(a) Subjective and Objective Approaches

Formation of a contract requires a manifestation of assent by each party. Assent is typically manifested by signing a document or saying certain words, but can be accomplished in other ways as well. The process by which parties manifest assent is often called "offer and acceptance."[213]

The FAA presupposes and incorporates state law regarding assent to form a contract.[214] In other words, mutual manifestation of assent is required to form an arbitration agreement, just as it is required to form any contract. The Uniform Arbitration Act and other typical state arbitration statutes also generally presuppose and incorporate the general contract law regarding assent.[215]

In contrast, some states' laws apply to arbitration agreements a higher standard of assent than that found in the pertinent state's general contract law. Consider for example, the Montana statute at issue in the Supreme Court case, *Doctor's Associates, Inc. v. Casarotto*[216]: "Notice that a contract is subject to arbitration * * * shall be typed in underlined capital letters on the first page of the contract; and unless such notice is displayed thereon, the contract may not be subject to arbitration."[217] The Supreme Court held that this Montana statute is preempted by the FAA because the Montana statute "conditions the enforceability of arbitration agreements on compliance with a special notice requirement not applicable to contracts generally."[218] As the *Casarotto* opinion stated, the FAA "precludes States from singling out arbitration provisions for suspect status, requiring instead that such provisions be placed 'upon the same footing as other contracts.' "[219]

Some courts, most frequently in the Ninth Circuit, take a different view. The Supreme Court's approach (in *Casarotto* and other cases) applies general contract law's standards of assent to arbitration agreements.[220] In contrast, the Ninth Circuit refused to enforce employees' agreements to arbitrate employment discrimination claims because the

§ 2.22

213. See generally Calamari & Perillo, supra note 28, ch.2.

214. See, e.g., First Options of Chicago, Inc. v. Kaplan, 514 U.S. 938, 944, 115 S.Ct. 1920, 131 L.Ed.2d 985 (1995)("[w]hen deciding whether the parties agreed to arbitrate a certain matter * * * courts generally * * * should apply ordinary state-law principles that govern the formation of contracts."); Doctor's Associates Inc. v. Casarotto, 517 U.S. 681, 685, 116 S.Ct. 1652, 134 L.Ed.2d 902 (1996)("state law, whether of legislative or judicial origin, is applicable if that law arose to govern issues concerning the validity, revocability, and enforceability of contracts generally.")

215. See Unif. Arbitration Act § 2, 7 U.L.A. 1, 109 (1997).

216. 517 U.S. 681, 116 S.Ct. 1652, 134 L.Ed.2d 902 (1996).

217. Mont.Code Ann. § 27–5–114(4) (1995). This language was deleted from the statute in 1997.

218. Doctor's Assoc., Inc. v. Casarotto, 517 U.S. 681, 683, 116 S.Ct. 1652, 134 L.Ed.2d 902 (1996).

219. Id. at 683.

220. See, e.g., First Options of Chicago, Inc. v. Kaplan, 514 U.S. 938, 944, 115 S.Ct. 1920, 131 L.Ed.2d 985 (1995)("[w]hen deciding whether the parties agreed to arbitrate a certain matter * * * courts generally * * * should apply ordinary state-law principles that govern the formation of contracts.")

employees did not "knowingly contract" for arbitration.[221] The Ninth Circuit's test appears to be a subjective test, one that turns on whether a particular employee actually knew of, *i.e.*, actually assented to, the arbitration clause. In contrast, general contract law turns, not on actual subjective assent, but on what would appear to an objectively reasonable person to be manifestations of assent.[222]

In particular, general contract law holds that parties manifest assent to standard forms they sign regardless of whether they read or understand the terms on the forms.[223] A party signing a standard form is, however, relieved of a particular term on that form if the party who drafted the form "has reason to believe" that the non-drafting party would not have signed if he had known "that the writing contained [the] particular term."[224] In other words, the non-drafting party is relieved of a particular term if the drafting party should have known that that term would have been a deal-breaker had the non-drafting party noticed it. To avoid an arbitration clause under this test, the non-drafting party must persuade the court that the drafting party should have known that if the non-drafting party had noticed the arbitration clause, the non-drafting party would have refused to sign the form. This objective test will only rarely result in the non-enforcement of an arbitration clause.

Departures from general contract law's objective test have been most prominent in cases alleging employment discrimination. The Ninth Circuit has used a subjective "knowing" assent test in cases in which employees sought to litigate, rather than arbitrate, claims under Title VII of the Civil Rights Act of 1964 and the Americans With Disabilities Act.[225] Agreements to arbitrate such claims were not enforceable until recently and some courts continue to resist enforcing them.[226] The "knowing" assent approach can be seen as a middle ground between (1) refusing to enforce agreements to arbitrate employment discrimination claims and (2) enforcing them under general contract law's standards. The "knowing" assent approach does enforce them, but under higher standards of assent than generally found in contract law.[227]

(b) Recurring Fact Patterns

There are a few recurring fact patterns that generate much of the litigation on assent to arbitration:

221. Prudential Insurance Co. of America v. Lai, 42 F.3d 1299, 1305 (9th Cir. 1994).

222. Macneil, Speidel & Stipanowich, supra note 1, at 17:21.

223. See § 2.14 (discussing Restatement (Second) of Contracts § 211 (1981)). General contract law does, however, include an unconscionability doctrine that often turns on actual subjective assent. See § 2.25.

224. Restatement (Second) of Contracts § 211(3) (1981).

225. Prudential Ins.Co.of America v. Lai, 42 F.3d 1299, 1305 (9th Cir.1994)(Title VII); Kummetz v. Tech Mold, Inc., 152 F.3d

1153, 1155 (9th Cir.1998)("agreements to arbitrate disputes arising under the ADA must at least be knowing, which means that 'the choice must be explicitly presented to the employee and the employee must explicitly agree to waive the specific right in question.'")(citation omitted). See also Penn v. Ryan's Family Steakhouses, Inc., 95 F.Supp.2d 940, 950 (N.D.Ind. 2000)(ADA).

226. See §§ 2.27—2.28.

227. Macneil, Speidel & Stipanowich, supra note 1, at 17:42—17:44.

—the document containing the arbitration clause was never signed by all of the parties and the issue is whether the parties manifested assent to arbitration by performing the contract;[228]

—the parties signed a document that did not contain an arbitration clause and the issue is whether that document effectively incorporated by reference a different document that does contain an arbitration clause;[229]

—the document containing the arbitration clause was signed but also contains language arguably stating that it is not a legally-binding contract;[230] and

—in a "battle of the forms" covered by Uniform Commercial Code § 2–207, one form contains an arbitration clause, while the other does not.[231]

§ 2.23 Consideration

Consideration is required to form a contract.[232] Perhaps the most obvious consideration for a promise to arbitrate is a reciprocal promise to arbitrate.[233] Most arbitration agreements obligate both parties to pursue their claims in arbitration. Each party's promise to do so serves as consideration for the other's promise to do so.

In contrast, some arbitration agreements obligate one party to pursue its claims in arbitration, while allowing the other party to pursue its claims in litigation.[234] Such agreements are said by some courts to "lack mutuality." Some of these courts refuse to enforce the promise to arbitrate on the ground that there is no reciprocal promise to arbitrate.[235] This is wrong as a matter of contract law.[236] Most courts

228. This issue arises when the arbitration clause appears on a "stuffer" mailed with a monthly bank statement or credit card bill, see, e.g., Badie v. Bank of America, 67 Cal.App.4th 779, 79 Cal.Rptr.2d 273 (Ct.App.1998), or an amendment to an insurance policy. See, e.g., Ex Parte Shelton, 738 So.2d 864 (Ala.1999).

For other fact patterns, see, e.g., Ex Parte Rush, 730 So.2d 1175 (Ala.1999); Dinong v. Superior Court, 102 Cal.App.3d 845, 162 Cal.Rptr. 606 (Ct.App.1980); Quality Truck and Auto Sales, Inc. v. Yassine, 730 So.2d 1164 (Ala.1999); Med Center Cars, Inc. v. Smith, 727 So.2d 9 (Ala.1998).

229. See, e.g., Kummetz v. Tech Mold, Inc., 152 F.3d 1153 (9th Cir.1998); Ex Parte Bentford, 719 So.2d 778 (Ala.1998); Hopper v. Woodmen of the World, 727 So.2d 9 (Ala.1998). See also Macneil, Speidel & Stipanowich, supra note 1, § 17.3.2.

230. See, e.g., Ex Parte Beasley, 712 So.2d 338 (Ala.1998); Ex Parte Grant, 711 So.2d 464 (Ala.1997). This most commonly occurs where the document in question is an employee handbook.

231. See, e.g., I.K. Bery, Inc. v. Boddy & Co., Inc., 2000 WL 218398 (S.D.N.Y.2000); Marlene Industries Corp. v. Carnac Textiles, Inc., 45 N.Y.2d 327, 408 N.Y.S.2d 410, 380 N.E.2d 239 (1978); Dorton v. Collins & Aikman Corp. 453 F.2d 1161 (6th Cir.1972). See also Macneil, Speidel & Stipanowich, supra note 1, § 17.5.

§ 2.23

232. See generally Calamari & Perillo, supra note 28, ch.4.

233. See Macneil, Speidel & Stipanowich, supra note 1, § 17.4.1.

234. Such agreements may be unconscionable. See § 2.25.

235. See, e.g., Stirlen v. Supercuts, Inc., 51 Cal.App.4th 1519, 60 Cal.Rptr.2d 138, 150 (Ct.App.1997); Hull v. Norcom, Inc., 750 F.2d 1547, 1550 (11th Cir.1985) ("the consideration exchanged for one party's promise to arbitrate must be the other party's promise to arbitrate at least some specified class of claims").

236. See note 236 on page 53.

recognize that the consideration for a promise to arbitrate can be anything that would constitute consideration for any sort of contract, *i.e.*, any promise or performance.[237]

The other set of cases raising doubts about consideration are those involving promises to arbitrate employment disputes where the employment is terminable at-will.[238] Suppose an at-will employee is asked to sign a document providing that she will arbitrate any claims she may have against her employer. If the employee later seeks to litigate such claims, she may argue that her promise to arbitrate was unsupported by consideration. The employer may point to its promise to pay salary and benefits as consideration. But courts may hold that this promise is illusory, *i.e.*, not a promise at all, because the employer could fire the employee at any time, even a moment after the arbitration agreement was signed.[239] If the employer has promised to arbitrate its claims against the employee, however, then that promise should serve as consideration for the at-will employee's promise to arbitrate.

3.   CONTRACT LAW DEFENSES TO ENFORCEMENT

Table of Sections

§ 2.24   Defenses Subject to Separability Doctrine

The defenses to enforcement of arbitration agreements are the same as the defenses to other contracts. They include: misrepresentation, duress, undue influence or overreaching, mistake, impracticability, frustration of purpose, illegality and the statute of frauds. These defenses to enforcement of arbitration agreements are, however, likely subject to the separability doctrine.[240] The separability doctrine holds that arbitrators, not courts, hear challenges to the enforceability of arbitration agreements unless those challenges are "directed to the arbitration clause itself" rather than to the whole contract containing that clause.[241] Under the separability doctrine, arbitrators rather than courts will address the

236. Macneil, Speidel & Stipanowich, supra note 1, § 17.4.2. See Restatement (Second) of Contracts § 71 (1981).

237. See, e.g., Doctor's Associates, Inc. v. Distajo, 66 F.3d 438 (2d Cir.1995); Wilson Elec.Contractors. v. Minnotte Contractors Corp., 878 F.2d 167 (6th Cir.1989); Green Tree Agency, Inc. v. White, 719 So.2d 1179 (Ala.1998); Willis Flooring, Inc. v. Howard S. Lease Constr. Co. & Assoc., 656 P.2d 1184 (Alaska 1983).

238. For a brief discussion of employment-at-will, see § 2.53(b)(2).

239. See Gibson v. Neighborhood Health Clinics, Inc., 121 F.3d 1126 (7th Cir.1997).

§ 2.24

240. See §§ 2.19—2.21.

241. See Prima Paint Corp. v. Flood & Conklin Manufacturing Co., 388 U.S. 395, 402, 87 S.Ct. 1801, 18 L.Ed.2d 1270 (1967).

aforementioned contract defenses in nearly all cases because those defenses are rarely "directed to the arbitration clause itself".[242] A party alleging that its arbitration agreement is unenforceable due to one of the grounds listed above will likely be sent to arbitration to make that argument. As arbitrators' decisions are rarely published,[243] there are few reported decisions applying these contract-law defenses to arbitration agreements.[244]

The one contract-law defense often directed to the arbitration clause itself and, therefore, likely to be heard by a court, is unconscionability.

§ 2.25   Unconscionability

(a) Generally

Unconscionability is often thought of as coming in two forms: procedural and substantive. Procedural unconscionability relates to the process of contract formation. It encompasses "not only the employment of sharp bargaining practices and the use of fine print and convoluted language, but a lack of understanding and an inequality of bargaining power."[245] Substantive unconscionability refers simply to terms that are "unreasonably favorable" to one side.[246] "Most cases of unconscionability involve a combination of procedural and substantive unconscionability, and it is generally agreed that if more of one is present, then less of the other is required."[247]

The separability doctrine holds that arbitrators rather than courts hear defenses to the enforceability of arbitration agreements unless those defenses are "directed to the arbitration clause itself" rather than to the whole contract containing that clause.[248] Unconscionability is often a defense directed to the arbitration clause itself.[249] Therefore, unconscionability arguments are often heard by courts, as opposed to arbitrators. This generates many reported decisions from which one can get an impression of the sorts of arbitration clauses that are, and are not, likely to be held unconscionable.

The Supreme Court seems to take a narrow view of the unconscionability doctrine.[250] Consider, for example, *Gilmer v. Interstate/Johnson*

---

242. See § 2.21. See also Macneil, Speidel & Stipanowich, supra note 1, § 19.2.1.

243. See § 2.37(e).

244. For cases not applying the separability doctrine, see Macneil, Speidel & Stipanowich, supra note 1, § 15.3.2.

§ 2.25

245. Farnsworth, supra note 127, § 4.28.

246. Id.

247. Id.

248. See Prima Paint Corp. v. Flood & Conklin Manufacturing Co., 388 U.S. 395, 402, 87 S.Ct. 1801, 18 L.Ed.2d 1270 (1967). See §§ 2.19—2.21.

249. Allegations of procedural unconscionability are rarely directed to the arbitration clause itself. So such allegations, if not combined with allegations that the arbitration clause is substantively unconscionable, may be subject to the separability doctrine. Cases applying the separability doctrine to allegations of unconscionability are cited in Macneil, Speidel & Stipanowich, supra note 1, § 15.3.2 n.18.

250. G. Richard Shell, Contracts in the Modern Supreme Court, 81 Cal.L.Rev. 431 (1993).

Lane Corp.,[251] which enforced a securities industry employee's agreement to arbitrate any dispute arising out of his employment.[252] The entire securities industry, at the time, required all employees in certain job categories to agree to arbitration as a condition of employment.[253] Justice Stevens' dissent in *Gilmer* raised "concern about the inequality of bargaining power between an entire industry on the one hand, and an individual * * * employee on the other."[254] The Supreme Court's majority responded that

> [m]ere inequality of bargaining power * * * is not a sufficient reason to hold that arbitration agreements are never enforceable in the employment context * * * . Of course, courts should remain attuned to well-supported claims that the agreement to arbitrate resulted from the sort of fraud or overwhelming economic power that would provide grounds for the revocation of any contract. There is no indication in this case, however, that Gilmer, an experienced businessman, was coerced or defrauded into agreeing to the arbitration clause in his registration application. As with the claimed procedural inadequacies discussed above, this claim of unequal bargaining power is best left for resolution in specific cases.[255]

Gilmer, then, indicates that parties raising unconscionability challenges to arbitration clauses face an uphill battle, and such challenges do seem to fail in most cases.[256] On the other hand, unconscionability challenges to arbitration clauses sometimes succeed.

These successes usually occur in the context of take-it-or-leave-it form contracts and are especially likely to occur if the arbitration clause lacks clarity or conspicuousness. Courts have held unconscionable arbitration clauses:

> —allowing the party drafting the clause to pursue its claims in litigation, while requiring the non-drafting party to pursue its claims in arbitration,[257]

> —requiring the non-drafting party to pay excessive fees,[258]

---

251. 500 U.S. 20, 111 S.Ct. 1647, 114 L.Ed.2d 26 (1991).

252. While *Gilmer* did not use the word "unconscionability", it discussed related concepts, like "inequality of bargaining power" and "overwhelming economic power". Regarding the interplay of state and federal law with respect to unconscionability, see § 2.25(b).

253. See Ware, supra note 203, at 114–15 & nn.151–52.

254. Gilmer, 500 U.S. at 43 (Stevens, J., dissenting).

255. Gilmer, 500 U.S. at 33.

256. See Macneil, Speidel & Stipanowich, supra note 1, § 19.3.1.1.

257. See, e.g., Armendariz v. Foundation Health Psychcare Services, Inc., 24 Cal.4th 83, 99 Cal.Rptr.2d 745, 6 P.3d 669 (2000); Iwen v. U.S. West Direct, 293 Mont. 512, 977 P.2d 989 (Mont.1999); Arnold v. United Companies Lending Corp., 204 W.Va. 229, 511 S.E.2d 854 (W.Va.1998); Fritz v. Nationwide Mut.Ins.Co., 1990 WL 186448, *6 (Del.Ch.1990). But see Harris v. Green Tree Financial Corp., 183 F.3d 173 (3d Cir.1999); We Care Hair Dev., Inc. v. Engen, 180 F.3d 838 (7th Cir.1999); Green Tree Agency, Inc. v. White, 719 So.2d 1179 (Ala.1998); Sablosky v. Edward S. Gordon Co., Inc., 73 N.Y.2d 133, 538 N.Y.S.2d 513, 516, 535 N.E.2d 643 (1989).

See also § 2.23.

258. See, e.g., Brower v. Gateway 2000 Inc., 246 A.D.2d 246, 676 N.Y.S.2d 569, 574 (App.Div.1998); Maciejewski v. Alpha Systems Lab., Inc., 87 Cal.Rptr.2d 390 (Ct.App.

—severely limiting discovery,[259]

—severely limiting remedies, such as punitive damages,[260]

—requiring the arbitrators to be members of occupations similar to that of the drafting party,[261]

—giving the drafting party greater control than the non-drafting party in the selection of the arbitrator,[262] and

—placing the location of arbitration far from the non-drafting party.[263]

(b) The FAA's Constraint on the Scope of the Unconscionability Doctrine

The FAA constrains the extent to which courts may hold arbitration clauses unconscionable. To see this, consider *Doctor's Associates, Inc. v. Casarotto*,[264] in which the United States Supreme Court enforced an arbitration clause in a take-it-or-leave-it franchise agreement. The Court did this despite the following protest by Montana Supreme Court Justice Trieweiler, who authored that court's opinion in *Casarotto*:

> In Montana, we are reasonably civilized and have a sophisticated system of justice * * *.
>
> * * *
>
> What I would like the people in the federal judiciary, especially at the appellate level, to understand is that due to their misinterpre-

1999), rev.granted, Maciejewski v. Alpha Systems Lab. Inc., 89 Cal.Rptr.2d 834, 986 P.2d 170 (Cal.1999). See also Green Tree Financial Corp. v. Randolph, ___ U.S. ___, 121 S.Ct. 513, ___ L.Ed.2d ___, 2000 WL 1803919, *6–7 (2000).

This argument has succeeded several times when a Title VII claim is involved. See 2.28(b).

259. See, e.g., Kinney v. United Health Care, Services, Inc., 70 Cal.App.4th 1322, 83 Cal.Rptr.2d 348 (Ct.App.1999); Gonzalez v. Hughes Aircraft Employees Federal Credit Union, 82 Cal.Rptr.2d 526 (Ct.App. 1999), review granted by, 83 Cal.Rptr.2d 763 (1999), appeal dismissed, 91 Cal. Rptr.2d 622, 990 P.2d 504 (1999). But see Farrell v. Convergent Communications, Inc., 1998 WL 774626, *5 (N.D.Cal.1998)("limitations on the amount of damages alone does not render an agreement to arbitrate per se unconscionable, as parties are generally free to contract as they see fit.")

See also § 2.36(d).

260. Stirlen v. Supercuts, Inc., 51 Cal. App.4th 1519, 60 Cal.Rptr.2d 138 (Ct.App. 1997). See also Graham Oil Co. v. ARCO Products Co., 43 F.3d 1244 (8th Cir.1994)(relying less on unconscionability,

more on Petroleum Marketing Practices Act).

See also § 2.38.

261. Broemmer v. Abortion Services of Phoenix, Ltd., 173 Ariz. 148, 840 P.2d 1013 (Ariz.1992)(characterizing its reasoning as one of the patient's "reasonable expectations", rather than "unconscionability").

See also § 2.36(a).

262. See, e.g., Hooters of America, Inc. v. Phillips, 173 F.3d 933, 938–39 (4th Cir.1999)(decided under duty of good faith and fair dealing, rather than unconscionability); Penn v. Ryan's Family Steakhouses, Inc., 95 F.Supp.2d 940, 950 (N.D.Ind.2000); Ditto v. RE/Max Preferred Properties, Inc., 861 P.2d 1000, 1004 (Okla.App.1993)(independent contractor's arbitration agreement was unconscionable because it "would exclude [her] from any voice in the selection of the arbitrators.").

See also § 2.36(a).

263. Patterson v. ITT Consumer Financial Corp., 14 Cal.App.4th 1659, 18 Cal. Rptr.2d 563 (Ct. App.1993), rev.denied, 14 Cal.App.4th 1659, 18 Cal.Rptr.2d 563 (1993).

264. 517 U.S. 681, 116 S.Ct. 1652, 134 L.Ed.2d 902 (1996).

tation of congressional intent when it enacted the Federal Arbitration Act, and due to their naive assumption that arbitration provisions and choice of law provisions are knowingly bargained for, [Montana's] procedural safeguards and substantive laws are easily avoided by any party with enough leverage to stick a choice of law and an arbitration provision in its pre-printed contract and require the party with inferior bargaining power to sign it.

The procedures we have established, and the laws we have enacted, are either inapplicable or unenforceable in the process we refer to as arbitration.

* * *

To me, the idea of a contract or agreement suggests mutuality. There is no mutuality in a franchise agreement, a securities brokerage agreement, or in any other of the agreements which typically impose arbitration as the means for resolving disputes. National franchisors, like the defendant in this case, and brokerage firms, who have been the defendants in many other arbitration cases, present form contracts to franchisees and consumers in which choice of law provisions and arbitration provisions are not negotiable, and the consequences of which are not explained. The provision is either accepted, or the business or investment opportunity is denied. Yet these provisions * * * do, in effect, subvert our system of justice as we have come to know it. If any foreign government tried to do the same, we would surely consider it a serious act of aggression.

Furthermore, if the Federal Arbitration Act is to be interpreted as broadly as some of the decisions from our federal courts would suggest, then it presents a serious issue regarding separation of powers. What these interpretations do, in effect, is permit a few major corporations to draft contracts regarding their relationship with others that immunizes them from accountability under the laws of the states where they do business, and by the courts in those states. With a legislative act, the Congress, according to some federal decisions, has written state and federal courts out of business as far as these corporations are concerned. They are not subject to California's labor laws or franchise laws, they are not subject to our contract laws or tort laws. They are, in effect, above the law.

These insidious erosions of state authority and the judicial process threaten to undermine the rule of law as we know it.[265]

Suppose that these views are widespread among Montana judges and suppose that Montana courts hold unconscionable every take-it-or-leave-it arbitration agreement before them. By so ruling, Montana courts could effectively nullify the FAA with respect to a huge class of contracts. FAA § 2 "precludes States from singling out arbitration provisions for suspect status, requiring instead that such provisions be placed

265. Casarotto v. Lombardi, 268 Mont. 369, 886 P.2d 931, 939–40 (Mont.1994).

'upon the same footing as other contracts.' "[266] As Montana courts enforce many take-it-or-leave-it contracts without arbitration clauses,[267] Montana courts would be singling out arbitration provisions for suspect status if they refused to enforce any take-it-or-leave-it contracts with arbitration clauses.

Notice, however, that Montana courts would be doing this through contract law's unconscionability doctrine, ordinarily an area of state, rather than federal, law. Ordinarily, the United States Supreme Court defers to state courts on matters of state law,[268] e.g., the United States Supreme Court accepts that Montana contract law is whatever the Montana Supreme Court says it is. But the FAA presupposes, and often incorporates, state contract law.[269] In effect, state contract law becomes federal law when the contract in question is an arbitration agreement. So the United States Supreme Court surely would review state courts' unconscionability rulings to the extent necessary to prevent the unconscionability doctrine from effectively nullifying the FAA with respect to a huge class of contracts. Indeed, the Court has twice stated that state courts may not "rely on the uniqueness of an agreement to arbitrate as a basis for a state-law holding that enforcement would be unconscionable, for this would enable the court to effect what * * * the state legislature cannot."[270]

§ 2.26 **Waiver of the Right to Arbitrate**

Contract rights can be waived.[271] Accordingly, one defense to the enforcement of an arbitration agreement is that the party seeking to enforce it has waived its right to do so.

(a) Participation in Litigation

Suppose that Buyer and Seller have an arbitration clause in their contract for the sale of goods. If Seller sues Buyer then Seller is in breach of its promise to arbitrate and Buyer has the right to compel arbitration of Seller's claim.[272] Suppose, however, that Buyer does not promptly ask the court to compel arbitration. Instead, Buyer participates in litigation before asking the court to compel arbitration. It is possible the court may refuse to compel arbitration on the ground that Buyer waived its right to compel arbitration by participating in litigation.

To determine whether a party's participation in litigation is extensive enough to constitute a waiver of the right to compel arbitration, courts often look to "whether the opposing party would be prejudiced by

266. Doctor's Associates, 517 U.S. at 682.

267. See, e.g., Counterpoint, Inc. v. Essex Insurance Co., 291 Mont. 189, 967 P.2d 393 (Mont.1998); Stutzman v. Safeco Insurance Co., 284 Mont. 372, 945 P.2d 32 (Mont.1997).

268. Chemerinsky, supra note 154.

269. See § 2.5(b).

270. Doctor's Associates, 517 U.S. at 687–88 n.3; Perry v. Thomas, 482 U.S. 483, 493 n. 9, 107 S.Ct. 2520, 96 L.Ed.2d 426 (1987).

§ 2.26

271. Farnsworth, supra note 127, § 8.19.

272. See § 2.4(b).

a subsequent order requiring it to submit to arbitration."[273] This is a fact-specific inquiry that generally turns on the costs the opposing party has incurred in litigating and whether the party now seeking arbitration has benefitted from features of litigation, such as extensive discovery, that may not be available to it in arbitration.[274]

Courts have held that parties waived the right to compel arbitration by filing pleadings,[275] engaging in discovery,[276] or removing to federal court.[277] In contrast, other courts have declined to find a waiver by parties who engaged in similar conduct.[278] Courts are more likely to find waiver by plaintiffs who initiate litigation before seeking arbitration than by defendants who respond in litigation before seeking arbitration.[279] If a court does find that a party has, by participating in litigation, waived the right to compel arbitration then the dispute will be resolved in litigation rather than arbitration.[280]

(b) Delay (Including Statute of Limitations)

The previous section discussed parties who waive the right to arbitrate by participating in litigation before asking the court to compel arbitration of the dispute.[281] The other sort of parties who waive the right to arbitrate are those who do nothing, *i.e.*, those who wait too long to assert their claims in arbitration or litigation. One way to wait "too long" is to allow the statute of limitations to expire. Courts send to arbitration the question whether a claim is time-barred by the statute of limitations or the related equitable doctrine of laches.[282] Some arbitration agreements shorten the limitations period by contract, *i.e.*, require claims to be asserted sooner than they would otherwise have to be.[283] Parties who fail to comply with statutes of limitations or contractual time limits lose the right to pursue their claims in any forum, arbitration or litigation.[284]

---

273. See, e.g., Mutual Assurance, Inc. v. Wilson, 716 So.2d 1160, 1163 (Ala.1998)(quoting Companion Life Ins. Co. v. Whitesell Manufacturing, Inc., 670 So.2d 897, 899 (Ala.1995)). But see Cabinetree of Wisconsin, Inc. v. Kraftmaid Cabinetry, Inc., 50 F.3d 388, 391–92 (7th Cir.1995)(not requiring prejudice).

274. Murray, Rau & Sherman, supra note 1, at 621.

275. Lapidus v. Arlen Beach Condominium Ass'n Inc., 394 So.2d 1102 (Fla.App. 1981); Ex Parte Prendergast, 678 So.2d 778 (Ala.1996).

276. Com–Tech Assoc. v. Computer Assoc. Int'l, Inc., 938 F.2d 1574 (2d Cir.1991); Ex Parte Smith, 706 So.2d 704, 705 (Ala. 1997).

277. Ex Parte Hood, 712 So.2d 341, 345 (Ala.1998).

278. See, e.g., Walker v. J.C. Bradford & Co., 938 F.2d 575 (5th Cir.1991); Stifel,

Nicolaus & Co., Inc. v. Freeman, 924 F.2d 157 (8th Cir.1991).

279. Macneil, Speidel & Stipanowich, supra note 1, § 21.3.2.1A (Supp.1999).

280. Of course, the parties can form a post-dispute agreement to use some other process, but if they do not then litigation is the default process. See § 1.5(b).

281. See Section 2.26(a).

282. Macneil, Speidel & Stipanowich, supra note 1, § 21.2.1.3. This is an application of the separability doctrine. See §§ 2.19—2.21.

283. See, e.g., PaineWebber Inc. v. Elahi, 87 F.3d 589 (1st Cir.1996)(describing Circuit-split over six-year period to bring securities claims).

284. See, e.g., PaineWebber Inc. v. Hartmann, 921 F.2d 507 (3d Cir.1990). See generally Macneil, Speidel & Stipanowich, supra note 1, §§ 21.2.1.2 & 21.2.2.

4. NON–CONTRACT LAW DEFENSES TO ENFORCEMENT:
FEDERAL STATUTORY CLAIMS AND PUBLIC POLICY

Table of Sections

The previous sections discuss contract law.[285] Those sections survey the law regarding the formation of enforceable contracts as that law applies to a particular species of contract, the arbitration agreement. In contrast, the next two sections note the rare occasions when non-contract law provides a defense to the enforcement of an arbitration agreement.

§ 2.27   Toward Universal Arbitrability

(a) The Mainstream

Consider domestic United States arbitration (as opposed to international arbitration) prior to the 1980's. Nearly all domestic arbitration occurred in two contexts: (1) labor disputes, and (2) disputes among businesses.[286] With arbitration limited to these contexts, the sorts of issues resolved in arbitration were also limited. Arbitration was basically limited to contract issues. Disputes in the labor context tend to focus on alleged breaches of collective bargaining agreements,[287] and disputes among businesses also tend to revolve around contract interpretation and performance. Prior to the 1980's, arbitration seemed largely confined to contract claims and little attention was given to the arbitration of non-contract claims. Then the Supreme Court revolutionized arbitration law.

The Court's 1980's revolution centered on "statutory arbitrability." An *arbitrable* claim is one with respect to which a pre-dispute arbitration agreement will be enforced.[288]

Consider, for example, a contract between Buyer and Seller obligating each party to arbitrate any "controversy or claim arising out of or relating to this contract, or the breach thereof." If a dispute arises and one party seeks to litigate, while the other seeks to arbitrate, a court will

---

285. See §§ 2.19—2.26.

§ 2.27

286. See Mitsubishi Motors Corp. v. Soler Chrysler–Plymouth, Inc., 473 U.S. 614, 650, 105 S.Ct. 3346, 87 L.Ed.2d 444 (1985) (Stevens, J., dissenting) (referring to "the undisputed historical fact that arbitration has functioned almost entirely in either the area of labor disputes or in 'ordinary disputes between merchants as to questions of fact' ").

287. See § 2.53.

288. This discussion of "statutory arbitrability" should be contrasted with § 2.29's discussion of "contractual arbitrability." The latter is the case-by-case question of whether the particular contract should be interpreted to send to arbitration a particular claim. Contractual arbitrability is a question of contract interpretation, while statutory arbitrability is a question of statutory interpretation.

have to decide whether to hear the case or to order arbitration. Assuming there is no generally applicable contract defense,[289] a court will order arbitration if, for example, Seller alleges that Buyer failed to pay, or Buyer alleges that Seller breached a warranty. By sending contract and warranty claims to arbitration over the objection of a party, a court holds that such claims are arbitrable.

But what if Buyer alleges that Seller violated the antitrust laws? Until the 1980's, courts held that antitrust claims were not arbitrable.[290] That is, if either party sought to litigate rather than arbitrate the antitrust claim, a court would have heard the antitrust claim on the merits, rather than ordering arbitration of it. In our example, the court may have concluded that Buyer and Seller agreed to arbitrate Buyer's antitrust claim because it, like the contract and warranty claims, "ar[ose] out of" the contract.[291] But the court would have refused to enforce the agreement to arbitrate antitrust claims because such enforcement would violate "public policy." In other words, courts held that antitrust claims were inarbitrable.

Antitrust claims were not alone in this regard. Other claims that courts held to be inarbitrable included: securities,[292] RICO,[293] patent,[294] copyright,[295] "non-core" bankruptcy proceedings,[296] Title VII,[297] ADEA,[298] and ERISA.[299] With such a long list of inarbitrable claims, arbitration was basically confined to resolving breach-of-contract claims.

In the 1980's, the Supreme Court revolutionized arbitration law to require enforcement of agreements to arbitrate regardless of the claims asserted. The Court drastically increased the variety of claims that are arbitrable.[300] The Court now holds that the FAA

289. See §§ 2.19—2.26.

290. See, e.g., American Safety Equip. Corp. v. J.P. Maguire & Co., 391 F.2d 821, 828 (2d Cir.1968) (declaring antitrust claims "inappropriate for arbitration"). But see Mitsubishi Motors Corp., 473 U.S. 614, 640, 105 S.Ct. 3346, 87 L.Ed.2d 444 (1985)(holding an agreement to arbitrate a claim arising under the Sherman Antitrust Act enforceable).

291. See §§ 2.29—2.31.

292. See Wilko v. Swan, 346 U.S. 427, 438, 74 S.Ct. 182, 98 L.Ed. 168 (1953).

293. See Page v. Moseley, Hallgarten, Estabrook & Weeden, Inc., 806 F.2d 291, 298–300 (1st Cir.1986). "RICO" is an abbreviation for "Racketeer Influenced and Corrupt Organizations." 18 U.S.C. §§ 1961–68 (1994).

294. See Beckman Instruments, Inc. v. Technical Dev. Corp., 433 F.2d 55, 63 (7th Cir.1970).

295. See Kamakazi Music Corp. v. Robbins Music Corp., 522 F.Supp. 125, 137

(S.D.N.Y.1981), aff'd, 684 F.2d 228 (2d Cir. 1982).

296. See Zimmerman v. Continental Airlines, 712 F.2d 55, 59 (3d Cir.1983). But see Hays and Co. v. Merrill Lynch, Pierce, Fenner & Smith, Inc., 885 F.2d 1149, 1155 (3d Cir.1989) (overruling and holding that non-core bankruptcy proceedings are arbitrable). A core proceeding involves "the administration of the estate; the allowance of claims against the estate; the voidance of preferences or fraudulent transfers; determinations as to dischargeability of debts; priorities of liens; or the confirmation of a plan." Id. at 1156 n.9.

297. See Utley v. Goldman Sachs & Co., 883 F.2d 184, 187 (1st Cir.1989).

298. See Nicholson v. CPC Int'l Inc., 877 F.2d 221, 231 (3d Cir.1989).

299. See Barrowclough v. Kidder, Peabody & Co., 752 F.2d 923, 941 (3d Cir. 1985).

300. See Macneil, Speidel & Stipanowich, supra note 1, ch.16.

mandates enforcement of agreements to arbitrate statutory claims. Like any statutory directive, the [FAA]'s mandate may be overridden by a contrary congressional command. The burden is on the party opposing arbitration, however, to show that Congress intended to preclude a waiver of judicial remedies for the statutory rights at issue * * * . If Congress did intend to limit or prohibit waiver of a judicial forum for a particular claim, such an intent will be deducible from [the statute's] text or legislative history, * * * or from an inherent conflict between arbitration and the statute's underlying purposes.[301]

Since first making a statement to this effect in 1985,[302] the Supreme Court has yet to discover a single instance in which "Congress intended to preclude a waiver of judicial remedies for the statutory rights at issue." In other words, the Supreme Court has consistently found that statutory claims are arbitrable.[303] Nearly all claims are now arbitrable.[304] In other words, courts' enforcement of arbitration agreements is nearly always without regard to the claims asserted.

Notice, however, that the Supreme Court acknowledges the possibility that Congress might create a claim that is inarbitrable. Congress can do this by merely saying so in the text of a statute, and bills have been introduced that do just that.[305] The possibility of *Congress* creating inarbitrable claims should be contrasted with the impossibility of a *state* legislature doing so. Any state law attempting to do so would, as discussed above,[306] be preempted by the FAA's command that arbitration agreements be enforced. The FAA's pro-enforcement command may, however, yield to a federal statute's anti-enforcement command.

(b) The Exception: Labor Arbitration

The previous section explained that nearly all claims are now arbitrable.[307] In other words, courts' enforcement of arbitration agreements is nearly always without regard to the claims asserted. The one national exception, the one place where the old "public policy" defense lives on, is labor arbitration.

---

301. Shearson/American Express Inc. v. McMahon, 482 U.S. 220, 226–27, 107 S.Ct. 2332, 96 L.Ed.2d 185 (1987)(citations omitted).

302. Mitsubishi Motors Corp. v. Soler Chrysler–Plymouth, Inc., 473 U.S. 614, 628, 105 S.Ct. 3346, 87 L.Ed.2d 444 (1985)("Having made the bargain to arbitrate, the party should be held to it unless Congress itself has evinced an intention to preclude a waiver of judicial remedies for the statutory rights at issue.")

303. Mitsubishi Motors Corp. v. Soler Chrysler–Plymouth, Inc., 473 U.S. 614, 105 S.Ct. 3346, 87 L.Ed.2d 444 (1985)(antitrust); Shearson/American Express, Inc. v.

McMahon, 482 U.S. 220, 107 S.Ct. 2332, 96 L.Ed.2d 185 (1987)(Securities Exchange Act and RICO); Rodriguez de Quijas v. Shearson/American Express, Inc., 490 U.S. 477, 109 S.Ct. 1917, 104 L.Ed.2d 526 (1989)(Securities Act); Gilmer v. Interstate/Johnson Lane Corp., 500 U.S. 20, 111 S.Ct. 1647, 114 L.Ed.2d 26 (1991)(employment discrimination).

304. Exceptions are discussed in § 2.28.

305. See, e.g., Civil Rights Procedures Protection Act of 1999, S. 121, 106th Cong., 1st Sess. §§ 2–9 (1999).

306. See § 2.12.

307. See § 2.27(a).

Here, it is crucial to distinguish between employment arbitration (individual employees not represented by a labor union) and labor arbitration (employees represented by a labor union).[308] Employment arbitration is part of the mainstream move toward universal arbitrability. In *Gilmer v. Interstate/Johnson Lane Corp.*,[309] the Supreme Court held that an individual employee's age discrimination claim was arbitrable. Since *Gilmer*, the vast majority of lower courts have held that individual employees' claims of race, sex, disability and other discrimination are also arbitrable.[310]

In contrast, labor arbitration retains the old public policy defense. When employees represented by a labor union have asserted federal discrimination claims in court they have been allowed to proceed with litigation despite arbitration clauses in their collective bargaining agreements.[311]

(c) Summary of the Move Toward Universal Arbitrability

The FAA directs courts to enforce arbitration agreements. It does not say arbitration agreements shall be enforced "only with respect to breach-of-contract claims" or "except with respect to statutory claims." Yet that is how the FAA was interpreted until the 1980's. Arbitration prior to the 1980's was largely confined to contract disputes. Agreements to arbitrate non-contract claims were generally unenforceable.

In the 1980's, the Supreme Court revolutionized arbitration law to require enforcement of agreements to arbitrate regardless of the claims asserted. Nearly all claims are now arbitrable. The one national exception, however, is labor arbitration. Courts have not sent to arbitration federal discrimination claims by employees covered by collective bargaining agreements.

§ 2.28　Current Inarbitrability

The previous section explained that nearly all claims are now arbitrable.[312] In other words, courts' enforcement of arbitration agreements is nearly always without regard to the claims asserted. There are, however, a few exceptions. The national exception for labor arbitration is noted above.[313] Other, more local, exceptions are discussed in this section.

(a) Simple Inarbitrability: Title VII and Magnuson–Moss

While the United States Supreme Court cases over the last generation have consistently held arbitrable every claim before the Court, some lower courts have broken ranks to hold certain claims inarbitrable. The

---

308. See § 2.50.

309. 500 U.S. 20, 111 S.Ct. 1647, 114 L.Ed.2d 26 (1991).

310. See § 2.28(a)(citing mainstream cases and Ninth Circuit's minority position).

311. See § 2.53(c).

§ 2.28

312. See § 2.27.

313. See § 2.27(b). This exception is also discussed in § 2.53(c).

most notable example is the Ninth Circuit's treatment of employment discrimination claims under Title VII of the Civil Rights Act of 1964. The Ninth Circuit refuses to enforce agreements to arbitrate such claims.[314] The other instance of localized inarbitrability is that state and federal courts in Alabama have refused to enforce agreements to arbitrate certain claims under a federal statute relating to consumer sales, the Magnuson–Moss Warranty—Federal Trade Commission Improvement Act.[315] With these two exceptions, all claims are now arbitrable in non-labor arbitration.

(b) Arbitrability With Strings Attached: Title VII and Truth in Lending

While nearly all claims are now arbitrable in non-labor arbitration,[316] some courts have made a few claims arbitrable only when certain conditions are met. Most notably, several courts have refused to enforce agreements to arbitrate Title VII claims where the agreement required the employee to pay an arbitration organization's filing fee plus half of the arbitrator's fees.[317] These courts seem to hold that Title VII claims are arbitrable only when arbitration is free to the employee. This would be a striking contrast from the custom in many arbitration contexts, which is that the claimant (plaintiff) pays the arbitration organization's filing fee and each of the two parties pays half the arbitrator's fee.[318] While this arrangement is customary and has been enforced in a variety of contexts, this arrangement is now doubtful when employment dis-

---

314. See Duffield v. Robertson Stephens & Co., 144 F.3d 1182 (9th Cir.1998). *Duffield*'s reasoning has been rejected by many other courts which hold Title VII claims arbitrable. See, e.g., Rosenberg v. Merrill Lynch, Pierce, Fenner & Smith Inc., 170 F.3d 1, 6–11 (1st Cir.1999); Seus v. John Nuveen & Co., Inc., 146 F.3d 175, 182 (3d Cir.1998); Paladino v. Avnet Computer Techs., Inc., 134 F.3d 1054, 1062 (11th Cir. 1998); Gibson v. Neighborhood Health Clinics, Inc., 121 F.3d 1126, 1130 (7th Cir. 1997); Patterson v. Tenet Healthcare, Inc., 113 F.3d 832, 837 (8th Cir.1997); Cole v. Burns Int'l Sec. Servs., 105 F.3d 1465, 1467–68 (D.C.Cir.1997); Austin v. Owens–Brockway Glass Container, Inc., 78 F.3d 875, 882 (4th Cir.1996); Metz v. Merrill Lynch, Pierce, Fenner & Smith, Inc., 39 F.3d 1482, 1487 (10th Cir.1994); Willis v. Dean Witter Reynolds, Inc., 948 F.2d 305, 307–12 (6th Cir.1991); Alford v. Dean Witter Reynolds, Inc., 939 F.2d 229, 230 (5th Cir.1991).

315. See Rhode v. E & T Investments, Inc., 6 F.Supp.2d 1322 (M.D.Ala.1998); Wilson v. Waverlee Homes, Inc., 954 F.Supp. 1530 (M.D.Ala.1997), aff'd, 127 F.3d 40 (11th Cir.1997) (table). See also Boyd v. Homes of Legend, Inc., 981 F.Supp. 1423 (M.D.Ala.1997). See also Southern Energy

Homes, Inc. v. Lee, 732 So.2d 994 (Ala. 1999), overruled by, Southern Energy Homes, Inc. v. Ard, 2000 WL 709500 (Ala. 2000).

316. See § 2.28(a).

317. Shankle v. B–G Maintenance Mgt., Inc., 163 F.3d 1230 (10th Cir.1999); Paladino v. Avnet Computer Technologies, Inc., 134 F.3d 1054, 1062 (11th Cir.1998)(finding that this "did not comport with the statutory policy" of Title VII). Contra Arakawa v. Japan Network Group, 56 F.Supp.2d 349, 351 (S.D.N.Y.1999) (rejecting *Paladino* and comparing authorities from various courts).

See also Cole v. Burns Int'l Sec. Serv., 105 F.3d 1465 (D.C.Cir.1997)(interpreting agreement to hold that employer would pay fees and then enforcing agreement); Armendariz v. Foundation Health Psychcare Services, Inc., 24 Cal.4th 83, 99 Cal.Rptr.2d 745, 6 P.3d 669 (Cal.2000)("when an employer imposes mandatory arbitration as a condition of employment, the arbitration agreement or arbitration process cannot generally require the employee to bear any type of expense that the employee would not be required to bear if he or she were free to bring the action in court.")

318. See §§ 2.36(a) & (c).

crimination claims are involved. This arrangement may also be in doubt when consumers assert federal statutory claims. In a Truth in Lending Act ("TILA") case, the Supreme Court stated that "the existence of large arbitration costs could preclude a litigant * * * from effectively vindicating her federal statutory rights in the arbitral forum."[319]

Importantly, the reasoning of the cases discussed in the previous paragraph can only be extended to *federal* statutory claims, not to claims arising under *state* law. The reasoning of these cases is that the policy of the federal statute in question, Title VII or TILA, would be undermined by enforcement of claimants' promises to pay significant arbitration fees[320] because such enforcement would deter some claimants from seeking to vindicate their claims. That policy clashes with the FAA's command that arbitration agreements, including those requiring claimants to pay significant arbitration fees, be enforced.[321] The holding of these cases is that the FAA must yield to the other federal statute with which it is in tension. But the FAA certainly does not yield to a state statute or state common law doctrine with which it is in tension. That is because the United States Constitution makes federal law supreme over state law.[322]

E. INTERPRETATION OF ARBITRATION AGREEMENTS

Table of Sections

1. CONTRACTUAL ARBITRABILITY

---

319. Green Tree Financial Corp. v. Randolph, ___ U.S. ___, 121 S.Ct. 513, ___ L.Ed.2d ___, 2000 WL 1803919, *7 (2000). The Court, however, held "that where, as here, a party seeks to invalidate an arbitration agreement on the ground that arbitration would be prohibitively expensive, that party bears the burden of showing the likelihood of incurring such costs." Id.

320. Claimants make such promises when they agree to arbitrate under rules of an organization that requires such fees.

321. 9 U.S.C. § 2 (1994). If an arbitration agreement incorporates the rules of an organization that requires claimants to pay significant fees, then that agreement must be enforced "save upon such grounds as exist at law or in equity for the revocation of any contract." Id.

322. See U.S. Const. art. VI, cl. 2. The Supreme Court of Alabama made this point in distinguishing *Paladino* , supra note 317. See Green Tree Financial Corp. of AL v. Wampler, 749 So.2d 409, 413 (Ala.1999)("Unlike *Paladino*, in which competing federal policies were in play, this present case arises under common-law principles governed solely by Alabama law and involves only one federal policy, that being a policy favoring arbitration.").

The FAA is not a complete statement of all the law governing arbitration.[323] The FAA presupposes, and often incorporates, existing law in areas such as contract, property, agency and tort. Most of the law in these areas is state common law. In other words, lots of general state law applies to arbitration. The area of general state law with the most frequent application to arbitration is contract law. The following sections discuss the law regarding contract interpretation as that law applies to arbitration agreements.

1. CONTRACTUAL ARBITRABILITY

Table of Sections

§ 2.29 Introduction

If a party seeks to litigate, rather than arbitrate, a particular claim, the court will send that claim to arbitration only if the parties agreed to arbitrate that claim.[324] That the parties agreed to arbitrate *some* claim is

---

323. See § 2.5(b).

324. See § 2.4(a)-(b).

not enough. They must have agreed to arbitrate *that* claim. Whether or not they did so is a question of contract interpretation, the question of "contractual arbitrability."

Contractual arbitrability should be distinguished from "statutory arbitrability", which is discussed in earlier sections.[325] Even if the parties did agree to arbitrate a particular claim, the court will still allow a party to litigate, rather than arbitrate, that claim if that claim is created by a federal statute that overrides the FAA's rule of enforcing arbitration agreements. Such claims are very rare. The discussion below assumes that no such claims are involved. If such claims are involved then the reader should consult both the following sections and the sections on statutory arbitrability.[326]

§ 2.30　Generally Decided by Courts

The threshold issue regarding contractual arbitrability is who, court or arbitrator, decides whether a claim is arbitrable. Consider, for example, a contract between Buyer and Seller obligating each party to arbitrate any "controversy or claim arising out of or relating to this contract, or the breach thereof." Suppose that Buyer sues Seller, alleging antitrust violations, and Seller moves to stay the litigation and to compel arbitration. Buyer may argue that, while the parties agreed to arbitrate breach-of-contract claims, they did not agree to arbitrate antitrust claims. Therefore, Seller's motion to compel arbitration should be denied. In other words, Buyer may argue contractual arbitrability.

If Buyer's case is brought outside the United States then the court is likely to grant Seller's motion. Most nations' laws give arbitrators, not courts, the power to rule on questions of contractual arbitrability.[327] Under such laws, Buyer must go to arbitration to persuade the arbitrator that the parties did not agree to arbitrate antitrust claims. In other words, Buyer must go to arbitration to persuade the arbitrator that the arbitration clause should be interpreted not to cover Buyer's claim. Only after getting a ruling from the arbitrator to that effect, or successfully challenging in court a contrary ruling,[328] can Buyer proceed to litigate the antitrust claim.

In contrast, the FAA sends contractual arbitrability disputes to courts, rather than to arbitrators.[329] In the United States, a court will interpret the arbitration agreement between Buyer and Seller. If the

---

325. See §§ 2.27—2.28.

326. See id.

§ 2.30

327. See Thomas E. Carbonneau, Beyond Trilogies: A New Bill of Rights and Law Practice Through the Contract of Arbitration, 6 Am.Rev.Int'l Arb. 1, 17 (1995)(most nations' laws "contain the *kompetenz-kompetenz* doctrine, under which arbitral tribunals are given the authority to rule initially at least upon questions of con-

tractual inarbitrability. These determinations are subject to judicial review * * * at the stage of enforcement when a final award can be challenged on the basis of an invalid or non-existent arbitration agreement or for excess of arbitral authority.")

328. See id.

329. First Options of Chicago, Inc. v. Kaplan, 514 U.S. 938, 115 S.Ct. 1920, 131 L.Ed.2d 985 (1995).

court interprets the arbitration clause to cover Buyer's antitrust claim, then the court will send that claim to arbitration, *i.e.*, grant Seller's motion. But if the court interprets the arbitration clause not to cover Buyer's antitrust claim then the court will deny Seller's motion. This approach follows from FAA § 3, which provides:

> If any suit or proceeding be brought in any of the courts of the United States upon any issue referable to arbitration under an agreement in writing for such arbitration, the court in which such suit is pending, *upon being satisfied that the issue involved in such suit or proceeding is referable to arbitration under such an agreement*, shall on application of one of the parties stay the trial of the action until such arbitration has been had in accordance with the terms of the agreement, providing the applicant for the stay is not in default in proceeding with such arbitration.[330]

FAA § 3 requires the court to satisfy itself that the issue involved in the suit is covered by the arbitration agreement before compelling arbitration.

While the FAA is not the primary law governing labor arbitration,[331] the rule that courts, rather than arbitrators, resolve contractual arbitrability disputes applies to labor arbitration, too.[332]

The rule that courts, rather than arbitrators, resolve contractual arbitrability disputes is merely a default rule. The parties can contract around this rule by using an arbitration agreement that says contractual arbitrability disputes shall be resolved by the arbitrator, rather than the court.[333] Had Buyer and Seller, in the example above, used such an agreement then the court would grant Seller's motion to compel arbitration. Buyer would have to go to arbitration to persuade the arbitrator that the arbitration agreement should be interpreted not to cover Buyer's antitrust claim. Only after getting a ruling from the arbitrator to that effect, could Buyer proceed to litigate the antitrust claim.[334]

§ 2.31   Contractual and Non–Contractual Approaches

The previous section explained that courts, as opposed to arbitrators, usually resolve contractual arbitrability disputes in the United

---

330. 9 U.S.C. § 3 (1994)(emphasis added).

331. See § 2.53(a).

332. AT & T Technologies, Inc. v. Communications Workers of Am., 475 U.S. 643, 106 S.Ct. 1415, 89 L.Ed.2d 648 (1986).

333. First Options of Chicago, Inc. v. Kaplan, 514 U.S. 938, 946–47, 115 S.Ct. 1920, 131 L.Ed.2d 985 (1995). See also AT & T Technologies, Inc. v. Communications Workers of Am., 475 U.S. 643, 106 S.Ct. 1415, 89 L.Ed.2d 648 (1986). For a case holding that the parties did contract around

the default rule, *i.e.*, did agree that the arbitrator should decide arbitrability, see Ex parte Waites, 736 So.2d 550 (Ala.1999).

334. While agreements sending contractual arbitrability disputes to the arbitrator are enforceable, there may in some cases be a dispute about whether the agreement does or does not do so. This dispute is also one of contract interpretation. Who resolves it, the court or the arbitrator? This question leads one into an infinite regression, a metaphysical quandary without end.

States.[335] In other words, courts interpret arbitration agreements to determine whether the parties did or did not agree to arbitrate a particular claim. One might suppose that this contract interpretation is no different from any other contract interpretation, as the court's job is to effectuate the apparent intentions of the parties by interpreting the contract's terms as those terms would ordinarily be understood by reasonable people in the positions of the parties.[336] A court taking this approach would apply the usual techniques of contract interpretation to the arbitration agreement.

While the usual techniques of contract interpretation do apply to the interpretation of arbitration agreements, there are also recurring departures from these usual techniques. To put it more directly, courts often seem to have an agenda, other than just effectuating the apparent intentions of the parties, when interpreting arbitration agreements. Courts often seem to have a finger on the scale.

Sometimes the court's agenda is to favor arbitration, *i.e.*, to interpret the arbitration clause broadly. This is the avowed policy of the Supreme Court. Its holdings establish that "in applying general state-law principles of contract interpretation to the interpretation of an arbitration agreement * * * , due regard must be given to the federal policy favoring arbitration, and ambiguities as to the scope of the arbitration clause itself [are] resolved in favor of arbitration."[337]

This interpretive agenda to favor arbitration is especially prominent in labor arbitration cases. Courts have long favored a broad interpretation of collective bargaining agreements' arbitration clauses.[338] In nearly all cases, a broader interpretation benefits the employee and union rather than the employer. That is because nearly all labor arbitration cases are grievances (claims) by the employee against the employer.[339] And if the arbitration clause is interpreted to cover the dispute, then the employee may win in arbitration. In contrast, if the arbitration clause is interpreted not to cover the dispute, then there will probably not be any adjudication of the dispute.[340] So in the labor context, a broad interpretation of the arbitration clause is nearly always favored by the employee and union. And the broad interpretation is often provided by courts who make statements like this oft-quoted one by the Supreme Court: "[a]n order to arbitrate the particular grievance should not be denied unless it may be said with positive assurance that the arbitration clause is not susceptible of an interpretation that covers the asserted dispute. Doubts should be resolved in favor of coverage."[341]

§ 2.31

335. See § 2.30.

336. Restatement (Second) of Contracts § 202(3)(1981).

337. Volt Information Sciences, Inc. v. Board of Trustees of the Leland Stanford Junior University, 489 U.S. 468, 476, 109 S.Ct. 1248, 103 L.Ed.2d 488 (1989).

338. See, e.g., United Steelworkers of America v. Warrior & Gulf Navigation Co.,

363 U.S. 574, 582–83, 80 S.Ct. 1347, 4 L.Ed.2d 1409 (1960).

339. See § 2.53(b).

340. See id. Adjudication is a process by which somebody (the adjudicator) decides the result of a dispute. See § 1.5(a), n.12.

341. United Steelworkers of America v. Warrior & Gulf Navigation Co., 363 U.S. 574, 582–83, 80 S.Ct. 1347, 4 L.Ed.2d 1409 (1960).

In other cases, by contrast, the court's agenda is to confine arbitration by interpreting the arbitration clause narrowly. This occurs when the court is straining to favor an employee or consumer plaintiff who seeks to litigate, rather than arbitrate, her claims despite having signed a take-it-or-leave-it arbitration agreement. For example, a New Jersey case interpreted an arbitration clause not to cover statutory employment discrimination claims because it did not, in "clear and unmistakable" language, include them.[342]

While a court's agenda in interpreting arbitration clauses affects the outcome in some cases, there are a great many cases in which the outcome is not controversial. That is to say, contractual arbitrability is clear in the bulk of cases. The typical arbitration clause is written broadly to cover any "controversy or claim arising out of or relating to this contract, or the breach thereof."[343] In the bulk of cases, all claims do plainly arise out of or relate to the contract or its breach so any fair-minded court (or arbitrator) will hold that the parties agreed to arbitrate the claims.

2. MULTI–PARTY DISPUTES

Table of Sections

§ 2.32   Claims By or Against Those Not Party to the Arbitration Agreement

The previous sections discuss contractual arbitrability, the question of whether a particular arbitration agreement covers a particular claim.[344] This is a question of contract interpretation. A specific application of that question is whether a particular arbitration agreement covers claims by or against a particular person who is not a party to the arbitration agreement.[345]

(a) Party Plaintiff vs. Non–Party Defendant

Consider, for example, an arbitration clause in a contract between Buyer and Seller for the sale of goods. If Buyer sues Seller, Seller will be

---

342. Alamo Rent A Car, Inc. v. Galarza, 306 N.J.Super. 384, 703 A.2d 961 (N.J. 1997). See also Wright v. Universal Maritime Service Corp., 525 U.S. 70, 119 S.Ct. 391, 142 L.Ed.2d 361 (1998)(requiring "clear and unmistakable" language encompassing statutory discrimination claims in labor arbitration context).

343. Macneil, Speidel & Stipanowich, supra note 1, § 20.2.2.

§ 2.32

344. See §§ 2.29—2.31.

345. Those not party to the arbitration agreement are often called "non-signatories" but this usage should be avoided if it misleads some into believing that the only way to be a party to an arbitration agreement is to sign it. Other methods of manifesting assent are also effective to make one a party to an arbitration agreement. See § 2.22.

able to obtain a stay of the litigation and an order compelling Buyer to arbitrate.[346] But what if Buyer also sues the manufacturer of the goods, the lender who financed Buyer's purchase, an insurance company involved in the transaction, or the individual salesperson who actually made the sale? Must Buyer arbitrate its claims against those third parties even though they are not parties to the arbitration agreement?

This is a question of contract law, particularly the law of third-party beneficiaries. Contracts often confer rights on those who are not party to it, "intended beneficiaries" in the current jargon.[347] To qualify as an intended beneficiary, one must show that "recognition of a right to performance in the beneficiary is appropriate to effectuate the intention of the parties."[348] In other words, whether a particular party may enforce a promise to arbitrate is a question of contract interpretation. Accordingly, if the arbitration clause in the agreement between Buyer and Seller is written broadly to cover "all disputes, claims, or controversies arising from or relating to this Contract or the relationships which result from this Contract", then Buyer is required to arbitrate its claims against defendants (such as the manufacturer or salesperson) who are not party to the arbitration agreement.[349] In contrast, if the arbitration clause is expressly limited to disputes between Buyer and Seller then Buyer is allowed to litigate against such defendants.[350] This approach of simply interpreting the contract to see if it covers claims against non-parties is taken by courts in most cases. Some cases, however, deviate from this approach, apparently because of the courts' anti-arbitration agenda.[351]

Note that intended third-party beneficiaries can compel arbitration but, without more, cannot be compelled to arbitrate.[352] In other words, those beneficiaries have the right, but not the duty, to arbitrate.

(b) Non–Party Plaintiff vs. Party Defendant

Plaintiffs, like defendants, can be intended third-party beneficiaries. If such a plaintiff brings a breach-of-contract action then that plaintiff "cannot pick and choose the portions of the contract that he wants to

---

346. See § 2.4(b).

347. See generally Farnsworth, supra note 127, ch.10.

348. Restatement (Second) of Contracts § 302(1) (1981).

349. Ex Parte Gates, 675 So.2d 371, 374 (Ala.1996).

350. Ex Parte Martin, 703 So.2d 883, 888 (Ala.1996).

This might not be true if the defendant who is not a party to the arbitration agreement is the agent of such a party. See, e.g., Pritzker v. Merrill Lynch, Pierce, Fenner & Smith, 7 F.3d 1110, 1121 (3d Cir.1993)("because a principal is bound under the terms of a valid arbitration clause, its agents, employees, and representatives are also covered under the terms of such agreements."); Macneil, Speidel & Stipanowich,

supra note 1, § 18.3.2.3 ("because of the liability of principals for the actions of their agents, an inference that the parties [to the arbitration agreement] intended the agent to be a beneficiary of the arbitration clause is quite reasonable.")

351. See, e.g., Ex Parte Herron, 1999 WL 6949 (Ala.1999)(arbitration clause in contract for sale of mobile home covered "[a]ll disputes, claims, or controversies arising from or relating to this contract or the relationships which result from this contract", yet court held that this language did not encompass the buyer's claim against the manufacturer).

352. Macneil, Speidel & Stipanowich, supra note 1, § 18.3.1.6 (Supp.1999).

apply."[353] If the contract contains an arbitration clause, the plaintiff must arbitrate its claim. This reasoning applies only to plaintiffs whose claims rest on the contract containing the arbitration clause. Plaintiffs whose claims rest on other grounds have no duty to arbitrate.[354]

§ 2.33   Consolidation of, and Stays Pending, Related Proceedings

In litigation, rules of civil procedure encourage courts to consolidate related cases and to join multiple parties in a single action if their disputes arise out of the same transaction or occurrence.[355] This consolidation and joinder avoids multiple litigation over the same facts, thus saving time and money and helping to avoid inconsistent results. These same goals also argue for arbitrators to consolidate cases and to join parties. The obstacle to doing so, however, is the contractual nature of arbitration. Parties who have not agreed to arbitrate have a right to litigate, *i.e.*, a right not to arbitrate.[356] And parties who have agreed to arbitrate have a right to arbitrate, *i.e.*, a right not to litigate.[357]

Consider, for example, a construction project in which the owner of the real estate has a contract with the general contractor and a separate contract with the architect.[358] Suppose that Owner's contract with Contractor has an arbitration clause but Owner's contract with Architect does not. Owner claims that Contractor breached the construction contract because the work had defects. Contractor replies that any defects are due to negligence by Architect in specifying the wrong materials, for example. Assume that either Architect or Contractor must be liable to Owner and the only question is to determine which one is liable.

Owner could pursue separate proceedings, suing Architect and asserting a claim in arbitration against Contractor. But this imposes on Owner the cost of two proceedings and the risk of inconsistent results. It might be that the court rules for Architect on the belief that Contractor (who is not a party to the litigation) is liable, while the arbitrator rules for Contractor on the belief that Architect (who is not a party to the arbitration) is liable. So Owner would lose both cases even though, as assumed above, one of the defendants must be liable to Owner.[359]

---

353. Ex Parte Dyess, 709 So.2d 447, 451 (Ala.1997). Accord District Moving & Storage Co. v. Gardiner & Gardiner, Inc., 63 Md.App. 96, 492 A.2d 319, 322–23 (Md.App. 1985).

354. Infiniti of Mobile, Inc. v. Office, 727 So.2d 42 (Ala.1999).

§ 2.33

355. See, e.g., Fed.R.Civ.P. 14 (third-party practice), 19 (joinder of persons needed for just adjudication), 20 (permissive joinder of parties), 22 (interpleader), 23 (class actions), and 24 (intervention).

356. See § 2.3(a).

357. See § 2.3(b).

358. These facts are loosely based on Moses H. Cone Memorial Hospital v. Mercury Construction Corp., 460 U.S. 1, 103 S.Ct. 927, 74 L.Ed.2d 765 (1983).

359. Owner is not saved from this result by ordinary principles of claim preclusion (res judicata) and issue preclusion (collateral estoppel) because preclusion may only be asserted against a party to the prior proceeding. See Jack H. Friedenthal, Mary Kay Kane & Arthur R. Miller, Civil Procedure § 14.14 (3d ed.1999). Contractor is not bound by the court's ruling because Contractor was not a party to the litigation. Architect is not bound by the arbitrator's

Under the FAA, Owner is stuck with these problems.[360] Owner may not compel all three parties into a single proceeding. Owner may not compel Architect to arbitrate because Architect never agreed to arbitrate. And Owner may not compel Contractor to litigate because Contractor has a contractual right to arbitrate its disputes with Owner. The FAA "requires piecemeal resolution when necessary to give effect to an arbitration agreement."[361]

In contrast, Owner's situation is more favorable under the arbitration law of certain states, such as California. A California statute allows a court to refuse enforcement of an arbitration agreement if one of the parties to it is also a party to pending litigation with a third party arising out of the same transaction.[362] So under California law, a court could order Contractor to litigate in one proceeding with Owner and Architect to prevent conflicting rulings.

Ordinarily, state law (such as California's) on consolidation is irrelevant because the FAA governs nearly all arbitration and preempts inconsistent state law.[363] But in *Volt Information Sciences, Inc. v. Board of Trustees of the Leland Stanford Junior University*,[364] the Supreme Court held that the parties were governed by California arbitration law, rather than the FAA, because of a provision in their agreement to that effect.[365]

If consolidation does not occur, the question arises which proceeding (arbitration or litigation) will reach a decision first.[366] The FAA does not directly address the question whether: (1) arbitration should be stayed

ruling because Architect was not a party to the arbitration.

360. Moses H. Cone Memorial Hospital v. Mercury Construction Corp., 460 U.S. 1, 103 S.Ct. 927, 74 L.Ed.2d 765 (1983).

361. Id. at 20. The Court went on to say:

> Under the Arbitration Act, an arbitration agreement must be enforced notwithstanding the presence of other persons who are parties to the underlying dispute but not to the arbitration agreement. If the dispute between [Contractor] and [Owner] is arbitrable under the Act, then [Owner's] two disputes will be resolved separately—one in arbitration, and the other (if at all) in state-court litigation.

Id.

362. Cal.Civ.Proc.Code Ann. § 1281.2(c). This provision provides, in pertinent part, that when a court determines that

> [a] party to the arbitration agreement is also a party to a pending court action or special proceeding with a third party, arising out of the same transaction or series of related transactions and there is a possibility of conflicting rulings on a

common issue of law or fact [,] * * * the court (1) may refuse to enforce the arbitration agreement and may order intervention or joinder of all parties in a single action or special proceeding; (2) may order intervention or joinder as to all or only certain issues; (3) may order arbitration among the parties who have agreed to arbitration and stay the pending court action or special proceeding pending the outcome of the arbitration proceeding; or (4) may stay arbitration pending the outcome of the court action or special proceeding.

Id.

363. See §§ 2.6—2.14.

364. 489 U.S. 468, 109 S.Ct. 1248, 103 L.Ed.2d 488 (1989).

365. See §§ 2.15—2.17.

366. The parties may care about this even though issues resolved in the first proceeding will not have preclusive effect on the second proceeding under the doctrine of collateral estoppel because the party against whom preclusion is asserted was not a party to the first proceeding. See § 2.42.

until litigation concludes, (2) litigation should be stayed until arbitration concludes, or (3) neither should be stayed. The Supreme Court has not directly addressed this question, either. The Supreme Court has held, in a two-party dispute, that arbitrable claims should not be stayed until litigation of non-arbitrable claims concludes.[367] In a multi-party dispute, a stay of arbitration pending litigation might "violate[] the spirit if not the letter" of this holding.[368] In contrast, a California statute allows a court to stay arbitration until litigation concludes.[369]

§ 2.34   Class Actions

Class actions may be pursued in arbitration. There is nothing in the process of arbitration inherently inconsistent with a class action. Courts have certified classwide arbitration.[370]

Many arbitration agreements expressly prohibit classwide arbitration.[371] Courts generally enforce these agreements to preclude both litigation and classwide arbitration, leaving only individual arbitration to resolve the claims.[372] In contrast, other courts have refused to enforce such agreements, often on unconscionability grounds.[373]

Arbitration agreements are often silent on whether classwide arbitration is permitted. Some courts have interpreted silence on the question of classwide arbitration as a prohibition of it and then enforced that prohibition.[374]

The Supreme Court has not definitively addressed the interplay of arbitration and class actions.[375]

367. See Dean Witter Reynolds Inc. v. Byrd, 470 U.S. 213, 105 S.Ct. 1238, 84 L.Ed.2d 158 (1985).

368. Macneil, Speidel & Stipanowich, supra note 1, § 10.9.1.

369. Cal.Civ.Proc.Code Ann. § 1281.2(c). This provision is quoted in note 362, supra.

§ 2.34

370. Lewis v. Prudential–Bache Securities, Inc., 179 Cal.App.3d 935, 225 Cal.Rptr. 69 (Ct.App.1986); Izzi v. Mesquite Country Club, 186 Cal.App.3d 1309, 231 Cal.Rptr. 315 (1986). See generally Macneil, Speidel & Stipanowich, supra note 1, § 18.9 (1994 & Supp.1996).

371. For examples, see Chris Drahozal, "Unfair" Arbitration Clauses, App. II, 2001 U.Ill.L.Rev. (forthcoming)

372. Doctor's Associates, Inc., v. Hollingsworth, 949 F.Supp. 77 (D.Conn.1996)(rejecting unconscionability argument); Lopez v. Plaza Finance Co., 1996 WL 210073, at 2–3 (N.D.Ill.1996); McCarthy v. Providential Corp., 1994 WL 387852 (N.D.Cal.1994); Meyers v. Univest

Home Loan, Inc., 1993 WL 307747 (N.D.Cal.1993)

373. In re Knepp, 229 B.R. 821 (N.D.Ala.1999); Powertel v. Bexley, 743 So.2d 570 (Fla.App.1999); Ramirez v. Circuit City Stores, Inc., 90 Cal.Rptr.2d 916 (Ct.App.1999), rev.granted, 94 Cal.Rptr.2d 1, 995 P.2d 137 (2000); In re Baldwin–United Corporation Litigation, 122 F.R.D. 424 (S.D.N.Y.1986). But see Johnson v. West Suburban Bank, 225 F.3d 366 (3d Cir.2000).

374. Champ v. Siegel Trading Co., Inc., 55 F.3d 269 (7th Cir.1995).

This issue is complicated in the securities arbitration context by a National Association of Securities Dealers rule. See, e.g., Nielsen v. Piper, Jaffray & Hopwood, Inc., 66 F.3d 145 (7th Cir.1995); In re NASDAQ Market–Makers Antitrust Litigation, 169 F.R.D. 493 (S.D.N.Y.1996); In re Regal Communications Corporation Securities Litigation, 1995 WL 550454 (E.D.Pa.1995).

375. Green Tree Financial Corp. v. Randolph, ___ U.S. ___, 121 S.Ct. 513, ___ L.Ed.2d ___, 2000 WL 1803919, *7 n.7 (2000); Gilmer v. Interstate/Johnson Lane Corp., 500 U.S. 20, 32, 111 S.Ct. 1647, 114 L.Ed.2d 26 (1991).

3. ARBITRATION PROCEDURE

Table of Sections

§ 2.35   Overview

Arbitration, like any *adjudication*,[376] involves the presentation of evidence and argument to the adjudicator. The presentation of evidence and argument in litigation is governed by rules of procedure and evidence enacted by government. In contrast, the rules of procedure and evidence in arbitration are, with few exceptions, whatever the parties' arbitration agreement says they are. The procedures of arbitration are largely determined by contract.

Arbitration agreements commonly provide for less discovery and motion practice than is typical of litigation and commonly provide for fewer rules of evidence than are typical of litigation. But the parties are free to draft their agreement almost any way they like. Arbitration privatizes procedural law by allowing parties to create their own customized rules of procedure and evidence.

There are, however, limits on the parties' freedom of contract. If the arbitration occurs and does not meet a court's definition of a "fundamentally fair hearing" then the court will grant a motion to vacate the arbitration award.[377] Also, courts have refused to send employment and consumer disputes to arbitration when persuaded that the agreed-upon procedures for arbitration would have been unfair. These cases rest on contract law's unconscionability doctrine,[378] or special concerns regarding the vindication of federal statutory rights.[379] For example, an oft-cited case is *Cole v. Burns Int'l Security Services*.[380] The *Cole* opinion was written by Judge Harry Edwards, an expert on labor arbitration. *Cole* did enforce an employee's agreement to arbitrate statutory employment discrimination claims, but only because:

> the arbitration arrangement (1) provides for neutral arbitrators, (2) provides for more than minimal discovery, (3) requires a written award, (4) provides for all of the types of relief that would otherwise be available in court, and (5) does not require employees to pay either unreasonable costs or any arbitrators' fees or expenses as a condition of access to the arbitration forum. Thus, an employee who is made to use arbitration as a condition of employment "effectively

---

§ 2.35

376.   See § 1.5(a), n.12.

377.   See § 2.44(c).

378.   See § 2.25.

379.   See § 2.28.

380.   105 F.3d 1465 (D.C.Cir.1997).

may vindicate [his or her] statutory cause of action in the arbitral forum."[381]

While other courts use different words, the substance of Judge Edwards' list is generally typical. The more of these five factors that are present, the less likely a court is to object to enforcing an arbitration agreement due to the arbitration procedures.

These five factors, along with other aspects of arbitration procedure, are discussed next.

§ 2.36   Pre–Hearing

(a) Selection of Arbitrator(s)

(1) Methods of Selection

Arbitration cannot occur without at least one arbitrator. Selection of the arbitrator(s) typically occurs through agreement of the parties. If the parties cannot agree on an arbitrator, however, the court will appoint one. The FAA gives courts the authority to do so:

> If in the agreement provision be made for a method of naming or appointing an arbitrator or arbitrators or an umpire, such method shall be followed; but if no method be provided therein, or if a method be provided and any party thereto shall fail to avail himself of such method, or if for any other reason there shall be a lapse in the naming of an arbitrator or arbitrators or umpire, or in filling a vacancy, then upon the application of either party to the controversy the court shall designate and appoint an arbitrator or arbitrators or umpire, as the case may require, who shall act under the said agreement with the same force and effect as if he or they had been specifically named therein; and unless otherwise provided in the agreement the arbitration shall be by a single arbitrator.[382]

Court appointment of an arbitrator is rarely necessary because the parties usually agree on an arbitrator.

Agreements for selecting an arbitrator fall into three categories. First, the parties can name an arbitrator (*e.g.*, "Donald Salvia",) in their arbitration agreement. While this is fairly common in post-dispute arbitration agreements, it is rarely done in pre-dispute arbitration agreements. At the time a pre-dispute agreement is formed, the parties probably hope and expect that no dispute will ever occur. Why take the time to negotiate agreement on who the arbitrator should be when arbitration is so unlikely to occur? And, to the extent a dispute is expected to occur, the parties do not know what the dispute will be. Maybe Donald Salvia would be the best arbitrator for one sort of dispute but not for another. Finally, at the time a pre-dispute agreement is

---

381. Cole, 105 F.3d at 1482 (quoting Gilmer v. Interstate/Johnson Lane Corp., 500 U.S. 20, 28, 111 S.Ct. 1647, 114 L.Ed.2d 26 (1991)).

§ 2.36

382. 9 U.S.C. § 5 (1994).

formed, the parties do not know *when* a dispute will occur. Perhaps by then, Donald Salvia will be unavailable or unwilling to serve as an arbitrator. For all these reasons, pre-dispute agreements rarely name an arbitrator.

What pre-dispute agreements typically do is specify a procedure for selecting an arbitrator. Many pre-dispute agreements commit the parties to arbitrate according to the rules of an arbitration organization, like the American Arbitration Association ("AAA"). AAA rules, like the rules of other arbitration organizations, contain procedures for selecting an arbitrator. The AAA Commercial Arbitration Rules serve as an example.

In cases where no claim exceeds $75,000 the AAA simply appoints a single arbitrator.[383] In other cases, the AAA sends the parties a list of potential arbitrators with some information about each person.[384] Then each party can strike the potential arbitrators to which that party objects.[385] Each party also ranks the remaining people in order of that party's preference.[386] The AAA invites those people with the highest combined ranking to serve as arbitrators.[387]

An alternative to using the rules of an arbitration organization for selecting arbitrators is to agree to *tripartite* arbitration. The agreement specifies that there will be three arbitrators: each party picks one arbitrator and those two agree on the third. Tripartite arbitration also occurs under the auspices of arbitration organizations.

Nearly all arbitrations have either one or three arbitrators, but any number is possible.

(2) Arbitrator Fees

Some arbitrators work for free. They provide their services on a pro bono basis as a way of serving others. These volunteer arbitrators range from merchant members of a trade association (who arbitrate disputes among members of that association) to a local lawyer who arbitrates consumer disputes for the Better Business Bureau. In AAA Commercial Arbitration, it is expected that arbitrators will serve for the first day of the hearing without charge in cases with no claim exceeding $10,000.[388] In many simple cases, a one-day hearing is enough.

In contrast, other arbitrators get paid a lot. One thousand dollars per day is common and many arbitrators earn much more than that. Particularly in multi-million-dollar cases, disputing parties are willing to pay high arbitrator fees to get high-quality arbitrators. But few arbitrators outside the labor context are in such demand that they can make a living out of arbitrating. Even well-respected arbitrators may be asked to

---

383. AAA, Commercial Arbitration Rule E–1 (1999).

384. AAA, Commercial Arbitration Rule R–13 (1999).

385. Id.

386. Id.

387. Id.

388. AAA, Commercial Arbitration Rule R–53 (1999).

arbitrate only one or two cases a year. Some well-respected labor arbitrators, in contrast, make a full-time career out of arbitrating.[389]

In many contexts, the custom is for the arbitrator's fee to be split equally between the parties. It is also common for arbitrators to order the losing party to pay the arbitrator's entire fee.[390] There are, however, some cases in which courts refuse to enforce employment arbitration agreements unless the employer relieves the employee of any obligation to pay arbitrator fees.[391]

(3) Courts' Constraints on Party Selection of Arbitrator(s)

Courts place limits on the arbitrators the parties may select. Courts place these limits in two ways. First, courts have refused to enforce arbitration awards when dissatisfied with the arbitrator. This topic is discussed in a later section.[392] Second, courts have refused to enforce executory arbitration agreements when dissatisfied with the agreement's method of selecting an arbitrator.

The most likely arbitration agreement to be unenforceable is the take-it-or-leave-it form contract selecting an arbitrator closely connected to the party drafting the contract. Some drafting parties even write contracts that reserve to themselves complete discretion over the selection of the arbitrator.[393] Only slightly less one-sided are agreements naming a close affiliate of the drafting party to be the arbitrator.[394] More debatable are agreements requiring the arbitrators to share with the drafting party, membership in a profession, if not in a particular organization.[395]

(b) Pleadings

Litigation generally begins with a complaint filed and served by the plaintiff, followed by an answer filed and served by the defendant. Arbitration is analogous but the terminology may be different. Arbitration generally begins with a *demand* for arbitration filed and served by the *claimant*, followed by an answer filed and served by the *respondent*.

The pleadings themselves typically cover the same ground as those in litigation: the basic factual allegations, the nature or source of the

---

389. The National Association of Arbitrators' membership consists of about 650 individuals who arbitrate the majority of labor arbitration cases. Dennis R. Nolan, Labor and Employment Arbitration in a Nutshell 24 (1999).

390. AAA, Commercial Arbitration Rule R–45(c) (1999).

391. See § 2.28.

392. See § 2.44(b).

393. Ditto v. RE/MAX Preferred Properties, Inc., 861 P.2d 1000, 1004 (Okla.App.1993)(independent contractor's arbitration agreement was unconscionable because it "would exclude [her] from any

voice in the selection of the arbitrators.") See also Hooters of America, Inc. v. Phillips, 173 F.3d 933, 938–39 (4th Cir.1999).

394. See, e.g., Graham v. Scissor Tail, Inc., 171 Cal.Rptr. 604, 623 P.2d 165 (1981)(refusing to enforce arbitration agreement between musician and concert promoter where agreement named musician's union as arbitrator).

395. For example, the drafting party in *Broemmer v. Abortion Services of Phoenix, Ltd.*, 173 Ariz. 148, 840 P.2d 1013 (Ariz. 1992), was an abortion clinic. Its arbitration clause required arbitration before "licensed medical doctors who specialize in obstetrics/gynecology." Id. at 104.

claims and defenses, the remedies sought, and the adjudicator's jurisdiction. While a court's jurisdiction is often shown by citing a statute, the arbitrator's jurisdiction is shown by the agreement to arbitrate.

The pleadings in arbitration tend to be written more concisely, with less legal jargon, than those in litigation.

(c) Filing Fees (and Un–Administered Arbitration)

Just as a plaintiff generally cannot commence litigation without paying a court's fee, a claimant generally cannot commence arbitration without paying the fee of the arbitration organization, such as the American Arbitration Association, that will administer the arbitration. These fees can run into the thousands of dollars, far exceeding court fees.[396] To complete the arbitration may require payment of additional fees to the arbitration organization beyond the initial filing fee.[397]

Parties can arbitrate without an arbitration organization. This un-administered (or ad hoc) arbitration saves the parties from paying the fees of an arbitration organization. But it also requires the parties to agree on their own to an arbitrator and to conduct the arbitration with the help of only the arbitrator. That is somewhat analogous to litigating with only a judge and no other court employees. As the arbitrator's hourly rate may be high,[398] the parties may find it cheaper to pay the fees of an arbitration organization.

(d) Discovery

"Limitations on discovery, particularly judicially initiated discovery, remain one of the hallmarks of American commercial arbitration."[399] While discovery in arbitration is usually minimal, it can be substantial. Discovery, like other aspects of arbitration, is primarily determined by the arbitration agreement.[400] Some arbitration agreements provide that discovery may be had in accordance with the Federal Rules of Civil Procedure.[401] Arbitration pursuant to these agreements is unlikely to have significantly less discovery than litigation.

Many arbitration agreements incorporate the rules of the American Arbitration Association or another arbitration organization. These rules typically provide for little discovery.[402] But these rules also typically grant the arbitrator wide discretion in authorizing discovery. The arbitrator's preferences may be the single strongest determinant of the

396. See, e.g., AAA, Commercial Arbitration Rules, Administrative Fees (1999).

397. See, e.g., National Arbitration Forum, Code of Arbitration, Fees.

398. See § 2.36(a)(2).

399. Macneil, Speidel & Stipanowich, supra note 1, § 34.1.

400. See, e.g., Robert A. Weiner & B. Ted Howes, Arbitration Discovery: When

should discovery provisions be included in an arbitration agreement?, Disp.Resol.Mag., Summer 1999, at 30–32.

401. See, e.g., Medicine Shoppe International, Inc. License Agreement, in Drahozal, supra note 371, App. II.

402. See, e.g., AAA, Commercial Arbitration Rule R–23 (1999).

amount of discovery in a particular case. And arbitrators seem to be authorizing more discovery in recent years. Perhaps this is a result of the increasing variety of parties and claims going to arbitration.[403]

Some courts, especially in the employment discrimination context, have indicated that they will not enforce arbitration agreements unless they have confidence that there will be sufficient discovery to allow claimants to gather necessary evidence.[404]

FAA § 7 authorizes the arbitrators to "summon in writing any person to attend before them or any of them as a witness and in a proper case to bring with him or them any book, record, document, or paper which may be deemed material as evidence in the case."[405] Courts are split on whether this provision authorizes pre-hearing deposition subpoenas of non-parties or only hearing subpoenas of non-parties.[406]

§ 2.37   Hearing

(a) General Comparison With Trial

A hearing is to arbitration what a trial is to litigation. Hearings look like trials in some respects: adversaries are trying to persuade a neutral adjudicator by presenting evidence and making arguments. But hearings generally look different from trials in other respects. One almost never sees a jury in arbitration. While judges sit up high, wear black robes and expect to be called "your honor", arbitrators do not. In contrast to trials, which are usually open to the public and the press, arbitration hearings are generally closed to non-participants. There typically is no transcript or other record of the hearing.[407]

---

403. See § 2.27. See also Edward Brunet, Replacing Folklore Arbitration with a Contract Model of Arbitration, 74 Tul. L.Rev. 39 (1999)(connecting increased discovery with broader changes in arbitration law and practice).

404. See, e.g., Cole v. Burns Int'l Security Services, 105 F.3d 1465 (D.C.Cir.1997); Kinney v. United Health Care Services, Inc., 70 Cal.App.4th 1322, 83 Cal.Rptr.2d 348 (Cal.Ct.App.1999); Gonzalez v. Hughes Aircraft Employees Federal Credit Union, 82 Cal.Rptr.2d 526 (Ct.App.1999), rev. granted by, 83 Cal.Rptr.2d 763 (Cal.1999), appeal dismissed, 91 Cal.Rptr.2d 622, 990 P.2d 504 (Cal.1999). See also Armendariz v. Foundation Health Psychcare Services, Inc., 24 Cal.4th 83, 99 Cal.Rptr.2d 745, 6 P.3d 669(Cal.2000).

405. 9 U.S.C. § 7 (1994).

406. Compare Meadows Indemnity Co. v. Nutmeg Insurance Co., 157 F.R.D. 42 (M.D.Tenn.1994)(enforcing subpoena of non-parties); Stanton v. Paine Webber

Jackson & Curtis, Inc. 685 F.Supp. 1241 (S.D.Fla.1988)(same), with COMSAT Corp. v. National Science Foundation, 190 F.3d 269, 275 (4th Cir.1999)("Nowhere does the FAA grant an arbitrator the authority to order non-parties to appear at depositions, or the authority to demand that non-parties provide the litigating parties with documents during prehearing discovery.")

§ 2.37

407. Murray, Rau & Sherman, supra note 1, at 640–41.

The FAA contains no provisions respecting maintenance or records of hearings or of records being furnished to the parties. Nor has any requirement that records of hearings be maintained or furnished to the parties been established by judicial decision. The maintenance of a record, if any, is strictly a matter for the agreement of the arbitrating parties.

Macneil, Speidel & Stipanowich, supra note 1, § 32.7.1 (1994).

(b) Role of Lawyers

Lawyers in many arbitration hearings do what they do at trial: make opening statements, call witnesses who testify under oath, cross-examine opposing witnesses, and make closing arguments.[408] But not all hearings look like this. In some arbitration contexts, such as trade association arbitration, lawyers often are not present.[409] If lawyers are present at the arbitration hearing, they are probably well-advised to behave somewhat differently than they do at trial. The rules of evidence in arbitration are likely to be minimal.[410] Lawyers making objections may find that doing so accomplishes nothing other than irritating the arbitrator. If the arbitrator has some expertise on the subject matter of the dispute, the lawyer may not need to lay the sort of factual and evidentiary foundations required in court. Also, lawyers may find that certain personal styles successful in front of a jury are less successful in front of an arbitrator. Many lawyers who succeed in arbitration remain seated and businesslike throughout the hearing, without the sort of movement or drama that might be effective in capturing a jury's attention.

(c) Rules of Evidence

Rules of evidence are historically intertwined with the jury. It is understandable then, that arbitration without a jury nearly always has less elaborate rules of evidence than those used in jury trials. In many arbitrations, there are no rules of evidence. The parties can present whatever evidence they like and the arbitrators can give to it whatever weight they like.[411] Arbitrators' tendency to admit all evidence may be caused in part by the fact that "refusing to hear evidence pertinent and material to the controversy" is a ground for vacating the arbitration award,[412] while hearing all evidence offered by the parties (no matter how long that takes) is not a ground for vacating.

Evidentiary rules, like other aspects of arbitration, are primarily determined by the arbitration agreement. Many agreements incorporate the rules of an arbitration organization such as the American Arbitration Association. The AAA's Commercial Arbitration Rules allow the parties to offer into evidence whatever is relevant and material.[413] These rules also say that the parties *shall* produce evidence the arbitrator deems necessary.[414] This is typical of most arbitration in that it contemplates a more active role by the arbitrator than is typical of judges and juries. Judges and juries are typically passive triers-of-fact, receiving only

---

408. See Jay E. Grenig, Arbitration Advocacy, Part II (2000).

409. See id., § 3.2 ("Rules of a few trade associations forbid representation by counsel in arbitration proceedings.") The law of many states provides that a pre-hearing waiver of the right to an attorney is void. See Unif. Arbitration Act § 6, 7 U.L.A. 1, 198 (1997). The FAA, by contrast, may require enforcement of an agreement to proceed without an attorney, see § 2.9, provided that enforcement would not be unconscionable, see § 2.25, or deprive the parties of a fundamentally fair hearing. See § 2.44(c).

410. See § 2.37(c).

411. Macneil, Speidel & Stipanowich, supra note 1, §§ 35.1.2.1. & 35.1.2.4.

412. 9 U.S.C. § 10(a)(3). See § 2.44(c).

413. AAA, Commercial Arbitration Rule R–33 (1999).

414. See id.

the evidence presented by the parties. In contrast, arbitrators tend to be more inquisitorial, sometimes questioning witnesses,[415] or making other investigations into evidence.[416]

If evidence is required from someone other than the parties, the arbitrator may obtain it through subpoena. Those who fail to comply with an arbitrator's subpoena may be compelled to do so by a court.[417]

(d) No Hearing; Dispositive Motions

Much litigation ends on a grant of a motion to dismiss or for summary judgment. Such motions rarely are granted by arbitrators. In other words, parties who want their "day in court" are more likely to get it in arbitration than in litigation.

Arbitration hearings do not, however, have to be live, face-to-face events. Hearings can be conducted across great distances through video teleconferencing. If the parties agree to forgo live testimony, they can have the hearing on the documentary evidence submitted. This is often called "desk arbitration".

(e) Written Awards; Reasoned Opinions

Arbitrator's decisions, called arbitration awards, generally are written.[418] But they rarely contain any reasoning.[419] For example, a typical arbitration award might consist of two sentences finding for the claimant and ordering the respondent to pay a particular dollar amount. In this respect, the typical arbitration award resembles the typical general verdict rendered by a jury.

The sort of reasoned opinions issued by judges are commonly issued by arbitrators in only two contexts: (1) labor and (2) international commercial and maritime arbitration.[420] Many labor arbitration opinions are published in the Bureau of National Affairs' *Labor Arbitration Reports*. International arbitrators' practice of writing reasoned opinions (which are sometimes published) conforms with practice of European arbitrators.

§ 2.38 Remedies

(a) Determined by Contract; the *Mastrobuono* Case

Remedies, like other aspects of arbitration, are primarily determined by the arbitration agreement. For example, the Supreme Court used a

---

415. Macneil, Speidel & Stipanowich, supra note 1, § 35.4.5.

416. See, e.g., AAA, Commercial Arbitration Rules R–35 (1999).

417. 9 U.S.C. § 7 (1994).

418. See, e.g., AAA, Commercial Arbitration Rules R–44 (1999).

419. See Macneil, Speidel & Stipanowich, supra note 1, § 3.2.3, at 3:13 & § 37.4.1, at 37:10.

420. "Only in a few, specialized types of arbitrations do arbitrators routinely craft written decisions—labor arbitrations, international commercial arbitrations, and maritime arbitrations." Edward Brunet & Charles B. Craver, Alternative Dispute Resolution: The Advocate's Perspective 324 (1997).

contractual analysis to determine whether the arbitrator could award punitive damages in *Mastrobuono v. Shearson Lehman Hutton, Inc.*[421] As the Court said, "the case before us comes down to what the contract has to say about the arbitrability of petitioners' claim for punitive damages."[422]

Mastrobuono held that this contractual analysis is mandated by the FAA and that it preempts any state law requiring a non-contractual analysis. New York law, at the time, required a non-contractual analysis. New York law prohibited arbitrators from awarding punitive damages regardless of the arbitration agreement's terms.[423] *Mastrobuono* stated that that New York law was preempted by the FAA.[424]

The challenging question in *Mastrobuono*, however, was whether the particular parties in that case had, by contract, avoided FAA preemption of New York law. *Mastrobuono* involved a contract between investors and their securities broker.[425] The contract contained both an arbitration clause and a New York choice-of-law clause.[426] When the arbitrator awarded punitive damages to the investor, the broker asked the federal district court to vacate that portion of the arbitrator's award on the ground that New York law governed because the parties had chosen to be governed by New York law.[427] The broker's argument was based on a prior Supreme Court case, *Volt Information Sciences, Inc. v. Board of Trustees of the Leland Stanford Junior University*,[428] in which a California choice-of-law clause had been interpreted by California state courts as the parties' choice to be governed by California arbitration law, rather than the FAA.[429] The Supreme Court in *Volt* deferred to the California court's interpretation of the choice-of-law clause and enforced the clause, so interpreted. The gist of *Volt* is that FAA preemption of state law is merely a default rule, *i.e.*, a rule the parties can avoid by contract.[430]

In *Mastrobuono*, however, the Supreme Court distinguished *Volt* and held that the parties did not contract around FAA preemption of New York law. Unlike *Volt*, which began in state court, the *Mastrobuono* case went to federal court. So in *Mastrobuono* the Supreme Court could interpret the contract as it wished, without having to defer to a state court's interpretation of the contract.[431] The Court began by suggesting

§ 2.38

421. 514 U.S. 52, 115 S.Ct. 1212, 131 L.Ed.2d 76 (1995).

422. Id. at 58.

423. See Garrity v. Lyle Stuart, Inc., 40 N.Y.2d 354, 386 N.Y.S.2d 831, 353 N.E.2d 793 (1976).

424. The Court said its "decisions in Allied–Bruce, Southland, and Perry make clear that if contracting parties agree to include claims for punitive damages within the issues to be arbitrated, the FAA ensures that their agreement will be enforced according to its terms even if a rule of state law would otherwise exclude such claims

from arbitration." 514 U.S. at 58. "[I]n the absence of contractual intent to the contrary, the FAA would pre-empt the Garrity rule." Id. at 59.

425. Id. at 54.

426. Id.

427. See id.

428. 489 U.S. 468, 109 S.Ct. 1248, 103 L.Ed.2d 488 (1989).

429. See §§ 2.15—2.17 (discussing Volt and the topic of choice-of-law clauses in arbitration agreements).

430. See § 2.16.

431. Mastrobuono, 514 U.S. at 60 n.4

that the choice-of-law clause was simply a choice of New York law over the law of other states, rather than a choice to avoid FAA preemption of New York law. The Court did this by pointing out that the securities broker interpreted the contract's choice of "the laws of the State of New York" to "include[] the caveat, 'detached from otherwise-applicable federal law.' "[432] The Court could have simply held that the contract did not include this caveat and then stopped. This interpretation would have been consistent with the ordinary understanding of such choice-of-law clauses as choices among states, not choices between state and federal.[433] And this interpretation would have led easily to the conclusion the Court reached, that the parties did not contract out of FAA preemption so the arbitrator could award punitive damages.

Instead of stopping with the point that the choice-of-law clause did not address the relationship between state and federal law, the Court spoke further on its interpretation of the contract. The Court pointed out that the contract authorized arbitration in accordance with the rules of the National Association of Securities Dealers ("NASD") and a NASD manual provided to NASD arbitrators contained this provision: "The issue of punitive damages may arise with great frequency in arbitrations. Parties to arbitration are informed that arbitrators can consider punitive damages as a remedy."[434] Thus the Court found that the arbitration clause "contradicts * * * the conclusion that the parties agreed to foreclose claims for punitive damages."[435] The Court then went on to cite two further reasons for interpreting the contract to permit arbitrators to award punitive damages: (1) "the federal policy favoring arbitration,"[436] which means that "ambiguities as to the scope of the arbitration clause itself are resolved in favor of arbitration", and (2) "the common-law rule of contract interpretation that a court should construe ambiguous language against the interest of the party that drafted it."[437] These final two points suggest that the Court favors interpretations of arbitration agreements that preserve the full remedies of the parties, especially parties who sign form arbitration agreements presented to them on a take-it-or-leave-it basis.

Some courts have gone beyond such interpretation of arbitration agreements to hold that certain contractual remedy-limitations are unenforceable.[438] These cases tend to arise in the context of take-it-or-leave-it arbitration agreements presented to employees and consumers. These cases rest on contract law's unconscionability doctrine,[439] special concerns regarding the vindication of federal statutory rights,[440] or a combi-

432. Id. at 59.

433. See § 2.16.

434. Mastrobuono, 519 U.S. at 61 (quoting Mastrobuono v. Shearson Lehman Hutton, Inc. 20 F.3d 713, 717 (7th Cir.1994).

435. Mastrobuono, 519 U.S. at 61.

436. Id. at 62.

437. Id.

438. See § 2.38. Remedies limited by agreement include punitive, special, exemplary, incidental and consequential damages, as well attorney's fees. The most commonly excluded remedy seems to be punitive damages.

439. See § 2.25.

440. See §§ 2.27—2.28.

nation of the two.[441] Other than these cases, the arbitrator's remedial power remains a matter determined by the arbitration agreement.

(b) Typical Contract Terms

Many arbitration agreements provide that the arbitrator may order any remedy that a court could order. And this is the default interpretation of arbitration agreements that are silent on remedies. For example, arbitrators routinely order parties to pay punitive damages[442] and issue injunctions[443] even though the arbitration agreement may not expressly authorize those remedies.

As discussed above,[444] some arbitration agreements expressly limit the remedies available in arbitration. Other than cases arising out of these agreements, it is rare that an arbitrator's choice of remedies is narrower than a court's.

(c) Consequences of Limiting Remedies in Arbitration

An arbitration agreement limiting the remedies available to an arbitrator may be unenforceable.[445] But if it is enforceable, an additional issue arises: may that remedy be awarded by a court on the same claim or has that remedy been waived altogether? This issue has arisen in the context of agreements that prohibit arbitrators from awarding punitive damages. May a court award punitive damages on the claim or has the right to recover them been waived altogether?

At least one court answers "waived altogether."[446] The alternative is to require arbitration of liability and other non-punitive damages issues, followed by judicial resolution of claims for punitive damages. At least one court has severed a claim for punitive damages to send the rest of the dispute to arbitration.[447] This bifurcation is inefficient. If, however, this bifurcation is chosen by the parties, courts are likely to enforce it to effectuate the FAA's primary command to enforce arbitration agreements.[448]

441. See Graham Oil Co. v. ARCO Products Co., 43 F.3d 1244 (8th Cir.1994).

442. See Todd Shipyards Corp. v. Cunard Line, 943 F.2d 1056 (9th Cir.1991); Raytheon Co. v. Automated Business Sys., Inc., 882 F.2d 6 (1st Cir.1989); Bonar v. Dean Witter Reynolds, Inc., 835 F.2d 1378 (11th Cir.1988).

443. Saturday Evening Post Co., v. Rumbleseat Press, Inc., 816 F.2d 1191 (7th Cir.1987); Matter of Sprinzen (Nomberg), 46 N.Y.2d 623, 415 N.Y.S.2d 974, 977, 389 N.E.2d 456 (1979).

444. See § 2.38(a).

445. See id.

446. See, e.g., Waltman v. Fahnestock & Co., 792 F.Supp. 31, 33–34 (E.D.Pa.1992), aff'd, 989 F.2d 490 (3d Cir.1993).

447. See DiCrisci v. Lyndon Guar.Bank, 807 F.Supp. 947, 953 (W.D.N.Y.1992) (severing claim for punitive damages pending completion of arbitration). See also Mulder v. Donaldson, Lufkin & Jenrette, 161 Misc.2d 698, 611 N.Y.S.2d 1019, 1021 (Sup. Ct.1994) (plaintiff's "appropriate recourse was to wait for a favorable award from the arbitrators, and then bring a plenary action in this court for punitive damages"); Singer v. Salomon Bros., Inc., 156 Misc.2d 465, 593 N.Y.S.2d 927, 930 (Sup.Ct.1992) ("At the conclusion of the arbitration, this court may award punitive damages, if proper.").

448. 9 U.S.C. § 2 (1994).

4. GOVERNING SUBSTANTIVE LAW, IF ANY

Table of Sections

§ 2.39 Substantive Law Applied in Arbitration

Some arbitration agreements state that the arbitrator is to apply the law of a particular jurisdiction, *e.g.*, New York or Switzerland.[449] Other agreements incorporate the rules of an arbitration organization, such as the National Arbitration Forum, that promises its arbitrators will apply the law.[450] But many arbitration agreements do not address the question of the law, if any, to be applied by the arbitrators.

Arbitrators often do not apply any law.[451] Many arbitrators believe they are free to ignore legal rules whenever they think that more just decisions would be reached by so doing.[452] Similarly, courts have acknowledged that "[a]rbitrators are not bound by rules of law."[453]

F. EFFECT OF ARBITRATION AWARD

Table of Section

1. ENFORCEMENT OF ARBITRATION AWARD

2. VACATUR OF ARBITRATION AWARD

§ 2.39

449. Mastrobuono v. Shearson Lehman Hutton, Inc., 514 U.S. 52, 58 n. 2, 115 S.Ct. 1212, 131 L.Ed.2d 76 (1995)("This agreement shall * * * be governed by the laws of the State of New York."); Mitsubishi Motors Corp. v. Soler Chrysler–Plymouth, Inc., 473 U.S. 614, 637 n. 19, 105 S.Ct. 3346, 87 L.Ed.2d 444 (1985)("This Agreement is made in, and will be governed by and construed in all respects according to the laws of the Swiss Confederation as if entirely performed therein.")

450. See <http://www.arb-forum.com>.

451. See § 2.45.

452. See id.

453. See id.

1.　ENFORCEMENT OF ARBITRATION AWARD

Table of Sections

§ 2.40　Confirmation

Arbitration awards can be enforced in court. This may not be needed because the party losing at arbitration often voluntarily complies with the arbitration award. But the winning party can get a court order *confirming* the award.[454] A confirmed award in favor of the plaintiff (or "claimant") is enforced in the same manner as other court judgments, through judgment liens, execution, garnishment, etc.[455]

Judicial enforcement of arbitration awards is an example of courts enforcing contracts. The parties agreed to comply with the arbitrator's decision and if a party refuses to do so then that party is in breach of contract. To put it another way, the arbitrator's decision is, with few exceptions, final and binding.[456]

---

§ 2.40

454. 9 U.S.C. § 9 (1994).

455. FAA § 13 provides:

The party moving for an order confirming, modifying, or correcting an award shall, at the time such order is filed with the clerk for the entry of judgment thereon, also file the following papers with the clerk:

(a) The agreement; the selection or appointment, if any, of an additional arbitrator or umpire; and each written extension of the time, if any, within which to make the award.

(b) The award.

(c) Each notice, affidavit, or other paper used upon an application to confirm, modify, or correct the award, and a copy of each order of the court upon such an application.

The judgment shall be docketed as if it was rendered in an action.

The judgment so entered shall have the same force and effect, in all respects, as, and be subject to all the provisions of law relating to, a judgment in an action; and it may be enforced as if it had been rendered in an action in the court in which it is entered.

9 U.S.C. § 13 (1994).

456. Those exceptions, *i.e.*, grounds for vacating arbitration awards, are discussed in §§ 2.43—2.46.

§ 2.41   Claim Preclusion (Res Judicata)

(a) Generally Applicable

The doctrine of claim preclusion bars adjudication of claims that have already been adjudicated in a prior proceeding. Arbitration awards, whether confirmed or not,[457] have claim-preclusive effect.[458] In other words, they are *res judicata*. Suppose that Ann asserts a claim in arbitration against Bob and that the arbitrator rules for Bob. If Ann then seeks to assert the same claim in litigation, a court will grant Bob's motion to dismiss the case. The court treats the prior arbitration award in Bob's favor just as it would treat a prior court decision in Bob's favor, as precluding further litigation of that claim. Finality is central to binding adjudication,[459] whether that adjudication be litigation or arbitration.

(b) The Labor Exception

There is a major exception to the claim-preclusive effect of arbitration awards. That is with respect to federal statutory claims asserted in labor arbitration. Courts have allowed employees to sue on such claims even after those claims are heard and rejected by arbitrators.[460] This is another dimension of the fact that labor arbitration is outside the mainstream with regard to the "public policy" defense discussed in a previous section.[461]

§ 2.42   Issue Preclusion (Collateral Estoppel)

The doctrine of issue preclusion bars adjudication of issues that have been decided in a prior case. The doctrine of issue preclusion can apply if that prior case was an arbitration.[462]

While issue preclusion can only be asserted *against* one who was a party to the prior case, it can be asserted *by* one who was a stranger to that prior case.[463] Suppose that Ann asserts a claim in arbitration against Bob and the arbitrator rules that certain conduct by Bob was negligent. If Claire then sues Bob for damages arising out of the same conduct, the court hearing Claire's case may hold, under the doctrine of issue preclusion, that Claire does not have to re-prove Bob's negligence. The court

§ 2.41

457. Rudell v. Comprehensive Accounting Corp. 802 F.2d 926 (7th Cir.1986); Central Transp., Inc. v. Four Phase Sys., Inc., 936 F.2d 256 (6th Cir.1990); Wellons, Inc. v. T.E. Ibberson Co., 869 F.2d 1166, 1169 (8th Cir.1989); Macneil, Speidel & Stipanowich, supra note 1, § 39.6.

458. Restatement (Second) of Judgments § 84 (1982); Charles Alan Wright, et al., Federal Practice and Procedure § 4475 (1981).

459. See §§ 1.5, 1.7 & 4.2.

460. Alexander v. Gardner–Denver Co., 415 U.S. 36, 50, 94 S.Ct. 1011, 39 L.Ed.2d

147 (1974). The *Gardner-Denver* Court did suggest that the arbitrator's findings could be admitted "as evidence" at trial and "accorded such weight as the court deems appropriate." Id. at 60 n.21.

461. See § 2.27.

§ 2.42

462. Macneil, Speidel & Stipanowich, supra note 1, § 39.3.1.2.

463. Macneil, Speidel & Stipanowich, supra note 1, § 39.3.1.1; Friedenthal, Kane & Miller, supra note 359, § 14.14.

adopts the arbitrator's ruling regarding Bob's negligence and moves on to the other issues of Claire's suit, such as whether her damages were caused by Bob's negligence. The court treats the prior arbitration ruling against Bob just as it would treat a prior court ruling against Bob, as precluding further litigation of that issue, even against a new party.

In practice, however, the likely challenge for Claire will be proving to the court that the arbitrator really did rule that Bob was negligent. Arbitration awards, outside the international and labor contexts, are rarely accompanied by reasoned opinions.[464] If the arbitration award for Ann contained no reasoning, a court may not be able to learn *why* the arbitrator ruled against Bob. Perhaps the arbitrator concluded that Bob was negligent or perhaps the arbitrator concluded that Bob was not negligent but was liable to Ann for some other reason. If the latter, Bob is not precluded from arguing the negligence issue in Claire's suit. Courts have denied issue-preclusive effect from arbitration awards because the court could not infer the factual basis for the arbitrator's decision.[465]

Issue preclusion from arbitration awards is a matter of judicial discretion,[466] and is applied less in labor arbitration than in other arbitration.[467] Under California law, arbitration awards have issue-preclusive effect only if the arbitration agreement provides that they will have that effect.[468]

2. VACATUR OF ARBITRATION AWARD

Table of Sections

§ 2.43   Introduction

(a) Vacatur is Rare

Courts do not vacate arbitration awards very often.[469] The gist of the caselaw is that the parties have agreed to accept the arbitrator's decision, right or wrong, so vacating the arbitration award would disregard that agreement. Courts recognize arbitration's appeal as a fast, low-cost

---

464. See § 2.37(e).

465. See, e.g., Hybert v. Shearson Lehman/American Express, Inc. 688 F.Supp. 320 (N.D.Ill.1988); Sports Factory, Inc. v. Chanoff, 586 F.Supp. 342, 346 (E.D.Pa. 1984).

466. Universal American Barge Corp. v. J–Chem, Inc., 946 F.2d 1131 (5th Cir.1991).

467. Macneil, Speidel & Stipanowich, supra note 1, § 39.1.2.

468. Vandenberg v. Superior Court, 21 Cal.4th 815, 88 Cal.Rptr.2d 366, 377–81, 982 P.2d 229 (Cal.1999).

§ 2.43

469. See generally Macneil, Speidel & Stipanowich, supra note 1, § 40.1.4. For a discussion focused on labor arbitration, see Nolan, supra note 389, at 180–216.

alternative to litigation. Courts are sensitive to the risk that, if they vacated a lot of arbitration awards, they would convert binding arbitration, an alternative to litigation, into non-binding arbitration, a preliminary step before litigation.[470]

(b) Statutory and Non–Statutory Grounds

The FAA contains the following narrow grounds for vacating an arbitration award:

(1) Where the award was procured by corruption, fraud, or undue means.

(2) Where there was evident partiality or corruption in the arbitrators, or either of them.

(3) Where the arbitrators were guilty of misconduct in refusing to postpone the hearing, upon sufficient cause shown, or in refusing to hear evidence pertinent and material to the controversy; or of any other misbehavior by which the rights of any party have been prejudiced.

(4) Where the arbitrators exceeded their powers, or so imperfectly executed them that a mutual, final, and definite award upon the subject matter submitted was not made.[471]

These are the *statutory grounds* for vacatur.[472] Courts have gone beyond the statutory grounds to create additional (*non-statutory*) grounds for vacatur.[473]

Judicial enforcement of arbitration awards is an example of courts enforcing contracts. The parties agreed to comply with the arbitrator's decision and if the losing party refuses to do so then that party is in breach of contract. When a court vacates an arbitration award then, the court is refusing to enforce a contract. The law permits this in only narrow situations.

§ 2.44 Statutory Grounds

(a) Corruption, Fraud or Undue Means

FAA § 10(a)(1) permits courts to vacate an arbitration award where the "award was procured by corruption, fraud, or undue means."[474] To vacate, there must be a close causal connection between the wrongdoing—corruption, fraud (including perjury) or undue means—and the award.[475] Also, the party seeking vacatur must show that the wrongdoing was "(1) not discoverable upon the exercise of due diligence prior to the

470. Non-binding arbitration is discussed in § 4.32.

471. 9 U.S.C. § 10(a) (1994).

472. See § 2.44.

473. See § 2.45.

§ 2.44

474. 9 U.S.C. § 10(a)(1) (1994).

475. See Macneil, Speidel & Stipanowich, supra note 1, § 40.2.2.

arbitration, (2) materially related to an issue in the arbitration, and (3) established by clear and convincing evidence."[476]

(b) Evident Partiality or Corruption

FAA § 10(a)(2) permits courts to vacate an arbitration award where "there was evident partiality or corruption in the arbitrators."[477] The leading partiality case is *Commonwealth Coatings Corp. v. Continental Casualty Co.*,[478] decided by the Supreme Court in 1968. In *Commonwealth Coatings*, a subcontractor sued a surety on the prime contractor's bond to recover money due for a painting job.[479] Each party appointed an arbitrator and the two party-appointed arbitrators appointed a third, neutral arbitrator.[480] The arbitrators unanimously ruled for the surety.[481] Then the subcontractor learned for the first time that the neutral arbitrator, an engineering consultant, had a business relationship with the prime contractor.[482] The prime contractor had paid the arbitrator consulting fees of about $12,000 over a period of four or five years.[483] Although there was no evidence of actual bias or prejudice, the Supreme Court reversed the lower courts and vacated the arbitration award. The plurality opinion of four justices held that non-disclosure of "any dealings that might create an impression of possible bias" or creating "even an appearance of bias" would warrant vacating.[484] The concurring opinion required disclosure of substantial relationships only.[485] What particular dealings or relationships trigger a duty to disclose can only be determined case-by-case in a fact-intensive inquiry.[486]

Many arbitration agreements incorporate the rules of organizations such as the American Arbitration Association or the National Arbitration Forum. "In most cases such contractual mechanisms, which permit issues of partiality and personal interest to be addressed as they arise, play a significant role in policing such conflicts and make recourse to the courts less likely."[487]

476. A.G. Edwards & Sons, Inc. v. McCollough, 967 F.2d 1401, 1404 (9th Cir. 1992).

477. 9 U.S.C. § 10(a)(2) (1994).

478. 393 U.S. 145, 89 S.Ct. 337, 21 L.Ed.2d 301 (1968).

479. Id. at 146.

480. Id.

481. Id.

482. Id.

483. Id.

484. Id. at 149.

485. 393 U.S. at 150 (White, J., concurring).

486. Compare, e.g., Schmitz v. Zilveti, 20 F.3d 1043, 1044 (9th Cir.1994), (vacating award where the arbitrator failed to disclose that his law firm had represented the corporate parent of the defendant corporation involved in the arbitration in 19 matters over a 35 year period ending some 21 months before the arbitration.); Neaman v. Kaiser Found. Hosp., 9 Cal. App.4th 1170, 11 Cal.Rptr.2d 879 (Ct.App.1992)(failure of neutral arbitrator to reveal that he had served as a party-arbitrator for one of the parties required the award to be set aside), with Apusento Garden (Guam) Inc. v. Superior Court of Guam, 94 F.3d 1346, 1352 (9th Cir.1996)(confirming award arbitrator failed to disclose that he and Apusento Garden's expert witness were both limited partners in a partnership unrelated to the arbitration); Woods v. Saturn Distribution Corp., 78 F.3d 424 (9th Cir.1996)(no evident partiality arising from arbitrators' financial dependence on Saturn where arbitrators, like Woods, were Saturn auto dealers).

487. Macneil, Speidel & Stipanowich, supra note 1, § 28.2.6.1.

(c) Fundamentally Fair Hearing

FAA § 10(a)(3) permits courts to vacate an arbitration award where "the arbitrators were guilty of misconduct in refusing to postpone the hearing, upon sufficient cause shown, or in refusing to hear evidence pertinent and material to the controversy; or of any other misbehavior by which the rights of any party have been prejudiced."[488] This provision has been summarized by courts as requiring arbitrators to provide the parties with a "fundamentally fair hearing", which requires only notice and an opportunity to be heard.[489] Courts are cautious about vacating an award due to an arbitrator's ruling on a procedural or evidentiary issue. As one court put it, "a challenge to an arbitrator's evidentiary rulings or limitations on discovery should not provide a basis for vacating an award unless the error substantially prejudiced a party's ability to present material evidence in support of its case."[490]

Rules of evidence in arbitration are discussed in an earlier section.[491]

(d) Exceeded Powers

FAA § 10(a)(4) permits courts to vacate an arbitration award where, among other things, "the arbitrators exceeded their powers."[492] These powers are, basically, whatever the arbitration agreement says they are.[493] Courts vacate awards under this provision "in cases where the arbitrators somehow alter the parties' contractual obligations" or "fail to meet their obligations, as specified in a given contract, to the parties."[494]

§ 2.45 Non–Statutory Grounds

Courts have gone beyond the statutory grounds, discussed in the previous section,[495] for vacating arbitration awards to create additional grounds for vacatur. These *non-statutory grounds* vary somewhat from

---

488. 9 U.S.C. § 10(a)(3) (1994).

489. See generally Macneil, Speidel & Stipanowich, supra note 1, § 32.4.1.1 (fundamental fairness requires that each party have an opportunity to present its case and offer its evidence to the arbitrator). See, e.g., FDIC v. Air Florida Sys., 822 F.2d 833 (9th Cir.1987)(upholding decision of arbitrator to deny one party's request to hold an oral evidentiary hearing and to require all evidence to be submitted in writing where sole issue involved valuation of corporate stock.), cert.denied, 485 U.S. 987, 108 S.Ct. 1289, 99 L.Ed.2d 500 (1988); Dexter v. Prudential Ins. Co., 1999 WL 156170, *2 (D.Kan.1999)("The courts seem to agree that a fundamentally fair hearing requires only notice, opportunity to be heard and to present relevant and material evidence and argument before the decision makers, and that the decisionmakers are not infected with bias.").

On the requirement of notice, see, e.g., American Postal Workers Union v. United States Postal Serv., 861 F.2d 211 (9th Cir. 1988); Macneil, Speidel & Stipanowich, supra note 1, § 32.4.1.2 ("In the absence of waiver, reliance by the arbitrators entirely on ex parte hearings is fundamentally unfair.").

490. Schlessinger v. Rosenfeld, Meyer & Susman, 40 Cal.App.4th 1096, 47 Cal. Rptr.2d 650, 659 (Ct.App.1995).

491. See § 2.37(c).

492. 9 U.S.C. § 10(a)(4) (1994).

493. Macneil, Speidel & Stipanowich, supra note 1, § 40.5.

494. See, e.g., Western Employers Ins. Co. v. Jefferies & Co., Inc., 958 F.2d 258, 262 (9th Cir.1992).

§ 2.45

495. See § 2.44.

court to court but generally fall under two headings. An arbitration award may be vacated if (1) the arbitrator "manifestly disregarded" applicable law, or (2) enforcement of the arbitration award would violate "public policy".[496] Some courts have also enforced agreements by which the parties add grounds for vacating that would not otherwise exist.

All three of these *non-statutory* grounds can be characterized as *statutory* because they define what constitutes arbitrators' "exceed[ing] their powers" under FAA § 10(a)(4).[497]

(a) Error of Law, Including Manifest Disregard

(1) Narrow Ground for Vacatur

The FAA's grounds for vacating arbitration awards do not include "error of law" by the arbitrator. In general, courts do not review whether the arbitrator's decision correctly applied the law.

Arbitrators often do not apply the law.[498] Many arbitrators believe they are free to ignore legal rules whenever they think that more just decisions would be reached by so doing.[499] Courts have directly acknowledged that "[a]rbitrators are not bound by rules of law."[500] This is consistent with the standard view that many parties choose arbitration because it provides a less legalistic process than litigation.[501]

In most cases in which an arbitrator does not apply the law, it will be very difficult for a court to discover that. Arbitrators generally do not

496. Macneil, Speidel & Stipanowich, supra note 1, § 40; Stephen L. Hayford, Law in Disarray: Judicial Standards for Vacatur of Commercial Arbitration Awards, 30 Ga.L.Rev. 731, 739 (1996).

497. Macneil, Speidel & Stipanowich, supra note 1, § 40.5.1.3. See § 2.44(d).

498. This does not necessarily mean that arbitrators under-enforce the policies embodied in certain substantive laws. Arbitrators may over-enforce these policies. Arbitrators may rule for plaintiffs/claimants more often than they would if they always applied the law.

499. See Murray, Rau & Sherman, supra note 1, at 636; see also Macneil, Speidel & Stipanowich, supra note 1, § 40.5.2.4, at 40:47; Martin Domke, Domke on Commercial Arbitration § 25.01 (Gabriel M. Wilner, ed., 1999).

500. Aimcee Wholesale Corp. v. Tomar Prods., Inc., 21 N.Y.2d 621, 289 N.Y.S.2d 968, 237 N.E.2d 223, 225 (N.Y.1968). See also Bowles Fin. Group, Inc. v. Stifel, Nicolaus & Co., 22 F.3d 1010, 1011 (10th Cir. 1994) ("Arbitration provides neither the procedural protections nor the assurance of the proper application of substantive law offered by the judicial system."); Stroh Container Co. v. Delphi Indus., 783 F.2d 743, 751 n. 12 (8th Cir.1986) ("[T]he arbitration system is an inferior system of justice, structured without due process, rules of evidence, accountability of judgment and rules of law."); In re Sprinzen, 46 N.Y.2d 623, 415 N.Y.S.2d 974, 976, 389 N.E.2d 456 (1979) ("[T]he arbitrator is not bound to abide by, absent a contrary provision in the arbitration agreement, those principles of substantive law or rules of procedure which govern the traditional litigation process."); Lentine v. Fundaro, 29 N.Y.2d 382, 328 N.Y.S.2d 418, 278 N.E.2d 633, 635 (N.Y. 1972) ("Absent provision to the contrary in the arbitration agreement, arbitrators are not bound by principles of substantive law."); Moncharsh v. Heily & Blase, 3 Cal.4th 1, 10 Cal.Rptr.2d 183, 832 P.2d 899, 919 (1992) ("[T]he existence of an error of law apparent on the face of the award that causes substantial injustice does not provide grounds for judicial review.").

501. "It is often said that the parties do not expect the arbitrators to make their decision according to rules but rather, especially when the arbitrators are not lawyers, on the basis of their experience, knowledge of the customs of the trade, and fair and good sense for equitable relief." Domke, supra note 499, § 25:01.

write reasoned opinions explaining their decisions.[502] Nor is there typically a transcript or other record of the hearing.[503]

While most cases of arbitrators failing to apply the law probably go undetected by courts, sometimes a court will realize that an award does not apply the law. In such a case, a court will likely confirm the award anyhow. Courts confirm arbitration awards that do not apply the law because "error of law" is not a ground for vacating them.[504]

There are circumstances in which a court will vacate an arbitration award for failure to apply the law, but these circumstances are very rare. While it varies somewhat from court to court, the usual doctrine is that courts vacate only where the arbitrator's failure to apply the law results from a "manifest disregard of the law" by the arbitrator.[505] As traditionally understood, this "manifest disregard" doctrine is extremely narrow. An oft-cited Second Circuit opinion says that an error of law should lead to vacatur for "manifest disregard" only if the error is "obvious and capable of being readily and instantly perceived by the average person qualified to serve as an arbitrator. Moreover, the term 'disregard' implies that the arbitrator appreciates the existence of a clearly governing legal principle but decides to ignore or pay no attention to it."[506] So not only does the arbitrator have to make an egregious error, the arbitrator must do so while consciously disregarding the correct law. This test is very difficult to meet. That difficulty explains why it was nearly impossible, until about 1997, to find a case vacating an arbitration award in reliance on the "manifest disregard of law" doctrine.[507]

(2) Recent Expansion

Since about 1997, some courts have expanded the "manifest disregard of law" ground for vacating arbitration awards. To put it another way, some courts are beginning to review arbitrators' legal rulings more closely. Perhaps the leading case is *Cole v. Burns International Security*

---

502. See § 2.37(e).

503. See § 2.37(a).

504. See, e.g., Todd Shipyards Corp. v. Cunard Line, 943 F.2d 1056, 1060 (9th Cir. 1991) ("[C]onfirmation is required even in the face of erroneous ... misinterpretations of law.... It is not enough that the Panel may have failed to understand or apply the law.... An arbitrator's decision must be upheld unless it is completely irrational, or it constitutes a manifest disregard for the law.") (internal citations omitted); Advest, Inc. v. McCarthy, 914 F.2d 6, 8 (1st Cir. 1990) (stating that courts are not authorized to reconsider the merits of arbitration awards "[e]ven where such error is painfully clear"); Miller v. Prudential Bache Secs., 884 F.2d 128, 130 (4th Cir.1989) (holding that "mere" error of law is insufficient to set aside arbitrator's award); Moseley, Hallgarten, Estabrook & Weeden, Inc. v. Ellis,

849 F.2d 264, 272 (7th Cir.1988) (holding that "mistake" of law is insufficient to vacate arbitration award); Siegel v. Titan Indus.Corp., 779 F.2d 891, 892–93 (2d Cir. 1985) (stating that "erroneous application of rules of law is not a ground for vacating an arbitrator's award").

505. Stephen L. Hayford, A New Paradigm for Commercial Arbitration: Rethinking the Relationship Between Reasoned Awards and the Judicial Standards for Vacatur, 66 Geo.Wash.L.Rev. 443, 466–76 (1998).

506. Merrill, Lynch, Pierce, Fenner & Smith, Inc. v. Bobker, 808 F.2d 930, 933 (2d Cir.1986).

507. See Macneil, Speidel & Stipanowich, supra note 1, § 40.7.

Services,[508] a 1997 D.C. Circuit opinion written by a labor arbitration expert, Judge Harry Edwards. *Cole* held that agreements to arbitrate statutory employment discrimination claims are enforceable "only if judicial review under the 'manifest disregard of the law' standard is sufficiently rigorous to ensure that arbitrators have properly interpreted and applied statutory law."[509] The opinion went on to assert that "the courts are empowered to review an arbitrator's award to ensure that its resolution of public law issues is correct."[510] *Cole,* in essence, converts the "manifest disregard of law" standard into a *de novo* "error of law" standard, at least with respect to claims under statutory or public law.

Cole has been cited with approval by other federal courts of appeals.[511] In one of those cases, *Halligan v. Piper Jaffray, Inc.,*[512] the Second Circuit stated that "when a reviewing court is inclined to hold that an arbitration panel manifestly disregarded the law, the failure of the arbitrators to explain the award can be taken into account."[513] The *Halligan* opinion seems to challenge the longstanding practice of arbitrators not to write reasoned opinions justifying their decisions.[514] That practice has largely ensured that parties criticizing arbitration awards have little to point to and, consequently, little chance of persuading a court to vacate the award. If arbitrators must write reasoned opinions, it seems that courts will be more likely to vacate awards on the ground that the arbitrator did not adequately apply the law.[515]

(b) Public Policy

Courts hold that they may vacate an arbitration award on the ground that its enforcement would violate "public policy."[516] While this ground for vacatur is not expressly stated in the FAA, it is an application of the established doctrine that courts will not enforce contracts that violate public policy. When a party asks a court to confirm and enforce an arbitration award it is asking the court to enforce a contract. The parties' contractual duty is to comply with the arbitrator's decision. If that compliance would violate public policy then a court will no more enforce that duty than a court would enforce a contract for the sale of cocaine.[517]

The public policy doctrine is rarely relied upon by courts to vacate

---

508. 105 F.3d 1465 (D.C.Cir.1997). This case is also discussed in § 2.35.

509. Id. at 1487.

510. Id.

511. See Montes v. Shearson Lehman Brothers, Inc., 128 F.3d 1456 (11th Cir. 1997).

512. 148 F.3d 197 (2d Cir.1998).

513. Id. at 204.

514. See § 2.37(e).

515. See generally Hayford, supra note 505, at 445.

516. See Hayford, supra note 505, at 476–480; see also Macneil, Speidel & Stipanowich, supra note 1, § 40.8.1.

517. United Paperworkers Int'l Union v. Misco, Inc., 484 U.S. 29, 42, 108 S.Ct. 364, 98 L.Ed.2d 286 ("A court's refusal to enforce an arbitrator's award * * * because it is contrary to public policy is a specific application of the more general doctrine, rooted in the common law, that a court may refuse to enforce contracts that violate law or public policy.").

arbitration awards.[518] Labor arbitration is the one context where the public policy doctrine is used fairly frequently.[519] But even in labor arbitration courts have been careful to confine narrowly the public policy ground for vacatur. An example is the 1987 Supreme Court decision in *United Paperworkers International Union v. Misco, Inc.*[520]

The employer (Misco) reprimanded an employee (Cooper) for deficient performance.[521] Then the police found marijuana in Cooper's house and caught him with two other men in a car (not Cooper's) in the company parking lot with marijuana smoke in the air.[522] Misco discharged (fired) Cooper who then pursued arbitration. Later, Misco learned that the police also found marijuana in Cooper's own car.[523]

The arbitrator refused to hear evidence of marijuana in Cooper's car because Misco had not known of that when it discharged Cooper.[524] The arbitrator ordered Misco to reinstate Cooper. The district court vacated the arbitration award and the Seventh Circuit affirmed because "to reinstate a person who had brought drugs onto [company] property was contrary to the public policy 'against the operation of dangerous machinery by persons under the influence of drugs or alcohol.' "[525] The Supreme Court reversed. It held that the arbitrator was free to disregard evidence of marijuana in Cooper's car. "The parties did not bargain for the facts to be found by a court, but by an arbitrator."[526] The *Misco* Court held that

> the assumed connection between the marijuana gleanings found in Cooper's car and Cooper's actual use of drugs in the workplace is tenuous at best and provides an insufficient basis for holding that his reinstatement would actually violate the public policy identified by the Court of Appeals "against the operation of dangerous machinery by persons under the influence of drugs or alcohol." A refusal to enforce an award must rest on more than speculation or assumption.[527]

In *Misco*, the Supreme Court confined the scope of the public policy ground for vacatur. It stated that this ground is limited to awards that "would violate some explicit public policy that is well defined and dominant."[528] This public policy must "be ascertained by reference to the laws and legal precedents and not from general considerations of supposed public interests."[529]

---

518. See Macneil, Speidel & Stipanowich, supra note 1, § 40.8.2.

519. See Macneil, Speidel & Stipanowich, supra note 1, § 40.8.3.

520. 484 U.S. 29, 108 S.Ct. 364, 98 L.Ed.2d 286 (1987).

521. Id. at 32.

522. Id. at 33.

523. Id.

524. Id. at 34.

525. Id. at 42 (quoting Misco, Inc. v. United Paperworkers Int'l Union, 768 F.2d 739, 743 (5th Cir.1985)).

526. Id. at 45.

527. Id. at 44.

528. Id. at 43 (quotations omitted).

529. Id. Accord Eastern Associated Coal Corp. v. United Mine Workers of America, ___ U.S. ___, 121 S.Ct. 462, ___ L.Ed.2d ___ (2000) (confirming arbitrator's decision to reinstate employee). "We agree, in principle, that courts' authority to invoke the

(c) Grounds Created by Contract

Some parties to arbitration agreements try to add grounds for vacating arbitration awards to the grounds already found in the law. For instance, the arbitration agreement in *Lapine Technology Corp. v. Kyocera Corp.*[530] provided that "The Court shall vacate, modify or correct any award: (i) based upon any of the grounds referred to in the Federal Arbitration Act, (ii) where the arbitrators' findings of fact are not supported by substantial evidence, or (iii) where the arbitrators' conclusions of law are erroneous."[531] The district court in *LaPine* refused to vacate the arbitration award for any ground other than those grounds listed in the FAA.[532] The Ninth Circuit reversed, instructing the district court to review the arbitration award by use of the standard agreed to by the parties.[533] A number of other cases also enforce agreements providing for judicial review of arbitrators' legal rulings.[534] In contrast, some courts are skeptical about enforcing such agreements.[535]

§ 2.46   Federal Preemption of State Law

The previous sections discuss the grounds for vacating arbitration awards.[536] That discussion addresses only federal, not state, law on the topic. State courts around the country frequently cite to their own state statutes when discussing the grounds for vacating arbitration awards.[537] State law regarding vacatur is generally similar to federal law.[538] But if a particular state law does differ from federal law, the question arises whether the state law is preempted by the federal law. State law might differ in one of two ways. It might add additional grounds for vacatur not found in federal law. Or it might recognize fewer grounds for vacatur than recognized by federal law.

(a) State Grounds for Vacatur Broader Than Federal

States may not add grounds for vacatur beyond those found in federal law.[539] To put it another way, federal law preempts state grounds

---

public policy exception is not limited solely to instances where the arbitration award itself violates positive law. Nevertheless, the public policy exception is narrow." Id. at 467.

530. 130 F.3d 884 (9th Cir.1997).

531. Id. at 887.

532. Id.

533. Id. at 891.

534. See Kyocera, 130 F.3d 884; Syncor Int'l Corp. v. McLeland, 120 F.3d 262 (4th Cir.1997)(unpublished); Gateway Techs., Inc. v. MCI Telecommunications Corp. 64 F.3d 993, 996–97 (5th Cir.1995); Fils et Cables d'Acier de Lens v. Midland Metals Corp., 584 F.Supp. 240 (S.D.N.Y.1984); New England Utils. v. Hydro–Quebec, 10 F.Supp.2d 53 (D.Mass.1998); Collins v. Blue Cross Blue Shield of Michigan, 228 Mich. App. 560, 579 N.W.2d 435 (Mich.App.1998).

Cf. Green v. Ameritech Corp., 200 F.3d 967 (6th Cir.2000).

535. See, e.g., Chicago Typographical Union No. 16 v. Chicago Sun–Times, Inc., 935 F.2d 1501, 1505 (7th Cir.1991)(Posner, J.)("If the parties want, they can contract for an appellate arbitration panel to review the arbitrator's award. But they cannot contract for judicial review of that award; federal jurisdiction cannot be created by contract.")

§ 2.46

536. See §§ 2.43—2.45.

537. See, e.g., Cal.Civ.Proc.Code § 1286.2 (West 1982 & Supp.1999)(containing many pages of case annotations).

538. See Unif. Arbitration Act § 12, 7 U.L.A. 280–283 (1997)(grounds for vacating award); See also 7 U.L.A. 1 (1997)(table of jurisdictions adopting the act).

for vacatur not found in federal law. An exception might be a case in which the parties agreed to be subject to state, rather than federal, arbitration law.[540]

(b) State Grounds for Vacatur Narrower Than Federal

Federal law preempts state grounds for vacatur not found in federal law.[541] In contrast, federal law may permit a state to recognize *fewer* grounds for vacating awards than are recognized by federal law. For example, California arbitration law lacks a ground for vacatur, "manifest disregard of law", found in federal law.[542] It is conceivable that a California court will confirm an arbitration award notwithstanding the court's finding that the arbitrator manifestly disregarded the law. If this occurs, the party seeking to vacate the arbitration award may argue that federal preemption of state arbitration law requires an order vacating the award. This argument was rejected by the California Court of Appeals in *Siegel v. Prudential Ins. Co.*[543]

> California's rule precluding on the merits review of an arbitration award does not stand as an obstacle to full effectuation of the purpose of the [FAA]—enforcement of arbitration agreements * * * . California's rule evidences no hostility towards arbitration. In fact, California's rule furthers the use of arbitration by somewhat more strictly limiting judicial review of the merits of an award. California's rule against on the merits review furthers rather than defeats full effectuation of the federal law's objectives.[544]

G. INTERNATIONAL ARBITRATION

Table of Sections

§ 2.47 Introduction

International disputes are often arbitrated. That generalization includes both disputes between countries ("States") and disputes between

---

539. See Collins v. Blue Cross Blue Shield of Michigan, 916 F.Supp. 638, 640–42 (E.D.Mich.1995)(as between Michigan's standard and federal "manifest disregard of law" standard, "the federal standard of review must prevail"), vacated on other grounds, 103 F.3d 35 (6th Cir.1996)(no federal jurisdiction); Macneil, Speidel & Stipanowich, supra note 1, § 40.1 ("the FAA preempts any state grounds for vacation unless the parties have clearly agreed to be bound by them.")

540. See §§ 2.15—2.17. See also Burlington Northern Railroad Co. v. TUCO Inc., 960 S.W.2d 629, 632 (Tex.1997)("The

parties' contracts provide that disputes 'shall be arbitrated pursuant to the provisions of the Texas General Arbitration Act,' and neither party disputes that the Texas Act is controlling.")

541. See § 2.46(a).

542. Moncharsh v. Heily & Blase, 3 Cal.4th 1, 10 Cal.Rptr.2d 183, 190, 832 P.2d 899 (1992). This ground is discussed in § 2.45(a).

543. 67 Cal.App.4th 1270, 79 Cal. Rptr.2d 726 (Ct.App.1998).

544. Id. at 735.

private parties who are citizens of different States. The "citizens" involved in international arbitration are often giant corporations and the disputes routinely involve amounts in excess of a million dollars. Rarely is an individual consumer or employee a party in international arbitration.[545]

§ 2.48   The New York Convention

(a) Basic Provisions

The most important body of law governing international arbitration is the United Nations Convention on Recognition and Enforcement of Foreign Arbitral Awards.[546] This treaty is referred to as the "New York Convention" after its birthplace. It has been ratified by approximately 120 States, including those with the most significant presence in international business, such as: the United States, Japan, Germany, France, Italy, Britain and the Netherlands.[547] States that have ratified the New York Convention are known as "Contracting States."

The primary purpose of the New York Convention is to make arbitration awards rendered in one State enforceable in the courts of other States. Accordingly, it begins "[t]his Convention shall apply to the recognition and enforcement of arbitral awards made in the territory of a State other than the State where the recognition and enforcement of such awards are sought."[548] It goes on to provide that "[e]ach Contracting State shall recognize arbitral awards as binding and enforce them."[549] It contains a narrow list of grounds upon which "[r]ecognition and enforcement of the award may be refused."[550]

In addition to requiring enforcement of arbitration awards rendered in another State, the New York Convention also requires enforcement of executory arbitration agreements.[551] The New York Convention's remedy for breach of such agreements, like the remedy under FAA §§ 3 and 4, is specific performance, *i.e.*, court orders to arbitrate.[552]

§ 2.47

545. The internet may change that as it enables large numbers of consumers to engage in cross-border transactions for the first time.

§ 2.48

546. Convention on the Recognition and Enforcement of Foreign Arbitral Awards, June 10, 1958, 21 U.S.T. 2517, 330 U.N.T.S. 38, No. 4739 (1959), available at <http://www.internationaladr.com/tc121.htm>.

547. See 9 U.S.C.A. § 201, note, revised annually (listing countries).

548. Convention, supra note 546, Article I(1).

549. Id. at Article III.

550. Id. at Article V.

551. Each Contracting State shall recognize an agreement in writing under which the parties undertake to submit to arbitration all or any differences which have arisen or which may arise between them in respect of a defined legal relationship, whether contractual or not, concerning a subject matter capable of settlement by arbitration.

Id. at Article II(1).

552. Id. at Article II(3). See also 9 U.S.C. §§ 206–07 (1994).

(b) Effect of United States Ratification

The United States ratified the New York Convention with the reservation that it would be applied, "on the basis of reciprocity, to the recognition and enforcement of only those awards made in the territory of another Contracting State."[553] Therefore, an arbitration award rendered in another Contracting State (or an agreement to arbitrate in another Contracting State) is generally made enforceable in United States courts by the New York Convention.[554] An arbitration award rendered elsewhere in the world may be enforceable in United States courts,[555] but the New York Convention does not make it so.[556]

The previous paragraph noted that an arbitration award rendered in another Contracting State (or an agreement to arbitrate in another Contracting State) is generally made enforceable in United States courts by the New York Convention. There are two main exceptions to that generalization. First, the New York Convention does not govern arbitration "entirely between citizens of the United States" unless their "relationship involves property located abroad, envisages performance or enforcement abroad, or has some other reasonable relation with one or more foreign states."[557] Second, the New York Convention does not govern "[i]f a majority of the parties to the arbitration agreement are citizens of a State or States" that have signed the Inter–American Convention on International Commercial Arbitration.[558] The Inter–American Convention, which also enforces arbitration agreements and awards, has been signed by about a dozen States, all in the Western Hemisphere, including the United States.[559]

(c) Significance

The primary significance of the New York Convention is that it makes enforcement of foreign arbitration awards easier than enforcement of foreign court judgments.[560] This is a major reason why parties to international contracts agree to arbitrate.[561] It is generally easier to persuade a United States court to enforce a foreign arbitration award than it is to persuade a United States court to enforce a foreign court's

---

553. In 1970, Congress enacted FAA §§ 201–208 to provide that the New York Convention "shall be enforced in United States Courts." 9 U.S.C. § 201 (1994).

554. It should be noted that the analysis of whether the New York Convention applies turns on where the arbitration award is made (or is to be made), not the citizenship of the parties. See, e.g., E.A.S.T., Inc. v. M/V Alaia, 876 F.2d 1168 (5th Cir. 1989); Ministry of Defense of the Islamic Republic of Iran v. Gould, Inc., 887 F.2d 1357 (9th Cir.1989).

555. Macneil, Speidel & Stipanowich, supra note 1, § 44.9.1.8.

556. There is doubt about whether the United States' reciprocity reservation ap-

plies to executory agreements as well as to completed arbitration awards. See Gary B. Born, International Commercial Arbitration in the United States 290 (1994).

557. 9 U.S.C. § 202 (1994).

558. 9 U.S.C. § 305(1) (1994).

559. Neil E. McDonnell, Obtaining Arbitral Awards Under the Inter–American Convention, Disp.Resol.J., Jan. 1995, at 19 n.1.

560. Murray, Rau & Sherman, supra note 1, at 529.

561. Christian Bühring-Uhle, Arbitration and Mediation in International Business 129–143 (1996).

judgment. Conversely, it is generally easier to persuade a foreign court to enforce an arbitration award made in the United States than it is to persuade a foreign court to enforce a United States court's judgment.

§ 2.49 Practice

As noted above,[562] international arbitration typically involves major disputes between large and sophisticated parties. While such arbitration is typically slower and more costly than domestic arbitration,[563] that is not a criticism of international arbitration. The alternative to international arbitration for parties engaged in international business is not domestic arbitration but international litigation. Parties often fear litigation in foreign courts both because they fear the application of foreign substantive law and they fear a local bias in the process of foreign litigation itself.[564] International arbitration can avoid application of foreign law through *amiable composition*, the arbitrator's power to ignore any State's law and apply instead the customs of international commerce, the *lex mercatoria*.[565] And international arbitration avoids the procedures and bias of foreign courts by substituting the procedures and arbitrators agreed to by the parties. International arbitration agreements often incorporate the rules of an organization such as the International Chamber of Commerce.

One of the major differences between international and domestic arbitration is that international arbitrators usually write reasoned opinions supporting their awards.[566]

H. EMPLOYMENT ARBITRATION AND LABOR ARBITRATION

Table of Sections

§ 2.50 The Conventional Distinction Between "Employment" and "Labor"

Law governing employment is often divided into two categories: "employment law" which applies to all employees, and "labor law" which applies only to employees represented by a labor union. Labor law has its own specialized terminology. Contracts between employers and

§ 2.49

562. See § 2.47.

563. Murray, Rau & Sherman, supra note 1, at 530.

564. Brunet & Craver, supra note 420, at 334–35.

565. See generally Thomas Carbonneau (ed.), Lex Mercatoria and Arbitration (Rev. ed.1998); Brunet & Craver, supra note 420, at 335. See also § 2.39.

566. See § 2.37(e).

unions are called "collective bargaining agreements." Claims alleging breach of these contracts are called "grievances."

The categories of "employment law" and "labor law" carry over into the terminology of arbitration. "Employment arbitration" arises out of a contract between an employer and an individual employee, while "labor arbitration" arises out of a collective bargaining agreement between an employer and a union. Employment arbitration, both in its practice and in the law governing it, is very much within the mainstream of arbitration. In contrast, labor arbitration is practiced quite differently from other arbitration and is governed by its own unique set of laws.

§ 2.51   The FAA's Exclusion of Certain "Contracts of Employment"

The FAA applies to an arbitration agreement "in any maritime transaction or a contract evidencing a transaction involving commerce."[567] FAA § 1 defines "commerce" to mean interstate or international commerce.[568] The Supreme Court interprets this language broadly to reach all transactions affecting interstate or international commerce.[569] So interpreted, FAA § 1's definition of commerce is extremely broad, bringing the vast majority of arbitration agreements within the coverage of the FAA.[570]

There is, however, an exception to the FAA's extremely broad reach. FAA § 1 says "nothing herein contained shall apply to contracts of employment of seamen, railroad employees, or any other class of workers engaged in foreign or interstate commerce."[571] Arbitration agreements falling within this "employment exclusion" are not governed by the FAA.

The caselaw interpreting the employment exclusion is somewhat complicated. First, the Supreme Court holds that labor arbitration is not primarily governed by the FAA.[572] The law governing labor arbitration is discussed in a later section.[573]

Turning from labor arbitration to employment arbitration, one finds further complications. Federal appellate courts are split in their interpre-

---

§ 2.51

567. 9 U.S.C. § 2 (1994).

568. "Commerce" is defined as commerce among the several States or with foreign nations, or in any Territory of the United States or in the District of Columbia, or between any such Territory and another, or between any such Territory and any State or foreign nation, or between the District of Columbia and any State or Territory or foreign nation, but nothing herein contained shall apply to contracts of employment of seamen, railroad employees, or any other class of workers engaged in foreign or interstate commerce.

9 U.S.C. § 1 (1994).

569. Allied–Bruce Terminix Cos. v. Dobson, 513 U.S. 265, 115 S.Ct. 834, 130 L.Ed.2d 753 (1995).

570. For rare exceptions, see Sisters of the Visitation v. Cochran Plastering Co., 2000 WL 681066 (Ala.2000); City of Cut Bank v. Tom Patrick Construction, Inc., 290 Mont. 470, 963 P.2d 1283 (Mont.1998).

571. 9 U.S.C. § 1 (1994).

572. See § 2.53(a).

573. See § 2.53.

tation of the FAA's employment exclusion. The Ninth Circuit holds that the FAA does not apply to any employment contracts.[574] In contrast, other federal circuit courts hold that the FAA applies to all employment contracts except for those of employees who work directly in interstate commerce, *i.e.*, those actually transporting goods across state lines.[575] The United States Supreme Court has granted certiorari in a case that may resolve this circuit split.[576]

Employment arbitration not governed by the FAA is governed by state arbitration law. Under the law of many states, employment arbitration is treated no differently from other arbitration.[577] For example, employment arbitration agreements are enforceable under California law,[578] and under the Uniform Arbitration Act,[579] neither of which contains an "employment exclusion" like that found in the FAA.

In sum, the Ninth Circuit holds that the FAA governs no labor or employment arbitration. Other courts hold that the FAA governs no labor arbitration but does govern all employment arbitration except for that of employees directly involved in transporting goods across state lines.

574. Craft v. Campbell Soup Co., 161 F.3d 1199 (9th Cir.1998).

575. Id. at 1202 n.5 (citing cases).

576. Circuit City Stores v. Adams, 194 F.3d 1070 (9th Cir.1999), cert.granted, ___ U.S. ___, 120 S.Ct. 2004, 146 L.Ed.2d 955 (2000).

The Supreme Court avoiding deciding the scope of the FAA's employment exclusion in *Gilmer v. Interstate/Johnson Lane Corp.*, 500 U.S. 20, 24 n. 2, 111 S.Ct. 1647, 114 L.Ed.2d 26 (1991). Gilmer enforced an employee's agreement to arbitrate age discrimination claims. Id. at 35. The parties to the arbitration agreement, however, were not the employee and employer. Id. at 24 n.2. Rather the parties were the employee and various securities exchanges. The employer was a member of the securities exchanges and, as a condition of membership, was required by the exchanges to hire for certain jobs only employees who signed the exchanges' arbitration agreement covering disputes between the employee and employer. See § 2.25(a)(discussing *Gilmer*). In effect, then, an agreement to arbitrate was a condition of employment. Nevertheless, Gilmer held that the agreement was not contained in a "contract of employment" so the Court did not have to determine the scope of the FAA's employment exclusion. 500 U.S. at 24 n.2.

577. For state statutes treating it differently, see § 2.13.

578. The California Code of Civil Procedure provides that "A written agreement to submit to arbitration an existing controversy or a controversy thereafter arising is valid, enforceable and irrevocable, save upon such grounds as exist for the revocation of any contract." Cal.Civ.Proc.Code § 1281 (West 1982). This provision, unlike the FAA, makes no exception for employment agreements. In contrast, an earlier California statute had provided that arbitration agreements are "valid, enforceable and irrevocable, save upon such grounds as exist at law or in equity for the revocation of any contract; provided, however, the provisions of this title shall not apply to contracts pertaining to labor." Former Cal.Civ. Proc.Code § 1280, repealed by Stats. 1961, c.461, p.1540 § 1 (emphasis added). Under ordinary principles of statutory construction, the replacement of a statute expressly excluding labor contracts by a statute silent on the question is a strong indication that such contracts are covered by the newer statute.

Since the Ninth Circuit has held that the FAA does not apply to any employment contracts, at least one California court has cited § 1281 in enforcing an employment arbitration agreement. See Lee v. Technology Integration Group, 82 Cal.Rptr.2d 387, 392 (Ct.App.1999).

579. Unif. Arbitration Act §§ 1–2, 7 U.L.A. 1, 6 (1997).

§ 2.52 Employment Arbitration

Unlike labor arbitration law,[580] employment arbitration law is very much within the mainstream of arbitration law.[581] This section collects the exceptions, the features peculiar to employment arbitration law. Most of these peculiarities seem to reflect judicial discomfort with employers conditioning employment on employees' agreements to arbitrate employment disputes, especially those involving discrimination claims.

The first peculiarity of employment arbitration law is the possibility that the employee's agreement to arbitrate will not be enforced even though the agreement would be enforceable under the standards of ordinary contract law. Ordinary contract law standards generally are used to determine whether an arbitration agreement is enforceable.[582] But in employment cases some courts have departed from ordinary contract law standards to require more for enforceability. For example, the Ninth Circuit has refused to enforce employees' arbitration agreements on the ground that there was not "knowing" assent by the employees to the agreements.[583]

The second, and perhaps most important, peculiarity of employment arbitration law is the possibility that particular claims will be inarbitrable. While the United States Supreme Court cases over the last generation have consistently held arbitrable every claim before the Court,[584] the Ninth Circuit has broken ranks to hold certain employment discrimination claims inarbitrable.[585] This means that an employee's agreement to arbitrate "all claims" may, for example, be unenforceable with respect to claims under Title VII of the Civil Rights Act of 1964 but enforceable with respect to tort or contract claims.

The third peculiarity of employment arbitration law is that enforcement of employees' agreements to arbitrate may be conditioned on procedural features not required of arbitration generally. For example, several courts have refused to enforce agreements to arbitrate Title VII claims where the agreement required the employee to pay an arbitration organization's filing fee plus half of the arbitrator's fees.[586]

Finally, it should be noted that the Equal Employment Opportunity Commission has sought to prevent enforcement of employment arbitration agreements.[587]

§ 2.52

580. See §§ 2.50 & 2.53.

581. For an overview, see Richard A. Bales, Compulsory Arbitration: The Grand Experiment in Employment (1997).

582. See §§ 2.22—2.26.

583. See § 2.22(a)

584. See § 2.27(a).

585. See § 2.28(a).

586. See § 2.28(b). See also § 2.35.

587. See EEOC Policy Statement on Mandatory Arbitration, 133 Daily Lab. Rep.(BNA) at E–4 (July 10, 1997); Richard A. Bales, Compulsory Employment Arbitration and the EEOC, 27 Pepp.L.Rev. 1 (1999). The EEOC obtained an injunction against an employer that prevents the employer from requiring employees to sign an arbitration agreement. See United States Equal Employment Opportunity Commission v. River Oaks Imaging and Diagnostic, 1995 WL 264003 (S.D.Tex.1995).

§ 2.53 Labor Arbitration

(a) LMRA Rather Than FAA

Labor arbitration is in many ways a world unto itself, apart from the mainstream of arbitration. Certainly, labor arbitration law differs in many important ways from other arbitration law. Most significantly, labor arbitration is not primarily governed by the FAA.

The seminal labor arbitration case is *Textile Workers Union v. Lincoln Mills*,[588] decided by the Supreme Court in 1957. *Lincoln Mills* held that courts must enforce arbitration clauses in collective bargaining agreements ("CBAs"), the contracts between employers and labor unions.[589] *Lincoln Mills* rested its holding on Section 301 of the Labor Management Relations Act of 1947 ("LMRA")[590]

While *Lincoln Mills* held that arbitration clauses in CBAs are enforceable under the LMRA, *Lincoln Mills* ignored the FAA. Because *Lincoln Mills* did not mention the FAA, the "most natural reading" of *Lincoln Mills* is that the FAA does not govern labor arbitration.[591] The Supreme Court's subsequent opinions on labor arbitration did not address the FAA until 1987.[592] That year, the Court suggested that, although the FAA does not govern labor arbitration, courts may look to the FAA for guidance in labor cases.[593]

While the LMRA, rather than the FAA, primarily governs labor arbitration, the LMRA says nothing about arbitration. It does not even

§ 2.53

588. 353 U.S. 448 (1957).

589. "Congress adopted a policy which placed sanctions behind agreements to arbitrate grievance disputes, by implication rejecting the common-law rule ... against enforcement of executory agreements to arbitrate." 353 U.S. at 456 (citation omitted) (footnote omitted).

590. 29 U.S.C. §§ 141–144, 171–188 (1994).

591. Macneil, Speidel & Stipanowich, supra note 1, § 11.3.1, at 11:9. See also, Lincoln Mills, 353 U.S. at 466 (Frankfurter, J., dissenting).

Naturally enough, I find rejection, though not explicit, of the availability of the Federal Arbitration Act to enforce arbitration clauses in collective-bargaining agreements in the silent treatment given that Act by the Court's opinion. If an Act that authorizes the federal courts to enforce arbitration provisions in contracts generally, but specifically denies authority to decree that remedy for 'contracts of employment,' were available, the Court would hardly spin such power out of the empty darkness of § 301. I would make

this rejection explicit, recognizing that when Congress passed legislation to enable arbitration agreements to be enforced by the federal courts, it saw fit to exclude this remedy with respect to labor contracts.

Id.

592. Macneil, Speidel & Stipanowich, supra note 1, § 11.3.1. See, e.g., United Steelworkers v. American Mfg. Co., 363 U.S. 564, 80 S.Ct. 1343, 4 L.Ed.2d 1403 (1960); United Steelworkers v. Warrior & Gulf Navigation Co., 363 U.S. 574, 80 S.Ct. 1347, 4 L.Ed.2d 1409 (1960); United Steelworkers v. Enterprise Wheel & Car Corp., 363 U.S. 593, 80 S.Ct. 1358, 4 L.Ed.2d 1424 (1960).

593. See United Paperworkers Int'l Union v. Misco, Inc., 484 U.S. 29, 108 S.Ct. 364, 98 L.Ed.2d 286 (1987).

The Arbitration Act does not apply to "contracts of employment of * * * workers engaged in foreign or interstate commerce," 9 U.S.C. § 1, but the federal courts have often looked to the Act for guidance in labor arbitration cases, especially in the wake of [*Lincoln Mills*].

Id. at 40 n.9.

mention the word "arbitration".[594] Because the LMRA says nothing about arbitration, courts must make common law to govern labor arbitration. *Lincoln Mills* held that this is *federal* common law. LMRA § 301 grants jurisdiction to federal courts and *Lincoln Mills* held that this provision does not merely give federal courts jurisdiction to apply *state* law, but rather gives them authority to create substantive *federal* law.[595] State courts have concurrent jurisdiction to enforce CBAs,[596] including arbitration clauses, but they must apply the federal common law of collective bargaining and enforcement.[597]

Although it is not the FAA that makes labor arbitration agreements enforceable, the FAA and labor arbitration law are similar in an important respect. Both require courts to use an especially powerful remedy, specific performance, in enforcing arbitration agreements. While money damages are the ordinary remedy for breach of contract,[598] specific performance, *i.e.*, a court order to arbitrate, is the remedy for breach of an arbitration agreement. That is true of non-labor arbitration under the FAA,[599] and it is true of labor arbitration under the LMRA, as interpreted by *Lincoln Mills*.[600] If, for example, Employee sues Employer over a grievance covered by the CBA's arbitration clause, the court will stay or dismiss Employee's case.[601] Alternatively, if Employee and her union seek to arbitrate Employee's grievance but Employer refuses to participate in arbitration, then a court will order Employee to do so.[602]

---

594. The portion of the LMRA on which Lincoln Mills relied (Section 301) provides in pertinent part:

(a) Suits for violation of contracts between an employer and a labor organization representing employees in an industry affecting commerce as defined in this chapter, or between any such labor organizations, may be brought in any district court of the United States having jurisdiction of the parties, without respect to the amount in controversy or without regard to the citizenship of the parties.

(b) * * * Any labor organization which represents employees in an industry affecting commerce as defined in this chapter and any employer whose activities affect commerce as defined in this chapter shall be bound by the acts of its agents. Any such labor organization may sue or be sued as an entity and in behalf of the employees whom it represents in the courts of the United States. Any money judgment against a labor organization in a district court of the United States shall be enforceable only against the organization as an entity and against its assets, and shall not be enforceable against any individual member or his assets.

29 U.S.C. § 185(a)-(b) (1994).

595. Lincoln Mills, 353 U.S. at 456 (the "substantive law to apply in suits under [the LMRA] is federal law, which the courts must fashion from the policy of our national labor laws.")

596. Charles Dowd Box Co. v. Courtney, 368 U.S. 502, 511–14, 82 S.Ct. 519, 7 L.Ed.2d 483 (1962).

597. Local 174, Teamsters v. Lucas Flour Co., 369 U.S. 95, 102, 82 S.Ct. 571, 7 L.Ed.2d 593 (1962).

598. Calamari & Perillo, supra note 28, ch.14.

599. See § 2.4(b).

600. Lincoln Mills, 353 U.S. at 451.

601. See, e.g., National Ass'n of Broadcast Employees & Technicians v. American Broadcasting Co., 140 F.3d 459, 462 (2d Cir.1998).

602. See, e.g., Lincoln Mills, 353 U.S. 448, 77 S.Ct. 923, 1 L.Ed.2d 972; Washington Hosp. Center v. Service Employees International Union, 746 F.2d 1503, 1506 (D.C.Cir.1984).

(b) The Practice of Labor Arbitration

Almost every CBA contains an arbitration clause.[603] Arbitration is routine in the labor context and has been for half a century. Available evidence, however, suggests that the number of labor arbitrations has declined over the last twenty years or so, as union membership has declined.[604]

(1) Two Peculiarities

The practice of labor arbitration is substantially different from the practice of other arbitration. From the perspective of arbitration generally, the practice of labor arbitration has two peculiarities. First, employees are the claimants (or "grievants") in the vast majority of labor arbitration cases. In other words, labor arbitration nearly always involves claims *against* employers and almost never involves claims *by* employers. Most CBA arbitration clauses do not even allow the employer to assert claims in arbitration.[605] That labor arbitration nearly always involves claims against employers distinguishes it from much other arbitration in which either side to a transaction might, depending on the case, assert a claim against the other. Labor arbitration is one-sided in a way that distinguishes it from much other arbitration.

What further distinguishes labor arbitration from other arbitration is the status of disputes that do not go to arbitration. Outside the labor context, "arbitration is the substitute for litigation."[606] Claims asserted in non-labor arbitration generally would have been asserted in litigation had the parties not agreed to arbitrate. In contrast, it is unlikely that grievances asserted in labor arbitration would have been asserted in litigation had the parties not agreed to arbitrate.

These two peculiarities of labor arbitration, its one-sidedness and its handling of claims that would not have gone to litigation, are related. Both result from the background legal rules against which CBAs are formed. These rules are discussed next.

(2) Labor Law and CBAs

Generally, the law's default rule is that employment is at-will.[607] That means, among other things, that the employer can fire the employee at any time, for any reason or no reason at all. It also means that the employer can unilaterally change the terms and conditions of employment at any time, for any reason or no reason at all. If, for example, Employer insists that Employee must take a pay cut and assume new

603. See Frank Elkouri & Edna Asper Elkouri, How Arbitration Works 8 (5th ed.1997); Macneil, Speidel & Stipanowich, supra note 1, § 11.1.

604. Nolan, supra note 389, at 6.

605. Id. at 165.

606. United Steelworkers v. Warrior & Gulf Navigation Co., 363 U.S. 574, 80 S.Ct. 1347, 4 L.Ed.2d 1409 (1960). See §§ 1.7(b)-(d).

607. See, e.g., Mark Rothstein et al., Employment Law § 1.27 (2d ed.1999); Andrew P. Morriss, Exploding Myths: An Empirical and Economic Reassessment of the Rise of Employment At–Will, 59 Mo.L.Rev. 679 (1994)(surveying history of the rule and its exceptions).

and more demanding job responsibilities, then Employee's only alternative to those new terms is to quit.

While employment-at-will is the law's default rule, the parties can contract around that rule. CBAs are such contracts. CBAs invariably contain terms by which employers give up some of the rights they would have had under the at-will rule. Most commonly, CBAs contain a promise by the employer to fire employees only "for cause."[608] The employer can no longer fire for any reason or none at all. Now the employer must have good cause for firing. But who is to determine what constitutes "good cause"? The arbitrator. CBAs provide for arbitration so that arbitrators will determine whether there was good cause to fire (discharge) or discipline the employee. And the most commonly arbitrated grievances arise out of the employer's discharge or discipline of the employee.[609] In essence, an arbitration clause in a CBA is the employer giving up its authority to decide certain matters and transferring that decision-making authority to the arbitrator.

Why do employers agree to this? Because, the usual answer goes, the employer gets something in return, a promise by the union not to strike. The standard view of CBAs is that the union gives up its right to strike in exchange for the employer giving up its discretion under the at-will rule and replacing that discretion with the arbitration of grievances. In reviewing the legislative history of the LMRA, the Supreme Court concluded that "the entire tenor of the history indicates that the agreement to arbitrate grievance disputes was considered as quid pro quo of a no-strike agreement."[610] This deal, no strikes in exchange for arbitration of grievances, is central to the Supreme Court's conception of labor law.

> The present federal policy is to promote industrial stabilization through the collective bargaining agreement. A major factor in achieving industrial peace is the inclusion of a provision for arbitration of grievances in the collective bargaining agreement.
>
> Thus the run of [non-labor] arbitration cases * * * becomes irrelevant to our problem. There the choice is between the adjudication of cases or controversies in courts * * * on the one hand and the settlement of them in the more informal arbitration tribunal on

608. Rothstein et al., supra note 607, § 8.1 ("Eventually, most collective bargaining agreements contained protection from discharge except for 'just cause,' with arbitration to resolve grievances."); Elkouri, supra note 603, 884–87 (union contracts almost always require cause for dismissal, and typically provide an arbitration mechanism as a method of review of employer decisions.)

609. Nolan, supra note 389, at 314. The most common remedies are reinstatement (perhaps with back pay) and restoration of the employee's seniority. Id. at 276. The employer might discipline the employee by suspending or demoting the employee or putting a letter of reprimand in the employee's personnel file. Elkouri, supra note 603, at 939.

610. Lincoln Mills, 353 U.S. 448, 455, 77 S.Ct. 923, 1 L.Ed.2d 972. See also Local 174, Teamsters v. Lucas Flour Co., 369 U.S. 95, 82 S.Ct. 571, 7 L.Ed.2d 593 (1962)(courts should imply a no-strike clause with respect to any dispute which a CBA "provides shall be settled exclusively and finally by compulsory arbitration.")

the other. In the commercial case, arbitration is the substitute for litigation. Here arbitration is the substitute for industrial strife.[611]

In sum then, grievances asserted in labor arbitration probably would not have been litigated had the parties not agreed to arbitrate. That is because the arbitration clause is part of a contract that gives employees rights they would not have had under employment-at-will. The creation of the rights asserted in grievance arbitration is tied to the agreement to arbitrate those grievances. This explains both peculiarities of labor arbitration: that it nearly always involves claims against employers and that it nearly always involves claims that would not have been asserted in litigation had the parties not agreed to arbitrate.

(c) Few Arbitrable Claims

(1) The Law

Nearly all claims are now arbitrable.[612] In other words, courts' enforcement of arbitration agreements is nearly always without regard to the claims asserted. The one national exception is labor arbitration.[613]

When employees represented by a labor union have asserted federal discrimination claims in court they have been allowed to proceed with litigation despite arbitration clauses in their collective bargaining agreements.[614] This law is most clearly stated in the Supreme Court's 1974 case, *Alexander v. Gardner–Denver* Co.[615] Labor cases like *Gardner–Denver* are based on the rationale that an employee's rights under anti-discrimination statutes are not "susceptible of prospective waiver" and that an arbitration agreement is such a waiver.[616] In non-labor cases, by contrast, the Court has repeatedly stated that an arbitration agreement is not such a waiver.[617] The Supreme Court recently conceded that

---

611. United Steelworkers v. Warrior & Gulf Navigation Co., 363 U.S. 574, 80 S.Ct. 1347, 4 L.Ed.2d 1409 (1960).

612. See § 2.27.

613. Local exceptions are discussed in § 2.28.

614. Wright v. Universal Maritime Service Corp., 525 U.S. 70, 119 S.Ct. 391, 142 L.Ed.2d 361 (1998)(leaving open whether "clear and unmistakable" language covering statutory discrimination claims would be enforced); Bratten v. SSI, 185 F.3d 625 (6th Cir.1999); Brown v. ABF Freight Systems, 183 F.3d 319 (4th Cir.1999). But see Austin v. Owens–Brockway Glass Container, Inc., 78 F.3d 875, 885 (4th Cir.) cert.denied, 519 U.S. 980, 117 S.Ct. 432, 136 L.Ed.2d 330 (1996).

And when employees pursue arbitration and lose, they have not been precluded from then pursuing their claims in court. See § 2.41.

615. 415 U.S. 36, 94 S.Ct. 1011, 39 L.Ed.2d 147 (1974).

616. Alexander v. Gardner–Denver Co., 415 U.S. 36, 51–52, 94 S.Ct. 1011, 39 L.Ed.2d 147 (1974).

617. Mitsubishi Motors Corp. v. Soler Chrysler–Plymouth, Inc., 473 U.S. 614, 628, 105 S.Ct. 3346, 87 L.Ed.2d 444 (1985)("By agreeing to arbitrate a statutory claim, a party does not forgo the substantive rights afforded by the statute; it only submits to their resolution in an arbitral, rather than a judicial, forum."); Shearson/American Express, Inc. v. McMahon, 482 U.S. 220, 229, 107 S.Ct. 2332, 96 L.Ed.2d 185 (1987)(same); Rodriguez de Quijas v. Shearson/American Express, Inc., 490 U.S. 477, 481, 109 S.Ct. 1917, 104 L.Ed.2d 526 (1989)(same); Gilmer v. Interstate/Johnson Lane Corp., 500 U.S. 20, 26, 111 S.Ct. 1647, 114 L.Ed.2d 26 (1991)(same).

A thoughtful labor arbitration scholar says that *Gilmer*, which held statutory discrimination claims arbitrable in the individual employment context, "came as a great surprise to most observers." Nolan, supra

"[t]here is obviously some tension between" labor cases like *Gardner-Denver* and the Court's mainstream arbitrability cases.[618]

There are, however, reasons to distinguish between labor and non-labor arbitration in holding certain claims inarbitrable only in the labor context. These reasons are discussed next.

(2) Union, Not Employee, Controls Arbitration

Under most CBAs, an employee with a claim has no individual right to arbitration; the employee must persuade the union to demand arbitration.[619] If the union refuses to demand arbitration, the employee can sue the employer only after proving that the union's refusal to arbitrate was a breach of its duty to the employee, the "duty of fair representation."[620] In short, an employee's claim is unlikely to receive a hearing unless the union wants it to. And the union may not pursue a particular employee's claim as vigorously as it pursues some other employees' claims.[621]

These, one might argue, are the prices employees pay for the benefits that come from union representation. But many labor law specialists distinguish between claims arising out of the CBA and claims arising out of "external law",[622] such as a statute prohibiting discrimination. The employee's rights under the CBA, one might argue, are derived from the union so it is appropriate to let the union control adjudication of those rights, while the employee's rights under anti-discrimination statutes are not derived from the union so it is not appropriate to let the union control their adjudication.

note 389, at 171. While that may describe most observers who specialize in labor arbitration, *Gilmer* was no surprise from the perspective of arbitration law, more generally. The reasoning of *Gilmer* closely followed the reasoning of *Mitsubishi, McMahon* and *Rodriguez.* See Nolan, supra note 389, at 173 ("Having become accustomed to arbitration of statutory issues [in other contexts], the Court had no trouble extending the development to employment cases.")

618. Wright, 525 U.S. at 76.

619. Mack A. Player, Employment Discrimination Law § 1.13(c) (1988); Elkouri, supra note 603, at 230–31.

620. Vaca v. Sipes, 386 U.S. 171, 87 S.Ct. 903, 17 L.Ed.2d 842 (1967). See Rothstein et al., supra note 607, § 8.18, at 729; Elkouri, supra note 603, at 252–57.

621. Gardner–Denver, 415 U.S. at 58 n.19. The union might even take a claim to arbitration hoping that the arbitrator will reject it. This might occur because the interests of the employees who control the union are opposed to the interests of the claimant.

A union can purposefully lose an arbitration a couple of ways. One is to simply signal to the arbitrator that this claim is a low priority one for the union. The arbitrator is probably a repeat player who arbitrates many disputes between this union and this employer. Such an arbitrator has an incentive (repeat business) to give each side (union and employer) victories on its high-priority cases. By signaling to the arbitrator that the union places a low priority on a particular claim, the union can substantially reduce the likelihood that the claim will prevail.

A union can also purposefully lose an arbitration by means of the "rigged award" which is simply an arbitration award incorporating a settlement agreement between the union and employer. The rigged award is deceiving, however, in that the arbitrator, union and employer pretend as though there was no settlement. They pretend as though the arbitrator reached that decision after vigorous advocacy by both sides. The rigged award is a way for a union to "sell out" a claimant while pretending that it was the arbitrator, not the union, who decided against the claimant.

622. See, e.g., Nolan, supra note 389, at 147–55. The use of this phrase "external law" is another peculiarity of labor arbitration.

This distinction fits comfortably within the traditional view of labor arbitration. Labor arbitrators have long thought of their jobs as interpreting CBAs, not statutes. Many labor arbitrators are not lawyers. Their expertise "pertains primarily to the law of the shop, not the law of the land."[623]

(3) Narrowly Drafted Arbitration Clauses

Even if *Gardner-Denver* is overturned and statutory discrimination claims become arbitrable in the labor context, there will still be the question whether particular agreements provide for the arbitration of such claims, *i.e.*, the question of "contractual arbitrability."[624] CBA arbitration clauses tend to be narrower than those found outside the labor context. While many non-labor arbitration clauses have broad language obligating each party to arbitrate "[a]ny controversy or claim arising out of or relating to this contract, or the breach thereof",[625] many labor arbitration clauses are limited to "differences arising with respect to the interpretation of this contract or the performance of any obligation hereunder."[626] Broad arbitration clauses generally are written with the intention that all claims will be arbitrable.[627] In contrast, labor arbitration clauses generally are written with the intention of making arbitrable only breach-of-contract claims.[628] This intent reflects the standard notion of a CBA as a deal in which the union gives up its right to strike in exchange for the employer giving up its discretion under the at-will rule and replacing that discretion with the arbitration of grievances.[629] This standard deal is not intended to encompass arbitration of claims arising out of anti-discrimination statutes or other law "external" to the CBA. As the Supreme Court put it, "an arbitrator is confined to interpretation and application of the collective bargaining agreement."[630] An arbitrator would "exceed[] the scope of the submission" by deciding a case "solely upon the arbitrator's view of the requirements of enacted legislation."[631] These sorts of statements by the Court make sense only in the context of CBA arbitration clauses confined to contract disputes. Outside the labor context, by contrast, the Court says it wants arbitrators to apply the requirements of enacted legislation.[632]

While CBA arbitration clauses tend to be drafted narrowly to cover contractual, but not statutory disputes, courts have interpreted CBA

623. Gardner–Denver, 415 U.S. at 56.

624. See §§ 2.29—2.31.

625. Macneil, Speidel & Stipanowich, supra note 1, § 20.2.2.

626. See, e.g., AT & T Technologies, Inc. v. Communications Workers of Am., 475 U.S. 643, 106 S.Ct. 1415, 89 L.Ed.2d 648 (1986). See also Nolan, supra note 389, at 293–94.

627. Some are even written to expressly cover claims based on "statutory law, common law, equitable claims, or claims for breach of fiduciary duty or other wrongful acts." Herrington v. Union Planters Bank, 113 F.Supp.2d 1026, 2000 WL 424232, *2 (S.D.Miss.2000).

628. Macneil, Speidel & Stipanowich, supra note 1, § 40.5.2.6 (Supp.1999)(in labor arbitration arbitrators are typically authorized only to interpret contracts, not to make other rulings of law).

629. See § 2.53(b)(2).

630. United Steelworkers v. Enterprise Wheel and Car Corp., 363 U.S. 593, 596, 80 S.Ct. 1358, 4 L.Ed.2d 1424 (1960).

631. Id.

632. See §§ 2.27—2.28.

arbitration clauses broadly on another issue. As explained above, a CBA arbitration clause is essentially the employer giving up its authority to decide certain matters and transferring that authority to the arbitrator.[633] When the contract interpretation issue is whether the clause covers a grievance, *i.e.*, whether the employer has given up its authority, courts tend to interpret CBA arbitration clauses broadly.[634]

(d) Interest Arbitration

Another unique feature of labor arbitration is "interest" arbitration. Labor law terminology distinguishes grievance arbitration from interest arbitration. Grievance arbitration is the usual labor arbitration, the labor arbitration discussed above.[635] Grievance arbitration resembles non-labor arbitration in that it resolves a particular claim. Because that claim generally alleges breach of the CBA, it is similar to the breach-of-contract claims often asserted in non-labor arbitration.

In contrast, interest arbitration does not resolve particular claims alleging breach of the CBA. Interest arbitration's task is to create a CBA. When a CBA expires, the union and employer have a duty to negotiate in good faith to try to form a new CBA.[636] If these negotiations fail, the union and employer may agree to send to arbitration the question of what the terms of the new CBA should be. Interest arbitration is a process for selecting contract terms, while grievance arbitration is a process for determining whether there has been a breach of those terms. Arbitration could be used as a process for selecting the terms of non-labor contracts. But it is not so used. Interest arbitration is used almost exclusively in the labor context, especially in the context of government employment.[637]

I. PROCESSES SIMILAR TO ARBITRATION

Table of Sections

§ 2.54 Private Judging ("Rent–A–Judge")

Litigation is *adjudication*[638] in a court or other government forum. Arbitration is adjudication in a private, *i.e.*, non-government, forum. Private judging is somewhere in between. It is adjudication in a quasi-government forum.

Arbitration, as this chapter repeatedly emphasizes, is a creature of contract. Not only does the parties' contract determine *whether* a dispute

---

633. See § 2.53(b)(2).

634. See § 2.31.

635. See § 2.53(a)-(c).

636. 28 U.S.C. §§ 158(a)(5),(b)(3) & (d) (1994).

637. Nolan, supra note 389, at 68–79.

§ 2.54

638. See § 1.5(a), n.12.

goes to arbitration, the contract also determines *what occurs* during arbitration.[639] Parties to arbitration agreements have the freedom of contract to determine the identity of the arbitrator(s), the rules of procedure and evidence and the secrecy of the proceedings. Judicial enforcement of arbitration awards is contractual in its rationale. The parties agreed to comply with the arbitrator's decision and if the losing party refuses to do so then that party is in breach of contract—even if the arbitrator's decision is wrong.

In contrast, private judging is a less contractual, less privatized, process. Party agreement, usually formed post-dispute, does send a case to private judging. And the parties have the freedom of contract to determine the time and place of trial, as well as the identity of the judge. Unlike arbitration, however, privately judged trials may (depending on the state[640] law) be: (1) required to use the same rules of procedure and evidence used in ordinary litigation,[641] (2) exposed to public view by court order,[642] (3) adjudicated only by a former judge,[643] and (4) subject to appeal in the same manner as other trial verdicts.[644] In sum, private judging is essentially an ordinary bench trial except that the parties select and, pay for, the judge.

Private judging "has been used primarily in technical and complex business litigation involving substantial amounts of money."[645] It allows parties to such disputes to "jump the line" waiting for a trial and get an early trial at the cost of paying (often $500 per hour) for the judge or "referee". Private judging has been labeled "Rent–A–Judge" and criticized as, "an unconstitutional, elitist institution that unfairly grants privileges to the wealthy."[646]

§ 2.55 Non–Contractual, Yet Binding, Arbitration

(a) Introduction

There are two types of arbitration, contractual and non-contractual.[647] The duty to arbitrate a dispute can be created by contract or by

---

639. See §§ 2.35—2.39.

640. Unlike the Federal Arbitration Act, which makes arbitration law nearly uniform around the country, the law on private judging varies from state to state. California is the leader in private judging. See Cal.Const.Art. VI, § 21 (1952 & Supp. 1996); Cal.Civ.Proc.Code §§ 638–645 (1976 & Supp.1996). Compare, e.g., N.H.Rev.Stat. Ann. § 519:9 (1974 & Supp.1995); N.Y.Civ. Proc.L. & R. 4301–21 (1992); Tex.Civ.Prac. & Rem.Code §§ 151.001—151.013 (West 1997); Wash.Rev.Code Ann. § 4.48.010 et seq. (West 1988).

641. Tex.Civ.Prac. & Rem.Code § 151.005 (West 1997).

642. Judicial Council of California Rule 532.1(d) (1993). Cal.R.Ct. 244(e).

643. Tex.Civ.Prac. & Rem.Code § 151.003 (West 1997).

644. Id.

645. Barlow F. Christensen, Private Justice: California's General Reference Procedure, 1982 Am.Bar Found.Research J. 79, 82.

646. Anne S. Kim, Note, Rent–A–Judges and the Cost of Selling Justice, 44 Duke L.J. 166 (1994). See also Note, The California Rent–A–Judge Experiment: Constitutional and Policy Considerations of Pay–As–You–Go Courts, 94 Harv.L.Rev. 1592 (1981).

other law. If the duty to arbitrate is created by contract, then enforcing that duty is unlikely to violate the constitutional right to a jury trial. Courts typically hold that, by forming a contract to arbitrate, a party waives its right to a trial by jury.[648] In contrast, the parties to non-contractual arbitration have rarely waived the right to a jury trial. Therefore, non-contractual arbitration generally must be non-binding to avoid violating this right.[649] Non-binding arbitration has less in common with arbitration than it does with mediation and other processes in aid of negotiation. Accordingly, non-binding arbitration is discussed, not in this chapter, but in Chapter 4.[650]

Non-contractual, yet binding, arbitration is discussed in this section. There are several examples of non-contractual, yet binding, arbitration. Some avoid violating the right to jury trial; others may not. The United States Constitution's Seventh Amendment, preserving the right to jury trial, and most state constitutional provisions recognizing this right,[651] were enacted prior to the merger of law and equity. Courts generally interpret these constitutional provisions to confer a jury trial right only in cases arising at law, as opposed to cases in equity.[652] This means, basically, that there is a right to a jury trial of claims for money damages, but not claims for equitable remedies like injunctions and specific performance.

Legislatures and administrative agencies have created new claims that did not exist at the time the constitutional provisions regarding the right to a jury trial were enacted. Whether there is a right to a jury trial of these claims is determined by the language of the statute creating the

§ 2.55

647. Many examples of "non-contractual" arbitration do involve a contract, such as an employment contract or a contract for the sale of an automobile. So in these contexts the duty to arbitrate is, in a sense, assumed by contract. The difference between "contractual" and "non-contractual" arbitration is whether it is possible to form a contract of the relevant sort without assuming the duty to arbitrate. For example, in transportation industries governed by the Railway Labor Act, it is not possible to form an employment contract without assuming the duty to arbitrate. See § 2.55(b)(4). In contrast, it is possible to form such an employment contract elsewhere in the private sector. See §§ 2.50–2.53. Accordingly, transportation employment arbitration is "non-contractual", while other labor and employment arbitration is "contractual".

648. See § 2.2.

649. See, e.g., GTFM, LLC v. TKN Sales, Inc., 2000 WL 364871 (S.D.N.Y.2000) (holding that Minnesota statute mandating binding arbitration violates constitutional

right to jury trial); Cooper v. Poston, 326 S.C. 46, 483 S.E.2d 750, 751 (S.C. 1997)(state statute allowing one party unilaterally to divert an action for monetary damages arising out a motor vehicle accident to binding arbitration would "abrogate another party's constitutional right to a jury trial").

650. See § 4.32.

651. While the Seventh Amendment is one of the few amendments in the Bill of Rights that constrains only federal, not state, government, see Curtis v. Loether, 415 U.S. 189, 192 n. 6, 94 S.Ct. 1005, 39 L.Ed.2d 260 (1974), nearly all state constitutions contain a provision that similarly protects the right to trial by jury. See Redish, supra note 6.

652. See, e.g., Feltner v. Columbia Pictures Television, Inc., 523 U.S. 340, 347–48, 118 S.Ct. 1279, 140 L.Ed.2d 438 (1998); Motor Vehicle Mfrs.Ass'n v. State, 75 N.Y.2d 175, 551 N.Y.S.2d 470, 550 N.E.2d 919 (1990).

claim and by whether these claims bear more resemblance to legal or to equitable claims.[653]

(b) Examples

(1) Federal Programs

Federal law requires arbitration of certain disputes under particular federal programs.[654] These disputes may involve claims by private parties against the federal government or claims between private parties relating to the rights and duties specified by the particular federal program. Examples of such federal laws include the Comprehensive Environmental Response, Compensation and Liability Act,[655] the Federal Insecticide, Fungicide, and Rodenticide Act,[656] and the Multiemployer Pension Plan Amendments Act.[657] In all these examples, the duty to arbitrate is created by statute in the absence of any contract providing for arbitration. This form of non-contractual arbitration does not, however, violate the constitutional right to a jury trial because that right does not attach to claims under these programs.[658]

(2) Government Employees—Federal

The Civil Service Reform Act ("CSRA") authorizes employees of the federal government to form labor unions and requires employers (the various federal government agencies) to bargain in good faith with these unions.[659] The CSRA states that the collective bargaining agreement "shall provide procedures for the settlement of grievances."[660] "[A]ny grievance not satisfactorily settled under the negotiated grievance procedure shall be subject to binding arbitration."[661] Herein lies the non-contractual source of the duty to arbitrate. A statute, rather than a contract, imposes the duty to arbitrate.

Either party to a federal employment arbitration may appeal to the Federal Labor Relations Authority and may further appeal that Authority's decision to a federal court.[662]

653. The Seventh Amendment's jury trial right applies not only to common-law causes of action, but also to actions brought to enforce statutory rights that are analogous to common-law causes of action ordinarily decided in English law courts in the late 18th century, as opposed to those customarily heard by courts of equity or admiralty. To determine whether a statutory action is more analogous to cases tried in courts of law than to suits tried in courts of equity or admiralty, we examine both the nature of the statutory action and the remedy sought. Feltner, 523 U.S. at 347–48.

654. See Macneil, Speidel & Stipanowich, supra note 1, ch.12.

655. 42 U.S.C. §§ 9601 et seq. (1994).

656. 7 U.S.C. §§ 136 et seq. (1994).

657. 29 U.S.C. §§ 1381—1461 (1994).

658. See, e.g., Thomas v. Union Carbide Agricultural Products Co., 473 U.S. 568, 105 S.Ct. 3325, 87 L.Ed.2d 409 (1985); Connors v. Ryan's Coal Co., 923 F.2d 1461 (11th Cir.1991).

659. 5 U.S.C. §§ 7101–14 (1994).

660. Id. § 7121.

661. Id.

662. Id. § 7122(a). See generally, Nolan, supra note 389, at 83–87 and 214–16.

(3) Government Employees—State and Local

Some state and local government employees are covered by grievance arbitration systems similar to those found in the private sector.[663] What stands out about arbitration in the context of state and local employees, however, is the prevalence of interest arbitration.[664] Interest arbitration is often used to determine the terms of employment for public school teachers, police, firefighters, etc. Such government employees

> are usually forbidden to engage in strikes; economic pressure, and the usual tests of economic strength used in the private sector to determine contract terms after a bargaining impasse, are therefore limited in the public interest. "Interest" arbitration to determine the terms of a new contract when bargaining fails provides a common alternative mechanism. In many cases, in fact, state statutes impose this as a *mandatory* means of settlement. * * * Such legislation in effect gives to public employee unions the "right" to resort to the arbitration mechanism to determine the future terms of employment.[665]

Such arbitration is not so much the application of law to resolve a dispute as it is quasi-legislative policymaking, requiring consideration of government spending and taxation priorities.[666]

(4) Railway Labor Act

Employers and employees in certain transportation industries, such as railroads and airlines, are governed by the Railway Labor Act ("RLA").[667] The RLA creates a National Railroad Adjustment Board consisting of representatives selected by the employers and representatives selected by the employees' labor unions.[668] The RLA requires employers and unions to submit certain disputes to the Adjustment Board for decision.[669] Thus, the RLA requires arbitration, rather than litigation, of these disputes. Appeals of Adjustment Board decisions may be taken to federal court. "Judicial review of these Boards' determinations has been characterized as 'among the narrowest known to the law.' "[670]

(5) State "Lemon" Laws

Many states have enacted "lemon" laws with the goal of ensuring that auto manufacturers satisfy their warranty obligations to consumers. New York State requires manufacturers to arbitrate lemon law disputes

663. Nolan, supra note 389, at 87–89.

664. See § 2.53(d).

665. Murray, Rau & Sherman, supra note 1, at 516. See, e.g., R.I.Gen.Laws §§ 28–9.1–1 & 28–9.2–1 (1995).

666. Clyde W. Summers, Public Sector Bargaining: Problems of Governmental Decisionmaking, 44 U.Cin.L.Rev. 669, 672 (1975).

667. 45 U.S.C. §§ 151—188 (1994).

668. Id. § 153(a).

669. Id. § 153(i).

670. Union Pacific R. Co. v. Sheehan, 439 U.S. 89, 91, 99 S.Ct. 399, 58 L.Ed.2d 354 (1978) (citation omitted).

with their customers if the customer chooses arbitration over litigation.[671] New York's highest court rejected the manufacturers' contention that this mandatory, binding arbitration violates their constitutional right to a jury trial.[672]

(6) State Auto Insurance Laws

Many states have enacted "no-fault" auto insurance. For example, New York State requires every vehicle owner to provide himself and certain others with compensation for economic loss resulting from injuries occasioned by the use or operation of that vehicle, regardless of fault.[673] The insurer is statutorily-required to arbitrate disputes as to benefits if the claimant chooses arbitration over litigation.[674] When insurers challenged this requirement on a number of federal and state constitutional grounds, a federal court abstained from ruling on whether the requirement conflicts with the state constitutional right to a jury trial.[675]

Some states mandate that certain auto insurance policies contain arbitration clauses.[676]

(7) Attorney Fee Disputes

Some states require lawyers to arbitrate fee disputes with their clients if the client chooses arbitration over litigation.[677] A federal court rejected the contention that this mandatory, yet binding, arbitration violates the lawyer's constitutional right to a jury trial.[678] The court held that by accepting a license to practice law the lawyer waived his or her jury trial right for these sorts of disputes.[679]

---

671. N.Y.Gen.Bus.L. § 198–a(k),(m) (1988); Lyeth v. Chrysler Corp., 929 F.2d 891 (2d Cir.1991).

672. Motor Vehicle Mfrs.Ass'n v. State, 75 N.Y.2d 175, 551 N.Y.S.2d 470, 550 N.E.2d 919 (1990).

673. N.Y.Ins.L. § 5103 (1985).

674. Id. § 5106(b).

675. Country–Wide Ins. Co. v. Harnett, 426 F.Supp. 1030, 1033–34 (S.D.N.Y. 1977)("Since this is a novel and important issue as to which the state law is evolving, it would appear that this Court should exercise its discretion to refuse to decide this pendent issue of state law.")

676. See, e.g., Steven M. Zipper, Note, Legislatively Mandated Arbitration in Oregon: The Unconstitutionality of the Unin-sured Motorist Arbitration and Personal Injury Protection Arbitration Statutes, 31 Willamette L.Rev. 737 (1995).

677. Anderson v. Elliott, 555 A.2d 1042 (Me.1989); In re LiVolsi, 85 N.J. 576, 428 A.2d 1268 (N.J.1981).

678. Kelley Drye & Warren v. Murray Indus., 623 F.Supp. 522, 525, 527 (D.N.J. 1985) (by voluntarily subjecting itself to the disciplinary jurisdiction of state Supreme Court, law firm has relinquished its Seventh Amendment right to jury trial in favor of arbitration where client elects latter under state Bar rule).

679. Id.

Chapter 3

NEGOTIATION

Table of Sections

Research References:

Key Number System: Compromise and Settlement ⊙ 1 et seq. (to(89))

Am Jur 2d, Alternative Dispute Resolution §§ 1 et seq.; Bankruptcy § 2279; Brokers §§ 227, 231; Contracts § 44; Job Discrimination §§ 1162–1167; Labor and Labor Relations §§ 715–722; Landlord and Tenant §§ 154, 355; Pollution Control § 201

Corpus Juris Secundum, Agency §§ 34, 212, 236; Bills and Notes, Letters of Credit §§ 143–147; Landlord and Tenant § 12; Railroads § 252; Treaties § 4

ALR Index: Alternative Dispute Resolution

ALR Digest: Arbitration §§ 1 et seq.; Bills and Notes §§ 82–85

Am Jur Legal Forms 2d, Attorneys at Law § 30:52; Labor and Labor Relations §§ 159:224, 159:535, 159:875

57 Am Jur Trials 255, Alternative Dispute Resolution: Employment Law; 53 Am Jur Trials 1, Evaluation and Settlement of Personal Injury and Wrongful Death Cases

25 POF2d 333, Good Faith in Collective Bargaining; 25 POF2d 241, Collective Bargaining Impasse

A. NEGOTIATION CONTEXTS

Table of Sections

§ 3.1 Dispute Negotiation and Transactional Negotiation

To negotiate is to "communicate or confer with another to arrive at the settlement of some matter."[1] So defined, negotiation is pervasive. Nearly everyone negotiates nearly every day. Lawyers negotiate especially frequently. There may be nothing more important to a lawyer's success than negotiation skills.

Some, but not all, negotiation relates to a *dispute*.[2] Negotiation is the most frequently used process of dispute-resolution and is the foundation for other important processes of dispute-resolution, such as *mediation* which is the focus of Chapter 4. The negotiation of disputes is the subject of this chapter.

Negotiation *un*related to any dispute is commonplace. Such *transactional* negotiation often precedes deals such as the hiring of an employee or the sale of a home or business. Transactional negotiation is central to the practices of many lawyers. It is not, however, a subject of this book. This book surveys Alternative Dispute Resolution, so this chapter focuses on the negotiation of disputes.[3]

---

§ 3.1

1. Webster's Third New International Dictionary 1514 (Merriam–Webster 1971).

2. See § 1.2 (defining dispute).

3. For surveys of legal negotiation generally, see, e.g., Donald G. Gifford, Legal

Dispute negotiation is more likely than transactional negotiation to be *zero-sum* negotiation, *i.e.*, the better a deal is for one party, the worse it is for the other party.[4] Dispute negotiation is less likely than transactional negotiation to involve parties who want or expect their relationship to continue after the negotiation.[5] Both these factors make dispute negotiation typically more adversarial and competitive than transactional negotiation, which tends to be more cooperative and problem-solving.[6]

§ 3.2 Dispute Negotiation and Lawyers

Most dispute negotiation occurs without the involvement of lawyers. Usually, the disputants—such as family members or co-workers—negotiate on their own. Only a small fraction of disputes ever come to the attention of lawyers and many of these disputes go to binding *adjudication*,[7] *i.e.*, *litigation*[8] or *arbitration*.[9] Thus, lawyers are likely to be involved in only the negotiation of a narrow class of disputes: those in litigation or arbitration, and those that are likely to go to litigation or arbitration if negotiation fails to reach a settlement. Negotiation of these disputes can be called *settlement negotiation*. Because of its importance to lawyers, settlement negotiation is emphasized in this chapter.

The reasoning of this chapter generally applies to both settlement negotiation of disputes headed to litigation and settlement negotiation of disputes headed to arbitration. To avoid wordiness and cumbersome sentence structure, however, the rest of this chapter is written entirely in terms of disputes headed to litigation.

Settlement negotiation is, in three respects, profoundly different from most other negotiation. First, settlement negotiation differs from much other negotiation simply because an agent is typically involved.[10] There will necessarily be interaction between principal and agent (client and lawyer) and there may be conflict between them. This interaction

---

Negotiation: Theory and Applications (1989); Larry L. Tepley, Legal Negotiation in a Nutshell (1992); Gerald R. Williams, Legal Negotiation and Settlement (1983).

4. Gifford, supra note 3, at 40. Zero-sum negotiation is discussed in § 3.8.

5. Gifford, supra note 3, at 40. The effect of continuing relationships on negotiation is discussed in § 3.24.

6. Accordingly, this chapter devotes more attention to the adversarial/competitive approach to negotiation, see §§ 3.15—3.22, and less attention to the cooperative and problem-solving approaches, see §§ 3.23—3.30, than it would if its subject were negotiation generally, rather than dispute negotiation in particular.

§ 3.2

7. Adjudication is the process by which somebody (the adjudicator) decides the result of a dispute. Rather than the disputing parties agreeing on the result of the dispute, as in negotiation, adjudication is the adjudicator telling the parties the result. See § 1.5(a), n.12.

8. Litigation is adjudication in a court or other government forum. See § 1.5(a).

9. Arbitration is adjudication in a private, *i.e.*, non-government, forum. See §§ 1.6(c) & 2.1—2.53.

10. See generally Ronald J. Gilson & Robert H. Mnookin, Disputing Through Agents: Cooperation and Conflict Between Lawyers in Litigation, 94 Colum.L.Rev. 509 (1994). Agency law governs the circumstances under which a lawyer has the power to bind a client to a settlement. See § 3.40.

affects approaches to negotiation,[11] preparation for negotiation,[12] and the choice of whether to settle or litigate.[13] In short, the relationship between lawyer and client thoroughly affects, and is affected by, settlement negotiation.

The next two sections address the other two ways in which settlement negotiation differs from most other negotiation.

§ 3.3 The Shadow of the Law

Settlement negotiation is negotiation about the sale of a claim by Plaintiff to Defendant. Claims, though, differ from other saleable assets in the legal consequences of not agreeing on price. If a car, for example, is not sold because the negotiators do not agree on price, the potential buyer will keep its money and the potential seller will keep its car. Nobody will force a sale. In contrast, if a claim is not sold because the negotiators do not agree on a price, the plaintiff can force a sale through litigation. The court's judgment will transfer (or "sell") the claim from Plaintiff to Defendant and will set the price Defendant must pay. This impending "forced sale" looms over settlement negotiation. Settlement negotiation is conducted "in the shadow of the law" because the negotiators' expectations about the results of litigation, *i.e.*, the forced sale, shape the negotiators' attitudes toward various settlement terms.[14] Negotiators' expectations about the price of a forced sale, if it comes to that, influence the price at which they will agree to settle. The "price" of a claim, whether agreed to in settlement or imposed by litigation, is not necessarily an amount of money. The price includes whatever the plaintiff receives in exchange for the claim.

While settlement negotiation is conducted in the shadow of the law, that is not true of all dispute negotiation. Ordinary day-to-day disputes one has with family members, co-workers, etc., will never be the subject of a court's judgment. Accordingly, negotiation of these disputes occurs beyond the shadow of the law. Therefore, law shapes most dispute negotiations very little but shapes a few of them very much. Those few tend to be the dispute negotiations involving lawyers.

§ 3.4 Bilateral Monopoly

Settlement negotiation is negotiation about the sale of a claim by Plaintiff to Defendant. The potential market for this claim typically consists of only one buyer (Defendant) and only one seller (Plaintiff). That is a bilateral monopoly, *i.e.*, the negotiating parties can only get what they seek by dealing with each other. In transactional negotiation, by contrast, sellers can play potential buyers off against each other, with credible statements like "you will have to raise your offer or I will sell to

11. See §§ 3.14—3.30.

12. See §§ 3.33—3.37.

13. See § 3.6.

§ 3.3

14. See § 3.11.

somebody else." And in transactional negotiation a buyer can often buy what she wants from a number of sellers.

In settlement negotiation, Defendant cannot "shop around" to find some other plaintiff who is charging less; only Plaintiff can provide what Defendant seeks, an end to Plaintiff's suit. Similarly, Plaintiff cannot shop around to find some other defendant willing to pay more.[15] The parties are stuck with each other. This bilateral monopoly characteristic strongly affects settlement negotiation and gives it a very different feel from most transactional negotiation.[16]

B.   THE SETTLEMENT/LITIGATION CHOICE

Table of Sections

§ 3.5   Valuing a Case

Litigation usually ends in a settlement, rather than proceeding to a trial's verdict or other conclusive ruling by the court.[17] Why do litigants typically settle, rather than pursue litigation to completion? Settlement is the sale of a claim by Plaintiff to Defendant. Sales occur when both buyer and seller believe that their interests are better served by the sale than by its absence. More specifically, settlements occur when both Plaintiff and Defendant believe that their interests are better served by the settlement than by litigating further.[18]

(a) Factors

Consider a litigant (the client, not the lawyer) who is thinking about making a settlement offer or accepting one made by the other side. In deciding whether to make or accept an offer, the client tries to foresee

---

§ 3.4

15. There are exceptions. With respect to some claims, Plaintiff can shop around. Breach-of-contract claims, for example, are assignable so that a merchant may find many collection agencies competing to buy the merchant's contract claims. See Restatement (Second) of Contracts § 317(2) (1981). Other claims, including many statutory claims and most tort claims for injury to person or reputation, are not assignable. This restraint on alienability is partially overcome by the contingency fee contract in which the plaintiff "sells" part of her claim to her lawyer. See § 3.6(b)(2). The lawyer pays, not with money, but with services.

16. See § 3.12. See also Richard A. Posner, Economic Analysis of Law 68–69, 607–09 (5th ed.1998).

§ 3.5

17. One oft-cited study found that about two-thirds of all cases filed in court settle. Many of the rest are resolved through adjudication (such as summary judgment, motion to dismiss and arbitration) and only about seven percent receive a full trial. Herbert M. Kritzer, Adjudication to Settlement: Shading in the Gray, 70 Judicature 161, 162–64 (1986). Even when it does not result in a settlement, negotiation often provides benefits for both parties. For example, negotiation can result in agreements that narrow and define the issues for trial or in agreements regarding discovery that save money for both parties.

18. The same point applies to settling disputes not yet in litigation, although the discussion that follows is cast in terms of settling disputes already in litigation.

the results of further litigation. Clients often ask their lawyers for help in this, *e.g.*, "how is a court likely to rule on my case?" Lawyers often resist making such predictions. Lawyers know that the results of litigation are difficult to predict,[19] especially when one "rolls the dice" by going to trial with a jury. So lawyers are understandably cautious about giving their clients predictions about the results of litigation. If the prediction turns out to have been overly optimistic, the client's expectations will have been raised so the client may conclude that the lawyer is a bad litigator for not achieving the predicted result. As a result, lawyers may have a tendency to be cautiously pessimistic in any predictions they do make to clients.[20]

Clients are not well-served by lawyers who resist predicting the outcome of litigation or whose predictions are overly pessimistic. The client thinking about making a settlement offer or accepting one made by the other side cannot make an informed decision without realistic expectations about the results of further litigation. The more complete and accurate the lawyer's prediction of those results, the better the client's decision-making will generally be.[21]

What is the likelihood the case will be dismissed before trial? If it does go to trial, what is the likelihood of a plaintiff's verdict? If Plaintiff does win a verdict, what remedy will the court order? How much money can a jury be expected to award? What is the likelihood that any award of damages will actually be paid? All these questions must be considered by the lawyer advising a client about a settlement offer.

These questions, however, do not exhaust the relevant considerations. Not only must lawyer and client compare the settlement offer to the likely results of litigation, they must consider what will happen on the way to those results. In particular, they must consider the litigation process itself. That process will cost the client additional time and, usually, additional legal fees. The litigation process may involve a grueling deposition of the client by hostile attorneys, or a trial in which the client's family secrets are exposed to the public. In short, the process of litigation can be devastating to a client, while the process of settling is usually quick and painless.

On the other hand, pursuing litigation to its conclusion can bring great satisfaction to the client. Some clients care less about the dollars that can be exchanged in settlement and more about the public vindica-

19. See e.g., Douglas E. Rosenthal, Lawyer and Client: Who's in Charge? 200–08 (1974)(survey of experienced lawyers reviewing identical case files revealing widely varying estimates of settlement value).

20. See Gifford, supra note 3, at 187–88.

21. We can imagine exceptions to this generalization. The lawyer may correctly realize that her client is congenitally over-optimistic and just refuses to hear that the case is anything less than a sure-winner. See § 3.6(a). The client refuses to process

and digest information indicating weakness in his case. The lawyer may have to emphasize the negative to offset the client's over-optimism. The client's decision-making may be better if the lawyer "slants" what she tells her client than if the lawyer discusses the case in a balanced, even-handed manner. On the other hand, a "client is entitled to straightforward advice expressing the lawyer's honest assessment." Model Rule of Professional Conduct 2.1, comment 1 (1999).

tion that comes from a favorable verdict. Other clients want to "make law" with a favorable precedent, or develop a reputation for being fierce litigators in order to intimidate future adversaries. And a few clients just like to litigate.

So the choice of whether to make a settlement offer (and if so what offer?) or to accept an offer made by the other side is often complex. It can be a difficult judgment call. Lawyers and clients agonize over the settlement/litigation choice. Sometimes the results of litigation lead to regret: "we should have taken their settlement offer" or "we should have made them a better offer." When one does settle, one never knows for sure what would have happened had litigation continued.

(b) Timing

Plaintiffs always face the settlement/litigation choice. At any time, from before a complaint is drafted until a judgment is satisfied,[22] the plaintiff can drop the case (sell the claim) in exchange for whatever consideration the defendant is willing to pay. Defendants, on the other hand, cannot unilaterally end litigation. Settlement requires the plaintiff's consent. But the defendant always has the option of making a more generous offer to the plaintiff. This option faces the defendant from the moment it learns of the dispute until a judgment is satisfied. In short, settlement options are ever-present for both parties.

The question of whether to make or accept a settlement offer should be considered, and reconsidered, throughout litigation because the answer may change during litigation.[23] The pleadings, discovery or the court's pre-trial rulings may influence the lawyer's prediction about the likely results of litigation. The passage of time may have changed the client's attitude toward the opposing party or the dispute. The question of whether to make or accept a settlement offer should be considered anew in light of such developments.

(c) Expected Value

A rational litigant facing the settlement/litigation choice will behave like a rational person facing any choice, *i.e.*, the litigant will assess the costs and benefits of each option and choose the one with the highest expected value.[24] What counts as a "cost" or "benefit," and how much it

---

22. Settlement can occur after a court has rendered judgment, but this is unlikely to nullify the precedential effect of that judgment or any opinion written by the court. Compare U.S. Bancorp Mortgage Co., v. Bonner Mall Partnership, 513 U.S. 18, 115 S.Ct. 386, 130 L.Ed.2d 233 (1994); Re Memorial Hospital of Iowa County, Inc., 862 F.2d 1299 (7th Cir.1988)("the judicial system ought not allow the social value of that precedent, created at cost to the public and other litigants, to be a bargaining chip in the process of settlement . * * * If the parties want to avoid stare decisis and pre-

clusive effects, they need only settle before the district court renders a decision, an outcome our approach encourages.") with Neary v. Regents of University of California, 3 Cal.4th 273, 10 Cal.Rptr.2d 859, 834 P.2d 119 (1992)(allowing parties to stipulate to reversal of trial court's judgment).

23. See § 3.36.

24. The expected value of an outcome is the value of that outcome multiplied by the probability that it will occur. For more on expected utility theory and its application to negotiation, see Chris Guthrie, Better Set-counts, will be determined by the litigant's own set of preferences. Whatever those preferences, they can be combined with predictions about the consequences of choosing each option to determine which option has the highest expected value to the litigant.

This can be illustrated with an example. Suppose a rational plaintiff owns lakefront property and sues to enjoin Defendant's pollution of the lake. Time is Plaintiff's only cost of litigating because her lawyer is working without pay (pro bono). Plaintiff's lawyer's best estimate is that there is a ten-percent chance of obtaining the injunction and a ninety-percent chance of a defendant's verdict. Assume that no other results are possible from litigation and that Defendant is certain to comply with an injunction. Assume also that Plaintiff is *risk-neutral*.[25]

Suppose Defendant offers Plaintiff $10,000 to settle the case. To decide whether to accept this offer, our rational Plaintiff must convert to dollars the values she places on:

-the time it will take her to complete litigation, and

-ending the pollution.

If Plaintiff values the time to complete litigation at $2,000 and ending the pollution at $80,000, then Plaintiff should settle because:

$$10,000 > (80,000 \times .1) - 2,000$$

$$10,000 > 8,000 - 2,000$$

$$10,000 > 6,000$$

The benefit to Plaintiff from settling is the $10,000 payment. The benefit to Plaintiff of not settling is an end to the pollution (worth $80,000) multiplied by the probability of attaining this result (.1) and then subtracting the time needed to attain this result (worth $2000). As the calculations show, the benefit to Plaintiff of litigating is only $6000. As that is less than the $10,000 benefit of settling, Plaintiff should settle.

If the preceding assumptions hold except that Plaintiff values ending the pollution at $150,000, then Plaintiff should litigate because:

$$10,000 < (150,000 \times .1) - 2,000$$

$$10,000 < 15,000 - 2,000$$

$$10,000 < 13,000$$

If the preceding assumptions hold except that Plaintiff values the time to complete litigation at $6,000, then Plaintiff should settle because:

$$10,000 > (150,000 \times .1) - 6,000$$

$$10,000 > 15,000 - 6,000$$

$$10,000 > 9,000$$

---

tle Than Sorry: The Regret Aversion Theory of Litigation Behavior, 1999 U.Ill.L.Rev. 43, 47–54.

25. See § 3.6(c).

Whether many actual litigants behave anything like our hypothetical rational litigant is an important topic for research.[26]

Expected value calculations get more complicated as more factors are added. The lake-pollution example is extraordinarily simple because it assumes only two possible rulings by the court: injunction or defendant's verdict. In most litigation, by contrast, the possible judicial rulings are endless. If there is a claim for money damages, the calculations would have to assign a probability that the court will award $1, a probability that the court will award $2, a probability that the court will award $3, and so on. Of course, it would be silly to perform such elaborate calculations because the time spent doing so would yield little additional accuracy. On the other hand, a rational choice about settling a claim for money damages does require an estimate of the likely dollar amount of a verdict. Lawyers often formulate such estimates by reading reports of similar cases. Especially in the personal-injury field, lawyers can obtain published reports showing in great detail the facts and the dollar amounts of verdicts in various categories of cases.

The lake-pollution example's simplicity is also achieved by assuming away questions about:

—attitudes toward risk,[27]

—legal fees[28] and other financial costs of litigating,

—non-financial costs of litigating, such as lost privacy, and

—benefits of litigating, such as a favorable precedent or an imposing reputation.

Each of these questions represents an additional factor that must be added to the rational litigant's calculation.[29] The rational litigant must, at least implicitly, place a numerical value on each. The numerical value will not necessarily be expressed in terms of dollars because not all tradeoffs involve money. There may be a tradeoff between, for example, time and publicity. So the rational litigant must determine where to strike the balance, *i.e.*, how much time is worth how much publicity. The rational litigant must, at least implicitly, quantify the value she places on both time and publicity.

§ 3.6 Disagreements Between Lawyer and Client

(a) Generally

The previous section analyzes the settlement/litigation choice and

---

26. For discussions of cognitive psychological research and its implications for negotiation, see Robert H. Mnookin, Why Negotiations Fail: An Exploration of Barriers to the Resolution of Conflict, 8 Ohio St.J.on Disp.Resol. 235, 243–47 (1993); Guthrie, supra note 24, at 54–59.

27. See § 3.6(c).

28. See § 3.6(b).

29. See § 3.5(a).

shows that choice to be often complex and difficult.[30] Given its complexity and difficulty, one should not be surprised that the settlement/litigation choice often provokes disagreements between lawyers and their clients. Many lawyers tell of clients who were so convinced of the merit of their cases that they would not believe their lawyers' warnings that a court might rule against them. Of course, as the lawyers tell these stories, the court did rule against the client, despite the lawyer's best efforts to persuade the client to take a very good settlement offer.

In many cases, the client is overly optimistic about the expected results of litigation and the lawyer is trying, unsuccessfully, to serve as an "agent of reality" who brings the client's expectations down to earth. Conversely, there are also cases in which the client benefits from disregarding the lawyer's advice to settle. And there are cases in which clients settle against their lawyers' advice to keep litigating. The fundamental point is that clients do not always follow their lawyer's advice with regard to the settlement/litigation choice.

A client and lawyer may disagree on the settlement/litigation choice because of "honest disagreements" like the ones just discussed. Or they may disagree because their interests diverge. Two common causes of this divergence are the method by which the lawyer is paid,[31] and the client's and lawyer's different attitudes toward risk. These two topics are discussed in the following two sections, which are followed by a discussion of the lawyer's professional responsibility when she and her client disagree about the settlement/litigation choice.

(b) Legal Fees

(1) Hourly Billing

Lawyers who bill by the hour are thought to resist settlement early in litigation.[32] Pleadings, discovery and motion practice can generate lots of billable hours. Settling early in the case deprives the lawyer of this income. Of course, there are only so many hours a lawyer can bill, so it may seem that early settlement is fine for a lawyer who has other cases. The hours that would have been billed on the settling case are, instead, billed on another case. But this fails to account for firm structure. Most lawyers who bill by the hour are not solo practitioners; they are owners (partners) or employees (associates) of a firm. While an individual lawyer can only bill so many hours, there is almost no limit to the number of hours a firm can bill because the firm can continue to add lawyers. For a law firm then, it seems that there is a financial incentive to avoid early settlement when billing by the hour.

§ 3.6

30. See § 3.5.

31. For overviews of the incentives created by these methods, see Geoffrey P. Miller, Some Agency Problems in Settlement, 16 J.Legal.Stud. 189 (1987); George B. Shepherd & Morgan Cloud, Time and Money: Discovery Leads to Hourly Billing, 1999 U.Ill.L.Rev. 91, 99–119.

32. Edward Brunet & Charles B. Craver, Alternative Dispute Resolution: The Advocate's Perspective 35 (1997). See generally William G. Ross, The Honest Hour: The Ethics of Time–Based Billing by Attorneys (1996).

There is, however, a significant constraint on a firm that seeks to prolong litigation in order to increase billable hours. That check is competition from other lawyers. Clients who believe their law firms are needlessly prolonging litigation can simply switch to another firm. This switch can occur during a single case or before the next case. Clients who litigate frequently, such as insurance companies, may be particularly aggressive in playing law firms off against each other to keep legal fees down. Clients who litigate rarely may be more vulnerable to lawyers who prolong litigation to increase their billable hours. It is doubtful whether such clients can easily obtain reliable information about the cost-effectiveness of various law firms, although a few litigators may have deserved reputations for cost-effectiveness. Many clients who litigate rarely do not face issues of hourly billing because they hire a lawyer on a contingent fee.[33]

(2) Contingency Fees

Assume that Plaintiff's fee agreement entitles her lawyer to receive a contingency fee of one-fourth of the recovery, however that recovery is obtained. Also assume that Plaintiff's lawyer must bear the expenses of litigation (photocopying, travel, fees charged by courts, investigators, expert witnesses, etc.), regardless of the outcome of litigation. These costs will be higher if litigation continues through trial than if a settlement is obtained before trial. Thus Plaintiff's lawyer has a financial incentive to settle even at an amount somewhat less than the expected result of trial.[34] In other words, Plaintiff's lawyer has an incentive to settle at a lower price than is in the client's interest.

Consider an unrealistically simple example.[35] Plaintiff's lawyer "expects" the case to yield a $100,000 judgment because she predicts a fifty-percent chance of a $200,000 judgment and a fifty-percent chance of a judgment for Defendant. If the lawyer's fee agreement entitles her to one-fourth of any recovery, then she expects to earn $25,000 if she pursues litigation. Suppose Defendant offers $80,000 to settle the case. Assuming that Plaintiff is *risk-neutral*,[36] and ignoring the *time-value of money*,[37] Plaintiff's interests would not be served by accepting this offer. Plaintiff would rather have three-fourths of $100,000 ($75,000) than three-fourths of $80,000 ($60,000). Accepting the settlement offer would, however, be in the interests of Plaintiff's lawyer if the cost of litigating further is expected to be, for example, $10,000. By settling, Plaintiff's lawyer will get one-fourth of $80,000 ($20,000). By litigating further, Plaintiff's lawyer expects to get one-fourth of $100,000 ($25,000) but will

33. Individual plaintiffs in personal injury actions nearly always pay their lawyers with contingent fees and often pay that way in other common actions, too. See Samuel R. Gross & Kent D. Syverud, Don't Try: Civil Jury Verdicts in a System Geared to Settlement, 44 UCLA L.Rev. 1, 16 (1996).

34. This is true even when accounting for the *time-value of money*. For more on that topic, see § 3.9.

35. See § 3.5(c)(discussing more complicated and realistic models).

36. See § 3.6(c).

37. See § 3.9.

have to pay $10,000 in litigation costs. That leaves $15,000 which is less than the $20,000 the lawyer gets by settling.

The Model Rules of Professional Conduct permit lawyers to pay the expenses of litigation only for indigent clients.[38] But, no matter who the client, "a lawyer may advance court costs and expenses of litigation the repayment of which may be contingent on the outcome of the matter."[39] Accordingly, many plaintiffs' contingency fee agreements provide that the lawyer shall bear the costs of litigation if there is no recovery but that any recovery shall be applied first to reimburse the lawyer for expenses, then the rest of the recovery is divided according to a formula, such as three-fourths for the client and one-fourth for the lawyer. Such an arrangement also gives the plaintiff's lawyer an incentive to settle at a lower price than is in the client's interest.[40] This divergence of interests is, however, less pronounced than in the situation of an indigent plaintiff whose lawyer pays the expenses of litigation even if the plaintiff recovers from the defendant.

While the contingent fee arrangements discussed thus far give the plaintiff's lawyer an incentive to settle at a lower price than is in the client's interest, this divergence of interests can be narrowed with a contingency fee agreement that gives the lawyer a higher percentage if the recovery is obtained through trial than if it is obtained through settlement. Accordingly, many contingency agreements give the lawyer forty percent of trial proceeds but thirty-three percent of settlement proceeds.[41]

(3) Retainers and Other Fixed–Fee Arrangements

Some lawyers agree to handle all the client's litigation during a certain time period for a fixed payment. Such "retainer" arrangements give the lawyer an incentive to settle and the client an incentive to shun settlement. The same can be said of arrangements whereby lawyers agree to handle a particular task, such as a single case or a single part of a single case, for a fixed payment.

(4) Liability Insurance

Many defendants have liability insurance. An insured defendant is entitled to have his insurer pay any settlement or judgment against the defendant up to the amount of the insurance policy. The typical liability

---

38. Model Rule of Professional Conduct 1.8(e)(2)(1999).

39. Model Rule of Professional Conduct 1.8(e)(1)(1999).

40. In the example in the text, assume that Plaintiff's lawyer "expects" a $100,000 judgment because she predicts a fifty-percent chance of a $200,000 judgment and a fifty-percent chance of a judgment for Defendant. If Plaintiff wins, her lawyer will get one-fourth of $190,000 ($47,500) and if Plaintiff loses her lawyer will lose $10,000.

As each of these outcomes is equally likely to occur, the expected value to Plaintiff's lawyer of litigating is (47,500/2) + (−10,000/2) which equals $18,750. That is less than the one-fourth of $80,000 ($20,000) Plaintiff's lawyer will get from a settlement, although not as much less as in the example in the text.

41. Samuel R. Gross & Kent D. Syverud, Getting to No: A Study of Settlement Negotiations and the Selection of Cases for Trial, 90 Mich.L.Rev. 319, 349 n.71 (1991).

insurance policy, however, gives the insurer complete control over settlement and litigation. The insurer hires any lawyer and, within broad limits,[42] the insurer decides whether to make settlement offers and, if so, at what amount. This arrangement can create a divergence between the interests of Defendant and his insurer.

Suppose, for example, that the limit of the insurance policy is $150,000 and Defendant and his insurer each "expect" a $100,000 judgment because each predicts a fifty-percent chance of a $200,000 judgment and a fifty-percent chance of a judgment for Defendant. In this case, the insurer's incentive is to offer Plaintiff at most $100,000, the expected value of the claim, and probably much less than that to strengthen the insurer's reputation as a fierce litigator.[43] While the insurer's incentive is to offer at most $100,000, Defendant's incentive is for his insurer to offer $150,000, the policy limit. The more money offered, the more likely Plaintiff is to accept, and offering $150,000 does not cost Defendant any more than offering $100,000 because it is his insurer's money. Defendant does pay his own money if his insurer's stinginess causes Plaintiff to go trial and Plaintiff wins a judgment in excess of $150,000. Defendant is personally liable for the excess.

(c) Risk Aversion

With regard to litigation, lawyers are *repeat players* while many of their clients are not. A particular lawsuit is likely to be one of many in a lawyer's career but may well be the only one in the client's life. The combination of repeat-player lawyers and *one-shot* clients can lead to disagreements about the settlement/litigation choice because, all other things being equal, one-shotters tend to be more *risk-averse* than repeat-players.

Risk aversion is the willingness to pay for increased certainty. Consider a choice between:

(a) receiving one million dollars, or

(b) flipping a coin and receiving two million dollars if it comes up heads and receiving nothing if it comes up tails.

Choosing (a) reveals risk-aversion. The expected value of each choice is one million dollars because choice (b) entails a fifty-percent chance of receiving two million dollars and a fifty-percent chance of receiving nothing.[44] So a risk-neutral person would find choices (a) and (b) equally appealing.

If choice (a) was $900,000, a *risk-neutral* person would choose (b) with its higher expected value of one million dollars. Yet many people

---

42. Courts have, to some extent, restricted insurers' discretion in settling. Robert E. Keeton & Alan I. Widiss, Insurance Law § 7.8 (1988).

43. The insurer is very much a *repeat player* litigant so it benefits from a reputation that intimidates future adversaries.

44. The expected value of an outcome is the value of that outcome multiplied by the probability that it will occur.

would choose a certain $900,000 over a fifty-percent chance of two million dollars, *i.e.*, they would pay for increased certainty. Risk-aversion manifests itself in countless ways. People reveal their risk-aversion when they buy insurance, or when they invest in bonds rather than stocks. The same person who is risk-averse in some contexts may be *risk-seeking* in another context. Risk-seeking behavior, such as gambling at a casino or in a lottery, is the willingness to pay for decreased certainty.

With respect to a particular lawsuit, one-shot clients tend (ignoring other factors) to be more risk-averse than repeat-player lawyers. That is because of *diversification*. Recall the choice between a certain $900,000 and a fifty-percent coin-flip chance of two million dollars. Now, imagine that this choice is broken down into a million separate choices, each one a choice between ninety cents and a fifty-percent coin-flip chance of two dollars. Many people who would take the certain $900,000 in the first scenario would, in the second scenario, choose the coin flip in each of their million choices. This is a rational response to diversification. Risk is highest when all one's "eggs are in one basket." That is the position of the one-shot client who has an enormous stake in one case and no other cases for diversification. In contrast, the lawyer is faced with something closer to the second scenario of a million coin-flips.[45] The lawyer has a portfolio of cases, much like a diversified investor has a portfolio of stocks. Thus the lawyer is likely to be less risk-averse than the one-shot client. This is especially true if the lawyer, rather than practicing solo, is part of a firm that spreads risk among its lawyers.

The more risk-averse one is, the more likely she is to choose settlement over trial. Consider the unrealistically simple case of a plaintiff with a fifty-percent chance of a verdict awarding her two million dollars and a fifty-percent chance of a defendant's verdict. Recall that risk-aversion is the willingness to pay to increase certainty. Accepting a settlement offer of one million dollars would allow Plaintiff to increase certainty without paying anything because the expected value of the claim she releases (.5 x $2,000,000) is equal to the money she receives. But how much less than one million dollars would Plaintiff accept in settlement? That is the amount Plaintiff is willing to pay to increase certainty. And that amount is higher than it would be if determined by someone less risk-averse. Plaintiff's lawyer, because of diversification, probably is someone less averse to risk than Plaintiff. In short, one-shot clients tend to be more risk-averse than their lawyers and thus more willing to settle. This divergence between client and lawyer may be compounded by the lawyer's desire for trial experience. The lawyer may prefer a million-dollar verdict to a million-dollar settlement because the former will help the lawyer's career more, or at least provide better stories for the grandchildren.

On the other hand, there may be factors offsetting the client's greater risk-aversion. For example, the client may be more confident

---

45. The same is true of repeat-player clients, such as insurance companies.

than the lawyer of a victory at trial,[46] or the client's contingency fee agreement may give her lawyer an incentive to settle at a lower price than is in the client's interests.[47] The mix of factors producing lawyer-client disagreement on the settlement/litigation choice varies from case to case.

(d) Professional Responsibility

When lawyer and client disagree on the settlement/litigation choice, the lawyer must, as a matter of professional ethics, defer to the client. The Model Rules of Professional Conduct provide that "[a] lawyer shall abide by a client's decision whether to accept an offer of settlement of a matter."[48] Presumably, the same applies to a client's decision whether to make a settlement offer.

Lawyers, especially litigators, sometimes need to be reminded that the client is the boss. Legally, the relationship between client and lawyer is one of principal and agent. Unless the principal has given the agent authority to make settlement decisions, the agent lacks the right to do so.[49]

Ultimately, disagreement over the settlement/litigation choice may lead a lawyer to stop working for the client. The lawyer must be aware, though, of limits on the circumstances under which she may terminate representation of a client.[50]

C. NEGOTIATION THEORY

Table of Sections

§ 3.7 Zero–Sum and Positive–Sum

In distinguishing *zero-sum* from *positive-sum* negotiation, a helpful metaphor is the contrast between dividing a pie and expanding it. In zero-sum negotiation, negotiators discuss only how to divide a pie, while in positive-sum negotiation, negotiators find ways to expand the size of the pie. In many negotiations, the negotiators both expand the pie and divide it. In other words, many negotiations have both a positive-sum part and a zero-sum part. Other negotiations are purely zero-sum. Few,

46. See § 3.6(a).

47. See § 3.6(b).

48. Model Rule of Professional Conduct 1.2(a)(1999).

49. See § 3.40.

50. See Model Rule of Professional Conduct 1.16 (1999).

if any, are purely positive-sum.[51]

Many people call zero-sum negotiation *distributive* bargaining and positive-sum negotiation *integrative* bargaining. This book uses the terms zero-sum and positive-sum, but the reader should be prepared to encounter the distributive/integrative terminology elsewhere.

§ 3.8 Zero–Sum

An example of zero-sum negotiation is the settlement of a lawsuit in which the lawyers negotiating on behalf of the parties assume that the only topic for negotiation is the amount of money Defendant will pay Plaintiff. In such a negotiation, any change in the proposed settlement terms results in increased value for one party and decreased value for the other party. This is depicted in Diagram 3–1.

Diagram 3-1

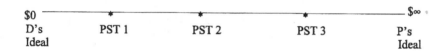

$0   PST 1   PST 2   PST 3 $∞
D's   P's
Ideal   Ideal

The horizontal line represents a continuum of all the possible settlement terms, from no payment (on the left) to payment of an infinite amount of money (on the right). Any place along the line, that is, any dollar amount, is a possible settlement term. Three possible settlement terms (PSTs) are shown. From Defendant's perspective, PST 1 is better than PST 2 and PST 2 is better than PST 3. Plaintiff's perspective is exactly the opposite: PST 1 is worse than PST 2 and PST 2 worse than PST 3. This complete opposition of interests applies to all possible settlement terms and is the essence of zero-sum negotiation. Any change in proposed settlement terms results in increased value for one party and decreased value for the other party. The more of the pie Plaintiff gets, the less Defendant gets, and vice versa.

In zero-sum negotiation, the interests of Plaintiff and Defendant are diametrically opposed with respect to all possible settlement terms. This does not necessarily mean, however, that settlement must harm one party or the other. It may be that settling at, for example, $50,000 benefits both parties *when compared to not settling at all*.[52] Plaintiff would rather take $50,000 than continue litigating and Defendant would

§ 3.7

51. David A. Lax & James K. Sebenius, The Manager as Negotiator: Bargaining for Cooperation and Competitive Gain 33 (1986)("No matter how much creative problem solving enlarges the pie, it must still be divided; value that has been created must be claimed.") Accord Leonard L. Riskin &

James E. Westbrook, Dispute Resolution and Lawyers 350–51 (2d ed.1997); Gerald B. Wetlaufer, The Limits of Integrative Bargaining, 85 Geo.L.J. 369, 373 (1996).

§ 3.8

52. See §§ 3.11—3.13.

rather pay $50,000 than continue litigating. Given these preferences, both parties make themselves better off by settling at $50,000 even though their negotiation is zero-sum.[53] In short, zero-sum negotiation can be quite rewarding to both parties.[54]

§ 3.9 Positive–Sum (With an Example on the Time Value of Money)

In zero-sum negotiation, negotiators discuss only how to divide a pie, while in positive-sum negotiation, negotiators find ways to expand the size of the pie they are dividing. Positive-sum negotiation finds those possible settlement terms that are better *for both parties* than other possible settlement terms. In many negotiations, the negotiators both expand the pie and divide it. In other words, many negotiations have both a positive-sum part and a zero-sum part. Other negotiations are purely zero-sum. Few, if any, are purely positive-sum.[55]

An example of positive-sum negotiation is the settlement negotiation discussed in the previous section,[56] with one change. The lawyers negotiating on behalf of the parties now assume that there are two topics for negotiation: the amount of money to be paid by Defendant to Plaintiff and the time of that payment. Diagram 3–2 adds to Diagram to 3–1 to reflect the additional consideration of time.

53. Of course, the results of trial might turn out better for one party than a $50,000 settlement. But at the pertinent time, the time at which the proposed settlement can be accepted, accepting it is better for both parties than the *expected value* of going to trial.

54. See § 3.12, especially the discussion of Diagram 3–3.

§ 3.9

55. See § 3.7, n.51.

56. See § 3.8.

Diagram 3-2

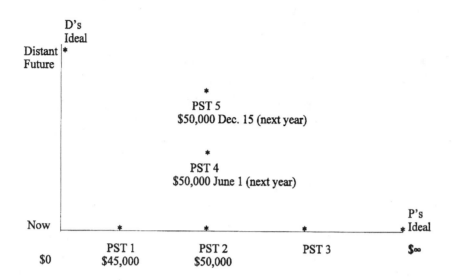

Along the left side of Diagram 3–2 is a vertical line not present in Diagram 3–1. The vertical line represents the time of payment by Defendant to Plaintiff, with the bottom of the line representing an immediate payment and the top of the line representing payment in the distant future. Any time in between is a point on the line.

Two of the possible settlement terms from Diagram 3–1 have been assigned values. PST 1 is an immediate payment of $45,000 and PST 2 is an immediate payment of $50,000. Two additional possible settlement terms are shown. PST 4 is a payment of $50,000 to occur on June 1 of next year and PST 5 is a payment of $50,000 to occur on December 15 of next year.

In general,[57] those receiving payment of a fixed amount of money prefer the payment as soon as possible, while those making payment prefer to delay payment as long as possible. (If it was otherwise, interest rates would be negative.) Accordingly, Diagram 3–2 reflects an assumption that Plaintiff prefers to receive the settlement payment as soon as possible, while Defendant prefers to delay paying as long as possible. In other words, Plaintiff's ideal settlement would be in the lower right corner of Diagram 3–2 (large payment now) while Defendant's ideal settlement would be in the upper left corner (low payment in distant future).

Compare the possible settlement terms involving $50,000. From Defendant's perspective, PST 5 is better than PST 4 and PST 4 is better

57. Tax laws may create exceptions to this generalization. See Javed A. Khokhar, Tax Aspects of Settlements and Judgments (Tax Management Portfolio No. 522–2nd, 1999). See also § 3.26(b).

than PST 2. Plaintiff's perspective is exactly the opposite: PST 5 is worse than PST 4 and PST 4 is worse than PST 2. This complete opposition of interests applies to all possible settlement terms involving payment of $50,000. In other words, the negotiation about time is zero-sum. Any change in the proposed time of payment results in increased value for one party and decreased value for the other.

Considered in isolation, both the amount of payment and the time of payment are topics for zero-sum negotiation. But considering them together may create a positive-sum negotiation. Compare, for example, PST 4 and PST 1. The choice between these two possible terms involves a tradeoff between time and amount. It may be that Plaintiff and Defendant weight (value) this tradeoff differently so that, for example, each prefers PST 4 to PST 1. Plaintiff may prefer receiving $50,000 next June 1 to receiving $45,000 now, and Defendant may prefer paying $50,000 next June 1 to paying $45,000 now.[58] One might say the issue of time is more important to Defendant while the issue of amount is more important to Plaintiff.[59] These differing preferences about time and money enable this negotiation to be positive sum. Because of these differing preferences, both parties prefer PST 4 to PST 1. That *both parties* prefer some possible settlement terms to other possible settlement terms is the essence of positive-sum negotiation.

If the negotiating lawyers had considered only the *amount* of the settlement payment, and assumed immediate payment, they might have agreed on $45,000 (PST 1). This would have squandered an opportunity to expand the pie. By choosing "$50,000 next June 1" over "$45,000 now", the negotiators created additional value, making each party better off than it would have been had the issue of time not been considered. The key to creating this additional value was considering an additional issue. Positive-sum negotiation almost never occurs if only one issue is considered, especially if that issue is the amount of money Defendant will pay Plaintiff. Considering multiple issues allows for the possibility of finding an issue on which the parties' interests coincide.[60] It also allows for what is often called *logrolling*.[61] Suppose Plaintiff cares a lot about Issue A, but not much about Issue B, while Defendant cares a lot about Issue B, but not much about Issue A. The parties can create value by having Defendant concede on Issue A in exchange for Plaintiff's concession on Issue B. Each party gives on something she cares little about to get what she cares about a lot. This is what happened in the example of choosing "$50,000 next June 1" over "$45,000 now." Plaintiff conceded on the issue of time, while Defendant conceded on the issue of amount. This sort of trade, logrolling, is the basis of most positive-sum negotia-

---

58. This might occur because Defendant—perhaps a large corporation—can invest $45,000 now with confidence that its investment will be worth more than $50,000 on June 1 of next year, while if Plaintiff—perhaps an individual of modest means—borrowed $45,000 now, the lender would insist on payment of more than $50,000 when the loan came due next June 1.

59. More precisely, Plaintiff's discount rate is lower than Defendant's.

60. See § 3.26(b).

61. Logrolling is discussed further in §§ 3.26(c) & 3.28.

tion. It works, even where the parties disagree on every issue, if they prioritize the issues differently.

The example of positive-sum negotiation just discussed, choosing "$50,000 next June 1", is exceptionally simple. In adding the issue of time, the lawyers still assumed that there would be only one payment by Defendant to Plaintiff. Expanding the options to include a series of installment payments might create still more value than that created by delaying a single payment. Settlements involving a series of installment payments are quite common, often have tax advantages, and are generally known as "structured settlements."[62]

The positive-sum negotiations discussed thus far involve nothing other than the payment of money. Looking beyond money opens countless other possibilities for creating additional value through negotiation. A settlement might involve the transfer of real estate, goods or intangible property, the performance of services, or even an admission of wrongdoing and an apology. The more topics considered, the more likely the negotiators are to find opportunities for positive-sum negotiation.

§ 3.10   Positive–Sum Negotiation is Not Always Worthwhile, or Even Possible

Negotiators do not have complete control over whether their negotiation is zero-sum or positive-sum. The interests of the parties may be so diametrically opposed that their negotiation must be zero-sum, no matter how sincerely the negotiators seek to find a positive-sum aspect to it. On the other hand, the interests of the parties may present opportunities for positive-sum negotiation that go unexploited because the negotiators do not find them. In such a case, there is a zero-sum negotiation in a positive-sum situation. To put it another way, positive-sum situations can yield either positive-sum or zero-sum negotiations, while zero-sum situations can yield only zero-sum negotiations. Having a zero-sum negotiation in a positive-sum situation is not necessarily a failure. The value created by exploiting a positive-sum opportunity may be lower than the value of the time and effort required to find it.

There is widespread agreement among negotiation theorists on the proposition that some situations are zero-sum, while others are positive-sum. Disagreement arises in generalizations about the frequency of each type of situation. This, in turn, is the source of some of the disagreement about the relative merits of different approaches to negotiation.[63] These

62. For an example of one, see § 3.39. See generally Richard G. Halpern, Structured Settlements in Henry G. Miller, The Art of Advocacy: Settlement ch.10 (1999).

§ 3.10

63. Compare, e.g., Carrie Menkel–Meadow, Toward Another View of Legal Negotiation: The Structure of Problem Solving, 31 UCLA L.Rev. 754, 784 (1984) ("true zero sum games are empirically quite rare"), with James J. White, The Pros and Cons of "Getting to Yes", 34 J.Legal Educ. 115, 115–117 (1984)(influential book "is frequently naive" for under-emphasizing prominence of zero-sum/distributive negotiation).

approaches are discussed in later sections.[64]

§ 3.11   Bottom Lines, Settlement Zones and Barriers to Settlement

When parties reach a settlement, whether through *zero-sum* or *positive-sum* negotiation, they do so because each party believes its interests are better served by settling than by litigating further. A settlement is the sale of a claim. The seller is the plaintiff (or potential plaintiff if the dispute is not in litigation.) The buyer is the defendant or potential defendant. Sales of claims, like other sales, occur only when buyer and seller agree on a price.

Settlements do not occur when there is no price acceptable to both parties. In a zero-sum negotiation, for example, Plaintiff may be unwilling to settle for anything less than $60,000 and Defendant may be unwilling to settle for anything more than $40,000. No settlement will occur because there are no possible settlement terms acceptable to both parties. In the example just given, $60,000 is Plaintiff's bottom line, while $40,000 is Defendant's bottom line. The *bottom line* is the worst deal a party will accept. It is also known as the "reservation price," "resistance point," or "BATNA" (Best Alternative To a Negotiated Agreement).[65]

In another zero-sum negotiation, assume that Plaintiff's bottom line is $150,000, while Defendant's bottom line is $200,000. This is depicted in Diagram 3–3.

Diagram 3-3

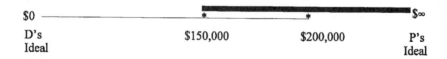

| $0 | | $150,000 | $200,000 | $∞ |
| D's Ideal | | | | P's Ideal |

The thin line represents possible settlement terms acceptable to Defendant. The thick line represents possible settlement terms acceptable to Plaintiff. The possible settlement terms from $150,000 to $200,000 comprise the *settlement zone*. It is impossible for a settlement to occur outside this zone. Any settlement must, by definition, be at least as good for each party than its bottom line because the bottom line is the worst deal a party will accept.

---

64. See §§ 3.14—3.30.

§ 3.11

65. But see Roger Fisher & William Ury, Getting to Yes: Negotiating Agreement Without Giving In 98–99 (2d ed.1991) (dis-

tinguishing BATNA from bottom line, while defining bottom line more narrowly than it is defined in this book). The role of bottom lines in positive-sum negotiation is discussed in § 3.13.

Thoughtful lawyers identify their clients' bottom lines before starting negotiation.[66] Lawyers help clients determine their bottom lines by considering questions like these:

> What is the likelihood the case will be dismissed before trial? If it does go to trial, what is the likelihood of a plaintiff's verdict? If Plaintiff does win a verdict, what remedy will the court order? How much money can a jury be expected to award? What is the likelihood that any award of damages will actually be paid?

> How much money will litigation cost? How much time will litigation cost? How will litigation affect reputations? Will it be traumatic, vindicating or both?

Notice that answers to all these questions are likely to be strongly influenced by expectations about the law. Substantive law shapes answers to the first group of questions and procedural law shapes answers to the second group of questions. In short, the law strongly influences bottom lines and, therefore, settlement zones. That is why settlement negotiations occur "in the shadow of the law."[67]

Consider what happens if the lawyers and parties on opposing sides of a case each come up with the same answers to the two groups of questions, *i.e.*, make the same predictions about the results of litigation. These lawyers and parties will probably formulate their bottom lines in a way that creates a settlement zone. If, for example, both Plaintiff and Defendant expect that litigation will result in Defendant paying $600,000 to Plaintiff, then they each benefit from settling at the *present value*[68] of $600,000 because each avoids the costs of going to trial. Settling helps both parties if they settle on the same outcome a court would have reached if, as is usually the case, the process of litigating is less attractive to the parties than the process of settling. Given the same result, most parties would rather reach that result through a settlement which typically is quick, cheap and private, than through litigation which typically is slow, expensive, and public.

In exceptional cases, though, one or more of the parties seeks something from a trial that, unlike money, cannot be provided by settlement. Some parties care about the public vindication that comes from a favorable verdict, want to "make law" with a favorable precedent, or develop a reputation for being fierce litigators in order to intimidate future adversaries. In these exceptional cases, opposing sides may not set their bottom lines in a way that creates a settlement zone

66. See § 3.34.

67. See Robert H. Mnookin & Lewis Kornhauser, Bargaining in the Shadow of the Law: The Case of Divorce, 88 Yale L.J. 950, 968 (1979)("the outcome that the law will impose if no agreement is reached gives each [party] certain bargaining chips—an endowment of sorts.") See also § 3.3.

68. The dollar amount of the settlement zone will be lower than $600,000 to reflect

the *time value of money*. See § 3.9. How much lower than $600,000 will be influenced by whether the law permits successful plaintiffs to recover pre-judgment interest and, if so, at what rate. Acknowledging the time-value of money does not detract from the prediction that lawyers and parties will set their bottom lines in a way that creates a settlement zone when both sides expect the same results from litigation.

even if they make the same predictions about the results of litigation. Outside these exceptional cases, though, opposing sides set their bottom lines in a way that creates a settlement zone when they each make the same predictions about the results of litigation.

Rarely do both sides of a case make exactly the same predictions about the results of litigation. For example, rarely will both Plaintiff and Defendant expect a $600,000 verdict. The odds of both sides predicting exactly the same number are quite low. But settlement zones occur beyond cases in which both sides make the same predictions about litigation. Settlement zones also occur in cases in which Plaintiff expects a less pro-Plaintiff result than Defendant expects. If, for example, Plaintiff expects a $550,000 verdict, while Defendant expects a $600,000 verdict, then Plaintiff will set its bottom line approximately $50,000 lower than when Plaintiff expected a $600,000 verdict.[69] This increases the size of the settlement zone, making settlement more likely than if each side made the same predictions about the results of litigation. So settlement zones occur in cases in which both sides make the same predictions about the results of litigation and in cases in which Plaintiff expects a less pro-Plaintiff result than Defendant expects.

Other than the exceptional cases in which a party seeks something from litigation that cannot be provided by settlement, the only cases lacking a settlement zone are those in which Plaintiff expects a more pro-Plaintiff result than Defendant expects. If, for example, Plaintiff expects a $650,000 verdict, while Defendant expects a $600,000 verdict, the settlement zone will shrink by approximately $50,000 when compared to the settlement zone created by both parties expecting a $600,000 verdict.[70] That $50,000 shrinkage may cause the settlement zone to disappear.[71] These cases in which Plaintiff expects a more pro-Plaintiff result than Defendant expects can be called cases of over-optimism. If Plaintiff expects a verdict of $650,000 and Defendant expects a verdict of $600,000, then at least one of the parties is overly optimistic about its likely success at litigation. Cases lacking a settlement zone are those in which at least one of the parties is in for a disappointment at trial.

To reiterate, other than the exceptional cases in which a party seeks something from litigation that cannot be provided by settlement, there are settlement zones in all cases in which Plaintiff expects a less pro-Plaintiff result from litigation than Defendant expects, and where both sides expect the same result. Notice that these settlement zones exist even if the parties' expectations are wrong. Settlement zones are created

---

69. The difference may not be exactly $50,000 because of the *time value of money*. See § 3.9.

70. The difference may not be exactly $50,000 because of the *time value of money*. See § 3.9.

71. Whether it disappears turns on how the two sides value the costs and benefits of the two processes: settlement and litigation. It may, for example, be that litigation is so costly that both sides are better off settling at any one of many possible settlement terms than they are litigating even though Plaintiff expects a higher verdict than Defendant expects.

by beliefs, not necessarily accurate beliefs. Notice also that these settlement zones exist even if the parties and their lawyers publicly deny that they exist. In a case where both sides expect a $600,000 verdict, Plaintiff's lawyer may be telling Defendant's lawyer that Plaintiff's lawyer expects a $8,000,000 verdict, while Defendant's lawyer may be telling Plaintiff's lawyer that Defendant's lawyer expects a verdict for Defendant.[72] Regardless of what the negotiators are telling each other about their expectations, if they both really expect a $600,000 verdict then there is a settlement zone.

§ 3.12 Settlement Zone Does Not Ensure Settlement

Bottom lines determine settlement zones. If Plaintiff's bottom line exceeds Defendant's bottom line, then there is no settlement zone and settlement is impossible.[73] Only if Defendant's bottom line exceeds Plaintiff's, as in Diagram 3–3,[74] is settlement possible.

The existence of a settlement zone does not mean the negotiators *will* reach an agreement, only that they *might* reach an agreement. In the case depicted by Diagram 3–3, for example, the range between $150,000 (Plaintiff's bottom line) and $200,000 (Defendant's bottom line) is the settlement zone, but the negotiators might be unable to agree on a settlement price for a number of reasons. First, the negotiators may not even realize a settlement zone exists. Negotiators typically conceal their true bottom lines from each other.[75] With each negotiator guessing about the other's bottom line, negotiators rarely are sure that a settlement zone exists and even less likely to know the precise boundaries of the zone.

Even if both negotiators discover that a settlement zone exists, and learn its precise boundaries, they still may not reach agreement. For example, a settlement of the case depicted in Diagram 3–3 will create $50,000 in value. But who gets how much of that value depends on where the price is in the zone between $150,000 and $200,000. If the parties settle at $150,001 then Defendant captures virtually all of the value created by settling. Plaintiff is barely made better off by the settlement.

The negotiators may spend much time and money negotiating within the settlement zone. Indeed, each negotiator may be so determined to capture the potential value from a settlement that they never reach a deal.[76] Defendant's lawyer may say to Plaintiff's lawyer "We will not pay more than $150,001. You should agree to it because it is better for your client than continuing litigation." Plaintiff's lawyer may say to

---

72. See § 3.20.

§ 3.12

73. See § 3.11.

74. See id.

75. See § 3.20.

76. Herein lie the transaction costs of the bilateral monopoly that is settlement negotiation. See § 3.4. See also Posner, supra note 16, at 68–69, 607–09.

Defendant's lawyer "We will not take less than $199,999. You should agree to it because it is better for your client than continuing litigation." These lawyers are playing the game of "chicken."

> The story behind this game comes * * * from an earlier time. Two teenagers drive cars headlong at each other. A driver gains stature when that driver drives headlong and the other swerves. Both drivers die, however, if neither swerves. Each player's highest payoff comes when that player drives head on and the other swerves; the second highest comes when that player swerves and the other [swerves] as well; and the third highest comes when that player swerves and the other drives. The lowest payoff results when both drive.[77]

As with the teenage drivers, so with lawyers. When negotiating within the settlement zone, whoever gives in first, loses. But if neither gives in, then both lose even worse. Going to trial is like crashing the cars because going to trial is worse for each party than accepting the other side's offer. Whoever gives in first, by accepting the other side's offer, loses most of the value created by settling, but if neither gives in then neither gets any of the value that could have been created by settling.[78]

§ 3.13   Bottom Lines in Positive–Sum Negotiation

Positive-sum negotiation nearly always requires consideration of multiple issues.[79] When multiple issues are considered, it is harder to determine whether a possible settlement is better or worse for a party than is her bottom line. To put it another way, bottom lines are more complicated in multiple-issue situations.

Suppose, for example, that a personal injury plaintiff genuinely wants from the defendant: (1) money, (2) a public admission of wrongdoing, and (3) changes in Defendant's internal procedures so this sort of injury is less likely to happen again. But suppose further that a court ruling for Plaintiff would not order any relief on Issues 2 and 3. In other words, assume that, while a court might order Defendant to pay Plaintiff money, it will not order Defendant to publicly admit wrongdoing or change its internal procedures. Plaintiff and her lawyer can formulate a bottom line based on their expectations of the dollar amount a court will award and the costs—financial and otherwise—of winning that award.[80] Suppose this analysis leads Plaintiff and her lawyer to determine that Plaintiff's bottom line is $50,000.

In settlement negotiation, Plaintiff may be able to achieve goals other than money. For instance, one possible settlement might be: (1) $30,000, plus (2) a full-page newspaper ad in which Defendant acknowl-

---

77. Douglas G. Baird, Robert H. Gertner & Randall C. Picker, Game Theory and the Law 44 (1994).

78. For tactics to win the game of chicken, see §§ 3.15—3.22.

§ 3.13

79. See §§ 3.9 & 3.26.

80. See § 3.5.

edges responsibility and (3) complete overhaul of Defendant's internal procedures. Plaintiff will have to determine whether she values the newspaper ad plus the overhaul of Defendant's procedures at more or less than $20,000. If she values them at less than $20,000, she should not agree to this possible settlement.[81] So positive-sum negotiation, like zero-sum negotiation, occurs within the constraints of bottom lines. And positive-sum negotiation poses the additional challenge of converting multiple goals into a single measure of value. That measure is, in settlement negotiation, usually money but it does not have to be.[82]

While positive-sum negotiation does not avoid the constraints of bottom lines, it does create settlement zones that would not otherwise exist. In the case just discussed, for example, it might be that Defendant's bottom line is $40,000. As Plaintiff's bottom line is $50,000, there is no settlement zone if money is the only possible settlement term. This is depicted in Diagram 3–4 (Part A), infra, where the thin line represents possible settlement terms acceptable to Defendant and the thick line represents possible settlement terms acceptable to Plaintiff.

Suppose further that Plaintiff values the newspaper ad plus the overhaul of Defendant's procedures at exactly $20,000. That means Plaintiff's bottom line can be expressed as "$30,000 plus the newspaper ad and overhaul of Defendant's procedures." This is depicted in Diagram 3–4 (Part B), infra, in which the thick line represents all possible settlement terms acceptable to Plaintiff. Also suppose that Defendant values the newspaper ad plus the overhaul of its procedures as a cost of only $5000. (This might be because Defendant believes the newspaper ad will help its image or because it sees benefits from overhauling its procedures.) Defendant's bottom line can be expressed as "$35,000 plus the newspaper ad and overhaul of Defendant's procedures." This is also depicted in Diagram 3–4, Part B, in which the thin line represents all possible settlement terms acceptable to Defendant.

---

81. Indeed, if she did agree to this possible settlement, her doing so would reveal that she does value the newspaper ad plus the overhaul of Defendant's procedures at more than $20,000. (Assuming, of course, that she has not changed her bottom line from $50,000. See §§ 3.5(b) & 3.36.)

82. See § 3.5(c).

Diagram 3-4

Part A

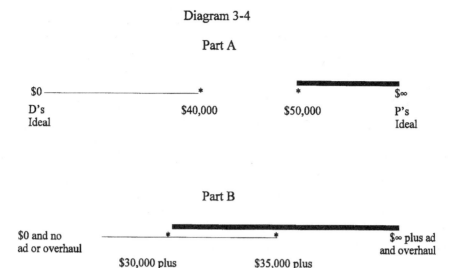

$0	$40,000	$50,000	$∞
D's Ideal			P's Ideal

Part B

$0 and no ad or overhaul $∞ plus ad and overhaul

$30,000 plus ad and overhaul $35,000 plus ad and overhaul

D's Ideal   P's Ideal

If multiple issues are considered, a party's bottom line can be expressed in multiple ways.[83] For example, the bottom line of Plaintiff in Diagram 3–4 could be expressed as either "$50,000" or "$30,000 plus the newspaper ad and overhaul of Defendant's procedures." Perhaps it could also be expressed as "$40,000 plus the newspaper ad." The more issues considered, the more different ways to express a party's bottom line. In other words, the more issues considered, the more possible settlement terms that a party will find acceptable. And the more possible settlement terms that a party will find acceptable, the more likely at least one of those terms will be acceptable to the other side. In sum, the more issues considered, the more likely there is to be a settlement zone.

D.   APPROACHES TO NEGOTIATION

Table of Sections

83. John S. Murray, Alan Scott Rau & Edward F. Sherman, Processes of Dispute Resolution: The Role of Lawyers 89 (2d ed.1996)("Bottom lines are no longer single figures, but a series of settlement packages that for the offering party represent the same utility value.")

§ 3.14 Terminology

Approaches to negotiation are as varied as negotiators themselves. Therefore, any attempt to categorize these approaches must make generalizations that do not always hold true. Many theorists have categorized various approaches to negotiation, but no theoretical framework has gained widespread acceptance. In short, there is no common language among negotiation theorists.

Many theorists posit two approaches to negotiation,[84] such as the ''adversarial'' and ''problem-solving'' approaches, the ''competitive'' and ''cooperative'' approaches, or ''positional bargaining'' and ''interests-

§ **3.14** at 149 & 160.
84. Riskin & Westbrook, supra note 51,

based bargaining." Still others use other terms, some of which are listed in Diagram 3–5.

Diagram 3-5

Adversarial	Problem-Solving
Competitive	Cooperative
Positional	Interest-Based
Distributive	Integrative
Value-Claiming	Value-Creating
Distributional	Principled
Win-Lose	Win-Win

Different negotiation theorists attach different meanings to these terms so students of negotiation must, when encountering any of these terms, seek a definition of how the term is being used. Some theorists seem to treat the terms on the left side of Diagram 3–5 as synonymous and the terms on the right side of Diagram 3–5 as synonymous.

This book discusses three negotiation approaches: (1) Adversarial/Competitive, (2) Cooperative, and (3) Problem–Solving.[85] The adversarial/competitive and cooperative approaches are, while quite different, both oriented toward *zero-sum* negotiation. In contrast, the problem-solving approach is oriented toward *positive-sum* negotiation. Each approach can be used in any kind of dispute negotiation and any kind of transactional negotiation. In keeping with the focus of this chapter, however, the approaches are discussed in the context of settlement negotiation.[86]

1.   THE ADVERSARIAL/COMPETITIVE APPROACH

Table of Sections

The adversarial/competitive approach is oriented toward *zero-sum* negotiation.[87] An adversarial/competitive negotiator treats negotiation as

85. Accord Gifford, supra note 3, at 14.

86. See § 3.2(defining settlement negotiation).

87. Zero-sum negotiation is defined and discussed in § 3.8.

a contest and focuses on defeating her counterpart. The adversarial/competitive approach often involves:

—an extreme opening offer,

—few and small concessions,

—false concessions and other concession tricks,

—attempts to obtain information about the other party's interests and bottom line, while concealing information about one's client's interests and bottom line,

—posturing about the strength of one's case and one's lack of interest in settling, and

—psychological warfare.

Bottom lines, discussed in an earlier section,[88] are central to the adversarial/competitive approach. The adversarial/competitive lawyer's goal is to push opposing counsel into settling at the opposing party's bottom line.

The tactics of the adversarial/competitive negotiator are discussed in more detail next.

§ 3.15 Opening Offers

An adversarial/competitive lawyer's opening offer proposes terms that are extremely favorable to her client, rather than proposing terms that are "fair" or "reasonable." Extreme opening offers have important advantages. In fact, empirical research shows a significant correlation between opening offers and the terms of an eventual deal.[89] An extreme opening offer allows the offeror room to later grant concessions, while still reaching a favorable settlement.

Any offer you make tells your counterpart something about your bottom line. For example, Plaintiff's offer of $30,000 tells Defendant that Plaintiff's bottom line is less than or equal to $30,000. The more extreme Plaintiff's offer ($50,000, $100,000, * * *), the less light it sheds on Plaintiff's bottom line. Suppose that, until hearing Plaintiff's opening offer of $30,000, Defendant was willing to pay up to $40,000. Upon hearing Plaintiff's opening offer of $30,000, Defendant's willingness to pay should immediately drop to $30,000 or lower. Plaintiff's opening offer cost Plaintiff $10,000 or more. The more extreme the opening offer, the less likely this sort of "give away" is to occur. An extreme opening offer conceals the offeror's bottom line.

The danger of an extreme opening offer, of course, is that it may lead the counterpart to conclude that the parties are simply too far apart to reach a settlement. So the counterpart may give up on settlement negotiations and pursue litigation as the only option.[90] This result is

88. See §§ 3.11—3.13.

§ 3.15

89. Brunet & Craver, supra note 32, at 69.

90. See § 3.20(d).

harmful to both parties in cases with a *settlement zone*[91] because the parties are forgoing an agreement that would have made them both better off than they are in the absence of an agreement. And even if extreme opening offers do not kill a deal, they delay it, making negotiation more costly and stressful for lawyers and clients.

There is debate among adversarial/competitive negotiators about whether it is advantageous to make the first offer, *i.e.*, for your opening offer to precede your counterpart's opening offer. The risk of making the first offer is revealed by the example of Plaintiff who "gave away" at least $10,000 by opening with $30,000. Had Plaintiff been able to first elicit an offer from Defendant, that offer might have been high enough to encourage Plaintiff to make his opening offer above $30,000, thus reducing or eliminating the "give away." The risk of a "give away" leads most adversarial/competitive negotiators to try not to make the first offer. On the other hand, making the first offer might influence your counterpart. Perhaps you can make your first offer the focus of subsequent negotiation and anchor discussion around it.

§ 3.16   Few and Small Concessions

When you make an offer less favorable to your client than your opening offer was, you have made a *concession*. The bigger your concessions, the worse for your client any deal will be. Accordingly, the adversarial/competitive lawyer makes as few concessions as possible and makes them as small as possible.

On the other hand, few settlements are reached without concessions. If you reached a deal without making any concessions from your opening offer then your opening offer was probably not ambitious enough.[92] You probably could have gotten a better deal than you did. So you do want to make some concessions, but you do not want to concede too much. The adversarial/competitive approach has guidelines to avoid conceding too much. These guidelines are discussed in this section.

When you make your first concession, you admit to your counterpart, opposing counsel, that you can be moved. You lead your counterpart to believe that you may not be tenacious. Your counterpart may believe you are on the slippery slope toward further concessions. After all, if you did not stick with your first position, why should your counterpart believe you will stick with your second position?

To avoid this sort of thinking, when you make a concession you may want to give your counterpart a "positional commitment," *i.e.*, a reason why you are not conceding more. Your determination to concede nothing more can be demonstrated by linking your concession to:

—a principle, ("I'm offering you the terms at which similar cases settle"),

91. See §§ 3.11—3.13.

§ 3.16

92. But see § 3.27, n.179 & § 3.38, n.221 (discussing "Boulwareism").

—your personal reputation, ("If I go any higher, I'll be known as a soft touch"), or

—a threat of ending negotiations, ("This is my final offer").

The adversarial/competitive approach also generally advises that each of your concessions should be smaller than the last. If, as the plaintiff's lawyer, you previously dropped your demand from $50,000 to $40,000, then your next concession should keep your position above $30,000. By conceding $10,000, and then conceding less than $10,000, you indicate that you are rapidly approaching your *bottom line*,[93] the point at which you will concede no more. You may succeed in persuading the defendant's lawyer that your bottom line is higher than it really is.[94]

If you are using the adversarial/competitive approach, you do not give away a concession. Instead, you extract something in exchange for it. You can say to your counterpart, "I'll give up my demand for X if you give up your demand for Y." In this manner, one concession is contemporaneously exchanged for another concession.[95]

Concessions can also be exchanged sequentially. For example, the parties may make offers in the following order: Plaintiff opens at $30,000, Defendant opens at $10,000, Plaintiff offers $23,000, Defendant offers $18,000, Plaintiff offers $20,000 and Defendant accepts. This process of "taking turns conceding" is a common way in which settlements are reached.

Suppose Plaintiff opens at $30,000 and then Defendant opens at $10,000. If Plaintiff then offers $23,000, Plaintiff should make no further concessions until Defendant offers more than $10,000. If, after Plaintiff's $23,000 offer, Defendant sticks at $10,000 and Plaintiff offers, say, $21,000 then Plaintiff is "bidding against himself." Defendant is being rewarded for her intransigence and is likely to become even more intransigent, hoping that Plaintiff will continue to bid against himself. Just as an adversarial/competitive negotiator will not bid against herself, so she will try to get her counterpart to bid against himself.

If negotiators are exchanging concessions sequentially, how quickly should the concessions come? The adversarial/competitive negotiator generally likes to make her own concessions more slowly than her counterpart's. Suppose Plaintiff made her most recent offer June 1 and Defendant made its most recent offer June 5. Plaintiff should, according to the adversarial/competitive approach, probably wait until after June 9 before making her next offer. This delay conveys to Defendant: "I am in less of a rush to make a deal than you are. That means I am more pleased with the status quo, the way litigation is proceeding, than you are." The adversarial/competitive lawyer does not want to seem to be in a rush to settle.[96] If she receives an encouraging offer, but one not good enough to accept, she does not reply right away. She waits, to make the

93. See §§ 3.11—3.13.

94. See § 3.20.

95. Compare *logrolling*, discussed in §§ 3.26(c) & 3.28.

96. See § 3.20(c).

opposing party "sweat". Conversely, when the opposing party seems to be rushing to settlement, the adversarial/competitive lawyer smells blood. She then demands large concessions and offers little or no concessions in return.

If negotiators are exchanging concessions either contemporaneously or sequentially, the adversarial/competitive negotiator wants her concession to be smaller than the concession for which it is exchanged. The "size" of a concession is not, however, easily measured. One might think that Defendant's lawyer who goes up from $10,000 to $15,000 concedes less than Plaintiff's lawyer who goes down from $30,000 to $20,000. This is because Defendant's lawyer conceded $5000, while Plaintiff's lawyer conceded $10,000. But the size of concessions must be assessed against the opening offer. Perhaps Plaintiff's lawyer's opening offer of $30,000 was extreme, while Defendant's lawyer's opening offer of $10,000 was reasonable. Given these opening offers, Plaintiff's lawyer might have expected that Defendant's lawyer's concessions would only be one-tenth the dollar-amount of Plaintiff's lawyer's. When Defendant's lawyer's concession turned out to be one-half the dollar-amount of Plaintiff's lawyer's, Plaintiff's lawyer was pleasantly surprised!

§ 3.17 False Concessions

One way to keep your concessions "smaller" than your counterpart's is to concede only on those issues you do not really care about.[97] The adversarial/competitive negotiator often begins negotiations by raising such issues. For example, assume that Plaintiff, who has an adversarial/competitive lawyer, cares only about how much money she can get from Defendant. Plaintiff's lawyer might open negotiations by saying "We'll settle for $30,000, plus a public admission of wrongdoing and changes in Defendant's internal procedures so this sort of injury does not happen to anyone else." Plaintiff does not value the admission or changes to Defendant's procedures, but Plaintiff's lawyer knows those things would be costly to Defendant. So early in negotiation, Plaintiff's lawyer pretends that her client strongly wants the admission and changes to Defendant's procedures. Later she agrees, with a great show of reluctance, to forgo those demands in exchange for Defendant raising its cash offer. Plaintiff gets a concession she cares about, money, by giving up things she never really wanted anyhow. Generally, the more convincingly one insists upon a particular demand early in negotiation, the larger the concession that ultimately will be obtained for dropping it. The danger of this false-concession tactic, especially if both parties use it, is that it hurts both parties by giving them what they said they want, while posturing, instead of giving them what they really want.[98]

§ 3.17   98. See § 3.28.
97. Compare *logrolling*, discussed in §§ 3.26(c) & 3.28.

§ 3.18   Concession Tricks and Escalation Tactics

Adversarial/competitive lawyers sometimes use tricks to keep their concessions "smaller" than their counterpart's. One trick is to convince your counterpart that you are conceding something, while not actually conceding it. In a patent-infringement case, for example, Plaintiff's lawyer's initial draft settlement agreement might, in clear and concise language, prohibit Defendant from exploiting certain technology. Plaintiff's lawyer might then delete this language in exchange for a monetary concession from Defendant, while simultaneously adding new language to the draft agreement. The new language, in a convoluted and complex way, also prohibits Defendant from exploiting the same technology. If Defendant's lawyer is not alert, Plaintiff's lawyer may succeed in "sneaking in" this nullification of its own concession.

Another tactic is to make a concession and then retract it. This is sometimes called the "backward step." In negotiation over the phone, for example, Plaintiff's lawyer might go down from $30,000 to $20,000, while Defendant's lawyer goes up from $10,000 to $20,000. Defendant is pleased to have a deal at $20,000. Plaintiff then refuses to sign a release for anything less than $25,000. Plaintiff's lawyer may tell Defendant's lawyer: "you've revealed your willingness to pay at least $20,000. Surely, you can move to $25,000 to make this case go away." There is not likely to be much evidence of the oral settlement agreement and, even if there is, a writing may be required for enforceability.[99]

A tactic similar to the retracted concession is to introduce a new issue late in negotiation, just as an agreement seems to be emerging. Consider negotiation of a patent-infringement case in which the only issue discussed was the scope of the technology Defendant would refrain from exploiting. These negotiations were long and difficult as lawyers and businesspeople struggled over scientific concepts and terminology. Just as the parties agreed on these matters, Plaintiff's lawyer demanded that Defendant make a cash payment of $10,000 and told Defendant's lawyer: "you wouldn't want to squander all this work reaching a deal for a mere $10,000, would you?"

The tactics discussed throughout this section are likely to anger opposing counsel and his client because they are generally considered beyond the bounds of "fair play." Their use by lawyers may raise issues of professional responsibility.[100]

§ 3.19   Deception and Information

Deception plays a central role in the adversarial/competitive approach. Deception feeds misinformation to opposing counsel and her client. Deception matters because information matters. All approaches to negotiation recognize the tremendous power of information. The ap-

§ 3.18

99. See § 3.39.

100. See Model Rule of Professional Conduct 4.1 (1999)(quoted in § 3.19).

proaches are dramatically different, though, in how they harness the power of information.[101]

In the adversarial/competitive approach, information is a weapon. The better your information, the stronger you are. This applies to all relevant information, including information about your client's interests as well as information about the other party's interests. The adversarial/competitive lawyer prepares for negotiation by thoughtfully considering her client's interests and priorities.[102] The adversarial/competitive negotiator also aggressively inquires into the other party's interests and priorities.[103] Means of inquiry include discovery, such as depositions and document requests. You can also use "informal discovery" such as searches of public records, inquiries to the other party's neighbors, employers or business associates, and even hiring an investigator to spy on the other party. To deprive her counterpart of information, the adversarial/competitive lawyer resists discovery requests by her counterpart and is careful not to discuss the case in public places. The adversarial/competitive lawyer keeps her cards close to the vest.

Other than discovery, there is little way of compelling the adversarial/competitive lawyer to disclose information. There are, however, a number of checks on the adversarial/competitive lawyer's desire to spread misinformation. One is conscience. Another is reputation.[104] Misrepresentations can also have legal consequences. If a fraudulent or material misrepresentation induces the other party to settle, the settlement is voidable at the option of the other party.[105] A misrepresentation may also lead to liability in tort. Finally, the Model Rules of Professional Conduct provide:

RULE 4.1 Truthfulness in Statements to Others

In the course of representing a client a lawyer shall not knowingly:

(a) make a false statement of material fact or law to a third person; or

(b) fail to disclose a material fact to a third person when disclosure is necessary to avoid assisting a criminal or fraudulent act by a client, unless disclosure is prohibited by rule 1.6 [which deals with the lawyer's obligation to keep client confidences].[106]

So a lawyer can be reprimanded, suspended from practice or even disbarred for his misrepresentations in settlement negotiations.[107] While

---

§ 3.19

101. See §§ 3.23—3.25 (discussing cooperative approach) and §§ 3.26—3.30 (discussing problem-solving approach).

102. See § 3.34.

103. See § 3.35.

104. See §§ 3.23—3.24.

105. See § 3.39.

106. Model Rule of Professional Conduct 4.1 (1999). See also Model Code of Professional Responsibility DR 7–

102(A)(5)(1969). The vast majority of states have adopted some or all of the American Bar Association's Model Rules of Professional Conduct, while a few states continue to use the older Model Code of Professional Responsibility. See American Bar Association, Compendium of Professional Responsibility: Rules and Standards 523–27 (1999).

107. The Model Rules are often thought to be *ethical* rules and they are. But they are also *legal* rules in that they are enacted by government. The state bar committees

the aforementioned factors deter misrepresentations, one cannot be sure that everything her counterpart says in settlement negotiations is true.[108] The adversarial/competitive negotiator remains suspicious of her counterpart's truthfulness.

§ 3.20   Misinformation About Bottom Lines and the Strength of Your Case

(a) Generally

If information is a weapon in the adversarial/competitive approach, then the nuclear weapon is information about *bottom lines*.[109] The adversarial/competitive lawyer is especially alert to anything that might reveal the other party's bottom line. Conversely, she is especially careful to prevent opposing counsel from learning anything that might shed light on her own client's bottom line.

The importance of information and misinformation about bottom lines can be illustrated with an example. Assume that Defendant's bottom line is $200,000 and that Plaintiff's bottom line is $150,000. So the *settlement zone* is from $150,000 to $200,000.[110] These assumptions are reflected in Diagram 3–6 in which the thin line represents possible settlement terms acceptable to Defendant and the thick line represents possible settlement terms acceptable to Plaintiff.

Diagram 3-6

$0			$∞
D's Ideal	$150,000	$200,000	P's Ideal

Assume that Plaintiff's lawyer knows Defendant's bottom line but Defendant's lawyer is ignorant of Plaintiff's bottom line. If Defendant learns that Plaintiff's bottom line is $150,000, then settlement may occur anywhere within the zone between $150,000 and $200,000. But if Defendant's lawyer comes to believe that Plaintiff's bottom line is $190,000, then Defendant's lawyer will believe the settlement zone is only between $190,000 and $200,000. This is reflected in Diagram 3–7 in

---

and courts that enforce these rules are government agencies administering occupational licensing regulations to determine who is, and is not, legally-permitted to practice law.

108. James J. White, Machiavelli and the Bar: Ethical Limitations on Lying in Negotiation, 1980 Am.B.Found.Res.J. 926, 935 (1980).

§ 3.20

109. Bottom lines are explained and discussed in §§ 3.11—3.13.

110. Settlement zones are explained and discussed in §§ 3.11—3.13.

which the thick dashed line represents possible settlement terms that
Defendant's lawyer believes are acceptable to Plaintiff.

Diagram 3-7

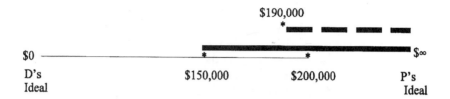

Defendant's lawyer's belief that Plaintiff will settle for no less than
$190,000 is advantageous to Plaintiff. It ensures that any settlement will
be near the high end of the real settlement zone.

The important practical question is how Defendant's lawyer came to
believe that Plaintiff's bottom line was $190,000. Perhaps Defendant's
lawyer reached that belief without any help from Plaintiff's lawyer. More
likely though, Plaintiff's lawyer tried to convince Defendant's lawyer
that Plaintiff's bottom line was higher than it really was. This is a
standard practice of the adversarial/competitive approach. In fact, it may
be the most common tactic used in settlement negotiation.

(b) Lying About One's Bottom Line

To make her client's bottom line appear tougher than it really is, an
adversarial/competitive lawyer may lie about it. For example, Plaintiff's
lawyer might say "$190,000 is as low as we can go," even though she has
been authorized by the client to go down to $150,000. This sort of lie
probably does not violate the Model Rules of Professional Conduct. Rule
4.1, quoted in an earlier section,[111] only prohibits false statements of
material fact, and Comment 2 to this Rule says:

> Under generally accepted conventions in negotiation, certain types
> of statements ordinarily are not taken as statements of material
> fact. Estimates of price or value placed on the subject of a transac-
> tion and a party's intentions as to an acceptable settlement of a
> claim are in this category.[112]

111. See § 3.19.

112. Model Rule of Professional Conduct 4.1, comment 2, (1999). Compare
Brunet & Craver, supra note 32, at 28 ("it
is ethically permissible for negotiators to
use deceptive tactics with respect to their
actual settlement intentions"), American
Bar Association Comm. on Ethics and Professional Responsibility, Formal Op. 93–370
(1993)("a party's actual bottom line or the
settlement authority given to a lawyer is a
material fact.")

Lying about bottom lines can be hard to distinguish from bluffing, which is generally considered "fair play" in negotiation, as in poker. Lying about bottom lines is routine.[113] Accordingly, few lawyers are naive enough to accept uncritically a counterpart's representation about the counterpart's bottom line. Understanding this, the adversarial/competitive lawyer seeks more imaginative ways to mislead opposing counsel. The most common way is to project confidence in one's case and lack of interest in settling.

(c) Projecting Confidence in One's Case and Lack of Interest in Settling

An adversarial/competitive lawyer exudes confidence. Whether she believes it or not, she acts as though she has a very strong case on the merits and that she is eager to litigate further. She acts as though she relishes the idea of trying the case. She goes out of her way to show that she has little or no desire to settle. She will not propose sitting down to discuss settlement and may reject the idea if raised by her counterpart. If she is brought to the negotiation table, she is quick to storm out of the room if her counterpart is not acceding to all her demands. Why should she waste time talking about a deal that will give her anything less than the total victory she is sure she will win in court?

If she and her counterpart have been through many grueling hours of negotiation and are only a few thousand dollars apart, her counterpart may be excited about the prospect of a deal and nervous that some last-minute disagreement might kill the deal that is starting to gel. Her counterpart feels invested in the deal they have worked so hard to produce. In contrast, the adversarial/competitive lawyer remains coolly uninterested in reaching a deal. She nonchalantly acts as though it would not bother her in the least to try a case that came within inches of settling. She patiently waits for her counterpart to make the last few concessions necessary to form a deal.

One common way to project confidence in one's case is to overstate its strength on the law and the facts. Adversarial/competitive lawyers often overstate the strength of their cases on the law. For example, Plaintiff's lawyer may confidently say to Defendant's lawyer "the *Jones* case is right on point for me as a precedent," even when Plaintiff's lawyer knows it is not. Plaintiff's lawyer may confidently deny the applicability of a statute that she knows provides a strong argument for Defendant. Plaintiff's lawyer tries to convince Defendant's lawyer that the law compels a ruling for Plaintiff or, at least, that Plaintiff's lawyer *believes* the law compels a ruling for Plaintiff. Even if Defendant's lawyer thinks Plaintiff's lawyer misunderstands the relevant cases and statutes, Plaintiff's lawyer will have succeeded in convincing Defendant's lawyer that Plaintiff's bottom line is higher than it really is. Plaintiff's lawyer will have failed if Defendant's lawyer realizes that Plaintiff's

113. James J. White goes so far as to make the following assertion. "To conceal one's true position, to mislead an opponent about one's true settling point, is the essence of negotiation." White, supra note 108, at 928.

lawyer knows the *Jones* case is distinguishable and the statute applies for Defendant. Defendant's lawyer will realize that Plaintiff's lawyer is just posturing.

What has just been said about overstating the strength of a case on the law applies as well to overstating the strength of a case on the facts. Plaintiff's lawyer will try to convince Defendant's lawyer that Plaintiff's lawyer thinks the jury will be outraged by documents Defendant created, even though Plaintiff's lawyer worries that the jury will not be interested in them. Plaintiff's lawyer will try to convince Defendant's lawyer that Plaintiff's lawyer thinks her client will perform marvelously on the witness stand, even though Plaintiff's lawyer expects her client to be a bad witness. In short, Plaintiff's lawyer will act as though she has much greater confidence in her case than she really does.

(d) Effect of Misinformation About Bottom Lines

All the adversarial/competitive tactics discussed above[114] can be used to mislead your counterpart about your bottom line. If they work, settlement will be far from your bottom line even if it is close to what your counterpart believes is your bottom line. These tactics can, however, work too well.

Reconsider the case depicted by Diagram 3–6[115] in which Plaintiff's bottom line is $150,000 and Defendant's bottom line is $200,000. Plaintiff's lawyer's tactics work if they convince Defendant's lawyer that Plaintiff's bottom line is $190,000.[116] But they work too well if Plaintiff's lawyer convinces Defendant's lawyer that Plaintiff's bottom line is $250,000. If this happens, Defendant's lawyer will believe no settlement is possible because Defendant is only willing to pay $200,000. Defendant's lawyer will give up on settlement negotiations and pursue litigation as the only option. This result is harmful to both parties because they are forgoing an agreement (anywhere between $150,000 and $200,-000) that would have made them both better off than they are in the absence of an agreement. Plaintiff's lawyer has outsmarted herself.

The chance of this failure occurring is even greater where Defendant's lawyer, as well as Plaintiff's lawyer, is trying to create misimpressions. If Plaintiff's lawyer succeeds in convincing Defendant's lawyer that Plaintiff's bottom line is $190,000, and Defendant's lawyer succeeds in convincing Plaintiff's lawyer that Defendant's bottom line is $160,000, then neither lawyer has succeeded at all. This is reflected in Diagram 3–8 in which a thin dashed line is added to Diagram 3–7 to represent possible settlement terms *Plaintiff believes* are acceptable to Defendant.

114. See especially §§ 3.15, 3.16 & 3.20(a)-(c).

115. See § 3.20(a).

116. See Diagram 3–7 in § 3.20(a).

Diagram 3-8

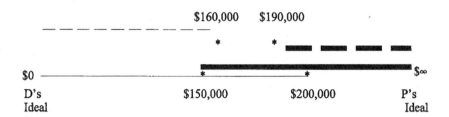

Each party has succeeded in bluffing the other. The result, no settlement, hurts both parties when compared to any settlement between $150,000 and $200,000.

§ 3.21   Psychological Warfare

Negotiation causes stress and anxiety in almost all people. To exploit this stress and anxiety, psychological warfare is part of the adversarial/competitive approach. The variety of tactics along these lines is endless.

(a) Anger, Threats, Ridicule, Accusation and Intimidation

Anger, threats, ridicule, accusation and intimidation may undermine the counterpart's confidence in the merits of his case and even in himself. If so, they may soften the counterpart's position and push him closer to his bottom line. They may work.

(b) Negotiate on Your Own Turf

Face-to-face negotiation should, according to the adversarial/competitive approach, occur in your office or some other place where you will feel more comfortable than your counterpart. This may put your counterpart at a psychological disadvantage "because he has had to come to you."[117] By negotiating on your own turf, you can gain a physical, as well as psychological, advantage by adjusting the seating or the thermostat so that your counterpart is uncomfortable. You can sit in your favorite chair and plan ahead to dress for the extreme temperature setting you choose.

(c) Outnumber Your Counterparts

Negotiation is hard work. Having more negotiators on your side than there are on the other side makes it more likely that you will be

§ 3.21

117. Michael Meltsner & Philip G. Schrag, Negotiating Tactics for Legal Services Lawyers, 7 Clearinghouse Rev. 259, 259 (1973).

able to control the flow of discussion and that the other side will tire while you remain energetic and sharp. Having multiple negotiators on your side also allows you to divide responsibilities. For example, you can do the talking, while your teammate carefully observes you (to ensure that you are not inadvertently revealing anything) and observes your counterpart (to pick up information you may miss).[118]

Having multiple negotiators on your side also enables you to do the "Mutt and Jeff" or "Good Cop, Bad Cop" routine. This is where one negotiator on your side is soft and cooperative while the other negotiator on your side demands an extremely one-sided deal. While the unreasonable negotiator is out of the room, the soft negotiator apologizes for his colleague and says that with a few more concessions from the other side he thinks he can persuade the unreasonable negotiator to calm down and go along with the deal.

Those who negotiate in teams must be careful in how they communicate with each other to avoid revealing confidential information to the other side.

(d) Negotiate When You Have Time and Your Counterpart Does Not

If opposing counsel is in more of a rush to reach a deal than you are, that eagerness is vulnerability you can exploit.[119] An application of this general tactic is to impose travel costs on your counterpart. If negotiations cannot be completed in one day, your counterpart will have to stay in a hotel, incurring expense and perhaps getting a bad night's sleep. In contrast, you will be home for dinner as usual.

(e) Lack of Authority

A lawyer may begin negotiating by saying that he lacks authority, *i.e.*, he will have to get his client's approval for any agreement.[120] When he and his counterpart reach a deal, he calls his client who (as planned) then refuses to sign the deal unless the other side makes a few additional concessions. This is a variant of the general tactic in which the adversarial/competitive lawyer attempts to squeeze concessions out of a counterpart who, after working hard to achieve a deal, feels invested in it.[121]

If your counterpart announces that he lacks authority, you might try one of three responses. One is to simply refuse to negotiate until the other side sends someone with authority. The other is to say that you, too, lack authority. The third is to keep some concessions in reserve when you reach a deal, the first deal, with the lawyer. That way, when the lawyer says his client will not sign unless you make further concessions, you can concede something you had planned to concede all along.

Lawyers frequently say "my client has only given me authority to settle above/below [a specific dollar amount]." Sometimes this is true.

---

118. Brunet & Craver, supra note 32, at 45.

119. See § 3.16 & 3.20.

120. See § 3.40 (without a grant of authority from the client, a lawyer cannot settle a claim).

121. See § 3.20.

But sometimes lawyers who say this are lying. The lawyer with (true or false) "limited authority" is trying to bias the negotiation in his favor by making "out of bounds" certain outcomes favorable to the other side. Responses to this tactic parallel the responses to the "lack of authority" tactic.

(f) Locked into Position

The *game of chicken* is presented by the case depicted by Diagram 3–3.[122] In that example, the plaintiff's bottom line is $150,000 and the defendant's bottom line is $200,000, so the range between $150,000 and $200,000 is the settlement zone. Assume the lawyers are each aware of the other's bottom lines. Defendant's lawyer may say to Plaintiff's lawyer "We will not pay more than $15,001. You should agree to it because it is better for your client than continuing litigation." Plaintiff's lawyer may say to Defendant's lawyer "We will not take less than $199,999. You should agree to it because it is better for your client than continuing litigation." These lawyers are playing the game of chicken because whoever gives in first, loses. But if neither gives in, then both lose even worse. Whoever gives in first loses most of the value created by settling, but if neither gives in then neither gets any of the value that could have been created by settling.[123]

If either side can show that it is credibly committed to its position, then it should win the game. Suppose, for an unrealistic example, that Plaintiff would lose his right arm if he accepted less than $199,999. This would make quite credible his lawyer's threat to try the case if he got anything less than $199,999. If Defendant really believed Plaintiff would lose his right arm if he accepted less than $199,999, Defendant would settle at that price because $199,999 is better for Defendant than going to trial and Defendant knows there is no chance of getting a settlement below $199,999. To gain credibility in the game of chicken, a negotiator must show her counterpart that she is locked in to her position. If that is not because loss of an arm will follow from abandoning this position, it is because some other great harm will follow. For example, in a case which has attracted publicity, a lawyer can announce to the tv cameras "we will pursue this litigation until we get an end to the pollution." Then the lawyer can tell his counterpart that he cannot accept a settlement that does not end the pollution; if he did, he would be publicly embarrassed and would lose all his professional credibility.

(g) Feign Irrationality

As noted in an earlier section,[124] adversarial/competitive lawyers routinely project confidence in their cases. The tactic of feigning irrationality takes this to the extreme. By seeming irrational, a lawyer hopes to convince his counterpart to accept his one-sided demands because the only alternative is to go to trial. There is no reasoning with this person

122. See § 3.12.

123. See Posner, supra note 16, at 68–69.

124. See § 3.20(c).

so the counterpart's choice is to settle around her bottom line or both sides will try a case that should settle.

Few successful lawyers convincingly portray themselves as irrational, but many convincingly portray their clients as irrational, which accomplishes the same goal. The feigned irrationality tactic is particularly useful in winning the *game of chicken*.[125]

(h) Wolf in Sheep's Clothing

Perhaps the most effective form of psychological warfare is to do none of the psychological tactics listed above, or at least not to do them in a way that allows your counterpart to realize that you are doing them. If your counterpart discovers that you are engaging in the tactics listed above, your counterpart will probably realize that you are taking an adversarial/competitive approach. For reasons discussed in later sections,[126] your adversarial/competitive approach is likely to be more effective if your counterpart does not realize you are using it. If you appear to be using either the *cooperative*[127] or the *problem-solving*[128] approach, while actually using the adversarial/competitive approach, you are likely to be quite effective in advancing your client's interests.

To pursue this wolf-in-sheep's-clothing strategy, you should be courteous and pleasant. You might also try some of the following tactics. But you cannot be too obvious about them or you will be unmasked as the wolf you are.

One tactic is to flatter your counterpart, to build her confidence. The rationale for this tactic is that negotiators are more likely to make concessions when they feel competent.[129] You might tell your counterpart, with a sense of frustration and respect in your voice, what a hard deal she is driving. If you can make her think she is succeeding, while you are actually taking her to the cleaners, then you are more likely to take her back to the cleaners the next time she is your counterpart. You may also be able to "generate greater concessions through disingenuous appeals to [your counterpart's] reputation for reasonableness and fair dealing."[130] In short, you may be able to exploit your counterpart's sense of guilt or shame.

§ 3.22 Drawbacks of the Adversarial/Competitive Approach

The adversarial/competitive approach is oriented to *zero-sum* negotiation.[131] Using this approach is likely to waste any available *positive-sum*

---

125. See § 3.12.

126. See §§ 3.23—3.25.

127. See id.

128. See §§ 3.26—3.30.

129. Jeffrey Rubin, Negotiation: An Introduction to Some Issues and Themes, 27 Am.Behavioral Scientist 135, 138–44 (Nov.-Dec. 1983).

130. Brunet & Craver, supra note 32, at 34.

§ 3.22

131. See § 3.8.

opportunities.[132] And even if there are no such opportunities, the adversarial/competitive approach still has its drawbacks. The major drawback of the adversarial/competitive approach, even in zero-sum situations, is its tendency to foster deadlocks. Adversarial/competitive lawyers are less likely than other lawyers to reach agreement. This result is harmful to both parties in cases with a *settlement zone* because the parties are forgoing an agreement that would have made them both better off than they are in the absence of an agreement.[133] And even if adversarial/competitive lawyers do reach settlement, they are likely to spend lots of time and effort in doing so. By constantly trying to battle and trick each other, adversarial/competitive lawyers end up delaying resolution of their clients' disputes, typically costing their clients extra legal fees and causing stress to all concerned.

Another drawback of the adversarial/competitive approach is its tendency to make enemies. A lawyer may use the adversarial/competitive approach to achieve a one-sided settlement by "running over" a counterpart who is not using the adversarial/competitive approach. But what about the next time she faces the same counterpart? Her counterpart is likely to use the adversarial/competitive approach.[134] The counterpart may be vengeful, fighting on every issue and refusing to extend routine professional courtesies. This danger faces the adversarial/competitive lawyer even if she never again crosses paths with the same counterpart. Lawyers talk with each other about other lawyers. A lawyer's reputation as an adversarial/competitive negotiator may be known to people she has not even met. The danger of having such a reputation is discussed below.[135]

2. THE COOPERATIVE APPROACH AND THE PRISONER'S DILEMMA

Table of Sections

§ 3.23 The Cooperative Approach

Many lawyers depart from the *adversarial/competitive* approach to negotiation.[136] Rather than making an extreme opening offer, they make a reasonable one. Rather than being stingy with concessions, they make concessions willingly. Rather than aiming for a one-sided agreement, they aim for one that is objectively fair or just. Rather than employing

---

132. See § 3.30.

133. See §§ 3.11—3.13.

134. See § 3.24.

135. See id.

§ 3.23

136. See Williams, supra note 3, at 18–23 (65% of surveyed lawyers use cooperative approach).

deception and psychological warfare, they are honest and civil. They are using the *cooperative* approach to negotiation. They do so, perhaps, because they believe it is the ethical or decent approach. Or they do so because they believe it is best-suited to advancing the interests of their clients.

The cooperative approach, like the adversarial/competitive approach, is oriented toward *zero-sum* negotiation.[137] The cooperative approach should be distinguished from the *problem-solving* approach, discussed in later sections,[138] which is oriented toward *positive-sum* negotiation.

If both lawyers use the cooperative rather than adversarial/competitive approach, both parties gain. In cases in which settlement benefits both parties when compared to further litigation, settlement is more likely to be achieved if both lawyers use the cooperative approach than if they use the adversarial/competitive approach. In other words, cases that should settle, those with a *settlement zone*,[139] are more likely to do so when both sides take the cooperative approach. Many cases with settlement zones do not settle because, for instance, the negotiators conceal their true bottom lines and play the *game of chicken*.[140] Each negotiator stubbornly tries to capture more of the potential value created by a settlement and neither gives in. So they both lose by trying a case in which both would have been better off settling. This is far more likely to happen with adversarial/competitive negotiators than cooperative ones because cooperative negotiators are more willing to make concessions are more candid about the case and their bottom lines.

Not only are cases that should settle more likely to do so when all sides take the cooperative approach, these settlements are likely to be reached quickly and inexpensively. As the lawyers build mutual trust, they can dispose of the costly and time-consuming tactics employed by adversarial/competitive negotiators to battle and trick each other.[141] This point also applies to cases that should not settle, those without a settlement zone. Two cooperative lawyers are likely to discover the lack of a settlement zone faster and cheaper than two adversarial/competitive lawyers. The cooperative lawyers will still go to trial, but without wasting as much time and money beforehand. Finally, whether the case settles or not, each cooperative lawyer will likely have built goodwill with the other and enhanced her reputation for the future.[142]

When two lawyers using the cooperative approach settle a case, the settlement terms are likely to be fair or reasonable, as opposed to one-sided. Cooperative lawyers use objective standards of fairness or reasonableness such as market value, precedents, professional standards, moral

---

137. Zero-sum negotiation is defined and discussed in § 3.8.

138. See §§ 3.26—3.30. The relationship between these approaches is discussed in § 3.30.

139. See §§ 3.11—3.13.

140. See § 3.12.

141. See §§ 3.15—3.22 (discussing these tactics).

142. See § 3.24 (discussing this reputational point).

standards, tradition, equal treatment, principles of reciprocity, scientific judgment, and efficiency.[143]

The danger, of course, is that a lawyer using the cooperative approach will have a counterpart who is using the adversarial/competitive approach. The cooperative lawyer makes a reasonable opening offer, but her counterpart responds with an extreme one. The cooperative lawyer makes concessions, but her counterpart does not. The result may be a one-sided settlement in which the cooperative lawyer quickly settles at his client's bottom line.[144] The adversarial/competitive lawyer celebrates her smashing victory and is rewarded for her choice of the adversarial/competitive approach. The cooperative lawyer rightly feels like a sap.

§ 3.24 The Prisoner's Dilemma and the Importance of Reputation

The analysis in the preceding section[145] suggests that, considering only a single negotiation, you fare best if you are adversarial/competitive and your counterpart is cooperative. Your second-best result is for both lawyers to be cooperative. Your third-best result is for both lawyers to be adversarial/competitive. And you fare worst if you are cooperative and your counterpart is adversarial/competitive. This is depicted in Diagram 3–9.

143. Fisher & Ury, supra note 65, at 88–91.

144. See §§ 3.24—3.25 for ways the cooperative lawyer can avoid this.

§ 3.24

145. See § 3.23.

Diagram 3-9

	Your counterpart uses Cooperative Approach	Your counterpart uses Adversarial/Competitive Approach
You use Cooperative Approach	Your second-best result	Your fourth-best (worst) result
You use Adversarial/Competitive Approach	Your best result	Your third-best result

Given this "payoff matrix," you should always choose to be adversarial/competitive. The adversarial/competitive approach is better for you than the cooperative approach, no matter what your counterpart does. If your counterpart chooses to be cooperative then your choice to be adversarial/competitive gives you your best result, rather than your second-best result. If your counterpart chooses to be adversarial/competitive then your choice to be adversarial/competitive gives you your third-best result, rather than your fourth-best (worst) result.

The problem is that the same analysis applies to your counterpart's choice between the adversarial/competitive and cooperative approaches. Just as you should choose the adversarial/competitive approach, so should your counterpart. The result is that you both choose the adversarial/competitive approach and you each get your third best result. If only you were both cooperative, then you could each get your second best result. What is best for the two parties in the aggregate is cooperation, but each party's incentive is to advance itself at the expense of the other. This quandary is known as the Prisoner's Dilemma.

The name comes from the story that was first told in the 1950s to illustrate the following strategic interaction: Two criminals are arrested. They both have committed a serious crime, but the district attorney cannot convict either of them * * * without extracting at least one confession. The district attorney can, however, convict them both on a lesser offense without the cooperation of either. The district attorney tells each prisoner that if neither confesses, they will both be convicted of the lesser offense. Each will go to prison for two years. If, however, one of the prisoners confesses and the other does not, the former will go free and the latter will be tried for the serious crime and given the maximum penalty of ten years in prison. If both confess, the district attorney will prosecute them for the serious crime but will not ask for the maximum penalty. They will both go to prison for six years.

Each prisoner wants only to minimize time spent behind bars and has no other goal. Moreover, each is indifferent to how much time the other spends in prison. Finally, the two prisoners have no way of reaching an agreement with each other.[146]

The Prisoner's Dilemma differs from negotiation insofar as negotiators can communicate with each other, while the prisoners cannot. In other respects, however, the Prisoner's Dilemma very much resembles the negotiator's choice of whether to use an adversarial/competitive or cooperative approach.[147] It is best for the prisoners in the aggregate (fewest total years in prison) if they cooperate with each other, but each prisoner's individual incentive is to be adversarial/competitive toward each other, *i.e.*, to confess to the district attorney.

The solution to the Prisoner's Dilemma of negotiation is to change the incentives to reward cooperation. This is not possible if the negotiator cares only about the single negotiation in which the negotiator is choosing to be adversarial/competitive or cooperative. Such a negotiator's incentive is, like the prisoner's, to be adversarial/competitive.[148] But most negotiators care about the future. They care not only about this negotiation, but about future negotiations and their reputations more generally. A negotiator who cares about the future has some incentive to be cooperative. Whether this incentive outweighs the incentive to be adversarial/competitive depends on how important the future is and how much is at stake in the current negotiation. The more important the future, the greater the incentive to cooperate, and the more at stake in the current negotiation, the greater the incentive to be adversarial/competitive.

The reason negotiators who care about the future have an incentive to cooperate is reputation. A reputation as a cooperative negotiator leads to rewards in the following way.

Before you begin negotiating, you are likely to consider your counterpart's reputation and your counterpart is likely to consider your reputation.[149] If you both have firmly established reputations as coopera-

---

146. Baird, Gertner & Picker, supra note 77, at 33.

147. Compare Lax & Sebenius, supra note 51, at 39.

148. See Diagram 3–9.

149. See §§ 3.33—3.37 on preparing for negotiation.

tive negotiators, then you are both likely to use the cooperative approach in this negotiation, because that will save you both time and money compared to what would have happened had you both taken the adversarial/competitive approach.[150] Through this process, cooperative lawyers repeatedly negotiating with each other provide their clients with better and cheaper results than adversarial/competitive lawyers repeatedly negotiating with each other. Lawyers using the cooperative approach get the corner office and the vacation home, while lawyers using the adversarial/competitive approach have to hustle to make ends meet. The meek inherit the earth.

When you start negotiating with a counterpart with whom you will be negotiating many times in the future, some theorists conclude that your best long-term strategy is "Tit for Tat." Tit for Tat is the strategy of cooperating in the first negotiation and then, in future negotiations, doing whatever your counterpart did in the previous negotiation.[151] If your counterpart cooperated in the first negotiation, then you cooperate in the second negotiation. If your counterpart used the adversarial/competitive approach in the first negotiation, then you use that approach in the second negotiation. Before cooperating in the first negotiation, you tell your counterpart that you are about to cooperate and that if he fails to cooperate, you will be adversarial/competitive the next time you meet.

The reasons for the success of Tit for Tat are many: It avoids unnecessary conflict as long as the other person cooperates; it responds immediately and firmly to provocation so that one is not exploited; it gives the other person an incentive to cooperate after you retaliate because he knows you will cooperate in response; and it adopts a clear, long-term strategy that elicits an easily understood and stable responsive pattern.[152]

The incentive to cooperate becomes even greater in light of the fact that one's approach to a particular negotiation will affect one's reputation not only with that counterpart but also with other future counterparts. Lawyers talk with each other about other lawyers.

To the extent reputations matter, we can make the following two predictions. First, the more adversarial/competitive you have been in the past, the more likely you are to face an adversarial/competitive counterpart in the future. Second, the more cooperative you have been in the past, the more likely you are to face a cooperative counterpart in the

150. See § 3.23.

151. See generally Robert Axelrod, The Evolution of Cooperation (1984).

152. Murray, Rau & Sherman, supra note 83, at 161. But see Stephen B. Goldberg, Frank E.A. Sander & Nancy H. Rogers, Teacher's Manual, Dispute Resolution: Negotiation, Mediation, and Other Processes 2 (3d ed.1999).

One problem with using the Tit-for-Tat strategy in face-to-face negotiations is that a strategy of punishing one's opponent for varying from a value-creating approach may lead to retaliation based on emotions that the computer does not possess. Your opponent may feel that his value-claiming approach was justified by his legitimate fears that you would engage in value claiming first, so that you were wrong to punish him, and he will react by continuing in a value claiming mode regardless of what you do thereafter.

Id.

future.[153] Having cooperative counterparts enables you to provide your clients with better and cheaper results than if you had adversarial/competitive counterparts.[154] Therefore, a negotiator who cares about the future has an incentive to be cooperative.

Of course, a lawyer who ordinarily uses the cooperative approach will adopt the adversarial/competitive approach when faced with a counterpart known to be adversarial/competitive.[155] This targeted use of the adversarial/competitive approach will not hurt the reputation of the ordinarily-cooperative lawyer among her fellow cooperatives, because they will recognize that she is just doing what is necessary in the circumstances. When she again negotiates with fellow cooperatives, she and they will all take the cooperative approach and enjoy its benefits.

In this regard, one can analogize lawyers with reputations for using the cooperative approach to members of a club. When interacting with each other, they cooperate because the failure to cooperate would destroy one's reputation and, therefore, lessen one's future success. The bonds of reciprocal cooperation, however, extend only to fellow members of the club. Lawyers with reputations for using the adversarial/competitive approach are not treated to the cooperative approach. Memberships in the club, and the benefits of cooperation that flow from them, are awarded only to applicants who painstakingly build an impeccable reputation through a track-record of engaging in the right sort of behavior, cooperation.

Notice that this story presumes lawyers' reputations are clearly-defined and widely-known. This may be true in a small town. The number of lawyers in town is low enough that each one has a clearly-defined reputation that is known by all the others in town. This is clearly not true in larger cities; there are simply too many lawyers for each to know the reputation of every other lawyer.[156] We would expect therefore, to find greater cooperation in negotiations between two lawyers practicing in the same small town than between two lawyers practicing in the same large city. If big-city lawyers are less cooperative, it is for good reason. It is entirely rational to take the adversarial/competitive approach when your future counterparts will not know what approach you have taken in the past.[157]

---

153. See § 3.25.

154. This raises an interesting ethical issue. In some situations, your current client would benefit if you used an adversarial/competitive approach but your future clients would benefit if you used a cooperative approach on behalf of your current client. You face a conflict between what is good for your current client and what is good for your future clients. For reactions to this conflict, see Brunet & Craver, supra note 32, at 39; Riskin & Westbrook, supra note 51, at 237, 239.

155. See § 3.25.

156. Although the reputation of a law firm can serve as a proxy for the reputation of a lawyer within that firm.

157. See Diagram 3–9. See also Meltsner & Schrag, supra note 117, at 259.

The more 'tricky' [negotiation] ploys are used most commonly in urban centers, where lawyers are not likely to be negotiating repeatedly with the same adverse attorneys who will eventually recognize their favorite tactics. Lawyers who have to deal with each other in case after case are more likely to conduct an open, straightforward discussion than those

The importance of reputation is not, however, determined only by the size of a city. Even in the biggest cities, a lawyer may find herself interacting with the same handful of other lawyers over and over again. This can be the result of a specialized practice. If, for example, you specialize in defending securities fraud claims, you may find that your counterpart is invariably one of the few lawyers who specializes in asserting securities fraud claims. If you specialize in international commercial arbitration, you may find that your counterpart is invariably one of the few lawyers who also specializes in international commercial arbitration. This sort of repeated interaction among a small group of lawyers creates a small town in the big city. Reputation, in short, matters more among *repeat players* than *one-shotters*.[158] If a small group of lawyers—even if they are separated by thousands of miles—repeatedly interact among themselves, you can expect to find that reputations are important and that there are significant incentives to take a cooperative approach to negotiation.

§ 3.25 Tactics For a Cooperative Lawyer With an Adversarial/Competitive Counterpart

A lawyer who regularly uses the cooperative approach will eventually have a counterpart using the adversarial/competitive approach. The result may be a one-sided settlement in which the cooperative lawyer settles at his client's bottom line.[159] The cooperative lawyer can avoid this by quickly identifying that his counterpart is using an adversarial/competitive approach and then withholding cooperation until his counterpart's approach becomes cooperative.

The first step for the cooperative lawyer is realizing that he is dealing with an adversarial/competitive counterpart. This may be harder than it seems. One should not assume that the adversarial/competitive negotiator is necessarily loud or abrasive or that the cooperative negotiator is necessarily courteous and pleasant. Adversarial/competitive negotiators have a variety of personal styles, as do cooperative negotiators. Do not be fooled by your counterpart's courteous or pleasant style into assuming that your counterpart has adopted a cooperative approach. Your counterpart may be a wolf in sheep's clothing.[160]

Once the cooperative lawyer realizes that he has an adversarial/competitive counterpart, he should stop cooperating.[161] For example, he

who may never negotiate with each other again.
Id.

158. For another distinction between repeat players and one-shotters, see § 3.6(c), discussing risk-aversion.

§ 3.25

159. See § 3.23 and Diagram 3–9.

160. See § 3.21(h).

161. Cooperative negotiators "are forced to assume a more competitive posture to avoid the exploitation that would probably result if they were too open and accommodating with their manipulative and greedy opponents." Brunet & Craver, supra note 32, at 37.

should stop making further concessions until his counterpart catches up with concessions of her own. He should punish his counterpart for taking an adversarial/competitive approach and offer the reward of further cooperation if his counterpart adopts a cooperative approach. In short, he should adopt the strategy of Tit for Tat.[162]

Essentially, what the cooperative negotiator should do is convert a single *prisoner's dilemma*[163] into a repeated one. He should treat the negotiation, not as one single event, but as a series of events, one after the other. The counterpart's adversarial/competitive approach in an early event is punished in the following event. If the counterpart cooperates in a later event, then that cooperation is rewarded in a still later event. The Tit-for-Tat strategy for multiple negotiations can be adapted and applied to a single negotiation. Notice, however, that it works only if the cooperative lawyer discovers that his counterpart is competitive before making too many concessions. So a cooperative lawyer must keep his concessions small early in negotiation until he is confident that his counterpart is reciprocating with a cooperative approach of his own.

Tit for Tat may not work. The counterpart may remain adversarial/competitive. If so, the cooperative lawyer can do either of two things. One is to simply stop negotiating and prepare for trial. The other is to offer to settle at his client's bottom line. If that offer is rejected, of course, the cooperative lawyer should stop negotiating and prepare for trial.

3. THE PROBLEM–SOLVING APPROACH

Table of Sections

§ 3.26 Overview of Problem–Solving

(a) Positive–Sum

Unlike the *adversarial/competitive* and *cooperative* approaches,[164] which are oriented toward *zero-sum* negotiation, the *problem-solving* approach is oriented toward *positive-sum* negotiation. Positive-sum negotiation finds those possible settlement terms that are better for both parties than other possible settlement terms.[165]

---

162. See § 3.24.

163. The prisoner's dilemma is discussed in § 3.24.

164. See §§ 3.15—3.25.

165. Positive-sum negotiation is defined and discussed in § 3.9.

§ 3.26

Negotiators do not have complete control over whether their negotiation is zero-sum or positive-sum. The interests of the parties may be so diametrically opposed that their negotiation must be zero-sum, no matter how sincerely the lawyers seek to find a positive-sum aspect to it. On the other hand, the interests of the parties may present opportunities for positive-sum negotiation that go unexploited because the lawyers do not find them. In such a case, there is a zero-sum negotiation in a positive-sum situation. To put it another way, positive-sum situations can yield either positive-sum or zero-sum negotiations, while zero-sum situations can yield only zero-sum negotiations. Having a zero-sum negotiation in a positive-sum situation is not necessarily a failure. The value created by exploiting a positive-sum opportunity may be lower than the value of the time and effort required to find it.

Problem-solving lawyers generally treat settlement negotiation as collaboration by the parties and their lawyers to solve their shared challenge of identifying positive-sum situations and exploiting the opportunities they present for creating additional value. The key to doing this is considering multiple issues. Positive-sum negotiation almost never occurs if only one issue is considered, especially if that issue is the amount of money Defendant will pay Plaintiff. The interests of the parties are almost certain to be diametrically opposed on the issue of money; Plaintiff wants to receive as much as possible, while Defendant wants to pay as little as possible. If issues other than money are considered, it may be possible to find one on which the parties' interests coincide or to engage in *logrolling*. Coinciding interests and logrolling are discussed in the following two sections.

(b) Coinciding Interests

For an example of an issue on which the parties' interests coincide, consider a negligence claim for compensatory damages arising from a personal injury Defendant caused while engaged in his ordinary business activities. Both Plaintiff and Defendant may prefer that a settlement payment occur in December, rather than in the next month, January. Ordinarily, the *time-value of money*[166] causes plaintiffs to want payments to occur sooner and defendants to want payments to occur later. This Defendant's payment, however, is probably tax deductible,[167] and taxpayers generally benefit from taking deductions in the current tax year, rather than waiting until next year.[168] In other words, Defendant's tax benefit of paying in December of this year may exceed the interest it could earn on the money by waiting until January of next year to pay. If so, Defendant prefers payment in December, rather than January. Plaintiff also prefers December to January because there is no tax consider-

---

166. See § 3.9.

167. Khokhar, supra note 57, at A–28.

168. See, e.g., James Edward Maule & Lisa Marie Starczewski, Deductions: Overview and Conceptual Aspects A–39 (Tax Management Portfolio No. 503, 1995)("One of the principal consequences of timing determinations is the availability of acceleration; for most taxpayers it is advantageous to accelerate deduction of an item to the earliest taxable year permitted by the tax law.")

ation offsetting Plaintiff's desire to start earning interest on the money sooner rather than later.[169] In short, both parties prefer that the payment occur in December, rather than January. A settlement providing for payment in January would make both parties worse off than a settlement providing for payment in December. Agreeing on payment in December is a clear example of positive-sum negotiating because the parties' interests coincide on this question of when the payment occurs.

Issues on which parties' interests coincide are rare. They tend not to become issues precisely because the parties' interests coincide and all parties quickly realize that. On the other hand, tax issues are examples of issues that litigators and their clients may forget.[170]

(c) Logrolling Multiple Issues

Even in the absence of issues on which the parties' interests coincide,[171] considering multiple issues can reveal opportunities for both parties to gain. This is because the degree of importance the parties attach to an issue may differ. Suppose Plaintiff cares a lot about Issue A, but not much about Issue B, while Defendant cares a lot about Issue B, but not much about Issue A. The negotiators can create value by having Defendant concede on Issue A in exchange for Plaintiff's concession on Issue B. Each party gives on something she cares about a little to get what she cares about a lot. This sort of trade, often called *logrolling*, is the basis of most positive-sum negotiation. It works even where the parties disagree on every issue, if they prioritize issues differently.[172]

Logrolling happens only when multiple issues are considered together, rather than each issue considered in isolation. Negotiators often make the mistake of considering one issue, resolving it, and moving on to the next issue without ever returning to reconsider the first issue. This approach, while neat and organized, precludes logrolling so problem-solving negotiators avoid this approach. Rather, they consider multiple issues simultaneously and trade concessions on low-priority issues for gains on high-priority issues.

(d) Tactics Listed

To exploit positive-sum opportunities, problem-solving lawyers generally:

—focus, not on the parties' positions, but on their underlying interests and priorities,

—identify the other party's interests and priorities through questions and attentive listening,

169. The personal injury settlement payment is not taxable income to Plaintiff. Khokhar, supra note 57, at A–3.

170. Tax law's impact on settlement can be significant and complicated. See generally, Khokhar, supra note 57.

171. See § 3.26(b).

172. For an example of logrolling, see § 3.9.

—openly communicate their own client's interests and priorities, and

—invent and explore a wide variety of potential solutions.

These tactics of the problem-solving negotiator are discussed in greater detail next.

§ 3.27 Interests, Not Positions

The parties' underlying interests and priorities are central to the problem-solving approach. *Interests* should be contrasted with *positions*. Examples of a negotiator's positions include: "I demand that Defendant stop releasing chemicals into the lake," and "I offer $30,000 to settle this case." In these examples, the clients' interests are the reasons why the clients want the other party to stop releasing chemicals or to drop the case. "Your positions are what you want. Your interests are why you want them."[173] One who knows only the parties' positions on various issues can rarely determine how strongly each party cares about each issue, *i.e.*, each party's priorities. If a discharged employee demands $50,000 and his job back, the employer cannot tell how important to the employee each item is. Would the employee be just as happy with $50,000 and a different job? Is the employee so focused on getting his old job back that he will take much less than $50,000 to avoid having to work a different job?

Positive-sum negotiation typically requires identifying issues about which one party cares more strongly than the other party.[174] So positive-sum negotiation typically requires negotiators to identify what is behind each party's positions. What underlying interests motivate the party to take a particular position? Those interests may reveal priorities, *i.e.*, which issues are of great importance to a party and which issues are of lesser importance.

The discharged employee demanding $50,000 and his job back, may have no family or friends other than his co-workers at that job. His job was his social life, a source of great joy, as well as a way to earn a living. He really wants that particular job so another job, even at higher pay, will not satisfy his interests. Central to the problem-solving approach of exploring underlying interests is the recognition that people are diverse. There are no standardized people with standardized goals. Some other discharged employee would have been more concerned with the money than with the friendships at that particular job.

Identifying the interests and priorities of the particular parties to a particular dispute is crucial to the problem-solving approach. You can and should identify your client's interests before you begin negotiation.[175]

§ 3.27

173. Stephen B. Goldberg, Frank E.A. Sander & Nancy H. Rogers, Dispute Resolution: Negotiation, Mediation, and Other Processes 36 (2d ed.1992). See also Riskin & Westbrook, supra note 51, at 10–11 ("A position is what someone says he wants or is entitled to have * * * . An interest is the need or motive that underlies the position.")

174. See §§ 3.9 & 3.26(c).

175. See § 3.34.

You will typically be less able to learn the other party's interests prior to negotiation.[176] So you may try learn more about them during negotiation.

When her counterpart states a position, the problem-solving lawyer neither accepts nor rejects it. Rather, she seeks to understand the interests behind it. She takes what her counterpart says and "reframe[s] it as an attempt to deal with the problem."[177] One way to do this is to ask direct questions. The questions most likely to be effective are broad and open-ended. "Why" questions are a common example: "Why are you concerned about pollution in the lake?" or "Why do you pick $30,000 as your settlement offer?" Sometimes more indirect questions elicit more telling information. If the discharged employee was asked about his life outside of work, *e.g.*, "what are your hobbies?", he might well reveal that his friendships all revolved around the job he wants back.

In seeking to understand the other party's interests, the main point to remember is that you do not learn much while you are talking. You gather information while your counterpart or his client is talking. The longer you can keep your counterpart talking, the more likely you are to pick up clues to his client's interests. Of course, you should listen carefully. Also, you should be alert to any non-verbal signals your counterpart may, intentionally or not, be conveying. Facial expressions and body language can be significant.[178] Overall, be patient and do not rush the process of gathering information.

In identifying the other side's interests, do not forget to distinguish between lawyer and client. Lawyers have interests, too. For example, lawyers do not like to appear unskilled in the eyes of their clients or other lawyers. Your counterpart may stand in the way of a settlement that advances his client's interests if that settlement, or the way it is generated, threatens his ego. For example, making your first settlement offer "take-it-or-leave-it" may preclude acceptance from your counterpart who feels a need to "wring concessions out of you" to satisfy his own ego and to show his client how skilled he is.[179] Finally, you must remember that your counterpart may have a financial incentive that diverges from his client's interests.[180]

§ 3.28 Communicating Your Side's Interests

The problem-solving lawyer communicates to her counterpart more than her client's *positions*. She also communicates the underlying *interests* motivating those positions. In fact, she may not take any positions until late in the negotiation. She will keep the focus on the interests she needs advanced by any settlement.

---

176. See § 3.35.

177. William Ury, Getting Past No: Dealing With Difficult People 144 (1991).

178. See Brunet & Craver, supra note 32, at 44–54; Gifford, supra note 3, at 127–32.

179. The practice of making an opening offer "take-it-or-leave-it" is known as "Boulwareism" and is prohibited in collective bargaining negotiation. See N.L.R.B. v. General Electric Co., 418 F.2d 736, 756 (2d Cir.1969), cert.denied, 397 U.S. 965, 90 S.Ct. 995, 25 L.Ed.2d 257 (1970).

180. See § 3.6(b).

For instance, a problem-solving lawyer representing the discharged employee in the previous section[181] will not begin with a demand for $50,000 plus reinstatement. The problem-solving lawyer will tell her client's story:

> Here is a man with no family or friends other than his co-workers at the job he lost. Here is a man whose job was his social life, a source of great joy, as well as a way to earn a living. He really wants that job back so any settlement must take that into account.

In short, the problem-solving lawyer is honest and forthcoming with information, even her client's most important information. And she asks her counterpart to be similarly honest and forthcoming. If neither side deceives or conceals, then everyone's underlying interests and priorities can be laid bare for all to see. This allows both lawyers to identify issues on which the parties interests coincide.[182] And it allows for *logrolling,* in which one party concedes on one issue in exchange for the other party's concession on another issue.[183]

Logrolling can occur without previously laying bare everyone's interests and priorities, but in that case the logrolling may not be positive-sum. Even where negotiators consider multiple issues simultaneously and trade concessions, they may make the wrong trades. If Plaintiff cares a lot about Issue A and Defendant cares a lot about Issue B, then value is created when Plaintiff concedes on Issue B in exchange for Defendant's concession on Issue A. In contrast, value is not necessarily created, and may even be destroyed, if Plaintiff concedes on Issue B in exchange for Defendant's concession on Issue C, D, or E. And value is certainly destroyed if Plaintiff concedes on Issue A (his high-priority issue) in exchange for Defendant's concession on Issue B (her high-priority issue). Negotiators risk making these "wrong trades"—trades that miss opportunities to create value and may even destroy value—if they have not revealed to each other their side's underlying interests and priorities.

§ 3.29 Variety of Solutions

The problem-solving lawyer is in no rush to take positions, *i.e.,* to begin the exchange of offers to settle the case.[184] The problem-solving lawyer defers such talk until both sides have thoroughly explored the underlying interests and priorities of all parties. Only then is it time to "generate solutions." The problem-solving lawyer thinks in terms of "solutions," rather than "offers to settle." While they may amount to the same thing, the term "solutions" implies that the parties' dispute is a problem to be solved. Also, the problem-solving lawyer seeks to generate, not one solution, but many solutions. These features of prob-

§ 3.28

181. See § 3.27.

182. See § 3.26(b).

183. See §§ 3.9 & 3.26(c).

§ 3.29

184. See §§ 3.27—3.28.

lem-solving negotiation—thoroughly exploring interests and generating multiple solutions—may be time-consuming.

The problem-solving negotiator seeks solutions that advance both parties' interests. Designing such solutions typically requires that numerous issues be considered simultaneously.[185] Designing such solutions is difficult under the pressure of negotiation. Accordingly, problem-solving negotiators may set aside a designated time for brainstorming.[186] Brainstorming can be done with your client in private, or even with all parties and their lawyers present. The problem-solving negotiator encourages each party to generate many possible solutions before assessing any of them. The crucial point is to separate the inventive phase of generating possible solutions from the evaluative phase of assessing the merits of those possibilities.[187]

When it does come time to assess the possible solutions, the problem-solving lawyer judges them by how well they advance the interests of both parties. And when the problem-solving lawyer finally takes a position, *i.e.*, suggests a particular solution to his counterpart, he justifies it by explaining how well it satisfies the interests of both parties.

§ 3.30   Drawbacks of the Problem–Solving Approach

The drawbacks of the problem-solving approach are similar to the drawbacks of the cooperative approach.[188] The primary danger is that a lawyer using the problem-solving approach will have a counterpart using the adversarial/competitive approach. The result may be unfortunate in two respects. First, no problem-solving occurs, *i.e.*, the lawyers have zero-sum negotiation in a positive-sum situation.[189] Second, the outcome of that zero-sum negotiation is a one-sided settlement in which the problem-solving lawyer quickly settles at his client's bottom line.

To avoid this result, the problem-solving lawyer should use many of the same tactics available to a cooperative lawyer confronted with an adversarial/competitive counterpart.[190] The lessons of the *Prisoner's Dilemma*,[191] apply to the interplay between the adversarial/competitive and problem-solving approaches, just as they do to the interplay of the adversarial/competitive and cooperative approaches.

When confronted with an adversarial/competitive counterpart, the problem-solving lawyer should quickly identify that his counterpart is

---

185. See § 3.26.

186. Fisher & Ury, supra note 65, at 60–65.

187. Id.

§ 3.30

188. See §§ 3.23—3.25.

189. Having a zero-sum negotiation in a positive-sum situation, *i.e.*, declining to

problem-solve, may have been the sensible thing for the lawyers to do. The value created by exploiting a positive-sum opportunity may be lower than the value of the time and effort required to find it.

190. See § 3.25.

191. See § 3.24.

using an adversarial/competitive approach.[192] Then he should stop those problem-solving tactics that are vulnerable to an adversarial/competitive counterpart.

Importantly, the very features of the problem-solving approach that make it effective in positive-sum negotiation make it risky in zero-sum negotiation. To honestly disclose one's interests and priorities, and reveal information, especially information about bottom lines, makes one vulnerable to an adversarial/competitive negotiator.[193] Accordingly, some theorists recommend reserving the problem-solving approach until after zero-sum negotiation.[194] Once the parties have reached tentative agreement on zero-sum issues, according to these theorists, the parties can begin problem-solving. If, however, the negotiators use the adversarial/competitive approach for zero-sum negotiation prior to engaging in problem-solving, their opportunities for positive-sum negotiation may have been reduced because adversarial/competitive tactics often conceal or distort the underlying interests and priorities that must be laid bare for problem-solving to work.[195] In short, it is difficult to fully employ the adversarial/competitive and problem-solving approaches in the same negotiation.

The cooperative and problem-solving approaches can more easily be used by the same lawyer in the same negotiation. While, the problem-solving lawyer faces less danger from a cooperative counterpart than from an adversarial/competitive one, the problem-solving lawyer should not mistake her counterpart's cooperativeness for problem-solving. The counterpart may be thinking in entirely zero-sum terms. The problem-solving lawyer may need to teach her counterpart about positive-sum negotiation, *i.e.*, opportunities for expanding the pie, rather than just dividing a fixed pie in a fair or reasonable way. Teaching your counterpart about positive-sum negotiation is, however, a delicate matter.

> Pedantic lectures to a more experienced attorney on the virtues of a new type of negotiation—whether termed "problem-solving" or "principled"—are likely to be ineffective. Implicit in such assertions is a thinly veiled sense of moral superiority and a rejection of how the other negotiator has operated during his professional life. At best, such proselytizing behavior is ineffective and looks silly or naive; at worst, it is offensive.[196]

A more effective way of trying to stimulate problem-solving is to ask the sort of questions discussed in an earlier section.[197]

192. See § 3.25.

193. See, e.g., Mnookin, supra note 26, at 240; Donald G. Gifford, A Context–Based Theory of Strategy Selection in Legal Negotiation, 46 Ohio St. L.J. 41, 70 (1985).

194. Brunet & Craver, supra note 32, at 125.

195. Lax & Sebenius, supra note 51, at 34.

196. Gifford, supra note 3, at 94. Reprinted from Legal Negotiation: Theory and Applications, Donald G. Gifford 94 (1989) with permission of the West Group.

197. See § 3.27.

4. GENDER, CULTURE, RACE AND ETHNICITY

Table of Sections

§ 3.31 Gender

Empirical tests reveal differences in the way women and men negotiate. Men are more likely than women to use the adversarial/competitive approach, while women are more likely than men to use the cooperative and problem-solving approaches.[198]

> Female negotiators speak less, show more self-doubt, make fewer explicit threats and derogatory putdowns, use fewer positional commitments, are less willing to form coalitions in three-or-more-party negotiations, and exhibit more persuadable and conforming behavior. Psychologists attribute these behavioral characteristics to a woman's greater concern for maintaining harmonious interpersonal relationships. Studies also indicate that males appear to be more oriented toward the impersonal task of maximizing their own earnings; females, in contrast, seemed more sensitive and reactive to the interpersonal aspects of their relationship.[199]

That men are more likely than women to use the adversarial/competitive approach, while women are more likely than men to use the cooperative or problem-solving approaches, is consistent with differences in society's expectations about proper behavior for women and men ("gender norms"). "The norms that guide competitive, win/lose negotiating were developed by men for men, and they are, therefore compatible with stereotypical gender norms for men. These norms, however are not compatible with gender norms for women."[200]

The foregoing generalizations about women and men are just that, generalizations. There are numerous counterexamples: men who shy away from the adversarial/competitive approach and women who swear by it. And it seems likely that gender differences in negotiation are less pronounced among lawyers than among the population as a whole.

§ 3.32 Culture, Race and Ethnicity

People in different cultures tend to have different approaches to negotiation. When Americans negotiate abroad, they may encounter an

§ 3.31

198. Murray, Rau & Sherman, supra note 83, at 175. Accord Brunet & Craver, supra note 32, at 58–59.

199. Murray, Rau & Sherman, supra note 83, at 175.

200. Carol Watson, Gender versus Power as a Predictor Of Negotiation Behavior and Outcome, 10 Neg.J. 117, 125 (1994). See also Carol M. Rose, Bargaining and Gender, 18 Harv.J.L. & Pub.Pol'y 547 (1995)(women are believed to value cooperation more than men do, so men negotiating with women can demand a disproportionate share of the value created by cooperation. The man can more credibly threaten deadlock because he is, or is thought to be, more tolerant of confrontation.)

approach that: "lays particular stress on long-term and affective aspects of the relationship between the parties; is preoccupied with considerations of symbolism, status and face; and draws on highly developed communications strategies for evading confrontation."[201] Negotiators accustomed to this approach may not react well to the (stereo)typical American who thinks of himself as direct and efficient, but who may come across as blunt, aggressive, impatient and insensitive.

Even within the United States, negotiating approaches may tend to differ among various cultural, racial or ethnic groups. For example, some studies have found that black Americans tend to negotiate more cooperatively than white Americans, while other studies have found no significant differences among members of various racial groups.[202]

E. PREPARING FOR NEGOTIATION

Table of Sections

§ 3.33   Introduction

Whichever negotiation approach, or mix of approaches, you choose, preparation is essential.[203] Thoughtful lawyers do not begin negotiation until they have:

—thoroughly considered their client's interests and priorities,

—identified their client's bottom line,

—researched the other party's interests and priorities,

—made an educated guess about the other party's bottom line,

—anticipated what negotiation approach(es) their counterpart is likely to use, and

—decided what negotiation approach(es) to use.

Preparation has a number of benefits. A poorly-prepared negotiator may fail to advance her client's interests simply because she does not know what they are. A well-prepared lawyer has a clear understanding of not only her own client's interests, but also the other party's interests. All approaches to negotiation rest on the insight that knowing your counterpart's goals helps you to achieve your own goals. Also, a negoti-

§ 3.32

201. Raymond Cohen, Negotiating Across Cultures: Communication Obstacles in International Diplomacy 153–54 (1991).

202. See Jeffrey Z. Rubin & Bert R. Brown, The Social Psychology of Bargaining and Negotiation 163 (1975); Charles

Craver, The Impact of Gender on Clinical Negotiating Achievement, 6 Ohio St.J.on Disp.Resol. 1, 17 n.81 (1990).

§ 3.33

203. Williams, supra note 3, at 20–30.

ator whose preparation gives her a good sense of her own client's bottom-line, and her counterpart's, has a better sense of when to take the offer on the table, when to push for a better deal, and when to turn from negotiation to trial.

§ 3.34 Identifying Your Client's Interests and Bottom Line

Identifying your client's interests may take some time and effort. It would make lawyering easier if all clients, upon retaining you, told you— in a clear, organized manner—all that is relevant and provided you with all relevant documents and materials. Unfortunately, it rarely works that way. Clients may not, for a variety of reasons, tell you what you need to know. For example, a divorcing client may say he most wants custody of the children because he is embarrassed to say what he really wants, which is to keep his wife from getting any money. Clients may fail to consider all available alternatives. For instance, a plaintiff may tell you she wants to sue for money, because that is what she thinks lawyers do, when what she really wants is equitable relief or even just an apology from the defendant. Sometimes a client will lie to his lawyer because the client is engaged in illegal or unethical activities and does not want the lawyer (or anyone else) to know about it.

To identify their clients' interests, lawyers should learn to interview their clients in a way that makes the client feel comfortable telling the lawyer the whole truth and nothing but the truth.[204] And forthright communication must go the other way, too. The Model Rules of Professional Conduct state that "[a] lawyer shall explain a matter to the extent reasonably necessary to permit the client to make informed decisions regarding the representation."[205]

Sometimes, lawyers and clients disagree about what the client's interests are. Some lawyers will quickly defer to the client as the best judge of his own interests. Other lawyers may try to persuade a client that what he thinks is in his interest really is not.

Once the client's interests are identified, the lawyer and client can formulate a *bottom line*.[206] This will require considering questions like:

> What is the likelihood the case will be dismissed before trial? If it does go to trial, what is the likelihood of a plaintiff's verdict? If Plaintiff does win a verdict, what remedy will the court order? How

§ 3.34

204. Books on the subject of interviewing and counseling include: Robert M. Bastress & Joseph D. Harbaugh, Interviewing, Counseling and Negotiating: Skills for Effective Representation (1990); David A. Binder, Paul Bergman & Susan C. Price, Lawyers As Counselors: A Client–Centered Approach (1991); Robert F. Cochran, Jr., John M.A. DiPippa & Martha M. Peters, The Counselor-at-Law: A Collaborative Approach to Client Interviewing and Counseling (1999); Thomas L. Schaffer & James R. Elkins, Legal Interviewing and Counseling in a Nutshell (1987).

205. Model Rule of Professional Conduct 1.4(b)(1999).

206. Bottom lines are discussed in § 3.11.

much money can a jury be expected to award? What is the likelihood that any award of damages will actually be paid?

How much money will litigation cost? How much time will litigation cost? How will litigation affect reputations? Will it be traumatic, vindicating or both?[207]

Answers to these questions will help the lawyer and client predict how well further litigation will advance the client's interests. This prediction can then be compared to possible settlement terms to see which better advances the client's interests.[208]

§ 3.35   Identifying Other Party's Interests and Bottom Line

As difficult as it may be to identify your client's interests, that is usually easier to do than identifying the other party's interests. To inquire about the other party's interests, you can use discovery, such as depositions and document requests. You can also use "informal discovery" such as searches of public records, inquiries to the other party's neighbors, employers or business associates, and even hiring an investigator to spy on the other party. During negotiation, you can obtain further information that may shed light on the other party's interests and bottom line.[209]

§ 3.36   Adjusting Approaches During Stages of Negotiation

Preparing for negotiation includes anticipating the negotiation approach(es) your counterpart will use. You may have repeatedly negotiated with this counterpart before and know that she always uses the same approach.[210] Or you may never have negotiated with this counterpart before, so you contact others to learn what you can about her approach to negotiation.

While you will have decided what negotiation approach(es) to use as part of your preparation, you must be prepared to adjust. For example, if you planned to use the cooperative or problem-solving approach because you expected your counterpart to do likewise, you may want to switch quickly to the adversarial/competitive approach if you discover that your counterpart is using it.[211] On the other hand, you may want to abandon your planned adversarial/competitive approach if you see that your use of it seems to be jeopardizing important relationships or just wasting time and money.[212]

207. These questions are discussed in § 3.5(a).

208. See §§ 3.5, 3.6 & 3.11—3.13.

§ 3.35

209. See §§ 3.19 & 3.27.

§ 3.36

210. See § 3.24.

211. See §§ 3.25 & 3.30.

212. See § 3.23.

Just as you must be prepared to adjust your negotiating approach, you must be prepared to adjust your bottom line. As a lawyer acquires more information over time, she should reconsider her client's bottom line.[213] Softening your bottom line is a sensible reaction to new information revealing weakness in your case. But you should be very cautious about softening your bottom line in the presence of your counterpart. Do not ever forget that your counterpart wants you to soften your bottom line. Your counterpart may be engaging in deception and psychological warfare to try to get you to soften your bottom line.[214] Do not fall for it. If your counterpart has you doubting your bottom line, take a break. Walk away from your counterpart or end the phone call. Give yourself time to think without pressure. Ask yourself, or a trusted confidant: are you softening your bottom line because of your counterpart's tactics? Or has something really changed since you originally determined your bottom line?

§ 3.37 Specific Preparations

You can make more specific preparations for your negotiation only after you have researched both parties' interests and priorities, formulated your bottom line, made an educated guess about your counterpart's bottom line and anticipated both lawyers' approaches to negotiation. Your specific preparations relate to questions like:

—What information do you to seek to obtain? How?

—What information will you disclose? When?

—What will be your opening offer/position? When will you communicate it?

—How will you defend your opening offer/position, *i.e.*, what are the arguments on behalf of it?

—What counter-arguments do you expect?

—When will you make concessions? How big will they be?

—What are the principled arguments for making your planned concessions but not conceding further?

No matter how thoroughly a lawyer prepares for negotiation, she will not be able to force the negotiation to follow her script. An overly-scripted negotiator will be less successful than one who easily adjusts as the negotiation develops.

F. LAW GOVERNING SETTLEMENT

Table of Sections

213. See § 3.5(b).   **214.** See §§ 3.15—3.22.

§ 3.38   Criminal and Tort Law; "Good Faith" in Negotiation

Many areas of law govern settlement negotiation. Most basically, criminal law and tort law prohibit negotiating tactics such as violence, extortion, and fraud.[215] Negotiators may engage in metaphorical arm-twisting, but they may not literally twist their counterparts' arms. Other negotiating tactics are less clearly prohibited. For example, negotiators may engage in various tactics that, in the eyes of some, constitute "bad faith." The leading case imposing liability on this theory is *Hoffman v. Red Owl*.[216]

Red Owl was a chain of grocery stores. Hoffman wanted to be a Red Owl franchisee. Hoffman said he had $18,000 to invest, and Red Owl assured him that this would be a sufficient amount of money to acquire a franchise.[217] Red Owl advised Hoffman to do a number of things to gain experience in the grocery business, and Hoffman did them.[218] Red Owl kept raising more demands of Hoffman before it would sell him the franchise. Red Owl finally insisted that his contribution be $34,000, instead of the originally promised $18,000.[219] Hoffman sued Red Owl and won on a theory of promissory estoppel.[220] According to the court, Red Owl made promises to Hoffman and Hoffman reasonably relied on those promises.

The *Hoffman* case remains a rarity; few courts impose liability for negotiating "in bad faith." The one significant exception is negotiation between labor unions and employers. The National Labor Relations Act imposes on these parties a duty to negotiate in good faith.[221] Outside the collective bargaining context, however, there is generally no duty to negotiate in good faith.[222] In settlement negotiations, the parties should

---

§ 3.38

215. The tort of fraud (deceit) is not discussed in this book but a related topic, misrepresentation as a ground for rescinding a settlement, is discussed in § 3.5(b). For an overview of the tort of fraud, see Robert E. Keeton et al., Prosser and Keeton on the Law of Torts ch.18 (5th ed.1984).

216. 26 Wis.2d 683, 133 N.W.2d 267 (Wis.1965).

217. Id. at 269.

218. Id. at 269–70.

219. Id. at 271.

220. See Restatement (Second) of Contracts § 90 (1981)("A promise which the promisor should reasonably expect to induce action or forbearance on the part of the promisee or a third person and which does induce such action or forbearance is binding if injustice can be avoided only by enforcement of the promise. The remedy granted for breach may be limited as justice requires.")

221. 28 U.S.C. §§ 158(a)(5),(b)(3) & (d)(1994). See, e.g., N.L.R.B. v. General Electric Co., 418 F.2d 736 (2d Cir.1969) ("Boulwareism", *i.e.*, take-it-or-leave-it bargaining, prohibited), cert.denied, 397 U.S. 965, 90 S.Ct. 995, 25 L.Ed.2d 257 (1970).

222. See, e.g., Restatement (Second) of Contracts § 205 (limiting duty of good faith and fair dealing to contract's "performance and enforcement", as distinguished from its formation). While liability insurers owe plaintiffs no duty to negotiate in good faith, liability insurers may owe their policyholders a duty to negotiate with plaintiffs in a certain way. See Keeton & Widiss, supra note 42, at § 4.8.

be keenly aware that they are negotiating at arms' length, *i.e.*, neither owes any fiduciary duty to the other, so courts should be especially reluctant to impose any good faith requirement in this context.

§ 3.39   Sales Law

A settlement is the sale of a claim. The seller is the plaintiff (or potential plaintiff if the dispute is not in litigation.) The buyer is the defendant or potential defendant. Sales of claims are governed by law similar to the law governing other sales, such as sales of real estate, goods or intangible property.[223]

Assume, for example, that Sykes rear-ends Epstein on Lake Shore Drive.[224] Epstein threatens to sue Sykes for negligence. To settle this dispute, Sykes might pay Epstein to complete, sign, notarize, and deliver the following document.

§ 3.39

223. For exceptions to this generalization, see Jeffrey A. Parness, Advanced Civil Procedure: Civil Claim Settlement Laws (2000)(frequently contrasting law governing civil claim settlements with law governing sales of "widgets").

224. This example is inspired by a Torts class taught by Alan O. Sykes at the University of Chicago Law School.

GENERAL RELEASE

TO ALL WHOM THESE PRESENTS SHALL COME OR MAY CONCERN, GREETING: KNOW YE, That _____ for and in consideration of the sum of _____

dollars ($_____) to _____ in hand paid, the receipt whereof is hereby acknowledged, have remised, released, and forever discharged, and by these presents do for _____ heirs, executors and administrators and assigns, remise, release and forever discharge _____, his successors and assigns, and/or his, her, their, and each of their associates, heirs, executors and administrators, and any and all other persons, associations and corporations, whether herein named or referred to or not, of and from any and every claim, demand, right, or cause of action, of whatsoever kind or nature, either in law or in equity, arising from or by reason of any bodily and/or personal injuries known or unknown sustained by me, and/or damage to property, or otherwise, as the result of a certain accident which happened on or about the ___ day of _____, 20__ for which I have claimed the said _____ to be legally liable, but this release shall not be construed as an admission of such liability.

In Witness Whereof _____ have hereunto set _____ hand and seal the _____ day of _____ in the year two thousand_____

Sealed and delivered in the presence of

_____   _____ (Seal)
(Witness)
_____   _____ (Seal)
(Witness)

State of
                          } ss.
County of

On this ____ day of _____, 20 ___ before me personally appeared

_____ to me known, and known to me to be the same person described in and who executed the within instrument and _____ acknowledged to me that _____ executed the same.

_____
_____
(Official Title)

If Epstein then sued Sykes for damages arising out of the Lake Shore Drive collision, Sykes would attach the release to his answer or motion to dismiss the lawsuit. The case would be dismissed unless Epstein could establish a ground to rescind the settlement. Grounds to rescind a settlement resemble grounds to rescind other sales. These grounds include duress, misrepresentation, mistake, and unconscionability. Such grounds are discussed in the following paragraph.

If Epstein signed the release while Sykes pointed a gun at Epstein, a finding of duress would allow Epstein to rescind the settlement. While settlements have been rescinded due to duress,[225] duress is far less

225. See, e.g., Willms Trucking Co. v. JW Construction Co., 314 S.C. 170, 442

common than misrepresentation. A settlement induced by a material misrepresentation is voidable by the party relying on the misrepresentation. Many common negotiation tactics at least border on misrepresentation.[226] Similarly, rescission may be available where both parties made a material mistake as to a basic assumption of the settlement. Epstein might make such an argument if his personal injuries turn out to be much more severe than anyone thought at the time of settlement.[227] Finally, an extremely one-sided settlement might be voidable on unconscionability grounds.[228]

Each of the grounds just discussed allows a party, at its option, to rescind. In contrast, some settlements are void, as against public policy, even if neither party seeks rescission. To put it another way, court approval is required to form a legally-binding settlement in some classes of disputes. In divorce proceedings, for instance, courts insist that settlements adequately serve the interests of children and, to a lesser extent, both spouses.[229] In class actions, courts insist that settlements adequately serve the interests of class members.[230] These examples are exceptions, though. Courts are generally happy to bless the parties' settlement. Judges are often quite eager to clear their dockets.

The settlement just discussed was a contemporaneous exchange. Epstein delivered the signed release to Sykes at the same time Sykes paid Epstein. The release imposed no affirmative duties to perform on either party. Other settlement agreements, in contrast, do involve promises to perform in the future. Suppose, for example, that Plaintiff sues Defendant for negligence causing an auto accident. At some point during litigation, the parties agree in writing to settle the claim for $300,000 payable in three annual installments of $100,000 each. The writing signed by the parties may resemble the following document with, of course, the blanks filled in.

S.E.2d 197 (S.C.App.1994); Service Fire Ins. Co. v. Reed, 220 Miss. 794, 72 So.2d 197 (Miss.1954).

226. See §§ 3.17—3.18.

227. See, e.g., Taylor v. Chesapeake & Ohio Railway Co., 518 F.2d 536 (4th Cir. 1975).

228. See, e.g., In re Marriage of Moran, 136 Ill.App.3d 331, 91 Ill.Dec. 234, 483 N.E.2d 580 (Ill.App.1985)(divorce settlement "manifestly unfair and unconscionable when considering the parties' relative circumstances and station in life"; also misrepresentation, duress and coercion).

229. See, e.g., Unif.Marriage and Divorce Act § 306(a)-(c)(1982). "[T]he terms of the separation agreement, except those providing for the support, custody, and visitation of children, are binding upon the court unless it finds, after considering the economic circumstances of the parties and any other relevant evidence produced by the parties, on their own motion or on request of the court, that the separation agreement is unconscionable." Id. § 306(b).

230. See, e.g., Fed.R.Civ.P. 23(e)("A class action shall not be dismissed or compromised without the approval of the court, and notice of the proposed dismissal or compromise shall be given to all members of the class in such manner as the court directs.")

Agreement made _____, 20__, between _____, of _____ [*address*], City of _____, County of _____, State of _____, referred to as plaintiff and _____, of _____ [*address*], City of _____, County of _____, State of _____, referred to as defendant.

RECITALS

A. On _____, 20__, plaintiff suffered _____ [*specify, such as:* personal injuries and damage to property as a result of an automobile accident at the intersection of _____ (*street*) and _____ (*street*) in the City of _____, County of _____, State of _____, involving plaintiff's automobile and an automobile owned and operated by defendant]. The damages suffered by plaintiff are listed in a schedule, marked Exhibit ____ and attached and made a part of this instrument.

B. On account of the occurrence described in Paragraph A, an action for the recovery of damages in the total amount of _____ Dollars ($____) was filed by plaintiff against defendant in _____ [*court*] as civil action No. ____, entitled _____ v _____.

C. Plaintiff contends that the sole cause of the occurrence described in Paragraph A was defendant's negligence, in that defendant _____ [*set forth alleged negligence of defendant*]. On the other hand, defendant contends that it is not liable to plaintiff because _____ [*set forth defense of defendant*].

D. Plaintiff and defendant are willing to compromise and settle their differences in the litigation at present pending between them.

AGREEMENT

In consideration of the mutual covenants set forth, the parties agree as follows:

SECTION ONE
PURPOSE

This agreement is made and executed for the sole purpose of settling between plaintiff and defendant the litigation at present existing between them arising from the occurrence described above and to terminate any controversy or claims for injuries or damages of any nature, whether now known or hereafter known, resulting from such occurrence, so that, by the execution of this agreement and the acceptance of the payments provided, plaintiff shall be barred completely and forever from making any further claims or bringing any other actions or suits in connection with such occurrence.

The execution of this agreement by defendant does not constitute an admission of negligence or liability to plaintiff as a result of the described occurrence.

SECTION TWO
TERMS OF SETTLEMENT

a. Payment for property damage. Defendant agrees to pay plaintiff on the execution of this agreement the amount of _____ Dollars ($_____) as compensation for the damages to plaintiff's automobile.

b. Payment for personal injuries. Defendant agrees to pay to plaintiff as compensation for plaintiff's personal injuries the following:

(1) The amount of _____ Dollars ($_____) for the medical, hospital, and nursing expenses of plaintiff resulting from the described occurrence.

(2) The amount of _____ Dollars ($_____) per year, beginning with the year 20__ and continuing up to

and including the year 20__, such annual payments to be made on or before the _____ day of _____ [*specify month*] of each year.

c. Payment for litigation expenses. Defendant agrees to pay to plaintiff the amount of _____ Dollars ($____) as reimbursement for actual litigation expenses, other than attorney fees, incurred by plaintiff.

d. Payment for attorney fees. Defendant agrees to pay to plaintiffs attorney the amount of _____ Dollars ($____) as and for claimant's attorney fees. Such payments shall be made as follows: _____ [*specify manner of payment*].

e. Death of plaintiff before receiving all payments. In the event plaintiff dies before receiving all the payments to which plaintiff is entitled as specified above, payment shall be made to _____ [*specify, such as:* plaintiff's executor or administer or _____ (*beneficiary*)].

SECTION THREE
RELEASE OF DEFENDANT

In consideration of the payments agreed to be made, plaintiff for plaintiff, and legal representatives, successors, and beneficiaries of plaintiff, agrees to release and discharge defendant, and heirs, and legal representatives of defendant, from any and all claims, damages, causes of action of any kind, for personal injuries or property damage suffered by plaintiff in connection with the described occurrence, whether now known or hereafter known, and whether existing or subsequently arising. Plaintiff further agrees to file a dismissal of the legal action against defendant now pending in _____ [*court*] on the happening of all of the following:

a. On receipt by plaintiff of the amounts agreed on to be paid as provided in Section Two, Paragraphs a, b, and c of this agreement.

b. On receipt by plaintiff's attorney of the amount agreed on to be paid by defendant as attorney fees as provided in Section Two, Paragraph d of this agreement.

SECTION FOUR
WAIVER

No waiver of any of the terms of this agreement shall be valid unless in writing and signed by all parties to this agreement. The failure of plaintiff to enforce at any time any of the provisions of this agreement, or to require at any time performance by defendant of any of the provisions, shall not be construed to be a waiver of such provisions, or the right of plaintiff to thereafter enforce each and every such provision. No waiver of any breach of this agreement shall be held to be a waiver of any other or subsequent breach.

In witness whereof, the parties have executed this agreement at _____ [*place of execution*] the day and year first above written.

[*Signatures*]

[*Acknowledgment*]

This agreement is technically known as an *accord*.[231] The most basic terms of this contract are Defendant's promise to pay and Plaintiff's promises to dismiss the suit and to "release and discharge" Defendant. The legal effect of this accord is not to discharge Defendant's underlying tort-law duty, but merely to suspend it. To discharge that duty, Defendant must perform the accord; *i.e.*, pay three annual installments of $100,000 each.[232] Performance of an accord is called *satisfaction*.

Instead of performing the accord, Defendant may breach it by failing to pay an installment when due. The legal effect of Defendant's material breach is to give Plaintiff a choice of suing in contract for breach of the accord or in tort on Defendant's underlying duty.[233] Recall that the

231. See Melissa K. Stull, Accord and Satisfaction, 1 Am.Jur.2d 465 (1994).

232. See Restatement (Second) of Contracts § 281(1)(1981).

233. See id. § 281(2).

underlying duty had been suspended, rather than discharged. That duty is revived by Defendant's breach of the accord. In contrast, as long as Defendant's underlying tort-law duty remains suspended, any suit to enforce that duty will be dismissed. Such a dismissal enforces Plaintiff's duty to perform the accord.

This agreement is a "structured settlement" because it provides for a series of installment payments, rather than one single payment. This example of three installment payments of $100,000 each is unrealistically simple. Structured settlements are often quite complicated and subject to important considerations of tax law.[234] Structured settlements usually provide that, rather than making a series of payments directly to the plaintiff, the defendant will make a single payment to an insurance company or other financial institution which will then pay plaintiff a series of payments. This is the defendant buying an "annuity" for the plaintiff.

The arguments available to parties seeking to rescind a settlement are also available as defenses to a breach of contract. The settlement agreement just discussed basically consists of Defendant's promise to pay and Plaintiff's promise to dismiss the tort claim. Plaintiff might breach by pursuing the tort claim. Defendant might breach by failing to make a payment when due. Either way, the breaching party might defend its breach with arguments of the sort discussed above: duress, misrepresentation, mistake and unconscionability. Contract law defenses shape litigation about settlement agreements.

Contract law defenses also shape the negotiation of settlement agreements. For example, lawyers who want their settlement agreements to be enforceable are careful to ensure that none of their statements during negotiation is a material misrepresentation. They also seek to foreclose any claims of mistake by anticipating contingencies and expressly addressing them in the settlement agreement.

Settlement agreements may have to be in writing to be enforceable. This varies from state to state.[235] Even in states enforcing oral settlements generally, a writing will be required if the subject matter of the settlement is within the Statute of Frauds,[236] like an interest in land or a promise that cannot be performed within a year.

§ 3.40 Agency Law

Settlements often implicate the law of agency because a lawyer negotiating on behalf of a client is the client's agent. Without a grant of

234. See generally Halpern, supra note 62; Khokhar, supra note 57.

235. Compare, e.g., Tex.R.Civ.P. 11 ("Unless otherwise provided in these rules, no agreement between attorneys or parties touching any suit pending will be enforced unless it be in writing, signed and filed with the papers as part of the record, or unless it be made in open court and entered of record."); Gordon v. Royal Caribbean Cruises Ltd. 641 So.2d 515 (Fla.Dist.Ct.App.1994); City of Delray Beach v. Keiser, 699 So.2d 855 (Fla.Dist.Ct.App.1997), with Lampe v. O'Toole, 292 Ill.App.3d 144, 226 Ill.Dec. 320, 685 N.E.2d 423, 424 (Ill.App. 1997)("oral settlement agreement is enforceable"); Kaiser Foundation Health Plan v. Doe, 136 Or.App. 566, 903 P.2d 375 (Ore.Ct.App.1995)(enforcing oral settlement agreement formed during mediation).

236. See, e.g., B–Mall Co. v. Williamson, 977 S.W.2d 74, 77 (Mo.App.1998).

authority from the client, a lawyer cannot settle a claim. Suppose Plaintiff's lawyer and Defendant's lawyer agree on a settlement. If Plaintiff disapproves of the settlement, she will not be bound by it unless she gave her lawyer authority to bind her.[237] That authority can be *actual* or *apparent*.[238] Plaintiff's lawyer would have actual authority if Plaintiff had told him, for instance, "I will go along with whatever deal you can get," or "I authorize you to settle anywhere over $30,000." Plaintiff's lawyer would have apparent authority if Plaintiff had led Defendant or Defendant's lawyer to reasonably believe that Plaintiff had given her lawyer authority to bind her to a settlement. Cases are split on the question of whether a client "clothes" her lawyer with apparent authority to settle a case merely by holding out that lawyer as the counsel representing her in the case.[239] Some cases distinguish settlement agreements made in open court from those made away from the courthouse, with the lawyer's authority to settle more readily found with respect to in-court settlements.[240]

Even if a lawyer lacks actual or apparent authority to settle, the client will be bound by the settlement if the client subsequently ratifies it.

§ 3.41 Multiple Parties: Indemnity, Contribution and Mary Carter Agreements

A Defendant making a settlement payment to Plaintiff may have a right to reimbursement from someone else, whom we will call Third Party. Such a right can be created by a contract. As an example, consider a contract clause obligating Third Party to "hold harmless" Defendant for liability Defendant incurs to Plaintiff as a result of Defendant's performance of its contract with Third Party. Another common example arises in insurance. Insurance companies paying claims of their policyholders generally acquire, *i.e.*, are "subrogated" to, the policyholder's rights against whomever injured the policyholder.[241] A right to indemnity can also be created by non-contract law. For instance, an employer who is vicariously liable for its employee's tort has a right to indemnity from the employee.[242]

§ 3.40

237. See, e.g., Fennell v. TLB Kent Co., 865 F.2d 498, 502 (2d Cir.1989).

238. See, e.g., United States v. Int'l Brotherhood of Teamsters, 986 F.2d 15 (2d Cir.1993)(both actual and apparent authority).

239. Compare, e.g., Capital Dredge & Dock Corp. v. City of Detroit, 800 F.2d 525, 530 (6th Cir.1986)(apparent authority), Clark v. Perino, 235 Ga.App. 444, 509 S.E.2d 707, 712 (Ga.App.1998)(same), with Fennell v. TLB Kent Co., 865 F.2d 498, 502 (2d Cir.1989)("client does not create appar-

ent authority for his attorney to settle a case merely by retaining the attorney."); Restatement of the Law Governing Lawyers § 39, comment d (Proposed Final Draft No.1, 1996)(no authority).

240. See, e.g., Koval v. Simon Telelect, Inc., 693 N.E.2d 1299 (Ind.1998).

§ 3.41

241. Keeton & Widiss, supra note 42, at § 3.10.

242. Keeton et al., supra note 215, § 51.

The law governing settlement acquires another layer of complexity in multi-party disputes. An example is contribution among joint tortfeasors. In most jurisdictions, joint tortfeasors are jointly and severally liable to the plaintiff, but they have, after paying a judgment, a right to contribution from each other in proportion to degree of fault. Contribution becomes more complicated when one defendant settles before judgment. Cases and statutes are divided on whether a settling defendant can recover contribution from non-settling defendants, and whether non-settling defendants have a right to contribution from the settling defendant.[243]

Sometimes one defendant will settle pursuant to an agreement with the plaintiff that makes the amount of the settling defendant's payment turn on the amount the plaintiff wins against the non-settling defendants. These so-called "Mary Carter" agreements are often unenforceable or enforceable only if promptly disclosed to the non-settling defendants.[244]

The Mary Carter agreement is an extreme example of what occurs during many multiple-party litigations, coalition building. Plaintiffs suing multiple defendants can "divide and conquer" in many ways. The plaintiff can release a particular defendant from litigation in exchange for: money to finance further litigation against the other defendants, information that will strengthen Plaintiff's case against the other defendants, and even the testimony of the settling defendant.

§ 3.42   Confidentiality

(a) Generally

Settlement negotiation is a means of discovery in litigation. Lawyers are very reluctant to reveal anything in settlement negotiations that could come back to haunt them if negotiations fail and litigation continues. On the other hand, the *problem-solving* approach to negotiation generally involves the free exchange of information between the parties.[245] It does so because *positive-sum* negotiation is inhibited by secrecy. In some cases, mutually-beneficial settlement options emerge only when each side reveals sensitive information to the other. So a problem-solving negotiator may be willing to reveal sensitive information to her counterpart.

Even if a negotiator is willing to reveal sensitive information to her counterpart, she may not want that information revealed to anyone else. Such information, if it becomes public, might cause her client embarrassment or financial loss. So settlement negotiation, especially the problem-

---

243. Keeton et al., supra note 215, § 50; Restatement (Second) of Torts § 886A, comment m, pp.343–344.

244. See June Entman, Mary Carter Agreements: An Assessment of Attempted Solutions, 38 Fla.L.Rev. 521 (1986).

§ 3.42

245. See § 3.28.

solving sort, benefits from tools to increase the certainty that what is revealed in settlement negotiation will not "leave the room."

(b) Confidentiality Agreements Prior to Negotiation or During Litigation

One tool to increase the certainty that what is revealed in settlement negotiation will not "leave the room" is the contract. At the outset of negotiation, participants may agree that any information revealed during the negotiation will remain confidential.

While confidentiality agreements may be generally enforceable,[246] they are unlikely to be enforced when the breach, *i.e.*, the disclosure of information, is introducing that information as evidence in litigation. Public policy generally voids agreements to withhold evidence from judicial proceedings.[247] The intrusive power of the subpoena trumps the protection of contract. Also, a confidentiality agreement only binds those who sign it. It does nothing to protect against discovery via a subpoena from someone not a party to the confidentiality agreement.

On the other hand, if the parties are litigating, they may jointly seek a court order requiring the confidentiality of information exchanged in discovery and settlement negotiations.[248] This order is called a "protective order" or "seal." "If a court orders a deposition or other discovery sealed it normally prohibits the parties and attorneys from making any disclosure of the contents of the discovery to any third party."[249] A party who breaches a protective order is in contempt of court. The seal agreed to by the parties is, however, sometimes overcome by a subpoena in another case if the party seeking the discovery can demonstrate a substantial need or that the protective order was improvidently granted in the first action.[250]

---

246. See C.R. & S.R. v. E., 573 So.2d 1088 (Fla.Dist.Ct.App.1991)(enforcing confidentiality agreement with injunction against disclosure).

247. 8 John H. Wigmore, Evidence in Trials at Common Law § 2286, at 528 (1964). But see Simrin v. Simrin, 233 Cal. App.2d 90, 43 Cal.Rptr. 376, 379 (Cal.1965)(enforcing agreement not to subpoena rabbi who acted as marriage counselor for parties).

248. The authority for such orders comes from Federal Rule of Civil Procedure 26(c) and its state counterparts, as well as from a court's inherent authority over litigation before it.

Protective orders are * * * often obtained by agreement, particularly regarding confidential information and in litigation likely to involve a large volume of documents. Frequently these take the form of "umbrella" protective orders that authorize any person producing information to designate that which is confidential as protected under the order. One distinguished judge noted in 1981 that he was "unaware of any case in the past half-dozen years of even a modicum of complexity where an umbrella protective order * * * has not been agreed to by the parties and approved by the Court. Protective orders have been used so frequently that a degree of standardization is appearing."

8 Charles A. Wright et al., Federal Practice and Procedure § 2035 (2d ed.1994)(quoting Zenith Radio Corp. v. Matsushita Elec. Indus. Corp., 529 F.Supp. 866, 889 (E.D.Pa. 1981)).

249. Wright et al., supra note 248, at § 2042.

250. For courts' diverging views on the standard for breaking the seal, see Wright et al., supra note 248, at § 2044.1. See also Citizens First National Bank of Princeton v. Cincinnati Ins. Co., 178 F.3d 943 (7th Cir.1999)(Posner, J.).

(c) Rules of Evidence and Discovery

Suppose settlement negotiations fail and the parties go to trial. One side may seek to introduce as evidence what the other side said during settlement negotiations. Such statements are not likely to be admitted into evidence. Federal Rule of Evidence 408 says "conduct or statements made in compromise negotiations" are not admissible "to prove liability or invalidity of the claim or its amount." The full text of Rule 408 is:

> Evidence of (1) furnishing or offering or promising to furnish, or (2) accepting or offering or promising to accept, a valuable consideration in compromising or attempting to compromise a claim which was disputed as to either validity or amount, is not admissible to prove liability for or invalidity of the claim or its amount. Evidence of conduct or statements made in compromise negotiations is likewise not admissible. This rule does not require the exclusion of any evidence otherwise discoverable merely because it is presented in the course of compromise negotiations. This rule also does not require exclusion when the evidence is offered for another purpose, such as proving bias or prejudice of a witness, negativing a contention of undue delay, or proving an effort to obstruct a criminal investigation or prosecution.[251]

Most states have adopted Rule 408 or something similar.[252] The policy behind this rule is to encourage settlement.

Note that Rule 408 does not invariably exclude from evidence all statements made in settlement negotiation. The statements must be related to settling a civil claim, not a criminal prosecution,[253] or a dispute not yet on the verge of litigation.[254] And even statements related to settling a civil claim are admissible if offered for purposes other than "proving liability for or invalidity of the claim or its amount." Such purposes include proving bias or prejudice, undue delay or obstruction of

---

251. Fed.R.Evid.408.

252. 4 Wigmore, supra note 247, § 1062 n.1 (Supp.1998). Some other states, however, do not exclude from evidence statements of fact made during settlement negotiations unless stated hypothetically or intertwined with an offer. See Batavia Turf Farms v. County of Genessee, 239 A.D.2d 903, 659 N.Y.S.2d 681 (N.Y.App.Div.1997); People v. Kilbride, 16 Ill.App.3d 820, 306 N.E.2d 879, 881 (Ill.App.1974); Rochester Machine Corp. v. Mulach Steel Corp. 449 A.2d 1366, 1371, 498 Pa. 545 (Pa.1982).

253. United States v. Peed, 714 F.2d 7, 9 (4th Cir.1983).

254. Crues v. KFC Corp., 768 F.2d 230 (8th Cir.1985)(Rule 408 does not apply); Cassino v. Reichhold Chems., Inc., 817 F.2d 1338, 1342–43 (9th Cir.1987)(Rule 408 does not bar evidence of termination package where employer offers to give severance pay in exchange for release of discrimination claims because plaintiff "had not asserted any claim at the time [defendant] asked for the release"); Pierce v. F.R. Tripler & Co., 955 F.2d 820, 827 (2d Cir.1992)(where a party threatens litigation and has initiated the first administrative steps in litigation, "any offer made between attorneys will be presumed to be an offer within the scope of Rule 408."); Affiliated Mfrs., Inc. v. Aluminum Co., of America, 56 F.3d 521, 527 (3d Cir.1995)(Rule 408 "applies where an actual dispute or a difference of opinion exists, rather than when discussions crystallize to the point of threatened litigation"); Winchester Packaging Inc. v. Mobil Chem. Co., 14 F.3d 316, 320 (7th Cir.1994)(reference to involving lawyers is not decisive on issue of whether there is a dispute, but is factor to be considered).

justice. Also, Rule 408, like any evidence rule, only applies to courts.[255] It does not apply to administrative hearings, for example.

Rule 408 and similar state statutes do nothing to protect statements made in negotiation from pre-trial discovery. Admissibility is much narrower than discover-ability.[256] Of course, the party to whom information is revealed in settlement negotiations will not need to discover it. But that party may receive discovery requests from other parties to that litigation or from parties to other cases. The information revealed in settlement negotiations will likely be discoverable because there is no "settlement privilege."[257]

(d) Confidentiality Clauses in Settlement Agreements

Once a settlement agreement is reached, the parties may wish to keep its terms confidential.[258] Many settlement agreements have such confidentiality clauses. On the other hand, parties often ask a court to enter their settlement as a judgment.[259] That makes the settlement a court record, presumptively open to the public.[260] Parties routinely request and receive court orders sealing their settlements from public access. Sometimes, however, the seal is broken in favor of a subpoena in another case.

G. THE SETTLEMENT/LITIGATION CHOICE: BROADER PERSPECTIVES

Table of Sections

255. See Fed.R.Evid.1101 (applicability of Rules).

256. The Federal Rules of Civil Procedure, for instance, allow discovery of, not just admissible evidence, but anything "reasonably calculated to lead to the discovery of admissible evidence." Fed.R.Civ.P.26(b).

Parties may obtain discovery regarding any matter, not privileged, which is relevant to the subject matter involved in the pending action, whether it relates to the claim or defense of the party seeking discovery or to the claim or defense of any other party, including the existence, description, nature, custody, condition, and location of any books, documents, or other tangible things and the identity and location of persons having knowledge of any discoverable matter. The information sought need not be admissible at the trial if the information sought appears reasonably calculated to lead to the discovery of admissible evidence.

Fed.R.Civ.P.26(b)(1).

257. Wayne D. Brazil, Protecting the Confidentiality of Settlement Negotiations, 39 Hastings L.J. 955, 987–1010 (1988).

258. See, e.g., Parness, supra note 223, at 367–68 (discussing settlement of child-molestation suit against pop star Michael Jackson).

259. Nancy H. Rogers & Craig A. McEwen, Mediation: Law, Policy & Practice § 4:13 (2d ed.1994).

260. Compare FTC v. Standard Financial Management Corp. 830 F.2d 404 (1st Cir.1987)(public access to settlement); Bank of America Nat. Trust & Sav. Ass'n v. Hotel Rittenhouse Associates, 800 F.2d 339 (3d Cir.1986)(same), with Minneapolis Star & Tribune Co. v. Schumacher, 392 N.W.2d 197 (Minn.1986)(keeping settlement private).

§ 3.43   Normative Views on the Prevalence of Settlement

Few cases go to trial; the vast majority of cases settle. Would it better if more cases went to trial? Would it be better if fewer cases went to trial? These questions do not concern lawyers insofar as those lawyers represent particular clients in disputes. Lawyers have ethical and contractual duties to advance their clients' interests, whether that be by settling or by litigating to the end, even when doing so harms society as a whole.[261]

Lawyers, however, often wear many hats. Lawyers do more than represent clients; they also make law. They do so as judges and legislators, of course. But lawyers also make law indirectly through their involvement with bar associations and other organizations involved in law reform efforts. For some lawyers, working as a lawmaker is just another way to advance their clients' interests. But other lawyers see lawmaking as a way to advance broader social interests. This latter group of lawyers should be especially interested in the issues raised in the remainder of this chapter.

§ 3.44   Resources

What would happen if every case went to trial? Would there be enough judges, jurors and courtrooms to handle the work? Most courts around the country say that they are operating at or near capacity. Many judges say they are overworked and cannot give each case the attention it deserves. Surely, the judicial system would be overwhelmed if cases never settled. Settlement and its criminal-law equivalent, the plea bargain, are practical necessities.

The conclusion that settlement is a practical necessity assumes that courts continue to receive the same level of resources. It would be possible to build more courthouses, elect and appoint more judges, and call jurors more frequently. In short, it would be possible to devote greater resources to the courts. This would enable the courts to try more cases.[262] Perhaps it would be possible to devote enough resources to courts to try all cases without delay. Of course, this would consume resources that are now devoted elsewhere. And one might argue that the court system is already consuming too many resources. Money now going to the courts might be better spent on, for example, better schools or a

---

§ 3.43

261. "As advocate, a lawyer zealously asserts the client's position under the rules of the adversary system." Model Rules of Professional Conduct, Preamble ¶ 2 (1999). See also James E. Westbrook, The Problems with Process Bias, 1989 J.Disp.Resol. 309, 313, 316.

§ 3.44

262. See, e.g., Albert Alschuler, Mediation with a Mugger: The Shortage of Adjudicative Services and the Need for a Two-Tier Trial System in Civil Cases, 99 Harv. L.Rev. 1808, 1818 (1986)("[t]he crisis in our courts that observers decry may be the product of an inadequate supply of adjudication rather than of the excessive litigiousness of our society.")

cleaner environment. Perhaps time people spend on jury duty would be better spent at their jobs or with their families. The court system's current level of resources is not the only possible level. Is the current level too high, too low, or about right? All other things being equal, the more resources devoted to courts, the more cases that can be tried.

Courts receive some of their revenue from fees paid by litigants, but most comes from the taxpayer. In short, litigation, and especially trials, are subsidized by government.[263] As with other subsidized goods and services, demand exceeds supply. Litigants must wait for a trial, sometimes for years. Trial time is allocated according to willingness to wait. In contrast, other goods and services are, in a market economy, allocated according to willingness to pay. If parties had to pay more to use the court system, fewer parties would use it so those who did would not have to wait as long.

§ 3.45 Dispute Resolution vs. Public Justice

If the court system's only purpose is to resolve disputes then settlement should be encouraged. Settlements and trials both resolve disputes and settlements generally do so at a lower cost of time, money and aggravation. So trials should be discouraged unless they accomplish something other than resolving disputes. They do, argues Owen Fiss in a frequently-cited article, *Against Settlement*.[264] Trials, not only resolve disputes, they also promote justice. Justice, Fiss argues, is not as well served by settlements as it is by trials and other dispositive rulings by courts.[265]

Despite such arguments, courts now use a variety of techniques to encourage settlement.[266] Sometimes it can be as simple (and ineffective) as the judge merely asking the lawyers at a pre-trial conference whether they have tried to settle the case. If the lawyers say they tried and failed, many judges will let the subject drop.

Increasingly, though, judges are more aggressive in encouraging settlement. Frequently, judges are present at "settlement conferences." The judge's mere presence can facilitate negotiation by encouraging the lawyers to be constructive and positive. The judge may require that the parties, as well as their lawyers, be present at the settlement conference.[267] The judge may become involved in the discussion, perhaps helping to focus issues or even offering a neutral assessment of the merits of the case. Some judges even propose terms of settlement.[268]

---

263. See, e.g., Richard A. Posner, Federal Courts: Crisis and Reform 132 (1985).

§ 3.45

264. 93 Yale L.J. 1073 (1984).

265. Id. at 1075.

266. See §§ 4.30—4.36.

267. See 28 U.S.C. § 473(b)(1994); G. Heileman Brewing Co. v. Joseph Oat Corp., 871 F.2d 648 (7th Cir.1989).

268. See, e.g., Kothe v. Smith, 771 F.2d 667 (2d Cir.1985)(reversing award of sanctions against party who refused to settle in range suggested by judge).

Occasionally a judge goes so far as to perform "shuttle diplomacy." Each side is in its own room and the judge travels back and forth.[269] The judge may tell Plaintiff how weak her case is and then, minutes later, tell Defendant that the judge expects the jury to bring a big verdict.

All the judges discussed in the preceding paragraphs are engaged in *mediation*, the focus of the next chapter.

269. Compare Peter H. Schuck, The Role of Judges in Settling Complex Cases: The Agent Orange Example, 53 U.Chi. L.Rev. 337, 345 (1986).

Chapter 4

MEDIATION AND OTHER PROCESSES IN AID OF NEGOTIATION

Table of Sections

198

Research References:

Key Number System; Insurance ⟳ 3333 (217k3333)

Am Jur 2d, Alternative Dispute Resolution §§ 1 et seq.; Consumer Product Warranty Acts § 62; Federal Courts §§ 2486–2488; Labor and Labor Relations §§ 31–33, 124–139, 153–156, 2596–2608, 3614–3616, 3629, 3630

Corpus Juris Secundum, International Law § 60; Labor Relations §§ 402–423

ALR Index: Alternative Dispute Resolution

ALR Digest: Arbitration §§ 1 et seq.; Labor § 73

Am Jur Legal Forms 2d, Arbitration and Award § 23:88.1; Partnership § 194:477

Am Jur Pleading and Practice (Rev), Alternative Dispute Resolution §§ 11–36; Workers' Compensation §§ 84, 85

57 Am Jur Trials 555, Mediation as a Trial Alternative: Effective Use of the ADR Rules; 57 Am Jur Trials 255, Alternative Dispute Resolution: Employment Law; 53 Am Jur Trials 1, Evaluation and Settlement of Personal Injury and Wrongful Death Cases; 31 Am Jur Trials 595, Evaluation of Structured Settlements

A. OVERVIEW

Table of Sections

§ 4.1   Mediation's Popularity

Mediation is popular. Its use grew significantly in the late 20th Century. Starting in the 1970's, an ADR Movement emerged.[1] This Movement consisted of some practicing lawyers, but also of judges, academics, psychologists, marriage counselors, social workers and others. The ADR Movement coalesced around mediation as its preferred dispute-resolution process. The ADR Movement built, and continues to build, a body of scholarship touting the benefits of mediation.[2]

Since the 1970's, the ADR Movement has succeeded in spreading enthusiasm for mediation among courts and legislatures who often seem to see mediation as a way to relieve court congestion, delay and expense.[3] More recently, many federal and state administrative agencies joined the mediation bandwagon.[4] Mediation has grown to the point that there are now many people for whom mediating is a full-time job. Some of these

---

§ 4.1

1. See, e.g., Nancy H. Rogers & Craig A. McEwen, Mediation Law, Policy, & Practice § 5:02 (2d ed.1994); Jeffrey W. Stempel, Reflections on Judicial ADR and the Multi–Door Courthouse at Twenty: Fait Accompli, Failed Overture, or Fledgling Adulthood? 11 Ohio St.J.on Disp.Resol. 297, 309–61 (1996).

2. Rogers & McEwen, supra note 1, §§ 5:02—5:03 (citing scholarship).

3. See § 4.6. See also Stempel, supra note 1, at 316 ("the thrust of the Pound Conference, even from speakers generally regarded as liberals, was that courts were becoming clogged"); Rogers & McEwen, supra note 1, § 5:03.

4. Rogers & McEwen, supra note 1,

mediators are employed by courts and other government agencies. Other mediators are employed by not-for-profit organizations, and still others are entrepreneurs who "hung out a shingle" and offered their services to the marketplace.[5] An increasing number of lawyers serve as mediators or represent clients in mediation. Mediation is now an important part of the practice of law.[6]

Of course, the story is not entirely one-sided. The "Second and Third Generations" of ADR scholarship raise serious concerns about mediation in certain circumstances.[7] And many lawyers remain skeptical of mediation.[8] But these are exceptions to the overall trend of recent decades which is steady growth in the use of, and enthusiasm for, mediation. Mediation remains the darling of the ADR Movement.[9]

§ 4.2 Mediation Defined

Until recently, many lawyers practiced their entire careers without ever hearing the word *mediation*, let alone participating in it. Some experienced lawyers still do not know what mediation is; they may even confuse it with *meditation*. But mediation is not all that different from something these experienced lawyers have been doing all their lives, *negotiation*. A mediator is simply someone who helps the negotiators negotiate.[10] Mediation is facilitated negotiation. While negotiation involves only the parties and their agents, such as their lawyers, mediation adds the mediator, who is not an agent of either party. The mediator is a neutral.

Because mediation is "negotiation plus", one's understanding of mediation typically builds on one's understanding of negotiation. Therefore, the reader may wish to read or skim Chapter 3, which discusses negotiation, before reading this chapter.

§ 5:03.

5. "[H]ourly rates for mediation services are right up there with fees for traditional legal services, often topping $300 per hour." Rita H. Jensen, Divorce—Mediation Style, A.B.A.J., Feb. 1997, at 55, 58. On the growth of private-sector mediation, see Janice A. Roehl, Private Dispute Resolution, in National Symposium on Court–Connected Dispute Resolution Research, A Report on Current Research Findings—Implications for Courts, and Future Research Needs 131 (Keilitz ed.1994).

6. Richard C. Reuben, The Lawyer Turns Peacemaker, A.B.A.J., Aug. 1996, at 54, 55.

7. Rogers & McEwen, supra note 1, § 5:02 (citing scholarship).

8. "Many lawyers, if they thought about it, would see mediation as an economic threat." Leonard Riskin, Mediation and Lawyers, 43 Ohio St.L.J. 29, 48 (1982).

9. See, e.g., various symposium authors, 19 Fla.St.L.Rev. 1 (1991); Thomas J. Stipanowich, The Multi–Door Contract and Other Possibilities, 13 Ohio St.J. on Disp.Resol. 303, 315 (1998)("Among ADR processes involving the intervention of third-party neutrals, mediation is far and away the most popular choice.")

§ 4.2

10. "The primary purpose of a mediator is to facilitate the parties' voluntary agreement." John D. Feerick et al., American Arbitration Assoc. et al., Model Standards of Conduct for Mediators Standard VI, comment (n.d.) (developed jointly by the American Arbitration Association, the American Bar Association's Sections on Litigation and Dispute Resolution, and the Society of Professionals in Dispute Resolution).

Mediation should be distinguished from *adjudication*. Adjudication is the process by which somebody (the adjudicator) decides the result of a dispute.[11] Adjudication typically is legally-binding. *Litigation*[12] and *arbitration*[13] are examples of binding adjudication. What makes litigation and arbitration *binding* is the fact that the adjudicator's decision in these processes is backed with the force of government.[14] The adjudicators' decisions in litigation and arbitration are enforced, ultimately, by sheriffs and marshals with guns and badges. Parties who fail to comply with these adjudicators' decisions may find themselves imprisoned or find their property forcibly taken from them. In contrast, *non-binding* adjudication lacks such enforcement.[15] The parties to non-binding adjudication get a decision from the adjudicator but a party's failure to comply with that decision does not subject that party to the barrel of the sheriff's gun. A party is free to disregard the non-binding adjudicator's decision and to pursue binding adjudication to its conclusion.

Mediation is certainly not binding adjudication. A mediator might say how the dispute should be resolved. But each party is free to disregard the mediator's statement or decision and to pursue litigation or arbitration to its conclusion.[16] Litigation and arbitration are the two processes capable of producing legally-binding results without a post-dispute agreement by the parties.[17] In contrast, mediation can produce a legally-binding result only with each party's post-dispute consent to that result through a settlement agreement.[18] In other words, mediation is a process that does not by itself resolve disputes. Rather, it is a "process in aid of negotiation", a process that helps the parties negotiate a resolution to the dispute. In stark contrast, binding adjudication (litigation and arbitration) resolves disputes wholly apart from any negotiation between the parties. So there is a sharp line distinguishing mediation from binding adjudication.[19]

The line between mediation and non-binding adjudication is fuzzier, but a line nevertheless. A mediator who says how the dispute should be resolved, *i.e.*, gives the parties a specific, concrete "decision", has crossed the line from mediation to (non-binding) adjudication. Those calling themselves "mediators" rarely cross this line. Mediators rarely make pronouncements specifying precisely how the dispute should be resolved.

---

11. See § 1.5(a).

12. See § 1.5(a)(defining litigation as adjudication in a court or other government forum).

13. See § 1.6(c)(defining arbitration as adjudication in a private, *i.e.*, non-government, forum). Arbitration is the focus of Chapter 2.

14. See §§ 1.5 & 1.7.

15. Non-binding adjudication is discussed at the end of this chapter. See §§ 4.31—4.36.

16. A party has the right to pursue litigation rather than arbitration unless that party has formed an arbitration agreement in which case it has the right to pursue arbitration rather than litigation. See § 2.3.

17. See § 1.7(c).

18. See § 1.7(a)(2) & 1.7(b).

19. See § 1.7 (comparing processes—litigation and arbitration—that cast "the shadow of the law" with processes—negotiation and mediation—that occur in that shadow).

Mediators do, however, often evaluate.[20] *Evaluation* is less precise than adjudication. Evaluation is an assessment of the merits of a case that does not go so far as to decree a specific, concrete result. For example, an adjudicator tells the parties that "Defendant is liable to Plaintiff in the amount of $250,000." In contrast, an evaluator might say "Plaintiff has a very strong argument that Defendant breached the contract and damages appear to be in the six figures", or "I've seen verdicts in similar cases range around two or three hundred thousand dollars." Other examples of evaluation include "Defendant's contributory-negligence argument is unlikely to persuade a jury", or "Plaintiff seems to have shown strong evidence of price-fixing." While some mediators are more evaluative than others, it is the rare mediator who never evaluates at all.[21] Evaluative mediation is still mediation and does not cross the line into (non-binding) adjudication.

§ 4.3 Dispute Mediation and Transactional Mediation

Mediation can be divided into two categories: *transactional* mediation and *dispute* mediation. Transactional mediation is when a mediator helps parties form a deal such as a collective bargaining agreement between a labor union and an employer. Transactional mediation is less common than dispute mediation and is only rarely mentioned in this chapter. This chapter focuses on the mediation of *disputes*.[22]

Only a small fraction of disputes ever come to the attention of lawyers and many of these disputes go to litigation or arbitration. Thus, lawyers are likely to be involved in the mediation of a narrow class of disputes: those in litigation or arbitration, and those that are likely to go to litigation or arbitration if mediation fails to reach a settlement. Mediation of these disputes can be called *settlement mediation* to emphasize its similarities to *settlement negotiation*.[23] Settlement mediation is the mediation most important to lawyers and is emphasized in this chapter.

The reasoning of this chapter generally applies to both settlement mediation of disputes headed to litigation and settlement mediation of disputes headed to arbitration. To avoid wordiness and cumbersome sentence structure, however, the rest of this chapter is written entirely in terms of disputes headed to litigation.

§ 4.4 Mandatory Mediation and Voluntary Mediation

Settlement mediation can be divided into two categories: mandatory and voluntary. Some settlement mediation occurs because a court or

---

20. See § 4.13.

21. See § 4.13(b)(2).

§ 4.3

22. Disputes are defined and discussed in § 1.2.

23. See § 3.2 (defining settlement negotiation).

other government agency requires it.[24] Other settlement mediation occurs because the parties agree to it. Mandatory mediation raises a number of legal and policy issues not raised by voluntary mediation.[25]

B. GOALS OF DISPUTE MEDIATION

Table of Sections

§ 4.5 Generally

Understanding the *goals* of mediation is helpful to understanding the *process* of mediation. Accordingly, the goals of mediation are discussed in the next four sections,[26] while the process of mediation is discussed thereafter.[27]

Of course, mediation itself has no goals. The goals belong to those who participate in mediation: mediators, parties, lawyers, and others. The participants in a given mediation may have different and even conflicting goals.[28] The goals of the participants in each mediation shape that particular mediation.

Settle case	Positive sum	Moral growth
Least ambitious		Most ambitious

The major goals of dispute mediation can be placed on a continuum from the least ambitious to the most ambitious. The least ambitious goal is to resolve the dispute, *i.e.*, to settle the case. All of the participants in nearly all mediations share the goal of settling, although parties obviously differ about the terms of settlement they seek. A more ambitious goal is not merely to settle, but to reach a settlement that exploits opportunities for *positive-sum*[29] negotiation. The third and most ambitious goal is to make the parties better people (moral growth). These three are not the only possible mediation goals, but they seem to be the most common.

One might argue that mediators and other participants in mediation should always pursue all three goals because, even if it turns out that

---

§ 4.4

24. See § 4.30.

25. These issues are discussed in § 4.30.

§ 4.5

26. See §§ 4.5—4.8.

27. See §§ 4.9—4.16.

28. For example, the lawyers may be focused on settling a case, while the parties are focused on problem-solving and the mediator seeks to engender moral growth.

29. See § 3.9.

they do not achieve any of them, there is no harm in trying. There may, however, be costs to pursuing the more ambitious goals. It is likely to cost more time and money to try to make the parties better people than it is to try to settle a case. It also costs time and money to search for positive-sum opportunities that may or may not exist.[30] By consuming time and money, the pursuit of more ambitious goals may actually make settlement less likely than if the participants had single-mindedly focused on settlement as the only goal. On the other hand, some cases can settle only after positive-sum negotiation.[31] And there may be other cases that can settle only after the parties themselves have changed in some important way. So pursuing goals more ambitious than merely settling may be the only way to achieve the less ambitious goal of settling.

§ 4.6   Settle Cases

The least ambitious mediation goal is to resolve the dispute, *i.e.*, to settle the case. All of the participants in nearly all mediations share the goal of settling, although parties obviously differ about the terms of settlement they seek.

In many cases, there exists at least one possible set of settlement terms that would make both parties better off than they would be by continuing to litigate. These are cases in which the parties' *bottom lines* create a *settlement zone*.[32] While it is in the interests of all parties for cases with a settlement zone to settle, such cases do not always settle. This failure of negotiation to reach a settlement is frequently due to a few common, well-understood causes.[33] These causes of the failure to settle can be overcome by mediation.[34] Mediation seems well-suited to getting cases that should settle to settle.

Nearly all mediators say that one of their goals is to resolve disputes, *i.e.*, to settle cases. Some mediators judge themselves by their "settlement rate." This is the percentage of mediated cases that settle. A mediator who judges herself primarily by her settlement rate can be called a *settlement-oriented* mediator.

While only some mediators emphasize settlement rates, many non-mediators emphasize them. Many parties and lawyers seek a mediator who is known for bringing the parties to a deal.[35] And many courts encourage, even require, cases to go to mediation because they want mediation to make cases settle and disappear from the court's docket.[36] The endorsement of mediation as a way to reduce court congestion, delay and expense is even found in legislation.[37]

---

30. See § 3.10.

31. See § 3.13.

§ 4.6

32. Bottom lines and settlement zones are discussed in §§ 3.11—3.13.

33. See §§ 3.12—3.13 & 3.22.

34. See §§ 4.11—4.13.

35. See § 4.13.

36. Kimberlee Kovach & Lela P. Love, Evaluative Mediation is an Oxymoron, 14 Alternatives to the High Cost of Litigation 31 (1996).

37. See 28 U.S.C. §§ 471–482 (1994).

In formulating the provisions of its civil justice expense and delay reduction plan,

§ 4.7 Positive–Sum or Problem–Solving

While settlement is the least ambitious mediation goal,[38] a more ambitious mediation goal is to reach a settlement that exploits opportunities for *positive-sum* negotiation. Positive-sum negotiation finds those possible settlement terms that are better *for both parties* than other possible settlement terms.[39] Positive-sum negotiation expands the pie, in contrast to zero-sum negotiation which divides it.

Negotiators, whether negotiating or mediating, do not have complete control over whether their negotiation is zero-sum or positive-sum. The interests of the parties may be so diametrically opposed that their negotiation must be zero-sum, no matter how sincerely the negotiators seek to find a positive-sum aspect to it. On the other hand, the interests of the parties may present opportunities for positive-sum negotiation that go unexploited because the negotiators do not find them. In such a case, there is a zero-sum negotiation in a positive-sum situation. To put it another way, positive-sum situations can yield either positive-sum or zero-sum negotiations, while zero-sum situations can yield only zero-sum negotiations. Having a zero-sum negotiation in a positive-sum situation is not necessarily a failure. The value created by exploiting a positive-sum opportunity may be lower than the value of the time and effort required to find it.

While having a zero-sum negotiation in a positive-sum situation is not necessarily a failure, it often is. Often the negotiators could, with little time and effort, exploit a valuable positive-sum opportunity, but they fail to do so. This is because positive-sum negotiation is unlikely to occur unless both negotiators use the *problem-solving* approach to negotiation.[40] And while both parties benefit if both use the problem-solving approach, each party's individual incentive may be to use the *adversarial/competitive* approach.[41] So there is a divergence between what is good for the parties in the aggregate (both using the problem-solving approach) and each negotiator's individual incentive (to use the adversarial/competitive approach). Mediation is well-suited to narrowing this divergence.[42]

The mediation process reduces the risk to a negotiator of using the problem-solving approach and being exploited by the other side's adversarial/competitive approach. The mediation process thus makes it more

each United States district court . . . shall consider and may include the following principles and guidelines of litigation management and cost and delay reduction:

. . .

(6) authorization to refer appropriate cases to alternative dispute resolution programs that—

(A) have been designated for use in a district court; or

(B) the court may make available, including mediation, minitrial, and summary jury trial. Id. § 473(a)(6).

§ 4.7

38. See § 4.6.
39. See § 3.9.
40. See § 3.30.
41. See id.
42. See § 4.12.

likely that both sides will use the problem-solving approach. Those mediators who encourage parties to use the problem-solving approach can be called *problem-solving* mediators. Just as problem-solving negotiators are oriented toward exploiting positive-sum opportunities, so are problem-solving mediators. Mediation with a problem-solving mediator seems well-suited to finding those settlement terms that are better for both parties than other settlement terms.[43] In short, mediation can expand a pie that negotiation would only have divided.

§ 4.8 Moral Growth

Some mediators seek not just to resolve disputes and facilitate positive-sum negotiation, but to change people. *Transformative mediation* is prominently advocated by Robert A. Baruch Bush and Joseph Folger, who contend that mediation has "a unique potential for transforming people—engendering moral growth."[44] Mediation does this through empowering the parties and evoking in each an appreciation for the problems of others. If this occurs, mediation succeeds even where it produces no settlement.[45] It succeeds in producing parties who may be able to later resolve this dispute on their own and who will be better equipped to resolve future disputes they have with each other and with others.

Transforming people to engender moral growth is the most ambitious of the three major mediation goals.[46] While many who study and practice mediation think that it sometimes, and to varying degrees, makes the parties better people, few are as optimistic and universalistic in this regard as Bush and Folger. For instance, Carrie Menkel–Meadow argues for more modest mediation goals based on the recognition that transformation is more likely in some contexts than others. "No process can do all things, or any one thing for all people."[47] Many mediators

---

43. See id.

§ 4.8

44. Robert A. Baruch Bush and Joseph P. Folger, The Promise of Mediation: Responding to Conflict Through Empowerment and Recognition 2–12 (1994). See also Institute for Christian Conciliation™, a division of Peacemaker® Ministries, Guidelines for Christian Conciliation (Revision 4.1 2000).

Christian conciliation is especially beneficial for people who sincerely want to do what is right and are open to learning where they may have been wrong. Conciliators can help them to identify improper attitudes or unwise practices, to understand more fully the effects of their decisions and policies, and to make improvements in their lives and businesses that will help them to avoid unnecessary conflict in the future.

Id. at 5, ¶ 21.

45. Bush & Folger, supra note 44, at 200–01; Institute for Christian Conciliation, supra note 44, at 5. See also Deborah M. Kolb & Kenneth Kressel, The Realities of Making Talk Work in When Talk Works: Profiles of Mediators 466–68 (Deborah M. Kolb et al. eds. 1994).

46. See § 4.5.

47. Carrie Menkel–Meadow, The Many Ways of Mediation: The Transformation of Traditions, Ideologies, Paradigms, and Practices, Neg.J. 217, 239 (July 1995). Menkel–Meadow also insightfully notes that "the act of training for and discussing mediation has itself created a 'community' of mediators. Thus, more than the parties in dispute, mediators themselves may be the most 'transformed' by mediative processes and ideologies." Id. at 231.

believe that mediation is well-suited to resolving disputes,[48] and to exploiting positive-sum opportunities,[49] but there is less consensus about the magnitude of mediation's prospects for engendering moral growth.

C. THE MEDIATION PROCESS

Table of Sections

§ 4.9   Goals Shape Process

The three major mediation goals are discussed in the previous sections.[50] Those goals are to settle cases, exploit positive-sum opportunities and engender moral growth. The participants in a given mediation—mediator, parties, lawyers, and others—may have some or all of these goals. In some cases, all participants have similar goals for the mediation. In other cases, they do not. For example, the lawyers may be focused on settling a case, while the parties are focused on positive-sum opportunities and the mediator seeks to engender moral growth. Whatever goals the participants have shape that particular mediation. So any description of the mediation process necessarily makes generalizations that do not always hold true. Nevertheless, there are some features common to most *settlement mediations*[51] and these features are surveyed next.[52] The succeeding sections then discuss important benefits of, and controversies about, the mediation process.[53]

§ 4.10   The Mediation Process Generally

(a) Participants

Mediation requires at least three people: a mediator and two negotiators. The only person indispensable to mediation is the mediator. Most mediators generally want the disputing parties to participate, but mediation can occur without the parties if they have authorized agents, such as lawyers, to participate for them.

Sometimes both parties and their lawyers participate in mediation. Some mediators try to increase the participation of the parties and decrease, even eliminate, the participation of the lawyers. This occurs

48. See § 4.6.

49. See § 4.7.

§ 4.9

50. See §§ 4.5—4.8.

51. See § 4.3.

52. See § 4.10.

53. See §§ 4.11—4.16.

most prominently in divorce, child custody, and other family mediation.[54] In contrast, other mediators try to increase lawyer involvement.[55]

Parties, lawyers and mediators are not the only possible participants in mediation. Anyone can participate with the permission of the parties and mediator. Depending on the sort of dispute, those participants might include anyone from family members to accountants, and from members of the clergy to business associates.

(b) Starting to Mediate

Mediation generally begins with the mediator introducing herself to those present. After welcoming everyone, the mediator explains the mediation process and her role in it. While her introductory explanation may be relaxed and informal, she has probably given it careful thought because she knows that it can set the tone for the entire mediation.[56] The mediator's introductory explanation often addresses, among other topics, the issue of whether, and to what extent, what is said during mediation will remain confidential.[57]

After the mediator's introduction, she may ask each party to take turns explaining the dispute, while the other participants listen quietly. These *opening statements* may be made by the lawyers, rather than the parties. In some cases the mediator will prefer that they be made by the parties, while in others the mediator will prefer that they be made by the lawyers. After opening statements, mediators typically ask those present to plan an agenda, *i.e.*, to discuss what issues must be discussed. Reaching agreement on an agenda may encourage the participants and generate momentum toward agreement on substantive issues. Mediators often like to put the easy issues early on the agenda. If the participants spend a little time reaching agreement on some issues, they may become encouraged and psychologically committed to reaching a deal that will resolve the whole dispute. They do not want their initial accomplishment to be wasted by a later deadlock.

Once an agenda is formulated, it may be necessary to gather additional information or additional participants. The mediation may need to break for the day to do so. While some mediations reach agreement in one session of a few hours, others have multiple sessions spread over weeks or months.

(c) Joint Sessions, Private Caucuses and Shuttle Diplomacy

A *joint* or *open session* is when both sides and the mediator are present. During joint sessions, the mediator typically keeps order and

§ 4.10

54. See § 4.17. For some of the reasons why mediators do this, see § 4.13(b)(1).

55. Craig A. McEwen, Nancy H. Rogers & Richard J. Maiman, Bring in the Lawyers: Challenging the Dominant Approaches to Ensuring Fairness In Divorce Mediation, 79 Minn.L.Rev. 1317 (1995).

56. See, e.g., Leonard L. Riskin & James E. Westbrook, Dispute Resolution and Lawyers 343 (2d ed.1997).

57. Confidentiality in mediation is discussed in § 4.28.

facilitates communication. This can be done in a variety of ways, some of which are discussed in the next section.[58]

There may also be private sessions, called *caucuses,* in which the mediator meets with one side only. Some mediations consist entirely of private caucuses with joint sessions only at the beginning and the end. In these mediations, the mediator conducts *shuttle diplomacy* by traveling back and forth between private caucuses with each side.

Shuttle diplomacy can prevent the parties from angering each other. "For instance, if Party A says, 'I think B is a filthy liar and I can't believe a word he says,' the mediator can explain that to B as follows: 'A has some doubts about whether she can rely upon your promises.' "[59] Shuttle diplomacy also allows the mediator to carry one party's settlement offer to the other party. This avoids hard feelings when the mediator, not the offeror, hears an initial reaction to the offer like: "That offer is insulting! We're going to trial unless they get realistic." The mediator can give a softer translation of that message back to the offeror, perhaps with a counter-offer.

The mediator is not the only one who can call for a private caucus. Parties and lawyers often ask for them. Before breaking into caucus, the mediator may re-visit the issue of whether, and to what extent, what is said during mediation will remain confidential.[60]

(d) Facilitating Communication

Much of what mediators do involves facilitating communication between the parties.[61] If this seems like an easy task, recall that many disputes get to mediation only after negotiation has failed and/or litigation has begun. The parties may hate each other. They may view each other as enemies to be destroyed. In this environment, facilitating communication can be a major accomplishment.

Mediators can facilitate indirect or direct communication between the parties.

(1) Indirect Communication

A very important way of facilitating indirect communication is to obtain each party's confidential information in private caucus and then combine all that information to identify settlement zones and positive-sum opportunities.[62] These settlement zones and positive-sum opportunities can then be communicated to each party in a way that gives only an imprecise or "noisy" translation of the other party's confidential infor-

---

58. See § 4.10(d).

59. Riskin & Westbrook, supra note 56, at 352.

60. Confidentiality in mediation is discussed in § 4.28.

61. Leonard L. Riskin, Understanding Mediator Orientations, Strategies, and

Techniques: a Grid for the Perplexed, 1 Harv.Neg.L.Rev. 7, 24 (1996)(facilitative mediators seek primarily "to enhance communication between the parties in order to help them decide what to do.").

62. See §§ 4.11—4.12.

mation. Delicate use of this important tactic is a mark of a mediator who excels at her craft.

(2) Direct Communication

Mediators generally try to facilitate *direct* communication between the parties. For example, the mediator may know about the dispute before the mediation begins because the mediator has received information about the dispute from the court, the lawyers or the parties.[63] Some mediators may be tempted to expedite mediation by starting with a summary, by the mediator, of the dispute at hand. Mediators generally resist this temptation in order to facilitate direct communication between the parties. Rather than characterizing the dispute, the mediator can ask each party to describe the dispute as he sees it. This tactic tends to foster communication for a variety of reasons.

First, it is the parties communicating directly with each other, rather than through their lawyers.[64] This may, for example, be the first time Plaintiff hears Defendant tell Defendant's side of the story, as opposed to hearing Defendant's lawyer tell Defendant's side of the story. Also, it allows the mediator to hear the parties' views of the dispute, not just the views of the court or the lawyers. This additional information for the mediator may enable the mediator to be more helpful in later stages of the mediation. One or both of the parties may characterize the issues differently from the way the court, the lawyers, or the mediator would have characterized them. Perhaps the parties see an issue the other participants do not see. That issue will have to be resolved before any settlement can occur. If the parties do not see an issue that the others do see, it is possible that it is not an issue at all, or at least not one that needs to be addressed.

When asked by the mediator to state the problem as he sees it, a party may not immediately respond with a thorough, well-organized answer. This might occur for a variety of reasons. It might simply be due to the party's weak communication skills. It might be due to his nervousness about mediation or his embarrassment about some part of the dispute. Or it might be due to an instruction from his lawyer to say as little as possible.[65] Probably, the mediator will want to know if any of these factors is present. Also, the mediator will still want to hear the party state the problem as he sees it. So the mediator's communication skills are called upon. The mediator may ask broad, open-ended questions. "Why" questions are a common example: "Why do you pick $30,000 as your settlement offer?" or "Why are you concerned about pollution in the lake?" Sometimes more indirect questions, such as "what are your hobbies?", elicit more telling information.[66] After asking

63. Kimberlee K. Kovach, Mediation: Principles and Practice 70–76 (1994).

64. For the benefits of parties communicating directly with each other, see Leonard L. Riskin, The Represented Client in a Settlement Conference: The Lessons of G.

Heileman Brewing Co. v. Joseph Oat Corp., 69 Wash.U.L.Q. 1059 (1991).

65. On such instructions, see § 4.25.

66. See § 3.27.

questions, the mediator listens carefully. She is alert to any non-verbal signals the party may, intentionally or not, be conveying. Facial expressions and body language can be significant.[67]

While gathering information from the parties, the mediator often summarizes what each party has said or encourages the party's communication with affirmations like "I see" and "I understand." These "active listening" tactics are designed to build the party's confidence in the mediator by showing him that the mediator listened to him and understands his perspective.[68]

The mediator may ask each party to summarize the views of the other side. This tests whether each party has listened to and understood the other side. Summarizing the views of the other side also tends to promote a little grudging respect for the interests and merits on the other side, thus bringing the parties a bit closer to each other and to settlement.

The mediator may try to facilitate communication with environmental factors. The classic example is to arrange the seating so the parties are not sitting directly across from each other at a rectangular table. Sitting next to each other at a round table is a less adversarial posture. The mediator may also seek to ensure that everyone is comfortable in terms of temperature, food, drink, etc.

Mediators also typically facilitate communication by clarifying issues and keeping order during joint sessions. The mediator might keep order the way a judge keeps order in a courtroom—by insisting that everyone communicate in a controlled, ritualized manner. More likely, though, the mediator sees value in spontaneity and informality. The mediator may even see value in angry or emotional outbursts by one or more of the parties.[69] The mediator may believe the problem cannot be solved until the parties "vent" their feelings and emotions. Many advocates of mediation favor it over *adjudication*[70] in part because it allows for the personal and the emotional, as well as the abstract and the rational.[71]

(e) Settlement Offers

Mediators may play a variety of roles in the formulation and communication of settlement offers.[72] If a party makes an offer, the mediator may evaluate it.[73] For example, the mediator may say "that offer is probably about as good a result as you're going to get from a court." Or the mediator may say "that sounds like a proposal that will

---

67. See Edward Brunet & Charles B. Craver, Alternative Dispute Resolution: The Advocate's Perspective 44–54 (1997); Donald G. Gifford, Legal Negotiation: Theory and Applications 127–32.

68. The mediator typically facilitates communication by being cautious about interjecting her own views. She accepts each party's characterization of the problem. If the parties insist on rejecting each others' characterization of the problem, the media-

tor is careful not to adopt one or the other characterization. That would risk appearing partial.

69. Kovach, supra note 63, at 25.

70. See § 1.5(a), n.12.

71. See, e.g., Riskin, supra note 8, at 43–48.

72. See §§ 4.10(c) & 4.16.

73. See § 4.13.

go a long way toward achieving both parties' goals.'' If an offer is rejected, the mediator may seek to improve upon it, to find a variation of it that is acceptable to both parties. The mediator may go so far as to make her own proposals for terms of settlement.

Many mediators, particularly problem-solving mediators and those concerned with moral growth,[74] are in no rush for the parties to exchange offers to settle the case. These mediators are happy to defer such talk until after a thorough exploration of the underlying interests of all parties.[75] Only then is it time to "generate solutions." The problem-solving mediator thinks in terms of "solutions," rather than "offers to settle." While they may amount to the same thing, the term "solutions" implies that the parties' dispute is a problem to be solved. Also, the problem-solving mediator seeks to generate, not one solution, but many solutions. These features of problem-solving mediation—thoroughly exploring interests and generating multiple solutions—may be time-consuming.

The problem-solving mediator seeks solutions that advance both parties' interests. Designing such solutions typically requires that numerous issues be considered simultaneously.[76] Designing such solutions is difficult under pressure. Accordingly, problem-solving mediators may set aside a designated time for brainstorming.[77] Brainstorming might be done in joint session, when both parties are present, and again in a private caucus when parties and lawyers feel more free to think out loud. The problem-solving mediator encourages each party to generate many possible solutions before assessing any of them. The crucial point is to separate the inventive phase of generating possible solutions from the evaluative phase of assessing the merits of those possibilities.[78] When it does come time to assess the possible solutions, the problem-solving mediator helps the parties judge them by how well they advance the interests of both parties. The mediator's assessments of the proposals may lead to the mediator making proposals of her own. But the problem-solving mediator typically prefers that proposals come from the parties to increase the parties' sense of ownership and to allow the mediator to remain more objective.[79]

(f) Agreements

Mediation may involve a number of agreements, typically written and signed. The agreement most everyone hopes to reach is an agreement to settle the dispute.[80] But, regardless of whether the mediation results in a settlement, there may be other agreements.

---

74. See §§ 4.7—4.8.

75. See § 4.12.

76. See id.

77. Roger Fisher & William Ury, Getting to Yes: Negotiating Agreement Without Giving In 62–65, 113–17 (2d ed.1991).

78. Id. at 60–80.

79. Riskin & Westbrook, supra note 56, at 351.

80. Mediated settlement agreements are discussed in § 4.16.

There may be an agreement between the parties, formed prior to any dispute, that requires any dispute arising between the parties to go to mediation.[81] In the absence of such a *pre-dispute* agreement to mediate, the parties may form a *post-dispute* agreement to mediate. And even if a court or other government agency orders the parties to mediate,[82] there may still be an agreement between the parties specifying who the mediator will be,[83] or how, when and where mediation will be conducted. There may also be agreements between each party *and the mediator* about how, when and where the mediation will be conducted. These agreements may address the issue of whether, and to what extent, what is said during mediation will remain confidential.[84]

Also, the mediator may have an agreement with the parties regarding the mediator's compensation. While some mediators are paid by the parties, other mediators are paid by a court, another government agency, or a non-profit organization. Some mediators perform their services without charge.

The following is a sample agreement to mediate.[85]

AGREEMENT

1.   The undersigned wish to retain the services of Mediator [*name*] to mediate disputed issues. The Mediator is an attorney licensed to practice law in the State of _____ . The parties acknowledge that the Mediator has discussed the advantages and disadvantages of the mediation process and compared that process with being represented by separate attorneys or having the issues resolved through negotiation between lawyers or by a judge in court.

2.   During the mediation, each party is encouraged to consult independent counsel at any time. Each party is entitled to the confidentiality of the attorney/client relationship in respect to any communication with an independent attorney. In particular, the parties should consult independent counsel before signing any final Agreement.

3.   The parties acknowledge that Mediator does not represent the interests of either party and is not acting as an attorney. The parties acknowledge that the purpose of mediation is to facilitate the ultimate resolution and agreement between parties regarding the issues, problems, and disputes presented in mediation. The parties acknowledge and agree that Mediator is not acting as an advocate, representative, or fiduciary, or lawyer for either party.

---

81. See § 4.29.

82. See § 4.30.

83. See § 4.27(c)(1).

84. See § 4.28(b).

85. Jay E. Grenig, West's Legal Forms: Alternative Dispute Resolution § 2.42 (1998).

4. Mediator agrees to keep all communications from the parties confidential unless express consent is given for disclosure of the communication.

5. Mediator will attempt to resolve any outstanding disputes as long as both parties make a good faith effort to reach an agreement based on fairness to both parties. Both parties must be willing and able to participate in the process. The mediated agreement requires compromise and both parties agree to attempt to be flexible and open to new possibilities for resolution of the dispute. If Mediator, in Mediator's professional judgment, concludes that agreement is not possible or that continuation of the mediation process would harm or prejudice one or both of the participants, Mediator shall withdraw and the mediation shall be concluded.

6. The mediation may be terminated without cause by either party at any time. No reason must be given to the other party or to the Mediator. A decision to terminate mediation must be in writing. Mediation may not resume following notification unless expressly authorized by both parties. Upon termination of mediation for any reason, Mediator agrees not to counsel either party or represent either party against the other in any court proceeding, adversary negotiation, or for any other reason involving a dispute between the parties.

7. While mediation is in progress, the parties agree that full disclosure of all information is essential to a successful resolution of the issues. Since the court process is not being used to compel information, any agreement made through mediation may be rescinded in whole or in part if one party fails to disclose relevant information during the mediation process. Because the voluntary disclosure of this information may give one party an advantage that the party may not have had in the traditional adversarial process, the parties agree to release and hold Mediator harmless from any liability or damages caused by voluntary disclosure of prejudicial information in the mediation process that may be used in subsequent negotiations or court proceedings. Mediator has no power to bind third parties not to disclose information furnished during mediation.

8. The parties agree that evidence of anything said or of any admission made in the course of this mediation process is not admissible in evidence and disclosure of any such evidence shall not be compelled in any civil action in which, pursuant to law, testimony can be given.

9. Concessions, offers of settlement, suggestions by Mediator, admissions by either party, or any other aspect of communication within the mediation process made for the purpose of settlement may not be used in any subsequent proceeding.

10. The parties agree not to call or subpoena Mediator to testify at any court proceeding or to produce any document obtained or prepared from any mediation session without the prior written authorization of both parties. If either party issues a subpoena regarding Mediator or his or her documents, that party shall pay Mediator the Mediator's current hourly rate for all hours expended and shall pay all reasonable, compliance, or resistance of the subpoena.

11. Once any agreement is reached, in whole or in part, or at any time the parties desire to file any court documents confirming the agreement and to obtain a court order or judgment based on the agreement, the parties understand that Mediator may not represent either party in a court of law.

12. The parties agree to reimburse Mediator for any and all costs expended on behalf of the parties. In addition, at Mediator's option, in place of and instead of charges for domestic telephone calls and long distance telephone (not to exceed $_____ per month), postage, mileage, parking, and in-firm photocopying or reproductions, a surcharge to the client's bill of four percent of the hourly billings per month for the client may be included. Examples of nonincluded costs are photocopying provided outside the office, messenger and delivery services, attorney service costs, witness and expert fees, deposition reporter fees, filing fees, and domestic long distance telephone calls exceeding 20 minutes and international telephone calls, which charges shall be itemized on the client's monthly statement in addition to the monthly surcharge.

13. Parties agree to be jointly and severally responsible for the fees for both Mediator and consulting professional. If for any reason the fee of Mediator is not paid within 15 days of billing, Mediator reserves the right to unilaterally refuse to render any further professional services for the parties. The parties agree that, in addition to the payment of any agreed upon fees, each of the parties shall be liable for any costs of collecting the total amount of the fee, including reasonable attorney fees for collecting the fees. The parties agree that a reasonable attorney fee is the hourly rate of $_____.

14. Mediator's hourly rate for mediation services is $_____, charged in minimum increments of .20 hours. The services of Mediator include, but are not limited to mediation sessions with either party, telephone conferences with either party or with third parties, coordination and referral with other resource persons.

15. Before commencing the mediation, the parties agree to pay an initial deposit. Parties shall deposit with Mediator an advance retainer to be credited against client's final bill. Parties will pay Mediator monthly in full for services rendered during

that month within 10 days of billing. At completion of Mediator's work with parties, the retainer will be credited towards parties' final bill and the remainder will be refunded to the parties.

16. Mediator shall bill the parties monthly, itemizing the services rendered on the parties' behalf for fees and reimbursements to which Mediator is entitled as a result of services rendered under this agreement.

Dated: _____

Dated: _____

_____

_____

§ 4.11 Identifying Settlement Zones and Overcoming Barriers to Settlement

In many cases, settlement would make both parties better off than they would be by continuing to litigate. It may be, for example, that Plaintiff is willing to settle for any amount over $40,000 and Defendant is willing to settle for any amount under $60,000. In other words, Plaintiff's *bottom line* is $40,000 and Defendant's bottom line is $60,000.[86] This is depicted in Diagram 4–1.

Diagram 4-1

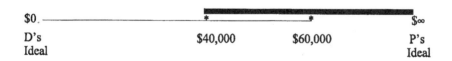

| $0 | | $40,000 | | $60,000 | | $∞ |
| D's Ideal | | | | | | P's Ideal |

The thin line represents possible settlement terms acceptable to Defendant. The thick line represents possible settlement terms acceptable to Plaintiff. The possible settlement terms from $40,000 to $60,000 comprise the *settlement zone*.[87] It is impossible for a settlement to occur outside this zone. Any settlement must, by definition, be better for each party than its bottom line, which is the worst deal a party will accept.

If the parties settle anywhere within the settlement zone, they have each made themselves better off than they would have been had they

---

§ 4.11

86. Bottom lines are discussed in §§ 3.11—3.13.

87. Settlement zones are discussed in §§ 3.11—3.13.

continued to litigate.[88] Settling at, for example, $50,000 benefits both parties when compared to not settling at all. Plaintiff would rather take $50,000 than continue litigating and Defendant would rather pay $50,000 than continue litigating. Given these preferences, both parties make themselves better off by settling at $50,000 or anywhere else between $40,000 and $60,000.

While it is in the interests of all parties for cases with a settlement zone to settle, such cases do not always settle. Negotiators may not even realize a settlement zone exists. Negotiators often conceal their true bottom lines from each other.[89] With each negotiator guessing about the other's bottom line, negotiators rarely are sure that a settlement zone exists and even less likely to know the precise boundaries of the zone. Mediation can overcome this problem. The mediator can hold a private caucus with each party.[90] Each party privately reveals its bottom line to the mediator who promises to keep this information secret from the other party.[91] The mediator can then assemble both parties in joint session and tell them only whether there is or is not a settlement zone. If there is a settlement zone, the parties now know that they are each better off with a settlement than they are going to trial. They become more committed to reaching a deal in mediation. If there is no settlement zone, the mediator and parties can try to create one. One way to do so is for the mediator to *evaluate* the merits of the case. The evaluation may cause one or both of the parties to move its bottom line in a way that creates a settlement zone.[92] The other way to try to create a settlement zone is to seek *positive-sum* opportunities.[93] If the participants choose not to try these options, or try them and still cannot create a settlement zone, the parties should prepare for trial. Any further negotiations are a waste of time unless and until one or both of the parties moves its bottom line.

Few mediators follow this stark procedure of simply asking each party in private caucus its bottom line and then telling the assembled parties nothing other than whether settlement is possible. But many mediators do variants of this procedure, along with other things. Variants of this procedure usually involve being more indirect and imprecise than bluntly asking a party what its bottom line is. Mediators usually get a more general feel of a party's bottom line, an approximation, rather

---

88. Of course, the results of litigation might turn out better for one party than accepting the other side's offer would have been. But at the pertinent time, the time at which the offer can be accepted, accepting it is better than the *expected value* of litigating further. See § 3.5(c).

89. See § 3.20.

90. See § 4.10(c).

91. See, e.g., Peter Contuzzi, Should parties tell mediators their bottom line? Disp.Resol.Mag., Spring 2000, at 30–32; <http://www.cybersettle.com>,

<http://www.clicknsettle.com>. See also Robert H. Gertner & Geoffrey P. Miller, Settlement Escrows, 24 J.Legal.Stud. 87 (1995).

On the topic of confidentiality in mediation, see § 4.28. On the party's incentives to be truthful about, or to misrepresent, its bottom line to the mediator, see Jennifer Gerarda Brown & Ian Ayres, Economic Rationales for Mediation, 80 Va.L.Rev. 323, 335 (1994).

92. See § 4.13.

93. See § 4.12.

than precise terms. And mediators do not often tell the parties whether they have a settlement zone in blunt yes-or-no terms. Mediators are, again, usually more indirect and imprecise in saying things like "I think we can work out a deal here."

In mediation, as in negotiation, discovering that a settlement zone exists does not ensure a deal.[94] For example, a settlement of the case depicted in Diagram 4–1 will create $20,000 in value. But who gets how much of that value depends on where the price is in the zone between $40,000 and $60,000. If the parties settle at $40,001 then Defendant captures virtually all of the value created by settling. Plaintiff is barely made better off by the settlement. If the parties settle at $59,999 then Plaintiff captures virtually all of the value created by settling. Defendant is barely made better off by the settlement.

The negotiators may spend much time and money negotiating within the settlement zone. Indeed, each negotiator may be so determined to capture the potential value from a settlement that they never reach a deal.[95] Defendant's lawyer may say to Plaintiff's lawyer "We will not pay more than $40,001. You should agree to it because it is better for your client than continuing litigation." Plaintiff's lawyer may say to Defendant's lawyer "We will not take less than $59,999. You should agree to it because it is better for your client than continuing litigation." These lawyers are playing the *game of chicken*.[96] Whoever gives in first, by accepting the other side's offer, loses most of the value created by settling, but if neither gives in then neither gets any of the value that could have been created by settling.

Mediators often stop the game of chicken from preventing agreement. With a sense of each party's bottom line, the mediator can guide the parties toward the middle of the settlement range. Again, few mediators will explicitly tell the parties: "you should settle at $50,000 because that's the middle of your settlement zone." But in a more indirect and imprecise way, the mediator can encourage a party who is making an offer toward the middle of the zone and caution a party who refuses to make such an offer that her inflexibility is preventing a deal that will be good for her. In other words, the mediator will preserve the confidentiality of each side's bottom line, while providing an imprecise or "noisy" translation of it for the other party.[97]

§ 4.12   Positive–Sum

(a) In General

Positive-sum negotiation finds those possible settlement terms that are better *for both parties* than other possible settlement terms.[98] Posi-

---

94. See § 3.12.

95. See § 3.4. See also Richard A. Posner, Economic Analysis of Law 68–69 & 607–09 (5th ed.1998).

96. See § 3.12. For tactics to win the game of chicken, see §§ 3.15—3.22.

97. Brown & Ayres, supra note 91, at 356–71.

§ 4.12

98. See § 3.9.

tive-sum negotiation expands the pie; zero-sum negotiation divides it. Positive-sum opportunities are exploited by negotiators who use the *problem-solving* approach to negotiation.[99] Problem-solving mediators encourage negotiators to use this approach.[100]

The key to positive-sum negotiation is considering multiple issues. Positive-sum negotiation almost never occurs if only one issue is considered, especially if that issue is the amount of money Defendant will pay Plaintiff. The interests of the parties are almost certain to be diametrically opposed on the issue of money; Plaintiff wants to receive as much as possible, while Defendant wants to pay as little as possible. If issues other than the amount of money are considered, it may be possible to find one on which the parties' interests coincide or to engage in *logrolling*. Coinciding interests and logrolling are discussed in the following two sections.

(b) Coinciding Interests

For an example of an issue on which the parties' interests coincide, consider a negligence claim for compensatory damages arising from a personal injury Defendant caused while engaged in his ordinary business activities. Both Plaintiff and Defendant may prefer that a settlement payment occur in December, rather than in the next month, January. Ordinarily, the *time-value of money*[101] causes plaintiffs to want payments to occur sooner and defendants to want payments to occur later. This Defendant's payment, however, is probably tax deductible,[102] and taxpayers generally benefit from taking deductions in the current tax year, rather than waiting until next year.[103] In other words, Defendant's tax benefit of paying in December of this year may exceed the interest it could earn on the money by waiting until January of next year to pay. If so, Defendant prefers payment in December, rather than January. Plaintiff also prefers December to January because there is no tax consideration offsetting Plaintiff's desire to start earning interest on the money sooner rather than later.[104] In short, both parties prefer the payment to occur in December, rather than January. A settlement providing for payment in January would make both parties worse off than a settlement providing for payment in December. Agreeing on payment in December is a clear example of positive-sum negotiating because the parties' interests coincide on this question of when the payment occurs.

99. See §§ 3.26—3.30.

100. See § 4.7.

101. See § 3.9.

102. Javed A. Khokhar, Tax Aspects of Settlements and Judgments A–28 (Tax Management Portfolio No.522–2nd, 1999).

103. See, e.g., James Edward Maule & Lisa Marie Starczewski, Deductions: Overview and Conceptual Aspects A–39 (Tax Management Portfolio No.503, 1995)("One of the principal consequences of timing determinations is the availability of acceleration; for most taxpayers it is advantageous to accelerate deduction of an item to the earliest taxable year permitted by the tax law.")

104. The personal injury settlement payment is not taxable income to Plaintiff. Khokhar, supra note 102, at A–3.

Issues on which parties' interests coincide are rare. They tend not to become issues precisely because the parties' interests coincide and all parties quickly realize that. On the other hand, tax issues are examples of issues that litigators and their clients may forget.[105] If the parties do not realize that their interests coincide on a particular issue, the mediator can point it out to the parties. Doing so is a clear example of the problem-solving mediator bringing something to the table, of adding value to the negotiation. In the absence of the mediator, the parties discussed above might have arranged for payment in January, rather than December.

(c) Logrolling Multiple Issues

Even in the absence of issues on which the parties' interests coincide,[106] considering multiple issues can reveal opportunities for both parties to gain. This is because the degree of importance the parties attach to an issue may differ. Suppose Plaintiff cares a lot about Issue A, but not much about Issue B, while Defendant cares a lot about Issue B, but not much about Issue A. The negotiators can create value by having Defendant concede on Issue A in exchange for Plaintiff's concession on Issue B. Each party gives up something she cares about a little to get something she cares about a lot. This sort of trade, often called *logrolling*, is the basis of most positive-sum negotiation. It works even where the parties disagree on every issue, if they prioritize issues differently.[107]

Logrolling happens only when multiple issues are considered together, rather than each issue considered in isolation. Negotiators often make the mistake of considering one issue, resolving it, and moving on to the next issue without ever returning to reconsider the first issue. This approach, while neat and organized, precludes logrolling so a problem-solving mediator discourages negotiators from using it. The problem-solving mediator encourages negotiators to consider multiple issues simultaneously and to trade concessions on low-priority issues for gains on high-priority issues.

Even where negotiators do consider multiple issues simultaneously and trade concessions, they may make the wrong trades. As just noted, if Plaintiff cares a lot about Issue A and Defendant cares a lot about Issue B, then value is created when Plaintiff concedes on Issue B in exchange for Defendant's concession on Issue A. In contrast, value is not necessarily created, and may even be destroyed, if Plaintiff concedes on Issue B in exchange for Defendant's concession on Issue C, D, or E. And value is certainly destroyed if Plaintiff concedes on Issue A (his high-priority issue) in exchange for Defendant's concession on Issue B (her high-priority issue). Negotiators risk making these "wrong trades"—trades that miss opportunities to create value and may even destroy value—if they have not revealed to each other their side's underlying interests and

---

105. Tax law's impact on settlement can be significant and complicated. See generally, Khokhar, supra note 102.

106. See § 4.12(b).

107. For an example of logrolling, see § 3.9.

priorities. This lack of openness is common.[108] A major problem with negotiation is that negotiators often have strong incentives not to reveal their underlying interests and priorities.[109] Mediation, as explained next, seems well-suited to solving this problem.

(d) Trusted Intermediary Combining Information

A negotiator who is open about his side's interests and priorities is using the *problem-solving* approach to negotiation, while a negotiator who conceals or misrepresents them is using the *adversarial/competitive* approach.[110] A problem-solving negotiator is often vulnerable to an adversarial/competitive counterpart who will exploit the problem-solver's openness by insisting on a settlement at the problem-solver's bottom line.[111] While there are tactics for the problem-solving negotiator to avoid vulnerability, these tactics are unlikely to work with a counterpart determined to remain adversarial/competitive. The problem-solving negotiator must basically give up on problem-solving, especially the disclosure of important information, unless and until the other side reveals its own important information.[112]

One can summarize as follows. Both sides would be better off if they each revealed their interests and priorities, *i.e.*, used the problem-solving approach. But in many cases each side's individual incentive is to conceal and misrepresent its interests and priorities, *i.e.*, to use the adversarial/competitive approach. As a result of each side following its individual incentives, neither side reveals its interests and priorities. Both take the adversarial/competitive approach, greatly reducing the likelihood of positive-sum negotiation.[113] This is an example of the *Prisoner's Dilemma*[114] because what is bad for both parties results from each trying to do what is good for itself.

Mediation can solve the dilemma through the use of private caucuses in which the mediator, but neither party, receives full information. If Plaintiff is sure that the mediator will keep confidences,[115] Plaintiff can be open about his interests and priorities to the mediator. Plaintiff can reveal even the most sensitive information, without worrying that Defendant will exploit it. Conversely, if Defendant is sure that the mediator will keep confidences, Defendant can be similarly open with the mediator. The mediator, in short, possesses the combined information of both parties.

Once the mediator has gathered all the relevant information, she can identify opportunities for positive-sum logrolling. She can see that Plaintiff's concession on Issue A in exchange for Defendant's concession on Issue B really will make both parties better off because Plaintiff really does care more about Issue A and Defendant really does care more

108. See §§ 3.15—3.22.
109. See § 3.30.
110. See §§ 3.15—3.30.
111. See id.
112. See id.

113. See § 3.30.
114. See §§ 3.24 & 3.30.
115. See § 4.28.

about Issue B. The mediator can also avoid "wrong trades." She can see that Plaintiff's concession on Issue A in exchange for Defendant's concession on Issue C would destroy value because Plaintiff never really cared much about Issue C.

The mediator can identify the possible settlement terms that are better for both parties than other possible settlement terms because she has received full disclosure from both sides.[116] This is disclosure that the parties refuse to make to each other simply because they do not trust each other the way they trust the mediator.

This function of combining information to create a complete picture of the parties' interests is an important way that mediators add value.[117] Many mediations achieve results better for both parties than negotiation would have achieved because the mediator combines each side's otherwise confidential information.[118]

Of course, the mediator is most likely to accomplish this if the parties are sure that what they tell the mediator will remain confidential. This is not just a question of whether the mediator will consciously break her promise not to tell one side's secrets to the other side. It is also a question of whether the mediator will inadvertently reveal something. And it is also a question of whether the mediator may reveal confidential information after the mediation is over. Suppose, for example, that the mediator is subpoenaed and asked under oath to reveal what she was told by one of the parties during a private caucus.

A discussion of the law governing confidentiality in mediation appears in a later section.[119]

§ 4.13   Evaluation by the Mediator

(a) The Appeal of Evaluation

Mediators have available to them a wide variety of "evaluative" tactics. An extreme example of mediator evaluation, bordering on (nonbinding) *adjudication*,[120] is when the mediator tells the parties and their lawyers something like: "I have considered the strengths and weaknesses of each party's arguments on the law and on the facts and, predicting how further litigation is likely to go, conclude that the current settlement value of this case is $200,000."[121] In contrast, a more mild form of evaluation might be "Plaintiff has a very strong argument that Defen-

---

116. See, e.g., <http://www.peacesummit.com> (discussing One Accord computer software designed to generate optimal settlement terms from confidential party disclosures made to neutral).

117. Cf. Brunet & Craver, supra note 67, at 205.

118. See also § 4.11 (mediator combines information about bottom lines).

119. See § 4.28.

§ 4.13

120. See § 1.5(a), n.12 (defining adjudication). See also §§ 4.2 & 4.31 (comparing adjudication and evaluation).

121. For an example of similar evaluation by the mediator, see Lavinia Hall, Eric Green: Finding Alternatives to Litigation in Business Disputes, in When Talk Works: Profiles of Mediators, supra note 45, at 295–99.

dant breached the contract and damages appear to be in the six figures", or "I've seen verdicts in similar cases range around two or three hundred thousand dollars." Other examples of mediator evaluation are when the mediator tells the parties and their lawyers something like: "Defendant's contributory-negligence argument is unlikely to persuade a jury" or "Plaintiff seems to have shown strong evidence of price-fixing."

Many parties and lawyers value a mediator who is willing to evaluate a case and is accurate in her evaluations.[122] The appeal of neutral-evaluation can be understood in light of the fact that a case cannot settle unless there is a *settlement zone*.[123] With few exceptions, the only cases lacking a settlement zone are those in which Plaintiff expects a more pro-Plaintiff result from litigation than Defendant expects.[124] If, for example, Plaintiff expects a $250,000 verdict, while Defendant expects a $200,000 verdict, there may be no settlement zone.[125] These cases in which Plaintiff expects a more pro-Plaintiff result than Defendant expects can be called cases of over-optimism. If Plaintiff expects a verdict of $250,000 and Defendant expects a verdict of $200,000, then at least one of the parties is overly optimistic about its likely success at litigation. Cases lacking a settlement zone are those in which at least one of the parties is in for a disappointment at trial.

Because parties' over-optimism about their success at litigation can prevent settlement zones, advocates of settlement seek to reduce party over-optimism and thus make the parties' expectations about the results of litigation converge. Neutral evaluation tends to do just that. It reduces the gap between the parties' expectations by giving them information (the neutral's evaluation of the case) that causes the parties' expectations about the results of litigation to converge around the neutral's evaluation. The neutral, because her judgment is respected by the parties, persuades the parties to change their expectations.

Suppose, for example, Plaintiff expected a verdict of $800,000, and Defendant expected a verdict of $100,000, before the neutral evaluator predicted a verdict of $300,000. The evaluation succeeded if it caused Plaintiff to now expect a verdict lower than $800,000 and Defendant to expect a verdict more than $100,000. The evaluation succeeded marvelously if it caused each party to now expect a verdict of $300,000. The

---

122. See, e.g., Majorie Corman Aaron, Evaluation in Mediation, in Dwight Golann, Mediating Legal Disputes: Effective Strategies for Lawyers and Mediators 267, 272–73 (1996); James Freund, The Neutral Negotiator: Why and How Mediation Can Work to Resolve Dollar Disputes (1994); Barbara McAdoo & Nancy Welsh, The Times They Are a Changin'—Or Are They? An Update on Rule 114, The Hennepin Lawyer, Jul.-Aug. 1996, at 9; McEwen, Mather & Maiman, Mediation, Lawyers, and the Management of Divorce Practice, 28 L. & Soc'y Rev. 149, 164–67 (1994); Hans U. Stucki, Mediator's Credibility is Key Predictor of Success in ADR, 13 Alternatives to the High Cost of Litig. 2, 8 (1995).

123. See § 3.11.

124. See id.

125. Whether there is a settlement zone turns on how the two sides value the costs and benefits of the two processes: settlement and litigation. It may, for example, be that litigation is so costly that both sides are better off settling at any one of many possible settlement terms than they are litigating even though Plaintiff expects a higher verdict than Defendant expects.

more the original $700,000 gap is reduced, the more the evaluation succeeded.

Successful evaluations come from a neutral whose judgment is respected by the parties as a good predictor of litigation. Suppose the case involves a personal injury arising out of an auto accident. If the neutral evaluator is a local judge who has presided over the trial of hundreds of similar cases, the parties and lawyers may have confidence that this neutral can predict quite well the results of litigating this case. The better a predictor of litigation the parties believe the evaluation to be, the better the evaluation is likely to be at reducing the gap in the parties' expectations.

Unsurprisingly, there is some evidence suggesting that mediators who evaluate have higher settlement rates than those who do not.[126]

(b) Concerns About Evaluation

(1) Interests vs. Rights

Mediators should not evaluate if they believe that mediation should focus on the parties' *interests*, as opposed to the parties' *positions* or *rights*.[127] A party may have no interest in something to which he has a right, for example reinstatement at the job from which he was fired. Conversely, he may have an interest in something to which he has no right, such as a public apology and admission of wrongdoing.[128] By evaluating, a mediator focuses the mediation on the parties' rights. Litigation *adjudicates* parties' legal rights,[129] and when a mediator predicts the results of litigation, she is saying what she thinks the parties' rights are. Even if she does not go so far as to predict specific results of litigation, but merely assesses the strength of a particular legal argument, she is giving her views on what she thinks the parties' rights are.

A focus on interests, rather than rights, is essential for *positive-sum* negotiation. Positive-sum negotiation requires the identification of issues on which the parties' interests coincide or on which they place a different level of priority.[130] Identifying such issues cannot be done by discussing the parties' rights, only by discussing their interests. Evaluative mediation, by focusing on rights rather than interests, encourages the parties to treat the situation as *zero-sum*, whether it is or not.

126. Jeanne M. Brett, Zoe I. Barsness & Stephen B. Goldberg, The Effectiveness of Mediation: An Independent Analysis of Cases Handled by Four Major Service Providers, Neg.J. 259, 261–62 (July 1996)(81 percent to 74 percent). See also Thomas J. Stipanowich, Beyond Arbitration: Innovation and Evolution in the United States Construction Industry, 31 Wake Forest L.Rev. 65, 122–24 (1996); Roselle L. Wissler, A Closer Look at Settlement Week: Study Finds Mediators' Style Can Have an Impact on Outcome of Dispute Resolution, Disp.Resol.Mag., Summer 1998, at 28.

127. See § 3.27 (defining and contrasting *interests* and *positions*).

128. Courts cannot order an apology. See Richard L. Abel, A Critique of American Tort Law, 8 Brit.J.of L. & Soc'y 199 (1981).

129. See § 1.5.

130. See § 4.12. For additional discussions, see §§ 3.9 & 3.26—3.30.

One might argue that a mediator can both (1) explore the parties' interests with an eye toward positive-sum opportunities and (2) evaluate the parties' rights. But this is usually not possible because evaluation generally prevents an exploration of interests. To see why, imagine yourself as the lawyer of a party to mediation in which the mediator will evaluate the merits of the case. You have a strong incentive to persuade the mediator that the merits are on your side, *i.e.*, that your client is in the right. If you persuade the mediator of this, you can make the mediator your ally against the other side. You can tell the mediator: "Of course we won't settle for anything less than X because we are entitled to X and our case is so strong that if we go to trial a court will give us X." Assume that you can persuade the mediator of all this. If the mediator wants, as most do,[131] for the case to settle then the mediator will try to persuade the other side to agree to a settlement that gives you X. The mediator knows that a settlement will not occur unless you get X because you cannot be talked into a settlement that is worse for you than the expected result of litigation.[132] Of course, the other side has an incentive to persuade the mediator that it is in the right and that you are not entitled to X. So both sides will be arguing their cases to the mediator. Both lawyers will be advocates.

Advocacy, especially by lawyers, prevents an exploration of the parties' interests. Rather than being open to the mediator about his side's interests and priorities, the lawyer-advocate resists disclosure of confidential information. Indeed, he conceals and misleads.[133] Or, as he would put it, he presents the case in the light most favorable to his client. Accordingly, the mediator who seeks to explore interests and exploit positive-sum opportunities tries to persuade the lawyers (and the parties) that advocacy is useless in mediation. There is no point in persuading the mediator that your side is in the right because the mediator will not be affected by those arguments. She does not think in those terms. She tells the lawyers and parties that if they want their dispute resolved according to arguments about rights then they should litigate, not mediate. The mediator will not do what a court does. The mediator is going to focus on the parties' interests to help them negotiate an agreement that, to the extent possible, satisfies all parties' interests, without regard to who has a right to what.

To keep the mediation focused on interests, non-evaluative mediators (often known as *facilitative* mediators[134]) generally seek to increase the participation of the parties and reduce the participation of lawyers.

---

131. See § 4.6.

132. See §§ 3.5 & 3.11—3.13.

133. See §§ 3.15—3.22.

134. Mediator approaches often are placed along a continuum with "facilitative" at one end and "evaluative" at the other, so that the more facilitative a mediator is, the less evaluative she is, and vice versa. See Riskin & Westbrook, supra note 56, at 314–28. This usage may imply that evaluation is inconsistent with facilitating agreement. In some cases, however, evaluation may be exactly what is needed to facilitate agreement. See § 4.13(a). Any mediator who helps the negotiation progress earns the label "facilitative" because "to facilitate" means to make easier, to help forward or to assist the progress of. See Webster's Third New International Dictionary 665 (Merriam–Webster 1971).

When it comes to the client's interests and priorities, the client typically knows better than the lawyer. In part, this is simply because every person knows his own values, preferences and tastes in a way that others can never know. But there is another reason why lawyers tend to be flawed sources of information about their client's interests and priorities. Lawyers are accustomed to thinking about rights, rather than interests. "Lawyers are trained to put people and events into categories that are legally meaningful, to think in terms of rights and duties established by rules, to focus on acts more than persons."[135] So, when the client's participation is overshadowed by the lawyer's participation, mediation typically becomes "a rights-based process."[136]

A lawyer may be so focused on rights that she never thought to ask her client about his interests and priorities.[137] And even if the lawyer does know her client's interests and priorities, she may be reluctant to disclose them to the mediator. Lawyers are trained to be adversarial and, even if the mediator stresses that she will not evaluate, some lawyers cannot break free of the adversarial mindset. They believe that they best represent their clients by giving the mediator zealous advocacy of the client's rights, rather than a forthright analysis of the client's interests and priorities. Finally, there is the possibility that the lawyer's interests differ somewhat from the client's interests and the lawyer is not whole-heartedly pursuing the client's interests.[138] Mediators should try to speak directly with clients to overcome such lawyers. In short, lawyers are often obstacles to the mediator's desire to shift the focus of dispute-resolution from rights to interests.

(2) Is "Evaluative Mediation" an Oxymoron?

Many scholars seek to emphasize the distinction between interests-based processes of dispute-resolution and rights-based processes.[139] Some of these scholars consider "evaluative mediation" an oxymoron.[140] According to these scholars, a neutral's evaluation of a case may sometimes be desirable, but it should not be called "mediation" because doing so blurs the distinction between an interests-based process, mediation, and a rights-based process, neutral evaluation, which is discussed in a later

135. Riskin, supra note 8, at 45. "This view requires a strong development of cognitive capabilities, which is often attended by the under-cultivation of emotional faculties. This combination of capacities joins with the practice of either reducing most nonmaterial values to amounts of money or sweeping them under the carpet." Id.

136. Jacqueline M. Nolan–Haley, Alternative Dispute Resolution in a Nutshell 83–90 (1992)(describing this as a "considerable downside[]" to heavy lawyer participation). But cf. McEwen, Rogers & Maiman, supra note 55, at 1364–75 ("lawyers do not 'spoil' mediation, but instead permit mediation to accomplish many of the goals surrounding party participation and empowerment.")

137. See § 3.34.

138. See § 3.6.

139. See § 3.27 (defining and contrasting *interests* and *positions*).

140. Kimberlee K. Kovach & Lela P. Love, "Evaluative" Mediation is an Oxymoron, 14 Alternatives to the High Cost of Litig. 31 (1996); Lela P. Love, The Top Ten Reasons that Mediators Should Not Evaluate: Reflections on the Evaluative–Facilitative Debate, 24 Fla.St.U.L.Rev. 937 (1997).

section.[141]

While there is much strength to this argument, because the distinction between rights and interests is important, this book uses the term "evaluative mediation." Evaluation is a matter of degree and once one concedes that some mild evaluation is consistent with being a "mediator," it is difficult, perhaps impossible, to draw the line at the maximum level of evaluation consistent with being engaged in "mediation," rather than "neutral evaluation."

Whether a mediator is evaluative is not a yes-or-no question, but a matter of degree. A mediator who puts a dollar amount on the settlement value of a case is as evaluative as possible. Such precise and all-encompassing evaluation borders on adjudication.[142] To a lesser degree, however, even mediators who consider themselves non-evaluative, often do some evaluating. For instance, a party who proclaims that he is certain to win a smashing victory in court may elicit a question from the mediator like: "Are you sure judges and juries never make mistakes?" The mediator is gently cautioning the party that there is always some uncertainty when going to trial. The mediator's reminder to the party about uncertainty may help moderate the party's unrealistic expectations. This is evaluation by the mediator. The mediator is talking about rights, rather than interests, and is doing so in a way calculated to reduce party optimism, *i.e.*, to make the parties' expectations about the results of litigation converge, however slightly.

Mediator evaluation may be inevitable. It is the rare mediator who never betrays even a hint of her views about the strengths of the parties' positions. Even mediators who do not think of themselves as evaluative often "aggressively prod one or more parties to reconsider its proposed position" or "challenge party proposals (perhaps in caucus) as unworkable or misleading."[143] The typical mediator cannot help but interject her views about the merits of the case by the questions she chooses to ask or not to ask, the statements she pursues or ignores, her tone of voice, her facial expressions, and so on. Despite the mediator's efforts to be non-evaluative, to focus on interests, she will usually betray at least some of hint of her views on the merits. Few people are capable of being purely non-judgmental.

(3) Mediator's Credibility

A mediator who does more than mild evaluation risks losing her credibility with at least one of the parties. At least one party is likely to feel that he has "lost" the evaluation. This "loser" and his lawyer may conclude that the mediator "decided against" them because she is biased toward the other side. Or perhaps she is incompetent; she did not listen to or understand them. Either way, it is unlikely the "loser" and his lawyer will participate constructively with the mediator after "losing"

141. See § 4.34.

142. See §§ 4.2 & 4.31.

143. Joseph B. Stulberg, Facilitative Versus Evaluative Mediator Orientations:
Piercing the "Grid" Lock, 24 Fla.St. U.L.Rev. 985, 1002–03 (1997).

the evaluation. If further mediation is to make any progress, it may have to be with a new mediator.

For this reason and others, extensive evaluation by the mediator, if it is to be done at all, may be better done toward the end of mediation.[144] If the mediator and parties have made a good faith attempt to resolve the dispute, without evaluation, and have truly reached impasse, then the choice is between litigation and an evaluation that might stimulate some additional offers of settlement.[145] But this should not lead one to conclude that there can be no harm to evaluation once mediation has exhausted without a deal. There is still the worry that parties who know an evaluation may occur will try to "win over" the mediator by arguing their rights and being less than candid about their interests.[146]

(c) Mediator's Evaluation Given to the Court

The mediator's evaluation is sometimes given to the court as well as to the parties. Such a practice can increase the effectiveness of evaluation in promoting settlement because the court is likely to be influenced by the mediator's report.[147] The parties' predictions about the results of litigation are especially likely to converge under this practice because the evaluation is not merely a prediction of how the case will be decided but an influence on how the case is decided. Conversely, the risks of evaluation are heightened by this practice which nearly guarantees that the mediation will focus on rights, rather than interests. "Mediation accompanied by this sort of settlement pressure thus becomes an adjudicatory process with the parties seeking to persuade a third-party while building a record to facilitate a challenge to the third-party if an unfavorable report results."[148]

§ 4.14 Broad or Narrow Scope of Issues

Depending on the goals of the participants in mediation,[149] these participants may seek to broaden or narrow the number of issues discussed in mediation. Those who see mediation primarily as a way of settling cases generally want to narrow the issues.[150] The fewer the issues, the less that needs to be resolved in order to reach an agreement. For this reason, most settlement-oriented participants try keep the discussion focused on the essentials and avoid being distracted by extraneous issues. On the other hand, sometimes settlement cannot be reached without positive-sum negotiation, such as *logrolling*.[151] Logrolling is the process in which the parties consider multiple issues simultaneously and make concessions on low-priority issues in exchange for

---

144. Aaron, supra note 122, at 283.

145. See § 4.13(a).

146. See § 4.13(b)(1).

147. Rogers & McEwen, supra note 1, § 7:05 (noting higher settlement rate in San Francisco, where custody mediators reported to the trier of fact, than in Los Angeles, where they did not).

148. Id. § 7:05 at 25–27.

§ 4.14

149. See §§ 4.5—4.8.

150. See Riskin, supra note 61, at 42–43.

151. See §§ 3.13 & 3.26(c).

gains on high-priority issues.[152] If settlement cannot be achieved without logrolling, the settlement-oriented participant is more likely to achieve her goal by broadening the discussion to include additional issues.

Those who see mediation as more than just a way to settle cases often see it as a way to achieve positive-sum solutions or even a way to transform the parties to engender moral growth.[153] These participants, unlike the settlement-oriented participant, generally want to broaden the number of issues discussed in mediation. The more issues considered, the more likely the negotiators and mediator are to identify opportunities for positive-sum negotiation. And moral growth also seems more likely to result from a holistic approach.

Sometimes the mediator seeks to broaden the number of issues discussed, but the parties and lawyers do not share that goal. The parties and lawyers may be accustomed to thinking in zero-sum terms and may believe that there is only one topic to negotiate, such as "how much money will Defendant pay Plaintiff?" or "how much pollution will flow into the lake?" The mediator must then decide how hard she can push the parties and lawyers toward considering additional issues without threatening the principles of party self-determination and mediator impartiality.

§ 4.15 Party Self–Determination and Mediator Impartiality

Three organizations prominent in ADR—the American Arbitration Association, the American Bar Association and the Society of Professionals in Dispute Resolution—approved Standards of Conduct for Mediators. The first two Standards state in part:

> -"Self determination is the fundamental principle of mediation. It requires that the mediation process rely upon the ability of the parties to reach a voluntary, uncoerced agreement."[154]

> -"The concept of mediator impartiality is central to the mediation process. A mediator shall mediate only those matters in which she or he can remain impartial and evenhanded."[155]

While these two Standards of self-determination and impartiality receive nearly universal assent, they are so general that they leave room for substantial disagreement.

Consider two views summarized by James Boskey. One view, which can be called the *libertarian* view, is that the parties "are capable of making their own decisions as to what does or does not constitute an appropriate or just result to their negotiations, and it would be presumptuous, to say the least, for the mediator to impose his or her sense of

152. See § 4.12(c).

153. See §§ 4.5—4.8.

§ 4.15

154. John D. Feerick et al., American Arbitration Assoc. et al., supra note 10, Standard I.

155. Id., Standard II.

fairness or justice on them."[156] The alternative view, which can be called the *egalitarian* view, "is that one of the primary purposes of mediation, if not the primary purpose, of mediation is to balance the power between the parties to insure that a 'fair' agreement results."[157] Power might be measured in a variety of ways including: the expected strength of one's case in court, one's financial and psychological resources to pursue that case, one's skill as a negotiator, and so forth.[158]

While the libertarian and egalitarian views are diametrically opposed to each other, each can claim fidelity to the Standards of self-determination and impartiality. Both views claim to provide self-determination, *i.e.*, a voluntary, uncoerced agreement, because each view rests on its own understanding of coercion and partiality.[159] The egalitarian view rests on the premise that the pre-existing inequality between the parties is inherently coercive to the less-powerful party. To the extent the mediator can reduce the pre-existing inequality, the mediator increases the voluntariness of any agreement that results. The mediator's failure to reduce the pre-existing inequality would be partiality toward the more powerful party.

In contrast, the libertarian view rests on the premise that the pre-existing inequality is not coercive, but that mediator attempts to equalize the parties are coercive and constitute partiality toward the less powerful party. A mediator who pursues her notions about what constitutes a fair result is no longer a mediator, but an advocate or moral judge.[160] So long as the resulting agreement does not trigger legal doctrines of duress, unconscionability and the like, the mediator should not try to stop the parties' relative strengths from being reflected in the terms of settlement.

While the libertarian view seems more common, especially among mediators handling cases in which all parties are represented by lawyers,[161] the egalitarian view is frequently voiced in contexts, such as

156. James B. Boskey, The Proper Role of the Mediator: Rational Assessment, Not Pressure, 10 Neg.J. 367, 367 (1994).

157. Id.

158. See § 3.5.

159. One interested in exploring the concept of coercion in law and philosophy has many excellent resources available. See, e.g., Alan Wertheimer, Coercion (1987); XIV Nomos: Coercion (J. Roland Pennock & John W. Chapman eds., 1972).

160. Joseph B. Stulberg, The Theory and Practice of Mediation: a Reply to Professor Suskind, 6 Vt.L.Rev. 85, 116 (1981). Accord Christopher W. Moore, The Mediation Process: Practical Strategies for Resolving Conflict 17–18 & 333–37 (2d ed.1996).

161. "[T]he dominant approach in statutes to defining fairness is consent (sometimes informed consent) by parties to settlements without pressures to settle created by special burdens of the mediation process." Rogers & McEwen, supra note 1, § 2:02 at 11. As mediation is usually an alternative to negotiation, "it is not surprising that the consent standard has emerged as dominant and does not impose on mediation substantially greater expectations for fairness than provided by negotiation. This approach is especially appropriate if attorneys are involved in the mediation sessions." Id. at 12–13. The libertarian view seems quite similar to what Rogers & McEwen call the "consent" approach to fairness, but the libertarian view differs from the "informed consent" approach.

divorce and child custody, in which parties often lack lawyers and the interests of young children must be protected.[162]

Whether the mediator takes the libertarian or egalitarian view will likely affect the mediator's conduct in a variety of situations. For example, suppose the parties are about to sign a settlement agreement and Defendant has told the mediator (in confidence) information that, if known by Plaintiff, would likely cause Plaintiff not to sign the settlement. A mediator with a libertarian view of self-determination and impartiality probably would keep the Defendant's secret so long as the resulting agreement would not be rendered unenforceable on the ground of misrepresentation or mistake.[163] In contrast, a mediator with an egalitarian view probably would reason that "an agreement is not truly voluntary if it is based on a factual misunderstanding * * * which the mediator had the opportunity to correct."[164]

§ 4.16   The Mediated Settlement Agreement

(a) Practice, Including the Single–Text Approach

In some mediations the parties reach an oral agreement and do not reduce it to writing. This is rare in settlement mediation, *i.e.*, mediation of a dispute in, or headed to, litigation or arbitration. Typically the parties to settlement mediation will sign a formal release or settlement agreement. In a simple case, this could be prepared and signed at the mediation session in which an oral agreement was reached. In many cases, though, drafting the agreement is left to the lawyers after the parties and mediator have moved on to other things. In these cases, the parties may write a short memo or outline of their deal at the end of the mediation and give that to their lawyers who will convert it into a formal, signed contract.

Some mediators are actively involved in writing the settlement agreement. The mediator may even draft a written proposal during mediation and use it as a starting point for the parties to critique. After each critique, the mediator re-writes the proposal to reflect those party suggestions the mediator wishes to incorporate. With this *single-text* approach, the mediator may control the drafting process from start to finish. One advantage of this approach is that, psychologically, parties may be more willing to consider proposals made by the mediator than those made by their adversaries. Other mediators object to the single-text approach on the ground that it raises the role of the mediator over that of the parties and threatens the principles of party self-determination and mediator impartiality.[165] Heavy mediator involvement in draft-

---

162. See, e.g., Cal.Fam.Code § 3162(b)(3)(West 1994)(mediator must "conduct[] negotiations in such a way as to equalize power relationships between the parties.") Family mediation is discussed in § 4.17.

163. See §§ 3.39 & 4.16.

164. Boskey, supra note 156, at 370.

§ 4.16

165. These principles are discussed in § 4.15.

ing is also likely to make the mediator more *evaluative*,[166] because it forces the mediator to make more decisions about how the dispute should be resolved. Every decision about whether to use this word or that word in the settlement agreement is a chance for evaluation by the mediator.

There are important legal risks for certain mediators who become involved in drafting settlement agreements. Non-lawyer mediators who do it may violate prohibitions on the un-licensed practice of law.[167] And lawyer-mediators who do it may violate their rules of professional conduct, especially if the parties are not represented by their own lawyers.[168]

(b) Enforceability

The law governing negotiated settlement agreements is discussed in the previous chapter,[169] and that law generally applies to mediated settlements. There are, however, exceptions. Mediated settlements sometimes must meet a higher standard than negotiated settlements to be enforceable. For example, some statutes say that a mediated settlement agreement is not legally-binding unless it contains a provision stating that it is.[170] Also, in some court-sponsored mediation programs, a settlement agreement is not enforceable unless approved by the court.[171] With negotiated settlements, court approval is typically required only for divorce and class action settlements.[172]

Ordinary contract-law defenses—such as misrepresentation, duress, unconscionability and mistake—apply to both negotiated and mediated settlements.[173] But some courts seem more ready find that these defenses are proven with respect to mediated settlements than negotiated settlements.[174] Perhaps that is because the mediator's conduct, as well as the parties' conduct, can supply the facts to prove the defense. On the other hand, the presence of even a minimally-competent mediator would seem to reduce the likelihood of an agreement induced by duress, misrepresentation, mistake or the like.

166. Evaluation by the mediator is discussed in § 4.13.

167. See § 4.27(c)(3).

168. See § 4.27(c)(2).

169. See §§ 3.38—3.42.

170. Cal.Bus. & Prof.Code § 467.4 (West 1990)(applies to mediations funded under the statute); Minn.Stat.Ann. § 572.35 (West 1998)(mediations under Civil Mediation Act). Compare Haghighi v. Russian–American Broadcasting Co., 577 N.W.2d 927 (Minn.1998)(enforcing Minnesota statute), with Haghighi v. Russian–American Broadcasting Co., 945 F.Supp. 1233 (D.Minn.1996)(avoiding Minnesota statute), rev'd, 173 F.3d 1086 (8th Cir. 1999).

171. Colo.Rev.Stat.Ann. § 13–22–308 (West 1999); Kan.Stat.Ann. § 23–603 (West 1985).

172. See § 3.39.

173. McEnany v. West Delaware County Community Sch. Dist., 844 F.Supp. 523 (N.D.Iowa 1994); Martin v. Black, 909 S.W.2d 192 (Tex.App.1995)(challenge to validity of mediated agreement governed by contract law); Sheng v. Starkey Laboratories, 117 F.3d 1081 (8th Cir.1997)(applying contract law of mutual mistake to mediated settlement agreement). See also § 3.39.

174. See, e.g., Wright v. Brockett, 150 Misc.2d 1031, 571 N.Y.S.2d 660, 665 (Sup. Ct.1991).

Negotiated settlements may have to be in writing to be enforceable.[175] Oral settlements are even less likely to be enforceable if they arise out of mediation. Some statutes and courts expressly state that mediated settlements are enforceable only if written.[176] And the requirement of a writing may also be an effect of law creating a *mediation privilege*[177] because the privilege precludes testimony necessary to prove that an oral agreement was formed. In short, the law may be developing what amounts to a Statute of Frauds for mediated settlements.

D. MEDIATION CONTEXTS

Table of Sections

§ 4.17   Family

The category of cases currently generating the most mediation is probably family law, especially divorce and child custody disputes. Divorce mediation is now common. Spouses frequently agree to mediate their divorce. In the absence of agreement, statutes and courts in many jurisdictions often require divorcing spouses to mediate.[178] The requirement to mediate applies only in contested cases, *i.e.*, cases in which the parties are headed to trial because they have not negotiated an agreement resolving all the issues attendant to divorce.[179]

The typical issues in family mediation are child custody and support, property division and alimony/maintenance. Child custody mediation, in particular, receives especially strong support from many states through

---

175. See § 3.39.

176. Barnett v. Sea Land Serv., Inc. 875 F.2d 741 (9th Cir.1989)(citing Washington District court Local Rule 39.1(d)(3)); Murphy v. Padilla, 42 Cal.App.4th 707, 49 Cal. Rptr.2d 722 (Ct.App.1996); Burckhard v. Del Monte Corp., 48 Cal.App.4th 1912, 56 Cal.Rptr.2d 569 (Ct.App.1996). As with other Statutes of Frauds, mediated oral agreements are enforceable if they are partially performed by the parties. See Kaiser Found. Health Plan v. Doe, 136 Or.App. 566, 903 P.2d 375 (Or.Ct.App.1995)(enforcing oral mediated settlement where subsequent behavior evidenced agreement).

177. See § 4.28(d).

§ 4.17

178. See, e.g., Cal.Fam.Code § 3170(a) (West 1994)(requiring the court to order mediation where custody or visitation issues are contested); Or.Rev.Stat. § 107.765(1)(1995)(mandating mediation in disputes regarding child custody or visitation); Maine Rev.Stat.Ann., Tit. 19–A, § 251 (West 1998); La.Rev.Stat.Ann. § 9:332(A) (West Supp.1996)(allowing court-ordered mediation in custody disputes).

179. See Rogers & McEwen, supra note 1, § 7:02. In uncontested cases, if the parties' agreement meets with the court's approval, the court simply grants the parties the divorce they seek, often incorporating the separation agreement into the judgment.

government funding, mandated participation and broad evidentiary privileges.[180] "Court sponsored family [mediation] programs often mediate only issues of custody or visitation and refuse to encourage negotiations regarding economic issues."[181]

Family mediation frequently involves no lawyers in any role. The vast majority of family mediators in many states are non-lawyers, typically mental health professionals such as marriage counselors, psychologists and social workers.[182] Moreover, lawyers for the parties often do not attend mediation sessions. Family mediators in some states even have authority to exclude lawyers.[183] The frequent absence of lawyers in family mediation is a striking contrast to most other settlement mediation, which involves lawyers for each party as well as a lawyer-mediator.[184] The prevalence of unrepresented parties in family mediation makes it the mediation context most likely to raise concerns about the unauthorized practice of law by non-lawyer mediators,[185] and about issues of professional responsibility for lawyer-mediators.[186]

If family mediation results in agreements on issues such as child custody and support, property division and alimony/maintenance, then these agreements must be approved by the court.[187] This should be contrasted with most settlement agreements which do not require court approval.[188]

Divorce mediation has a number of selling points when compared to trial.[189] Its advocates say its non-adversarial setting typically minimizes

180. Id. § 2:06 at 22–23.

181. Id. § 12:02 at 4. See also McEwen, Rogers & Maiman, supra note 55, at 1340.

182. Divorce Mediation: Theory and Practice 11 (Folberg & Milne eds.1988), referring to a survey in Jessica Pearson, et al., A Portrait of Divorce Mediation Services in the Public and Private Sector, 21 Conciliation Courts Rev., No. 1, at 1 (1983).

183. Kan.Stat.Ann. § 23–603(a)(6)(West 1995)(child custody mediator "shall * * * allow only the parties to attend the mediation sessions"); Wis.Stat.Ann. § 767.11(10)(a)(West 1993)(child custody mediator "may * * * [i]nclude the counsel of any party or any appointed guardian ad litem in the mediation.").

In some other jurisdictions lawyers have developed the practice of non-attendance on their own. See Craig A. McEwen, Lynn Mather & Richard J. Maiman, Mediation, Lawyers, and the Management of Divorce Practice, 28 L. & Soc'y Rev. 149, 180 (1994).

184. Similarly, divorce *negotiation* involves unrepresented parties more frequently than the negotiation of other cases. One study of divorce in sixteen urban areas

found that one or both parties was unrepresented in 72% of the cases. See John Goerdt, Divorce Courts: Case Management, Case Characteristics, and the Pace of Litigation in 16 Urban Jurisdictions 48 & 61–63 (1982). The typical party to a divorce proceeding is represented only if the divorce is contested or there is substantial property involved.

185. See § 4.27(c)(3).

186. See § 4.27(c)(2).

187. See, e.g., Unif.Marriage and Divorce Act § 306(a)-(c), 9A U.L.A. 248–49 (1998). "[T]he terms of the separation agreement, except those providing for the support, custody, and visitation of children, are binding upon the court unless it finds, after considering the economic circumstances of the parties and any other relevant evidence produced by the parties, on their own motion or on request of the court, that the separation agreement is unconscionable." Id. § 306(b).

188. See § 3.39.

189. On the comparison between mediation and negotiation, see § 4.24. See also § 1.7(d)(suggesting that litigation and arbitration are substitutes for each other, while

the emotional and financial trauma of divorce, benefitting both spouses and any children. Unlike litigation, divorce mediation can educate the parties about each other's interests and priorities and help them to work together in the future as, for example, children grow older and new parenting issues arise. By facilitating the parents' own decision-making and self-determination, mediation "should enhance continuing family ties and reassert the dignity and importance of the family as a self-governing unit."[190] While the remedies in litigation are limited, mediation can provide personalized, tailor-made arrangements for the particular parties involved. "Courts are ill-equipped to mandate particular visitation schedules and custodial arrangements, the wisdom of which depend on the situations of the parents and children rather than on legal rules."[191]

There are also strong critics of divorce mediation. "Many of these critics are leaders of the women's movement who contend that women will achieve worse results in mediation than in court."[192] This might occur for a variety of reasons, most based on the premise that wives tend to be less powerful—financially and otherwise—than their husbands.

First, men are more likely than women to use the *adversarial/competitive* approach to negotiation, while women are more likely than men to use the *cooperative* and *problem-solving* approaches.[193] There is a significant risk that the adversarial/competitive negotiator will exploit the cooperative or problem-solving one.[194] This risk is heightened in mediation if the parties do not have, or are unaccompanied by, their own lawyers.[195]

Another concern about mediation is the lack of compelled discovery. If the husband has more assets than the wife, or more knowledge about jointly-owned assets, then the litigation process enables the wife and her lawyer to acquire that knowledge through court-ordered discovery. In contrast, if mediation occurs prior to discovery, the husband may be able to conceal assets, or information about them, from the wife.[196]

Finally, divorce may follow domestic violence, typically a husband's abuse of his wife. "A view that victims of domestic violence are not well served in mediation has led several states to enact exceptions to mandated mediation in these cases."[197]

negotiation and mediation are substitutes for each other).

190. H. Jay Folberg, Divorce Mediation: A Workable Alternative, from American Bar Association, Alternative Means of Family Dispute Resolution 11, 17 (1982).

191. Rogers & McEwen, supra note 1, § 6:03 at 10.

192. Brunet & Craver, supra note 67, at 285.

193. See § 3.31.

194. See §§ 3.23—3.25 & 3.30. See also Trina Grillo, The Mediation Alternative:

Process Dangers for Women, 100 Yale L.J. 1545, 1603 (1991)("If she is easily persuaded to be cooperative, but her partner is not, she can only lose.")

195. McEwen, Rogers & Maiman, supra note 55.

196. See Laurie Woods, Mediation: A Backlash to Women's Progress on Family Law Issues, 19 Clearinghouse Rev. 431, 435 (1985).

197. Rogers & McEwen, supra note 1, § 12:02 at 9. The practice of sending to mediation criminal actions arising out of such abuse has also been criticized. See,

§ 4.18   Labor & Employment

Law governing employment is often divided into two categories: "employment law" which applies to all employees, and "labor law" which applies only to employees represented by a labor union. Labor law has its own specialized terminology. Contracts between employers and unions are called "collective bargaining agreements." Claims alleging breach of these contracts are called "grievances."[198] Mediation, in the labor context, is often called "conciliation."[199]

Mediation has been used to resolve labor disputes for at least a century.[200] The Federal Mediation and Conciliation Service ("FMCS") is part of the Department of Labor and it mediates disputes between labor unions and employers. Its statutory charge is "to assist parties to labor disputes in industries affecting commerce to settle such disputes through conciliation and mediation."[201] Its involvement is usually in *transactional* mediation, specifically the formation of a new collective bargaining agreement.[202] But it is also sometimes involved in *dispute* mediation, *i.e.*, the resolution of grievances under an existing collective bargaining agreement.[203] Grievances are also mediated by private-sector mediators, as many collective-bargaining agreements require that disputes be mediated.[204] Disputes between non-unionized employees and their employers are also mediated.

§ 4.19   Community

During the 1960's and 1970's, government and private money began funding "community mediation centers" or "neighborhood justice centers" around the country. These centers handle the sorts of disputes commonly found among neighbors, such as landlord-tenant, nuisance, small claims and misdemeanors. Disputes come to these centers largely through referrals by prosecutors, police and the courts.[205] The mediators are generally volunteers, usually non-lawyers. "The poor, unemployed, women, and ethnic minorities constitute a large proportion of disputants in many programs."[206] Rarely are any of the parties accompanied by lawyers during the mediation session.

e.g., Lisa G. Lerman, Mediation of Wife Abuse Cases: The Adverse Impact of Informal Dispute Resolution on Women, 7 Harv.Women's L.J. 57 (1984). On criminal mediation generally, see § 4.23.

§ 4.18

198.   See § 2.53.

199.   But see William E. Simkin & Nicholas A. Fidandis, Mediation and the Dynamics of Collective Bargaining 23–25 (2d ed.1986)(distinguishing between conciliation and mediation).

200.   Rogers & McEwen, supra note 1, § 5:01.

201.   29 U.S.C. § 173(a)(1998).

202.   See generally Simkin & Fidandis, supra note 199, at 195–217.

203.   The FMCS may provide its services for grievance disputes also, but "only as a last resort and in exceptional cases." 29 U.S.C. § 173(d)(1998). Parties are obligated to "participate fully and promptly" in the sessions called by the FMCS. Id. § 174(a)(3).

204.   Riskin, supra note 8, at 31–32 n.10.

§ 4.19

205.   Id. at 31–32.

206.   Richard Hofrichter, Neighborhood Justice in Capitalist Society: The Expansion of the Informal State 100 (1987).

§ 4.20 Business

Mediation of disputes among businesses seems to be growing. The variety of business contexts generating these disputes is endless: sales of goods and services, licenses of technology and intellectual property, real estate development and construction, franchising, financing through loans or securities, and so on. More and more business contracts include "two-step" ADR clauses, providing that the parties shall mediate any dispute that may arise and, if mediation fails to result in a settlement, the parties shall arbitrate the dispute.[207]

§ 4.21 Public Law (Including Environmental)

Much law is now made, not by legislatures or courts, but by the rulemaking of administrative agencies such as the Environmental Protection Agency and the Federal Trade Commission. Negotiated rulemaking ("reg-neg") is a form of *transactional mediation*[208] among the parties likely to be affected by a regulation on a particular issue. Instead of transactional mediation to form a private contract, the deal formed by the parties in reg-neg is a government regulation. Accordingly, the mediation sessions are open to the public. Reg-neg is encouraged by federal and state statutes, and many agencies use it.[209]

Administrative agencies also use mediation to resolve disputes. For example, several states have enacted statutes designed to encourage mediation of environmental disputes.[210] At the federal level, the Environmental Protection Agency uses mediation in its enforcement actions. Such disputes generally involve multiple parties: polluters, adjacent residents, public-interest groups, and federal, state and local agencies. The mediator may facilitate both multilateral (many parties) and bilateral (two parties) negotiation.[211]

§ 4.22 Any Civil Case

Many of the disputes discussed above—family,[212] labor,[213] community,[214] business,[215] environmental[216]—are widely-considered to be well-suit-

§ 4.20

207. See, e.g., California Association of Realtors, Residential Purchase Agreement, para. 21, reprinted in, Steven J. Burton & Melvin A. Eisenberg, Contract Law: Selected Source Materials 465–69 (2000). See also Stipanowich, supra note 9, at 372–78 (construction industry).

§ 4.21

208. See § 4.3.

209. See, e.g., 5 U.S.C. § 571 et seq. (Supp.II 1994); Administrative Dispute Resolution Act of 1990, Pub.L.No. 101–552, 104 Stat. 2736 (1990); Fla.Stat.Ann. ch.120.54 (West Supp. 2000); Neb.Rev.Stat.Ann. § 84–919.01 (Michie 1995); Idaho Code § 67–5206(3)(e), 67–5220 (1992); David M.

Pritzker & Deborah S. Dalton, Negotiated Rulemaking Sourcebook 9–10 (Administrative Conference of the United States 1995).

210. Rogers & McEwen, supra note 1, § 6:03 at 11 & § 12:07.

211. See, e.g., Lawrence Susskind, Environmental Mediation and the Accountability Problem, 6 Vt.L.Rev. 1 (1981).

§ 4.22

212. See § 4.17.

213. See § 4.18.

214. See § 4.19.

215. See § 4.20.

216. See § 4.21.

ed to mediation, especially the *problem-solving* approach. That is because they tend to be disputes between *repeat players*, that is, parties who want or expect to have relationships that continue after the dispute is resolved. Disputes between repeat players are more likely than disputes between *one-shotters* to involve multiple issues; they are less likely to be simple disputes about the amount of money one party will pay the other. Multiple issues are crucial to create opportunities for *positive-sum* negotiation,[217] and thus make the dispute more amenable to the *problem-solving* approach used by so many mediators.[218]

In contrast, other disputes involve parties who do not want or expect their relationship to continue after the dispute is resolved. A classic example of these *one-shot* parties is a personal injury arising out of an automobile accident. The plaintiff expects to have no further interaction with the defendant or the defendant's insurance company once the dispute is resolved. These one-shot disputes are often *zero-sum*[219] situations in which the only issue to be resolved is the amount of money one party will pay the other.

The parties to one-shot, zero-sum disputes do not much benefit from a problem-solving mediator and, until very recently, these disputes were not often mediated. These disputes may, however, be suited to a *settlement-oriented* mediator, especially an *evaluative* one.[220] And the last decade or so has seen some increase in mediation of personal injury and other run-of-the-mill civil cases. This development may be caused by courts' encouragement of mediation as a way to clear dockets.[221]

§ 4.23 Criminal

Plea-bargaining is to criminal litigation what settlement negotiation is to civil litigation, the way most cases are resolved. Plea-bargaining is negotiation between the government and the defendant. The government has a lawyer, the prosecutor, negotiating on its behalf and the defendant nearly always has a lawyer negotiating on his behalf. The mediation of criminal disputes is not mediation between the government and the defendant. Rather, it is mediation between the complainant or victim and the defendant.

Crimes have long been viewed as offenses against the state or society, rather than just offenses against the victim, so prosecutors, not complainants, have the authority to determine whether a prosecution will proceed.[222] Similarly, after conviction prosecutors, rather than victims, have the authority to determine what sentence to seek. Criminal

---

217. See §§ 3.9 & 3.26—3.30.

218. See §§ 4.7 & 4.12.

219. See § 3.8.

220. See §§ 4.11 & 4.13.

221. See, e.g., Robert B. Moberly, Ethical Standards for Court–Appointed Mediators and Florida's Mandatory Mediation Ex-

periment, 21 Fla.St.U.L.Rev. 701, 701–03 (1994).

§ 4.23

222. "Traditionally, the courts have treated agreements between the victim and the accused with suspicion." Rogers & McEwen, supra note 1, § 12:05, at 21.

mediation is an exception, authorized by legislatures or courts, to this government-dominated approach of modern criminal law.

Criminal cases are referred to mediation by courts, prosecutors and probation officers. Mediation can occur before trial, even before charges are filed. Agreements reached in such mediation typically remove the threat of prosecution in exchange for the payment of restitution to the complainant. Mediation is also used after conviction. Agreements reached in such mediation typically reduce or eliminate the offender's prison time in exchange for the payment of restitution to the victim. If a promise to pay restitution is a condition of probation then that promise can be enforced by the probation officer.[223] Critics argue that "[a]llowing offenders to buy their way out of prison" undermines the public goals of criminal law such as retribution, incapacitation, deterrence and rehabilitation.[224]

Some Victim–Offender Reconciliation Programs seek, as the name suggests, not just a restitution agreement, but some measure of reconciliation between the offender and victim. As some of its advocates put it, "we focus on the relational aspects of crime. Attitudes, feelings and needs of both victims and offender must be taken very seriously. Healing is important."[225]

Defendants/offenders are sometimes ordered by courts or pressured by prosecutors into participating in mediation.[226] Courts and prosecutors cannot compel complainants/victims to participate but can tell them that, in the absence of participation, the prosecution will dismissed or the sentence will be reduced.[227] There may even be pressure to reach an agreement if, in the event no agreement is reached, the mediator will report to the court or prosecutor, giving the mediator's view about which party was "uncooperative" during mediation. Lawyers are generally not present in criminal mediation.[228]

E. REPRESENTING CLIENTS IN MEDIATION

Table of Sections

§ 4.24 Whether to Mediate

You may find yourself representing a client in mediation even though your client never agreed to mediate. That is because some

---

223. Howard Zehr et al., The VORP Book at II–14 (1983).

224. Jennifer Gerarda Brown, The Use of Mediation to Resolve Criminal Cases: A Procedural Critique, 43 Emory L.J. 1247, 1253 & 1296–1301 (1994).

225. Zehr et al., supra note 223, at II–5.

226. Brown, supra note 224, at 1267.

227. Zehr et al., supra note 223, at II–7.

228. Compare Paul R. Rice, Mediation and Arbitration as a Civil Alternative to the Criminal Justice System—An Overview and Legal Analysis, 29 Am.U.L.Rev. 17, 64–66 (1979)(opposing lawyers), with Brown, supra note 224, at 1289–90.

statutes require mediation of certain types of cases and, in many state and federal courts, judges have authority to order most types of civil cases into mediation.[229] Leaving aside such *mandatory mediation*, the issue of whether to seek mediation arises in every dispute any of your clients has.

For you and your client to decide whether mediation would be worthwhile, you will have to examine the particular features of the dispute. Mediation is not for a client whose interests can only be served by a court's verdict. Some clients want, at nearly all cost, the public vindication that comes from a favorable verdict, to "make law" with a favorable precedent, or to develop a reputation for being fierce litigators in order to intimidate future adversaries. But most clients who want these things will give them up for a price, in the form of money or something else they want.[230] If settlement is truly out of the question for your client then mediation, like negotiation, is pointless. But it is the rare client who will flatly refuse any settlement offer, no matter how good and no matter when offered. For all but these rare clients, mediation is worth consideration simply because a settlement might be in the client's interests. Once you and your client have agreed to consider the possibility of settlement, how do you decide between negotiating with the other side and mediating with them?

Mediation has advantages over negotiation in all kinds of disputes, positive-sum and zero-sum. Some cases present opportunities for *positive-sum* negotiation, *i.e.*, for finding those settlement terms that are better for both parties than other settlement terms. Such cases tend to be those involving issues other than, or in addition to, money and such cases tend to involve *repeat players* (parties who expect or want to continue their relationship after the case is resolved).[231] Positive-sum opportunities may go unexploited in negotiation because negotiators often have strong incentives not to reveal their underlying interests and priorities.[232] Mediation, especially with a *problem-solving* mediator, can alter these incentives to facilitate positive-sum negotiation.[233] In short, mediation can expand a pie that negotiation would only have divided.

In zero-sum cases, *e.g.*, a case about nothing other than how much money Defendant will pay Plaintiff, dividing the pie is the only issue.[234] In these cases, negotiators often fail to discover whether a *settlement-zone* exists and, even if they discover that it does exist, they still often fail to reach a settlement.[235] A *settlement-oriented* mediation would likely be better than negotiation at quickly identifying whether a settlement zone exists, and narrowing differences between the parties' positions, *i.e.*, bringing them closer to agreement.[236]

§ 4.24

229. See § 4.30. See also Rogers & McEwen, supra note 1, §§ 6:04 & 7:02.

230. See § 3.5.

231. See §§ 3.9 & 3.26—3.30.

232. See § 3.30.

233. See §§ 4.7 & 4.12.

234. See § 3.8.

235. See §§ 3.12 & 3.15—3.22.

236. See §§ 4.11 & 4.13.

Mediation then, has advantages over negotiation in all cases, positive-sum and zero-sum. But the benefits of mediation must be weighed against the costs.

Mediation is likely to have costs not present in negotiation. For example, the cost of paying the mediator often must be borne by the parties. Another cost is time, both the lawyer's and the client's if they will both be participating in mediation. The relevant time includes, not just the mediation session(s), but also preparation for mediation, which can be much more elaborate than preparation for negotiation.[237] Preparing for mediation, if done thoroughly, can be quite time-consuming and, if not done thoroughly, can make mediation risky.[238]

Many lawyers who handle large numbers of small cases—such as auto accidents or slip-and-fall cases—spend little time negotiating settlements. They make settlement offers in two-minute phone calls or one paragraph letters. These lawyers, usually correctly, view most of their cases as zero-sum situations in which the only issue is the amount of money Defendant will pay Plaintiff. A trial of one of these cases may take a day or less of the lawyer's time. For these lawyers, spending just two hours and a few hundred dollars on mediation may be prohibitive. Unless the mediator's settlement rate is near 100 percent, she is not cost-effective. Outside these small cases, however, the money and time for a single mediation session are relatively minor costs.

The more serious cost is the risk that suggesting mediation, or participating in it, will hurt one's position against the other side. Many lawyers feel that suggesting mediation to the other side is a sign of weakness that an adversarial/competitive counterpart will exploit.[239] And there is the risk that participating in mediation will cause you or your client to reveal sensitive information to the mediator that, for whatever reason, does not remain confidential.[240]

§ 4.25   Preparing for Mediation

As a lawyer preparing to represent a client in mediation, you should do everything you would do to prepare for negotiation,[241] and more. The "more" is to learn about the mediator. You will want to learn about the mediator's background and her qualifications, of course. Is she an expert in the subject matter of this dispute? Such expertise is very important for an accurate *evaluation*,[242] and will be helpful even in a non-evaluative

---

237. See § 4.25.

238. See id.

239. Rogers & McEwen, supra note 1, § 4:07. This is an argument for judges ordering, or at least encouraging, mediation. If the idea comes from the judge, and both sides say they are mediating just to stay in the judge's good graces, then neither side looks weak. See Jeffrey Z. Rubin & Bert R. Brown, The Social Psychology of Bargaining and Negotiation 47, 58 (1975).

The worry that suggesting mediation makes one appear weak seems to decline as lawyers become more experienced with mediation. Rogers & McEwen, supra note 1, § 4:07.

240. See § 4.28.

§ 4.25

241. See §§ 3.33—3.37.

242. See § 4.13.

mediation.[243] More importantly, you will want to learn her usual approach to mediation.[244] Is she focused just on reaching settlement or does she emphasize positive-sum opportunities or even moral growth?[245] Does she evaluate?[246] Will she keep all communications in the strictest confidence?[247] You can gather information on these things by asking the mediator directly or asking parties and lawyers who have previously participated in mediations with this mediator.

You and your client will probably have a role in selecting the mediator. Voluntary mediation will not occur unless you agree (on behalf of your client) to the particular mediator. And even in mandatory mediation, a common procedure is for you and the other side to agree on a mediator; only if you cannot reach an agreement will one be appointed for you.[248] Prior to selecting a mediator you will want to learn about the candidates. You would like to learn, with respect to each candidate, all the information discussed in the previous paragraph. On the other hand, you may find that it costs too much time and money to gather so much information.

Preparing for mediation has an added dimension if your client will be participating in the mediation.[249] If you expect an *evaluative*[250] mediator or one who may reveal confidences then you might prepare your client for mediation as you would prepare your client for his deposition, *i.e.*, to vigorously advocate the merits of his case. In this mode, you will caution your client not to depart from his prepared script. If he wants to say anything not on the script, he should call for a break in which he will consult with you, his lawyer, privately. Preparation of your client is especially important if the mediator is likely to ask to meet with the parties without lawyers present. If you think your client would be disadvantaged in such a forum, you can refuse the mediator's request to leave the room.[251]

On the other hand, if you plan to take a *problem-solving*[252] approach then your discussions with your client would focus on his interests and priorities.[253] You will let him speak freely during the mediation so the mediator can identify positive-sum opportunities.

243. Stulberg, supra note 143, at 996–97.

244. See, e.g., Layn R. Phillips, Laying Foundation for Successful Mediation: Questions Neutrals and Parties Need to Ask, 13 Alternatives to the High Cost of Litig. 132 (1995).

245. See §§ 4.5—4.8.

246. See § 4.13.

247. Answering this question may require research about the law as well as about the mediator. Even a mediator who wants to keep confidences may be compelled by subpoena to reveal them. See § 4.28.

248. See § 4.30.

249. See § 4.13(b)(1) for reasons why some mediators seek to increase the participation of clients and reduce the participation of lawyers. For a list of questions the mediator is likely to ask your client, see Tom Arnold, 20 Common Errors in Mediation Advocacy, 13 Alternatives to the High Cost of Litig. 69, 71 (1995).

250. See § 4.13.

251. In the family law area, however, there are some jurisdictions in which the mediator has the authority to exclude lawyers. See § 4.17.

252. See §§ 3.26—3.30.

253. See § 3.27 (defining and contrasting interests and positions).

§ 4.26 During Mediation

How you best represent your client during mediation will depend on the specifics of that case and the participants. There are no hard-and-fast rules for representing clients in mediation. But there are some generalizations.

Your behavior should be influenced by at least two things about the mediator: the likelihood that she will *evaluate*[254] and the likelihood that she will keep confidential any sensitive information you give her. If the mediator is certain not to evaluate at all, and certain never to reveal any of your confidences, then you can be open to the mediator about your side's interests and priorities. In other words, you can take a *problem-solving* approach. This will best enable the mediator to help identify and exploit *positive-sum* opportunities.[255] On the other hand, if the mediator evaluates then the evaluation may be worse for your side than it would have been had you argued your case, rather than openly disclosed your side's interests and priorities.[256] And if the mediator, perhaps compelled by subpoena, reveals sensitive information you told her then you may regret your forthright disclosure.[257]

Finally, you, the lawyer, may not be present in mediation. For example, several states prohibit lawyers from attending family mediation sessions.[258] You may advise your client not to agree to anything until he has a chance to consult with you. Where lawyers are not present during mediation, clients often ask their lawyers to review the mediated settlement agreement before the client signs it. "Lawyers, however, express frustration over their limited ability to advise on these agreements, because they do not witness the give-and-take of the negotiations that created them and lack access to the information needed to evaluate properly alternatives to settlement."[259]

F. LAW GOVERNING MEDIATION

Table of Sections

§ 4.27 Mediators' Professional Duties

(a) Overview

This section discusses three ways to establish and enforce mediators' professional duties. The first way is the lawsuit. A private party suing a

---

§ 4.26

254. See § 4.13.

255. See § 4.12.

256. See § 4.13(b)(1); Riskin & Westbrook, supra note 56, at 433.

257. See § 4.28.

258. See § 4.17.

259. McEwen, Rogers & Maiman, supra note 55, at 1346.

professional for negligence, breach of contract or other legal violation is an important way in which various professionals' duties are enforced. It has been substantially disabled, however, as a way of enforcing mediators' professional duties.[260]

The second way of establishing and enforcing professional duties is administrative regulation, specifically occupational licensing. Lawyers, for example, must meet certain requirements to receive from the state a license to practice law and that license can be revoked if the lawyer violates certain professional duties, typically those in the Model Rules of Professional Conduct.[261] There is no analogous system of licensing for mediators generally, although there is something of a licensing requirement for many mandatory and court-sponsored mediation programs.[262]

The third way of establishing and enforcing professional duties is with private, rather than governmental, sanctions. This approach is developing with respect to mediation.[263]

(b) Liability Suits Against Mediators

Doctors, lawyers, psychologists, accountants, engineers, and architects are sued for alleged failures in their performance of professional services. In contrast, mediators rarely are sued.[264] One reason for this is a growing body of law largely immunizing mediators from suit. Some state statutes grant mediator immunity,[265] although often with an exception for "willful and wanton misconduct" or similar behavior.[266] Courts have generally endorsed mediator immunity,[267] even where not created by statute.[268]

Mediator immunity is an extension of judicial immunity. Judges are immune from suit for the performance of their judicial duties,[269] so the remedy for the party who dislikes a judge's ruling is to appeal, not to sue the judge. Immunity has spread from judges to other actors in the court system such as prosecutors, jurors, witnesses and court reporters.[270]

§ 4.27

260. See § 4.27(b).

261. See § 4.27(c)(1).

262. See § 4.27(c).

263. See § 4.27(d).

264. Rogers & McEwen, supra note 1, § 11:03 at 21. One example is Lange v. Marshall, 622 S.W.2d 237 (Mo.App.1981)(reversing jury verdict against divorce mediator in negligence claim). Cf. Tarasoff v. Regents of the Univ. of Calif., 17 Cal.3d 425, 131 Cal.Rptr. 14, 551 P.2d 334 (Cal.1976)(psychotherapist negligent in failing to warn woman of his patient's threats to murder her).

265. Rogers & McEwen, supra note 1, § 11:03.

266. Colo.Rev.Stat.Ann. § 13–22–305(6) (West 1999). See also Iowa Code Ann. § 13.16 (West 1995); Or.Rev.Stat. § 36.210 (1995).

267. See, e.g., Postma v. First Fed. Sav. & Loan of Sioux City, 74 F.3d 160 (8th Cir.1996); Howard v. Drapkin, 222 Cal. App.3d 843, 271 Cal.Rptr. 893 (1990).

268. The leading case is Wagshal v. Foster, 28 F.3d 1249 (D.C.Cir.1994). See also Meyers v. Contra Costa County Department of Social Services, 812 F.2d 1154 (9th Cir. 1987).

269. This immunity applies only to acts that are judicial in nature. A judge who fires a probation officer, for example, is acting in his administrative, rather than judicial, capacity so is not immune. Forrester v. White, 484 U.S. 219, 108 S.Ct. 538, 98 L.Ed.2d 555 (1988).

270. Caroline Turner English, Mediator Immunity, 63 Geo.Wash.L.Rev. 759, 765 (1995).

Mediator immunity, however, has been criticized on the ground that mediators do not perform functions comparable to others who have received immunity.[271]

(c) Occupational Licensing: Who May Mediate?

(1) Mandatory vs. Voluntary

The law permits anyone to mediate; no license is required. But that does not mean there is a free market for transactions between those who consume mediation services (disputing parties) and those who provide them (mediators). Much mediation is mandated by government and/or funded by government. In these cases, government intervenes in the market for mediation and often directly influences the choice of mediator.

In mandatory mediation, the mediator may be a government employee.[272] When courts in some jurisdictions order parties to mediate, a court employee selects the mediator.[273] More commonly, the parties are allowed to agree on a mediator but, if they cannot agree, the judge or other court employee will appoint one.[274] Even where the parties are permitted to select a mediator, they may be required to choose someone from a roster of mediators approved by the court or other government agency. To get on the roster, a mediator may have to meet certain qualifications. Getting on the roster amounts to getting a license to mediate this category of cases. The required qualifications might be:

-completing a mediator training course,[275]

-experience as a counselor or psychotherapist,[276]

-possessing a master's degree in psychology, social work, counseling, or other discipline,[277]

-complying with a mandatory disclosure requirement to reveal to the parties the mediator's qualifications, education and training.[278]

In short, government intervenes in the mediation market by requiring certain qualifications to mediate certain cases.

Government also intervenes in the mediation market by subsidizing certain mediators and mediation programs. This is clearest where mediators are government employees. "Many federal and some state and local mediation programs rely on direct legislative appropriations or budget allocations from the judiciary."[279] Other courts impose filing fee sur-

---

271. See id. at 777. See also Rogers & McEwen, supra note 1, § 11:03 at 12.

272. Rogers & McEwen, supra note 1, § 3:04 n.10.

273. Id. § 6:10.

274. See, e.g., Fla.R.Civ.P. 1.720(f)(2).

275. 710 Ill.Comp.Stat.Ann. 20/5(a)(2)(West 1999)(30 hours); Iowa Code Ann. § 679.8 (1998) (25 hours).

276. Cal.Fam.Code §§ 1815(a)(2) & 3164 (West 1994).

277. Cal.Fam.Code §§ 1815(a)(1) & 3164 (West 1994).

278. Minn.Stat.Ann. § 572.37 (West 1988).

279. Rogers & McEwen, supra note 1, § 6:13.

charges on all civil litigants and use that money to fund mediation programs.[280] Either way, by using some of this money to employ mediators, government influences who does and does not become a mediator.

In contrast, a free market for mediation exists outside the contexts of mandatory and other court-sponsored mediation. There are no government regulations on who can mediate or on standards for competence and ethics.[281] There are often, however, private regulations in the form of ethical standards or contractually-imposed duties.[282]

(2) Lawyer–Mediators

While no license is required to mediate,[283] a license is required to practice law.[284] A lawyer may lose her license, *i.e.*, be disbarred or suspended from practice, if she violates the conditions of her license, such as her state's Rules of Professional Conduct. The vast majority of states have adopted some or all of the American Bar Association's Model Rules of Professional Conduct, while a few states continue to use the older Model Code of Professional Responsibility.[285] The Model Rules and Model Code are often thought to be *ethical* rules and they are. But they are also *legal* rules because they are enacted by government. The state bar committees and courts that enforce these rules are government agencies administering occupational licensing regulations to determine who is, and is not, legally-permitted to practice law.

There is uncertainty about when lawyers who mediate violate the Model Rules. The Model Rules generally prohibit lawyers from representing multiple clients with conflicting interests.[286] Even the consent of all clients cannot overcome this prohibition if the clients' interests are fundamentally antagonistic to each other.

---

280. Id.

281. Riskin & Westbrook, supra note 56, at 380; Rogers & McEwen, supra note 1, § 2:08.

282. See § 4.27(d).

283. See § 4.27(c)(1).

284. See 2 Geoffrey C. Hazard, Jr. & W. William Hodes, The Law of Lawyering § 5.5 (Supp.1998); American Bar Association, Compendium of Professional Responsibility: Rules and Standards 523–27 (1999). See generally Deborah Rhode, Policing the Professional Monopoly: A Constitutional and Empirical Analysis of Unauthorized Practice Prohibitions, 34 Stan.L.Rev. 1 (1981).

285. American Bar Association, Compendium of Professional Responsibility: Rules and Standards 523–27 (1999).

286. Model Rule of Professional Conduct 1.7 provides:

(a) A lawyer shall not represent a client if the representation of that client will be directly adverse to another client, unless:

(1) The lawyer reasonably believes the representation will not adversely affect the relationship with the other client; and

(2) Each client consents after consultation.

(b) A lawyer shall not represent a client if the representation of that client may be materially limited by the lawyer's responsibilities to another client or to a third person, or by the lawyer's own interests, unless:

(1) The lawyer reasonably believes the representation will not be adversely affected; and

(2) The client consents after consultation. When representation of multiple clients in a single matter is undertaken, the consultation shall include explanation of the implications of the common representation and the advantages and risks involved

Model Rule of Professional Conduct 1.7 (1999).

[W]hen a disinterested lawyer would conclude that the client should not agree to the representation under the circumstances, the lawyer involved cannot properly ask for such agreement or provide a representation on the basis of the client's consent.[287]

For example, *a lawyer may not represent multiple parties to a negotiation whose interests are fundamentally antagonistic to each other*, but common representation is permissible where the clients are generally aligned in interests even though there is some difference of interest among them.[288]

In short, if the parties' interests are fundamentally antagonistic to each other, a lawyer cannot mediate the dispute if doing so constitutes "representation" of the parties.[289] The question then, is whether a lawyer-mediator "represents" the parties, *i.e.*, whether a lawyer-client relationship is formed between the lawyer-mediator and the parties.

The Model Rules do not define "representation" and state bar committees have reached differing conclusions.[290] But there does seem to be a consensus that lawyer-mediators are less likely to "represent" the parties if the parties have their own lawyers than if the mediator is the only lawyer involved. In other words, assuring that no lawyer-client relationship exists between the mediator and the parties is easier if the parties have their own lawyers than if they do not.

A distinction can be made between one-lawyer mediation, in which the mediator is the only lawyer, and three-lawyer mediation, in which

---

287. Model Rule of Professional Conduct 1.7, comment 5 (1999).

288. Id., comment 12.

289. While the Model Rules allow a lawyer to serve as an "intermediary" between clients, that is only when there is "little risk of material prejudice to the interests of any of the clients if the contemplated resolution is unsuccessful." Model Rule of Professional Conduct 2.2(a)(2)(1999). The full text of Model Rule 2.2 reads as follows:

(a) A lawyer may act as intermediary between clients if:

(1) the lawyer consults with each client concerning the implications of the common representation, including the advantages and risks involved, and the effect on the attorney-client privileges, and obtains each client's consent to the common representation;

(2) the lawyer reasonably believes that the matter can be resolved on terms compatible with the clients' best interests, that each client will be able to make adequately informed decisions in the matter and that there is little risk of material prejudice to the interests of any of the clients if the contemplated resolution is unsuccessful; and

(3) the lawyer reasonably believes that the common representation can be undertaken impartially and without improper effect on other responsibilities the lawyer has to any of the clients.

(b) While acting as intermediary, the lawyer shall consult with each client concerning the decisions to be made and the considerations relevant in making them, so that each client can make adequately informed decisions.

(c) A lawyer shall withdraw as intermediary if any of the clients so requests, or if any of the conditions stated in paragraph (a) is no longer satisfied. Upon withdrawal, the lawyer shall not continue to represent any of the clients in the matter that was the subject of the intermediation.

Model Rule of Professional Conduct 2.2 (1999). A comment to this Rule specifically excludes from the Rule's coverage situations in which the lawyer acts as a "mediator between or among parties who are not clients of the lawyer." Id., comment 2 (1999).

290. See Rogers & McEwen, supra note 1, § 10:02.

both parties have their own lawyers.[291] While three-lawyer mediation is the norm for most settlement mediation, one-lawyer mediation is common in family law matters.[292] It should be no surprise then, that issues surrounding the application of the Model Rules to lawyer-mediators have arisen most frequently in the family context.

To recap, the lawyer-mediator avoids possible violation of the Model Rules by avoiding an attorney-client relationship with the parties. It varies from state to state, and is often unclear, what the lawyer-mediator must do to avoid an attorney-client relationship with the parties.

A good first step is for the lawyer-mediator to explain to both parties that they are not her clients.[293] Although she is a lawyer, she is performing mediation services for them, not legal services.[294] Many agreements to mediate expressly state that no attorney-client relationship is formed between the mediator and any party.[295] Furthermore, the lawyer-mediator should explain to the parties that she cannot, in the future, represent either party in the matter.[296] There is also authority for the proposition that the lawyer-mediator cannot in the future represent either party in a related matter.[297]

In some states, a lawyer-mediator who wants to avoid an attorney-client relationship with the parties must refrain from giving the parties legal advice.[298] For example, parties lacking their own lawyers might ask the lawyer-mediator how their dispute would likely be resolved by a court. Rather than try to answer such a question, the lawyer-mediator should tell the parties that they each have the right to hire a lawyer if they want legal advice.[299] In contrast, other states permit lawyer-media-

---

291. With multiple parties, more than three lawyers can be involved. Two-lawyer mediation would be where the mediator is a lawyer and one of the two parties is unrepresented or where both parties are represented and the mediator is a non-lawyer.

292. See § 4.17.

293. And they must not have been her clients in the past. "In the event the mediator has represented one of the participants beforehand, the mediator shall not undertake the mediation." American Bar Association, Section of Family Law, Divorce and Family Mediation: Standards of Practice III.A. (1986)

294. See, e.g., State Bar of Michigan Ethics Opinion No. RI–256, 75 Mich.B.J. 364, 365 (1996); Arizona State Bar Committee on Rules of Professional Conduct, Op. No. 96–01 (1996). See also American Bar Association, Section of Family Law, Divorce and Family Mediation: Standards of Practice I.H. (1986)("The mediator cannot act as lawyer for either party or for them jointly and should make that clear to both parties.")

295. See § 4.10(f)(sample agreement to mediate, paragraph 3).

296. See § 4.10(f)(sample agreement to mediate, paragraph 6). See also American Bar Association, Section of Family Law, Divorce and Family Mediation: Standards of Practice I.G. & VI.B. (1986).

297. Rogers & McEwen, supra note 1, App. D, at 3; Poly Software Int'l Inc. v. Su, 880 F.Supp. 1487, 1494 (D.Utah 1995)("where a mediator has received confidential information in the course of mediation, that mediator should not thereafter represent anyone in connection with the same or a substantially factually related matter unless all parties to the mediation proceeding consent after disclosure.")

298. Rogers & McEwen, supra note 1, § 10:02 at 7 & nn.20–21.

299. If asked to recommend one or more lawyers, the lawyer-mediator should not refer a party to any particular lawyers. "[T]he parties should be referred to a bar association list if available. In the absence of such a list, the mediator may only provide a list of qualified family law attorneys in the community." American Bar Association, Section of Family Law, Divorce and Family Mediation: Standards of Practice VI.A. (1986).

tors to give legal advice, generally with the requirement that the advice be given in the presence of all parties.[300] An intermediate position allows lawyer-mediators to give legal information, but not legal advice.[301] There is a similar variety among the states in the extent to which the lawyer-mediator may be involved in drafting the settlement agreement while still avoiding an attorney-client relationship with the parties.[302]

As noted above, the issue under the Model Rules is whether the lawyer-mediator's giving legal advice or drafting the settlement agreement amounts to "representation" of the parties, *i.e.*, an attorney-client relationship. Certainly, giving legal advice and drafting settlement agreements have long been core activities of lawyers representing clients.[303] But there is something quite different about these activities when done by a neutral mediator than when done by an advocate seeking to advance one party's, and only one party's, interests. Accordingly, leading mediation scholars view the Model Rules' focus on whether the lawyer "represents" the parties as better suited to regulation of lawyers in their roles as advocates than to regulation of lawyers in their roles as mediators.[304] Along these lines, a few states "have abandoned efforts to interpret existing ethical provisions to apply to mediation and have amended them to provide specifically for mediation."[305]

(3) Non–Lawyer Mediators

A license from the state is required to practice law.[306] Only when one acquires this license, *i.e.*, becomes a lawyer, is she permitted to give legal advice,[307] draft legal documents,[308] and engage in the other activities constituting the practice of law. Non-lawyer mediators, like other non-lawyers, are subject to penalty if they engage in these activities. It should be noted, however, that prohibitions on the unlicenced practice of law seem to be enforced only sporadically.

There have been few cases in which courts have addressed the issue of what non-lawyer mediators can and cannot do without "practicing law." A Virginia court enjoined a non-lawyer mediator from "giving legal

300. Rogers & McEwen, supra note 1, § 10:02 at 9 n. 26 & 14 n.39.

301. Virginia State Bar Standing Committee on Legal Ethics, Op. Nos. LE–IO § #678 (1983) and § #590 (1985).

302. Rogers & McEwen, supra note 1, § 10:02.

303. See Carrie Menkel–Meadow, Is Mediation the Practice of Law?, 14 Alternatives to the High Cost of Litig. 57, 61 (1996)("When mediators engage in some prediction or application of legal standards to concrete facts—and especially when they draft settlement agreements, I think they are 'practicing' law.")

304. Rogers & McEwen, supra note 1, § 10:02 ("Abandoning the effort to determine whether the lawyer-mediator 'represents' the parties is sensible. Generally, the lawyer-mediator is providing a form of legal services, but regulation afforded advocacy representation is inappropriate for those services."); Menkel–Meadow, supra note 303, at 61 ("Ideally, we should analyze the work of third-party neutrals to see what they do, and then attempt to develop the appropriate regulatory models.")

305. Rogers & McEwen, supra note 1, § 10:02 at 17.

306. See generally Rhode, supra note 284; Hazard & Hodes, supra note 284.

307. See, e.g., Ga.Code Ann. § 15–19–51 (1999).

308. See, e.g., La.Rev.Stat.Ann. § 37:212 (West 1988 & Supp.1999).

advice to persons relating to the specific questions, problems or desires of such person."[309] The First Circuit dismissed a constitutional challenge to a bar association's warning to a non-lawyer mediator who was, the bar association concluded, practicing law.[310] Otherwise, the issue has been left to bar association opinions which have disapproved the giving of legal advice by non-lawyer mediators.[311] In short, the law has yet to develop much, and what law there is does not protect the non-lawyer mediator who gives legal advice or drafts settlement agreements.[312]

On the other hand, leading mediation scholars state that "[u]nauthorized practice prohibitions are avoided when the nonlawyer-mediator communicates legal advice of drafting suggestions to the parties' lawyers * * * . Court-employed mediators have also avoided unauthorized practice problems, presumably because their activities already are regulated by the courts."[313] In addition, bar associations and courts seem to apply unauthorized practice restrictions less rigorously to non-profit mediation programs than to for-profit mediators.[314] Thus, three large categories of non-lawyer mediators—those dealing with represented parties and those working for courts or non-profit programs—seem somewhat protected. The more serious risk is confined to private, for-profit mediators with one or more parties who is not represented by a lawyer.

(d) Private Duties (Including Ethical Standards)

Lawyers are obligated to follow their state's rules of professional conduct.[315] These are often thought to be *ethical* rules and they are. But they are also *legal* rules. They are enacted by government and breach of them can result in punishment by government, such as revocation of the license to practice law. The lawyer's Rules of Professional Conduct, then, should be distinguished from ethical obligations unbacked by the force of government. Ethical rules lacking government enforcement are the only sort of ethical rules applicable to all mediators.[316]

Many organizations have promulgated standards of ethics for mediators. Perhaps the most influential are the Standards of Conduct for Mediators, approved by the American Arbitration Association, the American Bar Association's Sections of Dispute Resolution and Litigation and the Society of Professionals in Dispute Resolution. The Standards explicitly acknowledge that they are not law: "in some cases the application of

---

309. Commonwealth of Virginia v. Steinberg, Va.Cir.Ct., Henrico Co., Case No. CL–96–504.

310. Werle v. Rhode Island Bar Ass'n, 755 F.2d 195, 199–200 (1st Cir.1985).

311. Connecticut Bar Ass'n Committee on Professional Ethics Informal Op. No. 83–1 (1982), 9 Fam. L. Rep. 2013 (1982); Boston Bar Ass'n Committee on Professional Responsibility Op. No. 78–1 (1979); Bar Ass'n of Nassau Co. [NY] Committee on Professional Ethics Op. No. 84–1 (1984).

312. See Menkel–Meadow, supra note 303.

313. Rogers & McEwen, supra note 1, § 10:05.

314. Id. at 34–36.

315. See § 4.27(c)(2).

316. An exception is if the mediator belongs to a profession, such as law, subject to its own set of government-backed ethical rules. See § 4.27(c)(2).

these standards may be affected by laws or contractual agreements."[317] The Standards are as follows:

I.   Self Determination: A Mediator Shall Recognize that Mediation is Based on the Principle of Self–Determination by the Parties.

II.   Impartiality: A Mediator Shall Conduct the Mediation in an Impartial Manner.

III.   Conflicts of Interest: A Mediator Shall Disclose all Actual and Potential Conflicts of Interest Reasonably Known to the Mediator. After Disclosure, the Mediator Shall Decline to Mediate Unless all Parties Choose to Retain the Mediator. The need to Protect Against Conflicts of Interest Also Governs Conduct that Occurs During and After the Mediation.

IV.   Competence: A Mediator Shall Mediate Only When the Mediator Has the Necessary Qualifications to Satisfy the Reasonable Expectations of the Parties.

V.   Confidentiality: A Mediator Shall Maintain the Reasonable Expectations of the Parties with Regard to Confidentiality.

VI.   Quality of the Process: A Mediator Shall Conduct the Mediation Fairly, Diligently, and in a manner Consistent with the Principle of Self–Determination by the Parties.

VII.   Advertising and Solicitation: A Mediator Shall Be Truthful in Advertising and Solicitation for Mediation.

VIII.   Fees: A Mediator Shall Be Truthful in Advertising and Solicitation for Mediation.

IX.   Obligations to the Mediation Process.

In addition to these Standards, there are other private devices to establish and enforce mediators' professional duties. For instance, many mediators are not hired directly by the parties but through an organization that sponsors mediation. Organizations such as the American Arbitration Association, JAMS/Endispute and the CPR Institute for Dispute Resolution maintain rosters of mediators. To be on the roster, the mediator may have to have certain qualifications relating to background, credentials, training and experience. There are also professional associations of mediators. For example, there is an Academy of Family Mediators, which has detailed membership requirements.[318] Membership in such an association may constitute something like a "Good Housekeeping Seal of Approval." Finally, the parties can, by contract, specify that their mediation will be conducted by someone who meets certain requirements.

317. John D. Feerick et al., American Arbitration Assoc. et al., supra note 10.

318. The members of the Academy of Family Mediators, the Society of Professionals in Dispute Resolution, and the Conflict Resolution Education Network, voted to merge their organizations into a new one, the Conflict Resolution Association as of January 1, 2001.

§ 4.28   Confidentiality

(a) Generally

Settlement mediation, like settlement negotiation, is a means of discovery in litigation. Lawyers are reluctant to reveal anything in mediation that could come back to haunt them if mediation fails and litigation continues. Lawyers are especially reluctant to make disclosures to the other side, but are also often reluctant to make disclosures to the mediator. On the other hand, mediators can often help the parties far more when the mediator learns the parties' sensitive information. For example, if the mediator learns each party's *bottom line*, she can quickly identify whether there is a *settlement zone* and, if so, where it is.[319] And if the parties are open to the mediator about their interests and priorities, the mediator can best help the parties identify and exploit *positive-sum* opportunities.[320] In sum, the more willing lawyers and parties are to make disclosures to the mediator, the better mediation works, but there are factors inhibiting such willingness.

The two major factors inhibiting disclosure to mediators are worries about confidentiality and the possibility of evaluation by the mediator. Evaluation is discussed in an earlier section.[321] Confidentiality is discussed in this section.

Mediators generally claim to be trustworthy, *i.e.*, good at keeping secrets. Mediators generally tell parties and lawyers that anything told to the mediator will remain confidential unless the mediator is given permission to reveal it.[322] Many mediations achieve results better for both parties than negotiation would have achieved because the mediator receives each side's otherwise confidential information in private caucus and then combines that information.[323] The mediator can only accomplish this if the parties and lawyers believe that what they tell the mediator will remain confidential. So mediation benefits from tools to increase the certainty that mediators can be trusted not to reveal confidences. Also, in some cases, parties are willing to reveal things to each other that they do not want revealed to others, such as journalists or competitors. So mediation also benefits from tools to increase the certainty that parties (and their lawyers) can be trusted not to reveal confidences.

(b) Confidentiality Agreements Prior to Mediation or During Litigation

One tool to increase the certainty that what is revealed in mediation will not "leave the room" is the contract. At the outset of mediation, participants may agree that any information revealed during the mediation will remain confidential. These agreements are often signed writ-

---

§ 4.28

319. See § 4.11.

320. See § 4.12.

321. See § 4.13.

322. See § 4.10(f)(sample agreement to mediate, paragraph 4).

323. See §§ 4.11—4.12.

ings, and may include express promises not to subpoena the mediator.[324] An agreement to mediate pursuant to the rules of an organization, such as the American Arbitration Association, may be a confidentiality agreement because the rules incorporated by reference into the contract require confidentiality.[325]

Confidentiality agreements in settlement negotiation are discussed in the previous chapter,[326] and that discussion generally applies to settlement mediation.

(c) Rules of Evidence and Discovery

Suppose mediation fails to achieve a settlement and the parties go to trial. One side may seek to introduce as evidence what the other side said during mediation. It might have been said either to the mediator in private caucus or to the other side in joint session. Either way, such statements are not likely to be admitted into evidence.

Federal Rule of Evidence 408 says "conduct or statements made in compromise negotiations" are not admissible "to prove liability or invalidity of the claim or its amount."[327] Rule 408 does not expressly state that it applies to statements in *mediation*, as well as to statements in *negotiation*. While courts have only begun to address the issue,[328] the policy behind Rule 408 certainly calls for its application to the mediation, as well as the negotiation, of disputes.[329]

Note that even if Rule 408 applies to mediation, it does not invariably exclude from evidence all statements made in mediation. The statements must be related to settling a civil claim, not a criminal prosecution, or a dispute not yet on the verge of litigation.[330] And even statements related to settling a civil claim are admissible if offered for purposes other than "proving liability for or invalidity of the claim or its amount." Such purposes include proving bias or prejudice, undue delay or obstruction of justice. Also, Rule 408, like any evidence rule, only applies to courts.[331] It does not apply to administrative hearings, for example.

Rule 408 and similar state statutes do nothing to protect statements made in mediation from pre-trial discovery. Admissibility is much nar-

---

324. See, e.g., § 4.10(f)(sample agreement to mediate, paragraph 10). See also American Bar Association, Section of Family Law, Divorce and Family Mediation: Standards of Practice II.A. (1986)("At the outset of mediation, the participants should agree in writing not to require the mediator to disclose to any third party any statements made in the course of mediation.")

325. See, e.g., AAA, Commercial Mediation Rules M.11 & M.12.

326. See § 3.42(b).

327. The full text of Rule 408 and further discussion of it, are contained in § 3.42(c).

328. Cf. United States Equal Employment Opportunity Comm'n v. Air Line Pilots Ass'n, Int'l, 489 F.Supp. 1003, 1008 (D.Minn.1980)(evidence arising in conciliation hearing "probably is inadmissible under Fed. R. Evid. 408."), rev'd on other grounds, 661 F.2d 90 (8th Cir.1981); In re The Hillard Development Co., 221 B.R. 282, 283 (S.D.Fla.1998)(apparently applying Rule 408 to mediation).

329. See also Haw.R.Evid. 408; Me. R.Evid. 408(b); Vt.R.Evid. 408.

330. See § 3.42(c).

331. See Fed.R.Evid. 1101 (applicability of Rules).

rower than discover-ability.[332] Having your adversary learn what you said to the mediator may harm you just as much as having your adversary learn it and introduce it into evidence.

(d) Mediation Privilege

The previous sections discuss the limitations of confidentiality agreements and rules of evidence and discovery as tools to ensure the confidentiality of mediation.[333] These limitations lead many people to advocate the development of a mediation privilege. Just as conversations between attorney and client or husband and wife are privileged, these advocates argue, so should conversations between party/lawyer and mediator be privileged. That way a mediator or party would not be compelled to testify about what was said at the mediation even if the evidence is offered for a purpose permitted by Federal Rule of Evidence 408 or similar state rules. A mediation privilege would also protect statements at mediation from the pre-trial discovery process and from disclosure outside of court, such as at administrative hearings or to journalists or competitors. A mediation privilege could go beyond protecting statements at mediation to protecting written records of the mediator or mediation program, agreements to mediate, settlement agreements formed at mediation, and so forth.[334]

Most states have created mediation privileges, either by statute or caselaw.[335] But these privileges usually do not apply to all mediations. "In the majority of statutes, the mediation privilege protects only a particular publicly administered program, such as family court custody and visitation mediation or state labor department mediation."[336] Other privileges are more broadly written to cover all mediators or mediation programs meeting certain requirements.[337] In other states, the privilege extends to mediations in which the parties expressly contract for the privilege.[338]

---

332. The Federal Rules of Civil Procedure, for instance, allow discovery of, not just admissible evidence, but anything "reasonably calculated to lead to the discovery of admissible evidence." Fed.R.Civ.P. 26(b).

Parties may obtain discovery regarding any matter, not privileged, which is relevant to the subject matter involved in the pending action, whether it relates to the claim or defense of the party seeking discovery or to the claim or defense of any other party, including the existence, description, nature, custody, condition, and location of any books, documents, or other tangible things and the identity and location of persons having knowledge of any discoverable matter. The information sought need not be admissible at the trial if the information sought appears reasonably calculated to lead to the discovery of admissible evidence.

Fed.R.Civ.P. 26(b)(1).

333. See §§ 4.28(b)-(c).

334. Rogers & McEwen, supra note 1, § 9:12.

335. See id. § 9:11 & App. A (1995 & Supp.1998).

336. Id. § 9:12, at 28.

337. See, e.g., Iowa Code Ann. § 679.12 (West Supp.1999); Iowa Code Ann. § 679C.2 (West Supp.1999); Mass.Gen.Laws ch. 233, § 23C (Law Co-op 1986). Perhaps the broadest privilege is in Texas. See Tex. Civ.Prac. & Rem.Code Ann. §§ 154.073(a)-(c), 154.053(b)(West 1997 & Supp.2000).

338. Cal.Evid.Code § 1119 (West Supp. 1999); Mo.Ann.Stat. § 435.014 (West 1992).

A privilege can be waived by the person holding the privilege. States vary on whether the mediation privilege is held by the party making the pertinent communication,[339] all the parties,[340] or the mediator.[341] Many mediation privilege statutes fail to identify the holder.[342]

The downside of any privilege, of course, is that it suppresses information that, if revealed, might have changed the outcome of a trial or other legal proceeding. The mediation privilege's suppression of information may even shield criminal or other wrongful activity. Suppose a parent admits to the child-custody mediator that the parent has physically abused his children and is not sure whether he will do it again. A broad mediation privilege would prevent the mediator from revealing that information to the court and, deprived of this information, the court may award custody to the abusive parent. A broad mediation privilege would also prevent the mediator from revealing this information to a state social services agency which, if it had the information, would monitor and counsel the parent. Accordingly, statutes creating a mediation privilege typically make an exception allowing for disclosure of such information.[343] Other privilege statutes make a broader exception for when allegations of crime are involved.[344] Still other privileges are defeated when the court finds that the need for evidence in a particular case outweighs the benefit created by the privilege.[345]

Another exception to some privilege statutes is when testimony goes to the question of whether a settlement agreement was actually formed in mediation.[346] Suppose that Plaintiff and Defendant sign a written settlement agreement at the conclusion of mediation. If Defendant, for example, breaches the agreement, Plaintiff may seek to enforce that agreement in court. Defendant may argue that no settlement agreement was formed and that the mediation privilege precludes admission of any

339. See, e.g., Conn.Gen.Stat.Ann. §§ 31–96 (West 1997).

340. See, e.g., Fla.Stat.Ann. §§ 44.102(3) (West Supp.2000); Colo.Rev. Stat. § 13–22–307 (Supp.1991).

341. Fenton v. Howard, 118 Ariz. 119, 575 P.2d 318, 319 (Ariz.1978); In re Marriage of Rosson, 178 Cal.App.3d 1094, 224 Cal.Rptr. 250 (Ct.App.1986).

342. Rogers & McEwen, supra note 1, § 9:16 & App. A.

343. The exception may allow for disclosure "when mandated by statute" because most states have statutes requiring the reporting of child abuse, even if learned during a confidential interview. See Alan Kirtley, The Mediation Privilege's Transition From Theory to Implementation, 1995 J.Disp.Resol. 1, 47.

344. N.C.Gen.Stat. 95–36 (199); N.D.Cent.Code § 31–04–11 (1996).

345. See, e.g., 5 U.S.C. § 574 (1994). Such privileges are "qualified," rather than "absolute."

346. See, e.g., N.D.Cent.Code § 31–04–11 (1996); Wyo.Stat.Ann. § 1–43–103 (Michie 1999). See Kaiser Found. Health Plan v. Doe, 136 Or.App. 566, 903 P.2d 375 (Or. Ct.App.1995); Few v. Hammack Enter. Inc., 132 N.C.App. 291, 511 S.E.2d 665 (N.C.Ct. App.1999).

Privilege issues arise with respect, not only to the formation of the settlement agreement, but also to contract-law defenses to enforcement, such as mistake. See, e.g., Scott H. Hughes, A Closer Look: The case for a mediation confidentiality privilege still has not been made, Disp.Resol.Mag. Winter 1998, at 14–16 ("Courts must be free to examine the contract formation to determine if the parties have complied with basic principles of contract law and, if compliance is not found, set the contract aside.")

evidence to the contrary. The privilege, Defendant argues, prevents Plaintiff or the mediator from testifying that an agreement was formed or from introducing the signed document into evidence. This argument must be rejected if mediated settlements are to be enforceable. On the other hand, courts have invoked the privilege to exclude evidence that an *oral* settlement agreement was formed at mediation.[347] Perhaps the mediation privilege, in its practical effect, amounts to a Statute of Frauds for mediated settlement agreements; such agreements are enforceable only if written or otherwise recorded.[348]

The start of this section noted that mediation benefits from tools to increase the certainty that mediators, *and other participants in mediation*, can be trusted not to reveal confidences.[349] Many privilege statutes, however, only apply to communications to mediators, not to communications to other participants in mediation.[350] These privileges encourage parties to be open in their disclosures to the mediator, but do nothing to encourage parties to be open in their disclosures to each other.

(e) Confidentiality Clauses in Settlement Agreements

Once a settlement agreement is reached at mediation, the parties may wish to keep the settlement's terms confidential. Many settlement agreements have such confidentiality clauses. On the other hand, parties often ask a court to enter their settlement as a judgment.[351] That makes the settlement a court record, presumptively open to the public.[352] Parties routinely request and receive court orders sealing their settlements from public access. Sometimes, however, the seal is broken in favor of a subpoena in another case.

§ 4.29 Agreements to Mediate

Parties with a dispute can agree to mediate that dispute. Such *post-dispute* mediation agreements can be formed before or after litigation starts. Much mediation is the result of such agreements, which may or may not be written. A sample post-dispute mediation agreement appears in an earlier section.[353]

347. Ryan v. Garcia, 27 Cal.App.4th 1006, 33 Cal.Rptr.2d 158 (Ct.App.1994); Hudson v. Hudson, 600 So.2d 7 (Fla.Dist. Ct.App.1992). See also Cohen v. Cohen, 609 So.2d 785 (Fla.Dist.Ct.App.1992).

348. See § 4.16(b)(discussing enforceability of mediated settlement agreements). See also Regents of the Univ. of Calif. v. Sumner, 42 Cal.App.4th 1209, 50 Cal. Rptr.2d 200 (Ct.App.1996)(enforcing settlement terms dictated into tape recorder); Bennett v. Bennett, 587 A.2d 463 (Me. 1991).

349. See § 4.28(a).

350. Rogers & McEwen, supra note 1, § 9:13.

351. Id. § 4:13.

352. Compare FTC v. Standard Financial Management Corp. 830 F.2d 404 (1st Cir.1987)(public access to settlement); Bank of America Nat'l Trust & Sav. Ass'n v. Hotel Rittenhouse Assoc., 800 F.2d 339 (3d Cir.1986)(same), with Minneapolis Star & Tribune Co. v. Schumacher, 392 N.W.2d 197 (Minn.1986)(keeping settlement private).

§ 4.29

353. See § 4.10(f).

More interesting, perhaps, are *pre-dispute* mediation agreements. Any sort of contract can include a clause obligating the parties to mediate any dispute that may arise between them.[354] It is an open question, however, whether these clauses are enforceable because there are few cases on point.

If a party who has formed a pre-dispute mediation agreement refuses to participate in mediation, what will the court do to enforce the agreement? One possibility is nothing. Another possibility is to award money damages to the non-breaching party. And a third possibility is to order the breaching party to participate in mediation so that a refusal to do so would be contempt of court.

Doing nothing to enforce a pre-dispute mediation agreement would conflict with the law's usual enforcement of contracts so some method of enforcement seems likely. The normal method of contract-enforcement is money damages. But how would these damages be calculated when the breach is the refusal to mediate? To put the non-breaching party in the position it would have been in had the contract had been performed,[355] the court would have to predict the results of both mediation and litigation, then award as damages the difference (in terms of value to the non-breaching party) between the two. The speculativeness of such an approach is daunting. The speculativeness of such an approach regarding agreements to *arbitrate* has led arbitration law to reject money damages in favor of specific performance, *i.e.*, ordering the breaching party to arbitrate.[356] Perhaps the same speculativeness in the mediation context, will lead courts to reject money damages in favor of ordering the breaching party to mediate.[357] Indeed, this is the result of the few cases on point.[358]

---

354. See generally, Rogers & McEwen, supra note 1, §§ 8:01—03. For sample clauses, see, e.g., American Arbitration Association, Drafting Dispute Resolution Clauses—A Practical Guide 9 (1998); Center for Public Resources, "Dispute Resolution Clauses: a Guide for Drafters of Business Agreements."

355. This is the way to calculate the "expectation damages" normally awarded for breach of contract. See Restatement (Second) of Contracts §§ 344 & 347 (1981).

356. See § 2.4(b).

357. See Whitmore Gray, Dispute Resolution Clauses: Some Thoughts on Ends and Means, 2 Alternatives to the High Cost of Litig. at 12, 13 (1984).

358. DeValk Lincoln Mercury, Inc. v. Ford Motor Co., 811 F.2d 326, 335–37 (7th Cir.1987). Cf. Annapolis Prof'l Firefighters Local 1926, IAFF, AFL–CIO v. City of Annapolis, 100 Md.App. 714, 642 A.2d 889, 894 (Md.Ct.Spec.App.1994)(dicta: mediation agreements should be enforced "in much

the same manner" as arbitration agreements.)

In the absence of cases on pre-dispute mediation agreements, the most analogous cases are those involving pre-dispute agreements to use other non-binding forms of ADR. Haertl Wolff Parker, Inc. v. Howard S. Wright Constr. Co., 1989 WL 151765 (D.Or.1989); AMF, Inc. v. Brunswick Corp., 621 F.Supp. 456 (S.D.N.Y.1985); Avitzur v. Avitzur, 58 N.Y.2d 108, 459 N.Y.S.2d 572, 446 N.E.2d 136 (1983).

Much less closely analogous are cases enforcing pre-dispute (binding) arbitration agreements because these cases are applying the dictates of long-established statutes covering arbitration, but not other forms of ADR. See §§ 2.1—2.53. But see CB Richard Ellis, Inc. v. American Environ. Waste Management, 1998 WL 903495 (E.D.N.Y.1998)(relying on Federal Arbitration Act to enforce agreement to mediate).

§ 4.30   Mandatory Mediation

(a) Generally

Courts and other government agencies often encourage, and even require, disputing parties to mediate. Some statutes require mediation of certain types of cases and, in many state and federal courts, judges have authority to order most types of civil cases into mediation.[359] Mediation is most frequently mandated for family disputes, especially child custody, but various state or local court rules require mediation of other types of cases, too.[360]

Sometimes, mediation is not required but encouraged. For example, a Florida statute provides that mobile home tenants are not entitled to recover statutory attorney's fees in actions against landlords unless they are first willing to use, and pay for, mediation.[361] Sometimes mediation is encouraged by a judge who suggests that the particular case "looks appropriate for mediation" and asks the lawyers if they and their clients would be willing to participate. Although the judge has been subtle about it, her message is received by the lawyers loud and clear: any party who refuses to mediate will have angered the judge. Each lawyer will likely advise her client to mediate, if only to stay in the good graces of the judge who will be presiding over the case if no settlement occurs.

(b) Policy Arguments For and Against

There are many reasons why courts and other government agencies often encourage, and even require, disputing parties to mediate. Many believe that doing so increases the percentage of cases that settle. The more cases that settle, the fewer that go to trial. That is attractive to judges and others who believe that the court system is overwhelmed with more cases than it can handle.[362] Increasing the number of cases that settle allows judges to devote more attention to those cases that remain.

There is reason to believe that mediation does facilitate settlement. *Evaluation* by the mediator is likely to cause a convergence in the parties' expectations about the results of litigation.[363] The closer the parties' expectations are to each other, the larger any settlement zone is likely to be. Also, mediation is more likely than negotiation to foster settlements because of mediation's tendency to facilitate communication and to exploit *positive-sum* opportunities.[364]

On the other hand, some studies indicate that mediation does little to encourage settlement. These studies indicate that settlement rates with mediation are only slightly higher than, or even the same as,

§ 4.30

359. Rogers & McEwen, supra note 1, §§ 6:04 & 7:02.

360. Id. § 7:02.

361. Fla.Stat.Ann.ch. 723.037 (West Supp.2000).

362. See §§ 3.43—3.45.

363. See § 4.13(a).

364. See § 4.12.

settlement rates without mediation.[365] In other words, mediated settlements largely replace negotiated settlements, not trials. The cases that settle in mediation may be the cases that would have settled without mediation. If the goal is to clear congested trial dockets or to save money in the court system, then encouraging or requiring mediation may do little to achieve the goal.

Another rationale for encouraging or requiring mediation is to achieve, not *more* settlements, but *better* settlements. And there is some empirical data suggesting that mediation tends to make settlements come earlier in litigation, rather than on the eve of trial.[366] Earlier settlements are, all other things being equal, better settlements because they save the parties time, money and aggravation. Second, mediated settlements are better settlements to the extent they tend to be more positive-sum than negotiated settlements.[367] There are, then, substantial reasons for courts to encourage, or even require, mediation. Doing so may produce a slightly higher settlement rate and seems to produce settlements that are faster and better than they would otherwise be.

The arguments against encouraging, and especially requiring, mediation reflect concerns about disempowered groups, party autonomy and cost.[368] The first set of arguments contend that mediation, when compared to litigation, "increase[s] the risk of unfair treatment for minority disputants, women and the poor."[369] The autonomy arguments against requiring mediation first note that parties can always choose mediation voluntarily. The parties know better than a judge or other court employee whether mediation is appropriate for their particular dispute so if they do not voluntarily choose it, they should not be forced into it.[370] This argument might be an application of a general distaste for coercion. Or it might be an argument that mediation, in particular, is especially incompatible with coercion.[371]

These party-autonomy arguments combined with concern for an especially disempowered group, domestic violence victims, have had some recent influence on the law. Several statutes exempt from the mandatory

---

365. Rogers & McEwen, supra note 1, § 2:02 at 12. See also id. § 6:02.

366. Rogers & McEwen, supra note 1, § 2:02 at 12. See also id. § 6:02.

367. See § 4.12.

368. See generally Society of Professionals in Dispute Resolution, Mandated Participation and Settlement Coercion: Dispute Resolution As It Relates to the Courts (1991).

369. Richard Delgado, et al., Fairness and Formality: Minimizing the Risk of Prejudice in Alternative Dispute Resolution, 1985 Wis.L.Rev. 1359, 1400. And there is one study suggesting "that minority participants generally fare worse than whites in both mediation and adjudication, and that

these effects are most severe in mediation." Michele Hermann et al., Metrocourt Project Final Report: A Study of the Effects of Ethnicity and Gender in Mediated and Adjudicated Cases at the Metropolitan Court Mediation Center viii–xii (1993).

370. Grillo, supra note 194, at 1582 ("It is presumptuous to assume that the state has a better idea than the parties themselves about whether mediation will work in their particular case.")

371. See, e.g., Mary Pat Truehart, In Harm's Way? Family Mediation and the Role of the Attorney Advocate, 23 Golden Gate U.L.Rev. 717, 761 (1993); Phyllis Gangel–Jacob, Some Words of Caution About Divorce Mediation, 23 Hofstra L.Rev. 825 (1995).

mediation of family disputes cases involving domestic violence,[372] the rationale being that it is wrong to force a victim of abuse to mediate with the abuser.[373] The party-autonomy principle also appears in Oregon legislation allowing a party to escape mandatory mediation by simply filing a written objection to it.[374] But these seem to be exceptions from a general trend of increased mandatory mediation. Lawmakers generally seem to believe that merely participating in mediation is quite a small burden and the coercion of requiring it is a price worth paying to achieve the likely gains of mediation. Notice, however, that the parties' burden from mandatory mediation may include some or all of the following costs:

— the parties' time,

— paying for the lawyers' time,

— paying for the mediator,[375]

— travel costs to the mediation, and

— the delay of another hurdle before trial.

(c) Who Must Participate?

One of the costs mandatory mediation inflicts on the parties is the consumption of their time. If a party can avoid participating in mediation by sending a lawyer, then the burden of mandatory mediation on the party's time is quite low. And many parties choose to have their lawyers participate in mediation on their behalf, just as they choose to have their lawyers participate in negotiation on their behalf. Some court orders mandating mediation, however, require participation of the client as well as the lawyer.[376] And some go so far as to require the participation of the client, instead of the lawyer.[377]

Some clients cannot participate in mediation except through agents. For example, corporations cannot participate except through the human beings who represent them. When a corporation is required to participate in mediation, can it send a low-level employee or must it send the Chief Executive Officer or even a quorum of the entire Board of Directors? The time of high-level executives and directors is quite precious to the corporation so any mediation rule that consumes a

---

372. Minn.Stat.Ann. § 518.619 (West 1990 & Supp.1999); N.D.Cent.Code § 14–09.1–02 (1997).

373. See Rogers & McEwen, supra note 1, §§ 7:02 & 12:02. See also Wis.Stat. § 767.11(8)(b)(West 1993 & Supp.1999)(exempting from mandatory mediation cases where mediation "will cause an undue hardship or would threaten health or safety.")

374. Or.Rev.Stat. § 36.185 (Lexis Supp. 1998).

375. For examples of mandatory mediation requiring parties to pay for the mediator, see, e.g., N.M. Stat. Ann. §§ 40–12–5, 40–12–6 (Michie 1996); Ohio Rev.Code Ann. § 3105.091 (West 1995).

376. Physicians Protective Trust Fund, v. Overman, 636 So.2d 827 (Fla.Dist.Ct.App.1994)(ordering attendance of entire Board of Directors). See also G. Heileman Brewing Co., v. Joseph Oat Corp., 871 F.2d 648 (7th Cir.1989)(Federal Rule of Civil Procedure 16 empowers trial judge to order client, as well as lawyer, to attend pretrial conference).

377. Mediators in some statutes have authority to exclude lawyers from child custody mediation. See § 4.17.

significant amount of that time imposes a severe burden.[378] On the other hand, sending an agent who lacks full settlement authority is an old trick to prevent settlement at anything but one-sided terms.[379]

(d) Good Faith

Suppose a party and his lawyer arrive for mandatory mediation at the appointed time but they refuse to speak and each insists on wearing earplugs to avoid hearing anything the mediator or other party says. Has that party satisfied his duty to mediate? If so, mandatory mediation is pointless. The presence at mediation of a party who refuses to speak or listen is not going to promote settlement, let alone a fast or good settlement. For this reason, some mandatory mediation requirements impose a duty to mediate in "good faith."[380] If the court finds that a party failed to make a good faith effort to mediate, the court may punish that party financially or even render a default judgment against that party.[381]

One practical problem with a "good faith" standard, of course, is that it is so indeterminate. Good faith is in the eye of beholder; what may look like good faith to you, may look like bad faith to me. Case law may or may not provide some guidance. For instance, one Fifth Circuit case holds that good faith does not require making a bona fide settlement offer.[382] But another Fifth Circuit case, only a year later, sanctioned a defendant that offered to pay only $100,000 (in a case resulting in a $6 million jury verdict) because the defendant "concealed its true position that it never intended to settle the case."[383]

Another practical problem with a "good faith" standard is that, to determine whether a party's participation was or was not in good faith, a court may have to learn things about the mediation that break the confidentiality of mediation.[384] Some jurisdictions with mandatory media-

---

378. Compare G. Heileman Brewing Co., v. Joseph Oat Corp., 871 F.2d 648, 655 (7th Cir.1989)(enforcing order that corporate party send to pretrial conference an agent with "full authority to settle the case or to make decisions and grant authority to counsel with respect to all matters that may be reasonably anticipated to come before the conference"), with id. at 663–65 (Easterbrook, J. dissenting)(sending agent with full settlement authority might require sending a quorum of the entire Board of Directors). See also Physicians Protective Trust Fund, v. Overman, 636 So.2d 827 (Fla.Dist.Ct.App.1994)(ordering attendance of entire Board of Directors).

379. See § 3.21(e).

380. See, e.g., Fla.Stat.Ann. 627.745(d)(West 1996 & Supp.2000); Kan. Stat.Ann. § 72–5430(c)(4)(1992); Me.Rev. Stat.Ann.tit. 19–A, § 251 (West 1998); Wash.Rev.Code 59.20.080(2). Federal Rule of Civil Procedure 16(f), which is often used as authority for ordering pretrial confer-

ences or mediation, goes further to sanction a party who is "substantially unprepared to participate." Fed.R.Civ.P. 16(f).

381. Me.Rev.Stat.Ann. tit. 19–A, § 251 (West 1998). Compare Robinson v. ABB Combustion Engineering Services, Inc., 32 F.3d 569 (6th Cir.1994)(reversing dismissal as too severe a sanction), with Wahle v. Medical Center of Delaware, Inc., 559 A.2d 1228 (Del.1989)(failure both to attend court-sponsored arbitration and to comply with other pretrial orders resulted in dismissal).

382. Dawson v. United States, 68 F.3d 886 (5th Cir.1995). See also Hess v. New Jersey Transit Rail Operations, Inc., 846 F.2d 114 (2d Cir.1988).

383. Guillory v. Domtar Industries Inc., 95 F.3d 1320, 1335 (5th Cir.1996).

384. Compare Graham v. Baker, 447 N.W.2d 397 (Iowa 1989)(refusing to defer to mediator on whether parties complied with

tion avoid these problems by refusing to impose any good-faith require-ment.[385] How those jurisdictions would deal with the party who insists on wearing earplugs to mediation remains to be seen.

(e) Additional Pressures to Settle

As noted in an earlier section,[386] requiring mediation may somewhat increase the likelihood of settlement. To further increase the likelihood of settlement, mandatory mediation can include *evaluation* by the media-tor. A mediator's evaluation tends to narrow the divergence between the parties' expectations about the result of litigation and this convergence makes settlement more likely.[387] The versions of mandatory mediation with the strongest pressures to settle exploit the mediator's evaluation. One way to do this is by reporting the evaluation to the judge.[388] That means the evaluation is not merely a prediction of how the case will be decided but an influence on how the case is decided. Mandatory media-tion with evaluation, especially if the evaluation is reported to the judge, resembles the processes of *non-binding arbitration* and *neutral evalua-tion* discussed at the end of this chapter.[389]

(f) Settlement Conference as Mediation

While not often called "mandatory mediation," the typical settle-ment conference before a judge or magistrate is just that. The judge is the mediator. The judge's mere presence can facilitate negotiation by encouraging the lawyers to be constructive and positive. The judge may require that the parties, as well as their lawyers, be present at the settlement conference.[390] The judge may become involved in the discus-sion, perhaps helping to focus issues or even evaluating the merits of the case. The most evaluative judges even propose terms of settlement.[391] Occasionally a judge goes so far as to perform "shuttle diplomacy." Each side is in its own room and the judge travels back and forth.[392] The judge may tell Plaintiff how weak her case is and then, minutes later, tell Defendant that the judge expects a big verdict.[393]

statutory requirements for participation), later proceeding 456 N.W.2d 364 (Iowa 1990), with Minnesota Bureau of Mediation Services v. Spellacy, Case No. C2–88–227 (Minn.App.1988)(mediation privilege bars testimony about whether party had bar-gained in good faith).

See § 4.28(discussing confidentiality).

385. Decker v. Lindsay, 824 S.W.2d 247 (Tex.Ct.App.1992); Graham v. Baker, 447 N.W.2d 397 (Iowa 1989).

386. See § 4.30(b).

387. See § 4.13(a).

388. See § 4.13(c). See also Rogers & McEwen, supra note 1, § 7:05 (noting high-er settlement rate in San Francisco, where custody mediators reported to the trier of fact, than in Los Angeles, where they did not).

389. See §§ 4.32 & 4.34.

390. See 28 U.S.C. § 473(b)(1995); G. Heileman Brewing Co. v. Joseph Oat Corp., 871 F.2d 648 (7th Cir.1989).

391. See, e.g., Kothe v. Smith, 771 F.2d 667 (2d Cir.1985)(reversing award of sanc-tions against party who refused to settle in range suggested by judge).

392. Compare Peter H. Schuck, The Role of Judges in Settling Complex Cases: The Agent Orange Example, 53 U.Chi. L.Rev. 337 (1986).

393. Kovach & Love, supra note 140, at 31.

These tactics tend to increase the likelihood of settlement. A neutral's evaluation tends to narrow the divergence between the parties' expectations about the results of litigation and this convergence makes settlement more likely.[394] This is especially true if the neutral is the judge who will be presiding over the case. The judge's evaluation is an excellent predictor of how the case will be decided because the judge can influence the case to be decided that way.

Instead of mediation by the judge, there is often mediation by the magistrate or special master. Indeed, ongoing litigation over school desegregation, prison reform and the like, is often primarily ongoing mediation by a magistrate or special master.

G. OTHER PROCESSES IN AID OF NEGOTIATION

Table of Sections

§ 4.31 Introduction to Other Processes

(a) Various Processes Providing Non–Binding Adjudication or Evaluation

The previous sections of this chapter discuss mediation, the most important process in aid of negotiation. This section discusses four other processes in aid of negotiation: non-binding arbitration,[395] the summary jury trial,[396] neutral evaluation,[397] and the mini-trial.[398] What all these processes (including mediation) have in common is that they do not by themselves resolve disputes. Rather, they help the parties negotiate a resolution to the dispute. Accordingly, they are called "processes in aid of negotiation".

Many of these processes are encouraged, and sometimes even required, by courts. As a result, these processes become intertwined with litigation.

(b) Defining Terms

The processes discussed in this section help parties negotiate a resolution to the dispute by providing non-binding adjudication or evaluation.

---

394. See § 4.13(a).

§ 4.31

395. See § 4.32.

396. See § 4.33.

397. See § 4.34.

398. See § 4.35.

(1) Non–Binding Adjudication

Non-binding adjudication should be contrasted both with the binding adjudication provided by litigation and arbitration and the lack of adjudication provided by negotiation and mediation.

Adjudication is a process by which somebody (the adjudicator) decides the result of a dispute.[399] Rather than the disputing parties agreeing on the result of the dispute, as in *negotiation*[400] or *mediation*,[401] adjudication is the adjudicator telling the parties the result. Judges and jurors are the adjudicators in *litigation*, which is adjudication in a government forum, such as a court.[402] *Arbitration* is adjudication in a private, *i.e.*, non-government, forum.[403]

What makes litigation and arbitration *binding* adjudication is the fact that the adjudicator's decision in these processes is backed with the force of government.[404] The adjudicators' decisions in litigation and arbitration are enforced, ultimately, by sheriffs and marshals with guns and badges. Parties who fail to comply with these adjudicators' decisions may find themselves imprisoned or find their property forcibly taken from them. In contrast, *non-binding* adjudication lacks such enforcement. The parties to non-binding adjudication get a decision from the adjudicator but a party's failure to comply with that decision does not subject that party to the barrel of the sheriff's gun. A party is free to disregard the non-binding adjudicator's decision and to pursue binding adjudication to its conclusion.

(2) Evaluation

Evaluation is less precise than adjudication. *Evaluation* is an assessment of the merits of a case that does not go so far as to decree a specific, concrete result. For example, an adjudicator tells the parties that "Defendant is liable to Plaintiff in the amount of $250,000." In contrast, an evaluator might say "Plaintiff has a very strong argument that Defendant breached the contract and damages appear to be in the six figures", or "I've seen verdicts in similar cases range around two or three hundred thousand dollars." Other examples of evaluation include "Defendant's contributory-negligence argument is unlikely to persuade a jury", or "Plaintiff seems to have shown strong evidence of price-fixing."

§ 4.32 Non–Binding Arbitration

Arbitration is adjudication in a private, *i.e.*, non-government, forum. There are two types of arbitration, binding and non-binding. Binding arbitration is far more common. Binding arbitration is the subject of Chapter 2. Non-binding arbitration is discussed in this section. Non-binding arbitration is a form of non-binding adjudication.[405]

---

399. See § 1.5(a), n.12.

400. See Chapter 3.

401. See §§ 4.1—4.30.

402. See § 1.5.

403. See §§ 2.1—2.53.

404. See §§ 1.5 & 1.7.

§ 4.32

405. See § 4.31(b)(1).

While parties can agree to non-binding arbitration, most non-binding arbitration is court-ordered, *i.e.*, mandatory. Courts in over twenty states and in some federal districts have authority to order parties (in certain classes of cases) to non-binding arbitration.[406] This arbitration is non-binding because the party that loses in arbitration may pursue the case in litigation and the court will hear the case *de novo*, giving no deference to the arbitrator's decision. However, most court-ordered arbitration rules impose some disincentive to deter the losing party from pursuing litigation. Generally, that party "must deposit with the court a sum equal to the fees of the arbitrators. The deposit is returned only if the result at the trial de novo is more favorable to the appellant than the award of the arbitrators."[407]

Some state statutes require non-binding arbitration of medical malpractice claims, in particular.[408] There is typically a panel of three arbitrators, at least one of whom is a physician. While the arbitrators' decision is non-binding, in some states that decision is admissible in any later trial.[409] Making the arbitrators' decision admissible increases the pressure to settle exerted by non-binding arbitration. The arbitrators' decision is not merely a prediction of how the case will be decided but an influence on how the case is decided.[410]

§ 4.33 Summary Jury Trial

The summary jury trial ("SJT") is a form of non-binding adjudication.[411] It is a non-binding jury trial that normally occurs after discovery has been completed and after rulings on any motions for summary

---

406. Ian R. Macneil, Richard E. Speidel & Thomas J. Stipanowich, Federal Arbitration Law § 2.4.2.1 (1995).

407. Macneil, Speidel & Stipanowich, supra note 406, § 2.4.2.2. See also Donna Sienstra, et al., ADR and Settlement in the Federal District Courts; a sourcebook for judges & lawyers (FJC 1996); John P. McIver & Susan Keilitz, Court-Annexed Arbitration: An Introduction, 14 Just.Sys.J. 2, at 130, Table 5 (1991). See, e.g., Ariz. Uniform Rules of Procedure for Arbitration, Rule 7(f)(if judgment on trial de novo is not more favorable by at least 10%, appellant must pay (1) to the county the compensation paid to the arbitrator ($75); (2) costs and reasonable attorney's fees, (3) expert witness fees); Haw. Arbitration Rules 25–28 (sanctions for failure to prevail in trial de novo include reasonable costs and fees incurred (e.g., expert witness fees, travel, and deposition costs), costs of jurors, attorneys' fees not to exceed $15,000); NC Court–Ordered Arbitration Rule 7 (party that asks for a trial de novo may be denied costs that could otherwise be recovered if the party does not improve his/her position at trial.); Or.Rev. Stat. § 36.425(4)(5)(1995).

408. See, e.g., Alaska Stat. § 09.55.535 (Lexis 1998); 710 Ill.Comp.Stat.Ann. § 15/1 (West Supp.2000); La.Rev.Stat. § 9:4232 (West 1997); Ohio Rev.Code Ann. § 2711.22 (West 1994); Cal.Civ.Proc.Code § 1295 (West 1982).

409. See La.Rev.Stat. § 40:1299.47(H)(West Supp.2000); Md.Code Ann.Cts. & Jud.Proc. § 3–2A–06(d)(1998).

410. A similar procedure occurs in Michigan's mandatory "mediation", which is better described as non-binding arbitration. See Wayne County, Mich.Local Court Rule 403.15–403.16; Mich.Gen. Court Rule 2.403(D). See also Mason v. Cass, 221 Mich. App. 1, 561 N.W.2d 402 (Mich.Ct.App. 1997)(plaintiff refused to settle at mediator's assessment then went to trial and won a verdict that was worse for plaintiff than mediator's assessment; therefore, the plaintiff was ordered to pay defendant's attorney's fees).

§ 4.33

411. See § 4.31(b). See generally Thomas D. Lambros, Summary Jury Trial—An Alternative Method of Resolving Disputes, 69 Judicature 286 (1986).

judgment. The speed of the SJT—it normally takes a day or less—"is achieved by using various procedural shortcuts, such as restricting questioning during jury selection, limiting evidentiary objections, omitting marginal evidence, and curtailing jury instructions. The most crucial element is the use of attorney summaries of evidence in lieu of live testimony."[412] The SJT may be confidential, closed to the press.[413]

There is a split of authority on whether federal courts have authority to order a SJT over a party's objection, *i.e.*, whether the SJT can be mandatory.[414]

§ 4.34 Neutral Evaluation

Neutral evaluation can be agreed to by the parties or required by the court. Courts use a variety of names to describe this process, including Early Neutral Evaluation ("ENE"). Generally, an attorney selected by the court serves as the evaluator. He or she meets with the parties and their lawyers for a few hours. This meeting generally occurs early in the case, before discovery. The meeting typically begins with the evaluator asking the clients to describe the case. Then the evaluator "asks questions of both sides to clarify issues, arguments, and evidence, to fill in evidentiary gaps, and to probe for strengths and weaknesses."[415] "The evaluator tries to help the parties to identify common ground, and to convert this to stipulations or informal agreements. The effort during the process is to isolate the areas of disagreement most central to the case."[416]

The evaluator writes an evaluation of the merits of the case. This evaluation can be quite detailed, predicting how the court will likely rule on each disputed issue and suggesting a range of damages. Before communicating the evaluation to the parties, the evaluator encourages the parties to discuss settlement. If the parties do not settle, the evaluator communicates the evaluation to the parties and encourages further settlement negotiation. If the parties still have not settled, the evaluator "outlines a case development plan, identifying key areas of disagreement and suggesting ways to posture the case and to conduct discovery as efficiently as possible."[417] ENE is designed, not only to promote settlement, but to streamline the litigation of cases that do not settle.

412. Thomas B. Metzloff, Improving the Summary Jury Trial, 77 Judicature 1, 9–12 (1993).

413. Cincinnati Gas and Electric Co. v. General Electric Co., 854 F.2d 900 (6th Cir.1988)(no First Amendment right of access to SJT).

414. Compare In re NLO, Inc., 5 F.3d 154 (6th Cir.1993) (no authority); Strandell v. Jackson County, 838 F.2d 884 (7th Cir. 1987)(same), with State of Ohio ex rel. Montgomery (Betty) v. Louis Trauth Dairy, Inc., 164 F.R.D. 469 (S.D.Ohio 1996)(authority); Arabian American Oil Co. v. Scar-

fone, 119 F.R.D. 448 (M.D.Fla.1988)(same); McKay v. Ashland Oil, Inc., 120 F.R.D. 43, 46 (E.D.Ky.1988)(same).

§ 4.34

415. Joshua D. Rosenberg & H. Jay Folberg, Alternative Dispute Resolution: An Empirical Analysis, 46 Stan.L.Rev. 1487 (1994).

416. Lawyers Get Tips on Using Early Neutral Evaluation, 4 ADR Rep. 124, 124–25 (Apr.12, 1990).

417. Id.

In a noteworthy case, *Wagshal v. Foster*,[418] the D.C. Circuit held that court-appointed evaluators enjoy quasi-judicial immunity.

§ 4.35   Mini–Trial

"Many business disputes are overly litigated and not settled because the corporate manager has given up and left the matter to his lawyers * * * . The mini-trial was specifically designed to bring the problem back to the corporate managers."[419] The mini-trial is not a trial at all; there is no judge or jury. It is, however, presided over by a neutral advisor. Each side presents its case in shortened form. The presentations are directed less to the neutral than to the corporate managers with settlement authority. These presentations may be the first time each manager is confronted with the arguments and evidence of the opposing side. After the presentations, the managers engage in settlement negotiations. They may ask the neutral to facilitate these negotiations by serving as a mediator or evaluator.

§ 4.36   Arguments For and Against Making These Processes Mandatory

(a) The Appeal of Mandatory Non–Binding Adjudication and Evaluation

Courts often require parties to use three of the processes discussed above: non-binding arbitration, summary jury trial and neutral evaluation.[420] The rationale for requiring these processes is to promote settlement and clear court dockets.[421] There is reason to believe that these processes, and other forms of non-binding adjudication and evaluation, do promote settlement.

A case cannot settle unless there is a *settlement zone*.[422] With few exceptions, the only cases lacking a settlement zone are those in which Plaintiff expects a more pro-Plaintiff result from litigation than Defendant expects.[423] If, for example, Plaintiff expects a $250,000 verdict, while Defendant expects a $200,000 verdict, there may be no settlement zone.[424] These cases in which Plaintiff expects a more pro-Plaintiff result

---

418. 28 F.3d 1249 (D.C.Cir.1994). See § 4.27(b).

§ 4.35

419. Ronald L. Olson, An Alternative for Large Case Dispute Resolution, 6 Litigation 22 (Winter 1980). See also Eric D. Green, Corporate Alternative Dispute Resolution, 1 Ohio St.J.on Disp.Resol. 203, 238–245 (1986).

§ 4.36

420. The mini-trial is rarely, if ever, ordered by courts except on the request of the parties. Mandatory mediation is discussed in § 4.30.

421. See, e.g., Riskin & Westbrook, supra note 56, at 3 ("a right to a trial de novo means that the process is fundamentally an effort to promote settlement.")

422. See § 3.11.

423. See id.

424. Whether there is a settlement zone turns on how the two sides value the costs and benefits of the two processes: settlement and litigation. It may, for example, be that litigation is so costly that both sides are better off settling at any one of many possible settlement terms than they are litigating even though Plaintiff expects a higher verdict than Defendant expects.

than Defendant expects can be called cases of over-optimism. If Plaintiff expects a verdict of $250,000 and Defendant expects a verdict of $200,-000, then at least one of the parties is overly optimistic about its likely success at litigation. Cases lacking a settlement zone are those in which at least one of the parties is in for a disappointment at trial.

Because parties' over-optimism about their success at litigation can prevent settlement zones, advocates of settlement seek to reduce party over-optimism and thus make the parties' expectations about the results of litigation converge. Non-binding adjudication and evaluation tend to do just that. They reduce the gap between the parties' expectations by giving them information (the neutral's adjudication or evaluation of the case) that causes the parties' expectations about the results of litigation to converge around the neutral's adjudication or evaluation. The neutral, because her judgment is respected by the parties, persuades the parties to change their expectations.

Suppose, for example, Plaintiff expected a verdict of $800,000, and Defendant expected a verdict of $100,000, before the neutral evaluator predicted (or adjudicator declared) a verdict of $300,000. The evaluation succeeded if it caused Plaintiff to now expect a verdict lower than $800,000 and Defendant to expect a verdict more than $100,000. The evaluation succeeded marvelously if it caused each party to now expect a verdict of $300,000. The more the original $700,000 gap is reduced, the more the evaluation succeeded.

Successful non-binding adjudications and evaluations come from a neutral whose judgment is respected by the parties as a good predictor of litigation. Suppose the case involves a personal injury arising out of an auto accident. If the neutral is a local judge who has presided over the trial of hundreds of similar cases, the parties and lawyers may have confidence that this neutral can predict quite well the results of litigating this case. The better a predictor of litigation the parties believe non-binding adjudication or evaluation to be, the better non-binding adjudication or evaluation is likely to be at reducing the gap in the parties' expectations.

(b) Concerns About Mandating Non–Binding Adjudication and Evaluation

Even assuming that non-binding adjudication and evaluation promote settlement,[425] one may still question whether courts should make such processes mandatory. After all, parties can always choose these processes voluntarily. One can argue that the parties know better than a judge or other court employee whether one of these processes is appropriate for their particular dispute so if they do not voluntarily choose it, they should not be forced into it. Moreover, mandating these processes may be especially harmful to poor plaintiffs because these processes increase the time and money plaintiffs must spend before trial.[426] Argu-

---

425. See § 4.36(a).

426. Lisa Bernstein, Understanding the Limits of Court–Connected ADR: A Critique

ments that this increased burden violates constitutional rights, including the right to a jury trial, have been rejected.[427]

There is also controversy about whether mandatory non-binding adjudication and evaluation do, in fact, promote settlement. There have been studies of court programs mandating non-binding arbitration,[428] summary jury trials,[429] and neutral evaluation.[430] These studies do not, on the whole, show that mandating these procedures leads to a significantly higher settlement rate than occurs without them. It may be that the cases settling after these procedures are those that would have settled without them. On the other hand, mandating these procedures may tend to make settlements come earlier in litigation, rather than on the eve of trial.[431] Earlier settlements are, all other things being equal, better settlements because they save the parties time, money and aggravation.

Of course, the earlier in litigation non-binding adjudication or evaluation is used, the less accurate a predictor it will be. If discovery has not yet occurred, there may be material information kept from the non-binding adjudicator or evaluator that would be introduced at trial. On the other hand, if non-binding adjudication or evaluation is delayed until right before trial then its success in promoting settlement is only a minor success in terms of the time, money and aggravation saved.

of Federal Court–Annexed Arbitration Programs, 141 U.Pa.L.Rev. 2169 (1993); G. Thomas Eisle, The Case Against Mandatory Court–Annexed ADR Programs, 75 Judicature 34, 40 (June 1991).

427. See, e.g., Riggs v. Scrivner, Inc., 927 F.2d 1146 (10th Cir.1991); Kimbrough v. Holiday Inn, 478 F.Supp. 566 (E.D.Pa. 1979); In re Smith, 381 Pa. 223, 112 A.2d 625 (Pa.1955); Eastin v. Broomfield, 116 Ariz. 576, 570 P.2d 744 (Ariz.1977); Davis v. Gaona, 260 Ga. 450, 396 S.E.2d 218 (Ga.1990); Firelock, Inc. v. District Court of 20th Judicial Dist., 776 P.2d 1090 (Colo. 1989); American Universal Insurance Co., v. DelGreco, 205 Conn. 178, 530 A.2d 171 (Conn.1987).

See also § 2.55(discussing constitutional right to jury trial in connection with mandatory, yet binding, arbitration).

428. See, e.g., Jane W. Adler, Deborah R. Hensler & Charles Nelson, Simple Justice: How Litigants Fare in the Pittsburgh Court Arbitration Program (1983); Lisa Bernstein, Understanding the Limits of Court–Connected ADR: A Critique of Federal Court–Annexed Arbitration Programs, 141 U.Pa.L.Rev. 2169 (1993); Deborah R. Hensler, Does ADR Really Save Money? The Jury's Still Out, Nat.L.J., act C2

(Apr.11, 1994); Keilitz, Court–Annexed Arbitration, in Nat'l Symposium on Court–Connected Dispute Resolution Research 43 (Nat'l Center for State Cts. and State Jus.Instit.1994); Levine, Court–Annexed Arbitration, 16 J. Law Reform 537, 542–43 (1983); Voluntary Arbitration in Eight Federal District Courts: An Evaluation 6 (Federal Judicial Center 1994).

429. See, e.g., Cook, A Quest for Justice: Effective and Efficient Alternative Dispute Resolution Processes, 1983 Detroit C.L.Rev. 1129, 1133; Summary Jury Trial Gain Favor, Nat.L.J. 1 (June 10, 1985); Thomas Metzloff, Reconfiguring the Summary Jury Trial, 41 Duke L.J. 806, 832–35 (1992); Richard A. Posner, The Summary Jury Trial and Other Methods of Alternate Dispute Resolution: Some Cautionary Observations, 53 U.Chi.L.Rev. 366, 377–85 (1986).

430. Joshua D. Rosenberg & H. Jay Folberg, Alternative Dispute Resolution: An Empirical Analysis, 46 Stan.L.Rev. 1487 (1994).

431. Rogers & McEwen, supra note 1, § 2:02 at 12. See also id. § 6:02.

Appendix

RESEARCHING ALTERNATIVE DISPUTE RESOLUTION ON WESTLAW®

Analysis

Section 1. Introduction

Alternative Dispute Resolution provides a strong base for analyzing even the most complex problem involving alternative dispute resolution. Whether your research requires examination of case law, statutes, expert commentary or other materials, West books and Westlaw are excellent sources of information.

To keep you abreast of current developments, Westlaw provides frequently updated databases. With Westlaw, you have unparalleled legal research resources at your fingertips.

Additional Resources

If you have not previously used Westlaw or have questions not covered in this appendix, call the West Group Reference Attorneys at 1–800–REF–ATTY (1–800–733–2889). The West Group Reference Attorneys are trained, licensed attorneys, available 24 hours a day to assist you with your Westlaw search questions. To subscribe to Westlaw, call 1–800–344–5008 or visit the West Group Web site at **www.westlaw.com**.

Section 2. Westlaw Databases

Each database on Westlaw is assigned an abbreviation called an *identifier*, which you use to access the database. You can find identifiers for all databases in the online Westlaw Directory and in the printed *Westlaw Database Directory*. When you need to know more detailed information about a database, use Scope. Scope contains coverage information, lists of related databases and valuable search tips.

The following chart lists Westlaw databases that contain information pertaining to alternative dispute resolution. For a complete list of alternative dispute resolution databases, see the online Westlaw Directory or the printed *Westlaw Database Directory*. Because new information is continually being added to Westlaw, you should also check Welcome to Westlaw and the online Westlaw Directory for new database information.

Selected Alternative Dispute Resolution and Related Databases on Westlaw

Database	Identifier	Coverage
Federal and State Case Law Combined		
Federal & State Case Law	ALLCASES	Begins with 1945
Federal & State Case Law– Before 1945	ALLCASES–OLD	1789–1944
State Case Law		
State Case Law	ALLSTATES	Begins with 1945
State Case Law Before 1945	ALLSTATES–OLD	1821–1944
Individual State Cases	XX–CS (where XX is a state's two-letter postal abbreviation)	Varies by state
Federal Case Law		
Federal Case Law	ALLFEDS	Begins with 1945
Federal Case Law– Before 1945	ALLFEDS–OLD	1789–1944
State Statutes and Regulations		
State Statutes–Annotated	ST–ANN–ALL	Varies by state
Individual State Statutes– Annotated	XX–ST–ANN (where XX is a state's two-letter postal abbreviation)	Varies by state
State Administrative Code Multibase	ADC–ALL	Varies by state

Database	Identifier	Coverage
Individual State Administrative Code	XX–ADC (where XX is a state's two-letter postal abbreviation)	Varies by state

Federal Statutes and Regulations

Database	Identifier	Coverage
United States Code Annotated®	USCA	Current data
Code of Federal Regulations	CFR	Current data
Federal Register	FR	Current data

Other Legal Materials

Database	Identifier	Coverage
Federal Labor & Employment–Federal Service Impasses Panel	FLB–FSIP	Begins with 1970
Federal Labor & Employment–National Mediation Board Decisions	FLB–NMB	Begins with 1935
Federal Securities and Blue Sky Law–Arbitration Awards	FSEC–ARB	Begins with 1989
International Economic Law Documents	IEL	Varies by document
National Association of Securities Dealers (NASD)–Arbitration Awards	NASD–ARB	Begins with 1981
WTO & GATT Panel Decisions	WTO–DEC	GATT: 1948–1994 WTO: Begins with 1995

Legal Periodicals, Texts and Practice Materials

Database	Identifier	Coverage
Alternative Dispute Resolution with Forms, Second Edition	ADR	Current through 2000 pocket part
American Arbitration Association Publications	AAA–PUBS	Current data
American Review of International Arbitration	AMRIARB	Full coverage begins with 1997 (vol. 7)
Commercial Leasing Law and Strategy	COMLLST	Begins with March 1995
Corporate Counsellor	CORPCOUN	Begins with March 1995
CPR Model ADR Procedures and Practice Series	CPR–MAPP	1998 edition
Dispute Resolution Journal	DRJ	Selected coverage begins with 1993 (vol. 48)
Dispute Resolution Magazine	DISPRES	Begins with 1996 (vol. 3)
Harvard Negotiation Law Review	HVNLR	Full coverage begins with 1996 (vol. 1)
International Arbitration Law Review	INTALR	Selected coverage begins with 1998 (vol. 1)
Journal of Dispute Resolution	JDR	Selected coverage begins with 1991 (vol. 1991); full coverage begins with 1993 (vol. 1993, no. 2)

Database	Identifier	Coverage
Journal of Divorce & Remarriage	JDIVREMAR	Begins with January 1997
Lowell & Governale: U.S. International Taxation: Practice and Procedure	WGL–INTPRAC	Current edition
Nichols Illinois Civil Practice with Forms	NICHOLS–ILCP	Current through 2000 supplement
PLI Litigation and Administrative Practice: Litigation Course Handbook Series	PLI–LIT	Begins with June 1984
Regulation, Litigation and Dispute Resolution Under the Americans with Disabilities Act: A Practitioner's Guide to Implementation	ABA–DISIMPL	1996 edition
The Rutter Group–California Practice Guide: Alternative Dispute Resolution	TRG–CAADR	1999 edition
Texas Practice Guide: Alternative Dispute Resolution	TXPG–ADR	1998 edition
Willamette Journal of International Law and Dispute Resolution	WMTJILDR	Full coverage begins with 1997 (vol. 5)

Directories

BNA Labor Relations Reporter: Directory of Arbitrators	LRR–DIR	Current edition
Labor Arbitration Information System	LAIS	Begins with 1960
West Legal Directory®– Alternative Dispute Resolution	WLD–ADR	Current data

News and Information

Andrews Publications Multibase	ANDREWS	Varies by publication
Andrews International Reinsurance Dispute Reporter	ANIRDR	Begins with November 1996
BNA Combined Labor Arbitration Decisions	LA–COMB	Varies by source
BNA Labor Relations Reporter: Labor Arbitration Reports	LRR–LA	Begins with 1979
BNA Unpublished Arbitration Decisions	LA–UNP	Begins with 1988
Combined Jury Verdicts and Settlements	JV–ALL	Varies by source
Daily Labor Report	BNA–DLR	Begins with January 1986
Jury Verdicts Northwest	JVN	Begins with 1988
Legal Services Industry News	WNS–LG	Varies by source

Database	Identifier	Coverage
Mealey Publications Multibase	MEALEYS	Varies by publication
Mealey's International Arbitration Report	MINTARBR	Begins with January 1993
Mealey's Litigation Reports: Reinsurance	MLRREINS	Begins with January 1993

Section 3. Retrieving a Document with a Citation: Find and Hypertext Links

3.1 Find

Find is a Westlaw service that allows you to retrieve a document by entering its citation. Find allows you to retrieve documents from anywhere in Westlaw without accessing or changing databases. Find is available for many documents, including case law (state and federal), the *United States Code Annotated*, state statutes, administrative materials, and texts and periodicals.

To use Find, simply access the Find service and type the citation. The following list provides some examples:

To Find This Document	Access Find and Type
Security Watch, Inc. v. Sentinel Systems, Inc. 176 F.3d 369 (6th Cir. 1999)	**176f3d369**
Vernon v. Acton, 732 N.E.2d 805 (Ind. 2000)	**732ne2d805**
28 U.S.C.A. § 651	**28 usca 651**
13 C.F.R. § 134.216	**13 cfr 134.216**
Minn. Stat. Ann. § 484.76	**mn st s 484.76**
Cal.Penal Code § 14151	**ca penal s 14151**

For a complete list of publications that can be retrieved with Find and their abbreviations, consult the Publications List after accessing Find.

3.2 Hypertext Links

Use hypertext links to move from one location to another on Westlaw. For example, use hypertext links to go directly from the statute, case or law review article you are viewing to a cited statute, case or article; from a headnote to the corresponding text in the opinion; or from an entry in a statutes index database to the full text of the statute.

Section 4. Searching with Natural Language

Overview: With Natural Language, you can retrieve documents by simply describing your issue in plain English. If you are a relatively new Westlaw user, Natural Language searching can make it easier for you to retrieve cases that are on point. If you are an experienced Westlaw user, Natural Language gives you a valuable alternative search method.

When you enter a Natural Language description, Westlaw automatically identifies legal phrases, removes common words and generates variations of terms in your description. Westlaw then searches for the concepts in your description. Concepts may include significant terms, phrases, legal citations or topic and key numbers. Westlaw retrieves the 20 documents that most closely match your description, beginning with the document most likely to match.

4.1 Natural Language Search

Access a database, such as Journals & Law Reviews (JLR). In the text box, type a Natural Language description such as the following:

are confidential statements made in mediation privileged

4.2 Next Command

Westlaw displays the 20 documents that most closely match your description, beginning with the document most likely to match. If you want to view additional documents, use the Next command, click the **Document** or **Doc** arrow at the bottom of the page or click the right arrow in the left frame.

4.3 Natural Language Browse Commands

Best Mode: To display the best portion (the portion that most closely matches your description) of each document in your search result, click the **Best Section** or **Best** arrow at the bottom of the window or page.

Standard Browsing Commands: You can also browse your Natural Language search result using standard Westlaw browsing commands, such as citations list, Locate and term mode.

Section 5. Searching with Terms and Connectors

Overview: With Terms and Connectors searching, you enter a query, which consists of key terms from your issue and connectors specifying the relationship between these terms.

Terms and Connectors searching is useful when you want to retrieve a document for which you know specific details, such as the title or the fact situation. Terms and Connectors searching is also useful when you want to retrieve documents relating to a specific issue.

5.1 Terms

Plurals and Possessives: Plurals are automatically retrieved when you enter the singular form of a term. This is true for both regular and irregular plurals (e.g., **child** retrieves *children*). If you enter the plural form of a term, you will not retrieve the singular form.

If you enter the nonpossessive form of a term, Westlaw automatically retrieves the possessive form as well. However, if you enter the possessive form, only the possessive form is retrieved.

Automatic Equivalencies: Some terms have alternative forms or equivalencies; for example, *5* and *five* are equivalent terms. Westlaw automatically retrieves equivalent terms. The *Westlaw Reference Manual* contains a list of equivalent terms.

Compound Words, Abbreviations and Acronyms: When a compound word is one of your search terms, use a hyphen to retrieve all forms of the word. For example, the term **along-side** retrieves *alongside, alongside* and *along side*.

When using an abbreviation or acronym as a search term, place a period after each of the letters to retrieve any of its forms. For example, the term **a.d.r.** retrieves adr, a.*d.r.*, *a d r* and *a. d. r.* Note: The abbreviation does *not* retrieve *alternative dispute resolution*, so remember to add additional alternative terms to your query such as **"alternative dispute resolution"**.

The Root Expander and the Universal Character: When you use the Terms and Connectors search method, placing the root expander (!) at the end of a root term generates all other terms with that root. For example, adding the ! to the root *confiden* in the query

confiden! /s mediat! /s privileg!

instructs Westlaw to retrieve such terms as *confidence, confident, confidential* and *confidentiality*.

The universal character (*) stands for one character and can be inserted in the middle or at the end of a term. For example, the term

withdr*w

will retrieve *withdraw* and *withdrew*. Adding three asterisks to the root *elect*

elect* * *

instructs Westlaw to retrieve all forms of the root with up to three additional characters. Terms such as *elected* or *election* are retrieved by this query. However, terms with more than three letters following the root, such as *electronic*, are not retrieved. Plurals are always retrieved, even if more than three letters follow the root.

Phrase Searching: To search for an exact phrase, place it within quotation marks. For example, to search for references to *arbitration clause*, type **"arbitration clause"**. When you are using the Terms and Connectors search method, you should use phrase searching only if you are certain that the terms in the phrase will not appear in any other order.

5.2 Alternative Terms

After selecting the terms for your query, consider which alternative terms are necessary. For example, if you are searching for the term *a.d.r.*, you might also want to search for the terms *alternative dispute resolution, mediation* or *arbitration*. You should consider both synonyms and antonyms as alternative terms. You can also use the Westlaw thesaurus to add alternative terms to your query.

5.3   Connectors

After selecting terms and alternative terms for your query, use connectors to specify the relationship that should exist between search terms in your retrieved documents. The connectors are described below:

Use:	To retrieve documents with:	Example:
& (and)	both terms	**arbitrat! & award!**
or (space)	either term or both terms	**a.d.r. "alternative dispute resolution"**
/p	search terms in the same paragraph	**contract! /p "arbitration clause"**
/s	search terms in the same sentence	**negotiat! /s disput!**
+s	the first search term preceding the second within the same sentence	**damages +s exceed! excess!**
/n	search terms within "n" terms of each other (where "n" is a number)	**breach! /5 contract**
+n	the first search term preceding the second by "n" terms (where "n" is a number)	**mediator +5 bias! partial!**
" "	search terms appearing in the same order as in the quotation marks	**"binding arbitration"**

Use:	To exclude documents with:	Example:
% (but not)	search terms following the % symbol	**arbitrat! % union labor**

5.4   Field Restrictions

Overview: Documents in each Westlaw database consist of several segments, or fields. One field may contain the citation, another the title, another the synopsis and so forth. Not all databases contain the same fields. Also depending on the database, fields with the same name may contain different types of information.

To view a list of fields for a specific database and their contents, see Scope for that database. Note that in some databases not every field is available for every document.

To retrieve only those documents containing your search terms in a specific field, restrict your search to that field. To restrict your search to a specific field, type the field name or abbreviation followed by your search terms enclosed in parentheses. For example, to retrieve a U.S. Supreme Court case titled *Thomas v. Union Carbide,* access the U.S. Supreme Court Cases database (SCT) and search for your terms in the title field (ti):

ti(thomas & "union carbide")

The fields discussed below are available in Westlaw databases you might use for researching alternative dispute resolution issues.

Digest and Synopsis Fields: The digest (di) and synopsis (sy) fields, added to case law databases by West's attorney-editors, summarize the main points of a case. The synopsis field contains a brief description of a case. The digest field contains the topic and headnote fields and includes the complete hierarchy of concepts used by West's editors to classify the headnotes to specific West digest topic and key numbers. Restricting your search to the synopsis and digest fields limits your result to cases in which your terms are related to a major issue in the case.

Consider restricting your search to one or both of these fields if

• you are searching for common terms or terms with more than one meaning, and you need to narrow your search; or

• you cannot narrow your search by using a smaller database.

For example, to retrieve federal cases that discuss actions to vacate an arbitrated or mediated award, access the Federal Case Law database (ALLFEDS) and type the following query:

sy,di(arbitrat! mediat! /p award! /p vacat!)

Headnote Field: The headnote field (he) is part of the digest field but does not contain topic numbers, hierarchical classification information or key numbers. The headnote field contains a one-sentence summary for each point of law in a case and any supporting citations given by the author of the opinion. A headnote field restriction is useful when you are searching for specific statutory sections or rule numbers. For example, to retrieve headnotes from federal cases that cite 29 U.S.C.A. § 108, access the Federal Case Law database (ALLFEDS) and type the following query:

he(29 +7 108)

Topic Field: The topic field (to) is also part of the digest field. It contains hierarchical classification information, including the West digest topic names and numbers and the key numbers. You should restrict search terms to the topic field in a case law database if

• a digest field search retrieves too many documents; or

• you want to retrieve cases with digest paragraphs classified under more than one topic.

For example, the topic Arbitration has the topic number 33. To retrieve cases that discuss arbitration provisions included in employee handbooks, access the Federal and State Case Law database (ALLCASES) and type a query like the following:

to(33) /p employ! /s manual hand-book

To retrieve cases classified under more than one topic and key number, search for your terms in the topic field. For example, cases discussing arbitration clauses or agreements may be classified to Arbitration (33), Insurance (217) or Labor Relations (232A), among other topics. To retrieve recent federal cases classified to any of these topics, access the Federal Case Law database (ALLFEDS) and type a query like the following:

to(arbitrat! /5 clause agreement) & da(aft 1998)

For a complete list of West digest topics and their corresponding topic numbers, access the Key Number Service.

> *Note*: Slip opinions, cases not reported by West and cases from topical services do not contain the digest, headnote and topic fields.

Prelim and Caption Fields: When searching in a database containing statutes, rules or regulations, restrict your search to the prelim (pr) and caption (ca) fields to retrieve documents in which your terms are important enough to appear in a section name or heading. For example, to retrieve Illinois statutes regarding alternative dispute resolution, access the Illinois Statutes–Annotated database (IL–ST–ANN) and type the following:

pr,ca("alternative dispute resolution")

5.5 Date Restrictions

You can use Westlaw to retrieve documents *decided* or *issued* before, after or on a specified date, as well as within a range of dates. The following sample queries contain date restrictions:

da(2000) & enforc! /s arbitrat! mediat! /s award!

da(aft 1998) & arbitrator mediator /5 discretion

da(9/13/2000) & compel! /5 arbitration

You can also search for documents *added to a database* on or after a specified date, as well as within a range of dates. The following sample queries contain added-date restrictions:

ad(aft 1999) & arbitrat! mediat! /p malpractice

ad(aft 12/31/1999 & bef 4/1/2000) & "arbitration clause"

Section 6. Searching with Topic and Key Numbers

To retrieve cases that address a specific point of law, use topic and key numbers as your search terms. If you have an on-point case, run a search using the topic and key number from the relevant headnote in an appropriate database to find other cases containing headnotes classified to that topic and key number. For example, to search for cases containing headnotes classified under topic 33 (Arbitration) and key number 6 (Requisites and Validity), access the State Case Law database (ALL-STATES) and enter the following query:

33k6

For a complete list of West digest topic and key numbers, access the Key Number Service.

> *Note*: Slip opinions, cases not reported by West and cases from topical services do not contain West topic and key numbers.

Section 7. Verifying Your Research with Citation Research Services

Overview: A citation research service is a tool that helps you ensure that your cases are good law; helps you retrieve cases, legislation or articles that cite a case, rule or statute; and helps you verify that the spelling and format of your citations are correct.

7.1 KeyCite

KeyCite is the citation research service from West Group.

KeyCite for cases covers case law on Westlaw, including unpublished opinions.

KeyCite for statutes covers the *United States Code Annotated* (USCA®), the *Code of Federal Regulations* (CFR) and statutes from all 50 states.

KeyCite Alert monitors the status of your cases or statutes and automatically sends you updates at the frequency you specify when their KeyCite information changes.

KeyCite provides the following:

- Direct appellate history of a case, including related references, which are opinions involving the same parties and facts but resolving different issues

- Negative indirect history of a case, which consists of cases outside the direct appellate line that may have a negative impact on its precedential value

- The title, parallel citations, court of decision, docket number and filing date of a case

- Citations to cases, administrative decisions and secondary sources on Westlaw that have cited a case

- Complete integration with the West Key Number System® so you can track legal issues discussed in a case

- Links to session laws amending or repealing a statute

- Statutory credits and historical notes
- Citations to pending legislation affecting a federal statute or a statute from California or New York
- Citations to cases, administrative decisions and secondary sources that have cited a statute or federal regulation

7.2   Westlaw As a Citator

For citations not covered by KeyCite, including persuasive secondary authority such as restatements and treatises, use Westlaw as a citator to retrieve cases that cite your authority.

For example, to retrieve cases citing the law review article "Enforcing Small Print to Protect Big Business: Employee and Consumer Rights Claims in an Age of Compelled Arbitration," 1997 Wis. L. Rev. 33 (1997), access the Federal & State Case Law database (ALLCASES) and type a query like the following:

consumer /s compelled /s 1997 /5 33

Section 8. Researching with Westlaw—Examples

8.1   Retrieving Law Review Articles

Recent law review articles are often a good place to begin researching a legal issue because law review articles serve 1) as an excellent introduction to a new topic or review for a stale one, providing terminology to help you formulate a query; 2) as a finding tool for pertinent primary authority, such as rules, statutes and cases; and 3) in some instances, as persuasive secondary authority.

Suppose you need to gain background information on the arbitration of employment contract disputes.

Solution

- To retrieve recent law review articles relevant to your issue, access the Journals & Law Reviews database (JLR). Using the Natural Language search method, enter a description like the following:

arbitration of employment contract disputes

- If you have a citation to an article in a specific publication, use Find to retrieve it. For more information on Find, see Section 3.1 of this appendix. For example, to retrieve the article found at 73 N.C. L. Rev. 443, access Find and type

73 nclrev 443

- If you know the title of an article but not which journal it appeared in, access the Journals & Law Reviews database (JLR) and search for key terms using the title field. For example, to retrieve the article "The Federal Arbitration Act and Individual Employment Contracts: A Better Means to an Equally Just End," type the following Terms and Connectors query:

ti("individual employment" & "better means")

8.2 Retrieving Case Law

Suppose you need to retrieve state cases discussing unconscionable arbitration clauses.

Solution

- Access the State Case Law database (ALLSTATES). Type a Natural Language description such as the following:

unconscionable arbitration clause

- When you know the citation for a specific case, use Find to retrieve it. For more information on Find, see Section 3.1 of this appendix. For example, to retrieve *Place St. Charles v. J.A. Jones Construction Co.*, 823 F.2d 120 (5th Cir. 198), access Find and type

823 f2d 120

- If you find a topic and key number that is on point, run a search using that topic and key number to retrieve additional cases discussing that point of law. For example, to retrieve state cases containing headnotes classified under topic 232A (Labor Relations) and key number 454 (Authority of Arbitrators), access the Federal Case Law database (ALLFEDS) and type the following query:

232ak454

- To retrieve cases written by a particular judge, add a judge field (ju) restriction to your query. For example, to retrieve cases written by Judge Posner that contain headnotes classified under topic 33 (Arbitration), type the following query:

ju(posner) & to(33)

8.3 Retrieving Statutes and Regulations

Suppose you need to retrieve California statutes addressing alternative dispute resolution.

Solution

- Access the California Statutes–Annotated database (CA-ST-ANN). Search for your terms in the prelim and caption fields using the Terms and Connectors search method:

pr,ca("alternative dispute resolution")

- When you know the citation for a specific statute, regulation or code section, use Find to retrieve it. For example, to retrieve California Code of Civil Procedure § 1731, access Find and type

ca civ pro s 1731

- To look at surrounding sections, use the Table of Contents service. Click a hypertext link in the prelim or caption field, or click the **TOC** tab in the left frame. You can also use Documents in Sequence to retrieve the section following § 1731, even if that subsequent section was not retrieved with your search or Find request.

● When you retrieve a statute on Westlaw, it will contain a message if legislation amending or repealing it is available online. To display this legislation, click the hypertext link in the message.

Because slip copy versions of laws are added to Westlaw before they contain full editorial enhancements, they are not retrieved with Update. To retrieve slip copy versions of laws, access the United States Public Laws database (US–PL) or a state's legislative service database (XX–LEGIS, where XX is the state's two-letter postal abbreviation). Then type **ci(slip)** and descriptive terms, e.g., **ci(slip) & arbitrat! "alternative dispute resolution" mediat!**. Slip copy documents are replaced by the editorially enhanced versions within a few working days. Update also does not retrieve legislation that enacts a new statute or covers a topic that will not be incorporated into the statutes. To retrieve this legislation, access US–PL or a legislative service database and enter a query containing terms that describe the new legislation.

8.4 Using KeyCite

Suppose one of the cases you retrieve in your case law research is *Dayhoff Inc. v. H.J. Heinz Co.*, 86 F.3d 1287 (3rd Cir. 1996). You want to determine whether this case is good law and to find other cases that have cited this case.

Solution

● Use KeyCite to retrieve direct history and negative indirect history for *Dayhoff v. Heinz.*

● Use KeyCite to display citing references for *Dayhoff v. Heinz.*

8.5 Following Recent Developments

As the alternative dispute resolution specialist in your firm, you are expected to keep up with and summarize recent

legal developments in this area of law. How can you do this efficiently?

Solution

One of the easiest ways to stay abreast of recent developments in alternative dispute resolution is by accessing the Westlaw Topical Highlights–Litigation database (WTH–LTG). The WTH–LTG database contains summaries of recent legal developments, including court decisions, legislation and materials released by administrative agencies in the area of alternative dispute resolution.

Some summaries also contain suggested queries that combine the proven power of West's topic and key numbers and West's case headnotes to retrieve additional pertinent cases. When you access WTH–LTG, you will automatically retrieve a list of documents added to the database in the last two weeks.

*

Table of Cases

*

Index

References are to Section Number

297